WINES OF THE
GRAVES

PAMELA VANDYKE PRICE

WINES OF THE
GRAVES

SOTHEBY'S PUBLICATIONS

First published 1988 for Sotheby's Publications
by Philip Wilson Publishers Ltd
26 Litchfield Street
London WC2 9NJ

Available to the USA book trade from
Harper & Row, Publishers, Inc.
10 53rd Street
New York
NY 10022

Exclusive distribution to the wine trade in the USA:
THE WINE APPRECIATION GUILD
155 Connecticut Street
San Francisco
California 94107
(415) 864–1202

ISBN 0 85667 334 X

Library of Congress Catalog Number 88–060435

Endpapers
Design from toile de Beautiran, now in Château Mongenan

Designed by Keith Pointing
Filmset and printed by
BAS Printers Limited,
Over Wallop, Hampshire
Bound by
Dorstel Press Ltd, Harlow

CONTENTS

ACKNOWLEDGEMENTS   9

INTRODUCTION

1 THE REASON WHY   15
   Sources and dates   20
2 THE SCENE IS SET   23
3 WHERE IT IS AND WHAT IT IS   31
4 CLIMATE   43

HISTORY

5 IN THE VERY BEGINNING   51
6 THE TWILIGHT TIME: from the sack of Bordeaux to
   the ducal dynasty   61
7 THE DUKES – AND THE LAST DUCHESS
   (Eleanor of Aquitaine)   73
8 MEDIEVAL WINES and the end of English domination   89
9 THE GASCON POPE – Pape Clément   105
10 AQUITAINE BECOMES FRENCH: the end of English
   rule in 1453   121
11 'GRAVES' AS DISTINCT FROM 'BORDEAUX'   131
12 THE BEGINNING OF MODERN WINES: from the
   eighteenth century to the present day   141

THE WINES

13 THE GRAVES VINEYARD TODAY   163
   Demarcation   163
   The organisations   164
   The shrinking vineyard   165
   The 'technopole'   169
   The A.O.C.s   169
   Machines in the vineyard   175
14 THE VINES   177
   The market's dilemma   177

The vineyards		179
The grapes		181
Historic plagues		188
What contribution the grapes make		191
Tasting descriptions		193
A personal view of the different wines of the Graves		194
The black grapes		194
The white grapes		198
15	THE WINE	203
	The red wines	204
	The white wines	211
	New methods	213
	The role of the oenologist	216
16	WHAT ARE THE WINES LIKE?	219
	Dry white Graves	223
	Slightly sweeter white Graves	225
	Small-scale red Graves	225
	Fine red Graves	226
17	CLASSIFICATION: the 'most delicate' question	233
	The significance of the A.O.C.s	249
	The Cérons region	255
18	THE ESTATES	257
	Arrangement	258
	Non-classified growths	259
	A note about capacity	260
	The Classed Growths	262
	Some other properties	288
19	LILLET: the Graves aperitif	297
20	TOURISM	307
	The Lord of La Brède	307
	Planning a visit	320
	Timing	321
	Starting from Bordeaux	322
	Guides and visits	322
	Maps	323
	Some centres and places of interest	324
	Excursions in the south	327
	Just outside the Graves region	332

APPENDICES

Appendix I Family trees: the French and English royal houses   337

Appendix II *Stow's Survey of London* Vintry Ward   339

Appendix III Synonyms of grapes of the Gironde in former times   342

Appendix IV The growth of a dry white Bordeaux   352

Appendix V Décret of 8 July 1984   354

Appendix VI Décret of 9 September 1987   356

Appendix VII The non-classified growths of the Graves   361

Appendix VIII Production of vintages in the Graves 1976–86   368

Appendix IX Export of Graves wines 1980–6   369

Appendix X Stendhal's visit to La Brède   370

Glossary   374

Bibliography   376

Index   379

This book is dedicated to
Susan and Peter Vinding-Diers
in admiration and gratitude
and with my love

ACKNOWLEDGEMENTS

Many people have made major contributions to my efforts to compile this book and although I hope that I have acknowledged their help in the relevant pages, there are some to whom special thanks are due.

For many years, *Food & Wine from France* in London have been a constant source of reference for me. A long while ago they provided many introductions within Bordeaux in general and the Graves in particular, notably arranging for me to meet the great historian, Louis Desgraves, at the public library. More recently they effected more introductions and provided my transport in my latest visit to the Graves, as well as allowing me to draw on their files and photographic library. It would not have been possible for me to have undertaken this book, as well as several others, without their advice and co-operation throughout. I am fortunate to have many friends within their organisation.

The Maison des Vins de Graves made a major contribution to this book by means of an important London tasting, by frequent hospitality in London and by enabling me to visit the Graves in 1986. While there, they not only entertained me most generously and officially, but individual members of the organisation, under the aegis of Monsieur Pierre Guignard, extended much hospitality to me – it was my loss that I was not able, through lack of time, to accept all their invitations, but these are most gratefully acknowledged. Over the period of my visit and subsequently, on numerous occasions, Madame Monique Achard, who became a dear friend, acted as guide and driver, supplied illustrations and statistics, as well as giving up much of her time to providing material that this book would otherwise have lacked. The organisation at Podensac was, throughout, the most helpful and meticulous of colleagues and I trust that their efforts have been justified in this book.

The proprietors of the great Graves estates whom I was able to meet or meet again gave unstintingly of information and help – I only regret that I was not able to spend as much time as I should have liked in visiting their properties and, indeed, in seeing so many of the other estates that have had to be briefly described here, although all of them are recorded with thanks and respect. Among so many, I must record special thanks to M. J. B. Delmas of Haut Brion and his colleagues, Tony Perrin of Carbonnieux and his family, including his son who was an impeccable guide to many properties that had to be briefly visited, and Yves Kressmann, an old friend for many years. M. Claude Ricard and his family gave me an unforgettable tasting at Domaine de Chevalier and M. Olivier Bernard has followed up this contact with much valuable comment. The officials at the Maison du Vin in Bordeaux were also generous with their time and patient with answering my many questions. M. Pierre Coste supplied a unique piece of text on his own important work in the region. MM. Borie and Lillet gave me a fascinating visit to their revitalised establishment and have kindly checked the relevant text for me.

Those who assist research are usually so helpful that it was odd to find one 'learned establishment' that was not when I was trying to find out about soils and geology! Never mind, the contempt with which this one institution received my query, dismissing me as 'not one of our members' and sarcastically referring me to 'a book you will have to go to Paris to consult' was more than made up for by the patience and wealth of material supplied by a librarian who wished to remain nameless at Imperial College, who have often in the past proved courteous and of great assistance. As on many previous occasions, the Guildhall Library was also most co-operative and so was the Kensington & Chelsea Public Library. As an 'elephant's child' by nature, I have made use of very many anecdotes, snippets of information and history, both in Britain and in France which have come my way from all those aware of the gestation of this book who have sympathetically made contributions that have certainly added to its worth.

Other Bordeaux friends who have contributed to sections of this book include William and Trudy Bolter, who have so often been my instructors on much that relates to Bordeaux life and, in this instance, especially to Montesquieu. Baron Eric de Rothschild, who shares my enthusiasm for Eleanor of Aquitaine, not only read the chapter on Montesquieu, but most kindly supplied me with some of the white wine of La Brède; if he and I had not had a brief meeting before a dinner in London, I might never have been able to make even an approximate study of Montesquieu. I am proud to include all three of these friends as scrupulous and severe judges of what I write.

To Susan and Peter Vinding-Diers I have expressed my debt in the dedication to this book: their hospitality and unending kindness on many occasions has been as encouraging as it has been invaluable, both in my explorations of Graves wines and the regional way of life. Margaret Howard, who accompanied me on one visit to the Graves, is another of the many friends who have, by providing company and a sounding board for many conclusions and opinions, enabled me to present my impressions to readers who I hope may share some of my travels in the south-west of France.

A number of colleagues have given me permission to quote from their writings, both in books and periodicals. It is typical of the world of wine that they have so willingly shared their work with me and throughout I have cited my indebtedness to them, though I must pay particular tribute to the work of Jancis Robinson M.W., Edmund Penning-Rowsell, James Seely and David Peppercorn M.W.; also I owe much to the help of friends in the U.K. who have recommended wines of specific interest and drawn my attention to certain aspects of the Graves that I might otherwise have omitted. Charles Sichel has checked a number of my definitions, translations and accounts of the vineyard work most patiently and politely. Thank you Steven Spurrier, Graham Chidgey, Michael Broadbent M.W., David Molyneux-Berry M.W., Martin Wright, John Avery M.W., W. I. Baverstock Brooks and your many colleagues.

To Clive Coates M.W. I owe more thanks than can be expressed. Not only has he prompted many most rewarding explorations of the history concerned with the Graves and checked a vast number of references, but he read through the manuscript of this book and, in addition to correcting certain technicalities, contributed both ideas and the way in which these might most agreeably be presented to the ultimate reader, always making constructive comments and providing encouragement in what was sometimes an intimidating task. To him and to Juliet Coates this book owes a very great deal.

It is to be regretted that space and production costs prohibited the inclusion of colour plates or black-and-white photographs.

Those who assisted with the typing and duplicating also made contributions that I do not forget. But to my dear agent, Carole Blake, whose enthusiasm throughout has never flagged, I must also add a heartfelt 'Thank you'.

London 1987

INTRODUCTION

Bordeaux c.1550 from Sebastian Münter's Cosmographia Universalis *(reproduced with the kind permission of Wine Arts Ltd). Note the Palais de l'Ombrière, the Piliers de Tutelle, the Palais Gallien, the cathedral and the layout of the streets much as they are today.*

THE REASON WHY

WHY a book about the Graves? There isn't one or, rather, there has as yet not been one conceived and written in English. Even a French author, Florence Mothe, herself of the region, has divided her descriptive study into two parts, concentrating on what the Graves is today.

Yet although the Graves gets somewhat short measure in many reference books on Bordeaux and its wines, the tag that most writers cite is that it is *le berceau de Bordeaux* (the cradle of Bordeaux). And then they concentrate on some of the world-famous properties in the north of the region, tending to ignore the vast numbers of estates in the south, which, to this day, remain virtually unknown even to many French wine lovers and certainly to those in export markets whose buying is so much dictated by picking out 'known names'. Throughout the Graves there is a great deal of wine made, although in the U.K., so fortunate in having a range of wines of the world available in supermarkets, retail chains, wine warehouses and historic merchants, in all price categories, it is not usual to find the area 'Graves' denoted in displays or on lists where wines are picked out by region or even by commune. Even the sought-after 'tutored tastings' in Britain seldom concentrate on the Graves.

Indeed, although it's an easy French word to say, is it too easy? Does it sound plain, almost dull? Many years ago there was an amusing article in *Punch*, prompted by an attempt in the United States to tell would-be wine buyers how to pronounce some of those 'difficult' French names: 'Shotto nerf, doo, Pop' was tagged as a 'Yiddish folksong'; 'Bow Jo Lay' as a primitive sea-shanty; but 'Grahv' was a mere 'Latvian dirge'.

The Graves is a slightly withdrawn, almost hidden region. Even the 'regional specialities' tend to blur into Gironde or Landes recipes in general. The novels of the great French writer François Mauriac are often set in the odd, enclosed, spiritually desolate life of certain dwellings in the pine forests of the Landes which hold back the encroaching sand and I have sometimes wondered whether the grimness and, often, the horror of these human dramas may have inclined some of those who have read them to shudder away from the area.

In the middle of the Graves the regions of Sauternes and Barsac erupt, golden and opulent, hillocky and in more open country; they are easier to observe and visit, especially now that the luscious sweet wines are once more being appreciated. But you can drive down the autoroute to Toulouse and hardly see a row of vines. The N.113, quieter these days, is seldom a highway to prompt lingering, although there are some charming patches of countryside.

Even those in the wine trade who are perennially seeking out 'new' wines have seldom spent much time there, at least as far as buyers from export markets are concerned. Many select from samples sent up to the offices of their associates or to the great shippers in Bordeaux and then confirm orders after re-tasting when they return home.

The naturalist may venture to explore the region. But there's nothing to lure the archaeologist. There are fine things to see for the amateur of art and architecture – but one has mostly to go off the beaten track. English-speaking travellers tend to hasten southwards, to the Basque country, the Pyrenees and the Spanish frontier. The Graves is still a hidden region, though there is much to discover within it.

This is not, however, and cannot be, the 'definitive' book on the Graves. 'Definitive' is casually applied to many volumes on wine but as it in fact means the last word, the final ever-afterwards-to-be-accepted authority, those writers who allow it to be applied to their work (as I once did) are to my mind being impudently arrogant. Not only am I incapable of writing a 'definitive' book on wine but, when wine is the subject, no text can possibly be accepted in this way: wine changes, not just from year to year but, more often than many may suppose, from half-year to half-year, or even more frequently: there are alterations made in wineries, changes of ownerships, adjustments and revisions of regulations; there are redirected policies on the part of major holding companies (the interests of the shareholders being, naturally, in the minds of the directors); there are variations in fashions of drinks and drinking that, once created, ripple along to affect the wines concerned; there are reactions to changing economic conditions, both good and bad, currency fluctuations, innovations in the patterns according to how people eat and drink and entertain, within which wines must be fitted. All these factors influence wine. Many of them will be affecting and, albeit slightly, changing the wines of the world, including the wines of the Graves, during the time that this book is being written, while it is being prepared for publication and when it eventually appears on sale – and, of course, the public may not buy it immediately, so that, by the time they do, further changes will have taken place.

Sometimes, I admit, I am tempted to think that books about wine should not be written at all if they attempt to include such ephemera as vintages (how long will certain wines be on sale or, if they are, be affordable?); any arbitrary assertions on style (how soon may such styles change, subject to what is in demand or what can be an appealing price?); and, most of all, what the writer, writing at a particular time, thinks that the reader in that particular time – across the table from the typewriter or the pen and paper – may wish to know; that reader will change too – as well as the writer.

For example, a few years ago – as few as ten or fifteen – I myself had no notion what terms such as clonal selection, organic wine making, or mechanical harvesting actually meant and even less idea of these and other terms now in current wine usage could and did affect the wines we drink at the time I am writing this text.

And what about the reader?

A book about wine that was published in, say, 1938 or 1939 could still provide the layman with information about what was going on in the wine world then and, for all that writers and readers knew, what might continue for the next decade or so. But today books published ten years ago are substantially out of date and I am at a loss as to what to say when some of mine are still produced for me to sign by people who say they have learned from them: do I urge the charming readers to chuck the book into the incinerator, or mistrust every statement, because the text is so out of date – and, too, because I now think I know more about the subject as a whole? In the past thirty years changes in the wine world have been as radical and fantastic as those in other fields – art, technology, ordinary everyday life. Yet it is a stimulus that things do change and we who write should change as well – in our methods of presentation as well as our added knowledge and experience; we should not bluntly condemn changes that we find we cannot like – we should seek to understand them, though this may take much of that precious commodity, time.

Wine is a personal subject. Separating personal preference from an impersonal appraisal of quality is difficult, even more so now that there are many more wines to like and enjoy rather than to condemn – although one might not think so if reading certain wine writers! – and it should be understood that many wines, apparently superficially in opposition or at least in competition with each other, are aimed at the same target. Still, people do go on reading or referring to books. Few, true. But those of us whose trade is words write for the few. Shippers whose customers want the known names for their public continue to buy for the few as well as the masses and, with the increase in lectures and study sessions on wine, despite the anti-drink campaigners in many sections of 'the media', public interest in wine exists and is growing. The Graves deserves to be known, more than it is already. Nor should any pundit or 'expert' – a term of contempt among genuine wine lovers, for we are all students of wine, some merely having a little more experience than others – generalise once and for all. The constant questioning is what keeps wine and wine lovers alert and alive and, as wine is something that goes into the body, the study of it is as intimate as that of any other appetite – and often less disappointing. We are fortunate in that our age is that of a renaissance of inquiry about our physical composition – and what certain wines do to us should be of importance.

Books, including this one, must then inevitably be out of date by the time they reach the public, even if people rush to buy within the week of copies first being on sale. But, like wines, books must challenge readers: they should test themselves against any assertions, accepting some for the time, leaving others that they do not understand. In the end conclusions may be formed, subject I trust to frequent reappraisal, that may often be at variance with the text that started a train of thought, but this will give the reader who loves wine a far deeper knowledge and love of the subject than the acceptance of a series of glib generalisations. No one should suppose that anybody, no matter who, no matter how qualified, is the ultimate authority on wine. Years ago, at Oxford University, I was abjured 'Beware somewhat of the Germanic tradition of scholarship – because a text is within hard covers, it doesn't mean that it is always and forever right.' So with wine. I was taught to justify my likes and dislikes, to explain my reasons in detail – hard going sometimes, but it makes you think!

So if even an out-of-date book can jolt readers out of an acceptance of received ideas – from even the most exalted authorities – this is good. I can't go along with the laziness of anyone who simply follows what somebody else has written about a wine – if you don't like a world-famous Graves, own to this but, at the same time, justify your lack of affection and enthusiasm, while admitting its quality. If you revel in the drinking of a small-scale wine of the region, analyse why you love it – and do not overlook what may be its shortcomings.

My hope, in writing this book, is that readers may find in it something that may not previously have occurred to them and that may enlighten enjoyment or, at least, understanding. For no one writing about wine can know everything – in spite of what some seem to claim! – and, along the way of learning, there may be discoveries, the discarding of prejudices, the acceptance of limitations. Reappraisal of a subject that one may suppose oneself to know can be humiliating (salutary) and can be exhilarating! Before I started to write this book I had enjoyed certain Graves wines, white and red – but I don't think that I had come to grips with them. I had, maybe, thought seriously about certain of the greater and well-known wines. I knew nothing about the lesser-known ones, and, although I had studied the history of the Bordeaux region a little, I had not appreciated how the progress of the wines of the Graves had played a major part in this. Even now I feel inadequate at pronouncing about the wines and the area – but at least I have come to know both a little more than I did thirty years ago and have begun to understand as well as to love them.

Bear in mind, dear reader – as the Victorian writers used to urge – that what I write now, you may disagree with tomorrow; you may evolve great discoveries of your own among the wines. Even last week I would have written this book differently, because I am always sampling the wines. It may, incidentally, astonish some to know that, although writers on wine enjoy magnificent hospitality and many opportunities to sample wines, both when these are young and when they become mature, yet scribes such as myself are hesitant about demanding 'free' bottles. I know that some do – but in the comments voiced in this book it should be understood that many of the ready-to-drink wines on which I comment have been ordered and paid for by me from merchants in the United Kingdom; some, thoughtfully, gave me a 'trade discount', for which I thank them. Sometimes I simply went into a shop and bought a bottle. But it would have been unthinkable to me had I required any estate to provide me with a range of samples of vintages of even the more modest wines – apart from anything else, my bottles of cooking wine and, even, my various vinegar crocks, would have eventually been overflowing!

What I thought about the Graves I have expressed here as my impressions while I was there. Tastings were done in the Graves region and in the U.K. The experiences of the reader may be different. I hope they are as agreeable and as rewarding.

SOURCES AND DATES

In working on this book I have tried to consult as many relevant sources as possible, although inevitably some remain untapped. Authors quoted are mentioned in the text, with the date of publication of their work when this can be definitely given, otherwise their own dates must suffice. This seems to make for easier reading than do footnotes to the pages and would otherwise considerably bulk out the bibliography, which mainly lists works of general reference (although, with some books of major importance, such as the big histories, they have been listed again).

In some instances, in citing differing opinions, the references may seem to clash and in a few places I myself think that the writers may have been in error, either because of lack of information then available to them or because they were writing from a prejudiced position; it is sometimes surprising to see how, for many years, even centuries, writers go on quoting without query from the past, even when their predecessors could not always have had access to original material, were repeating hearsay, were insufficiently educated or, sometimes, were deliberately writing so as to influence their readers. No one can know everything, no one can be infallible; a 'known name' in the writing of history or about wine can be occasionally as unreliable as the 'known name' on a wine's label! Sometimes I have ventured to disagree with certain sources, at others I have admitted my own lack of sympathy with or understanding of them; without doubt, some readers will find fault with or disagree with me. I have, though, occasionally tried to give a contemporary interpretation to some of the events of the past; trade talk and human reactions don't change very much throughout history but when opinions are expressed and reports prepared in what to us now seems an archaic form, in the language of many years ago, it is not always easy for the reader in the late twentieth century to grasp the meaning of what has been recorded.

Then there's the difference in dating. The Gregorian calendar was introduced in 1582 but it was then mainly the Catholic countries that henceforth used it. Not until 1752 did the British adopt it and even then there were fiercely conservative opponents – 'Give us back our eleven days!' – rather like the members of the public who tried to resist metrication and the use of Centigrade instead of Fahrenheit, or the systems of measuring alcoholic strength that have recently made the matter much simpler for me. So, in dating events in relation to both France and England, there may be some inconsistency.

It should be borne in mind that this is not at all an overall history of the Bordeaux region, nor of France, nor of England or Britain. But as many lovers of wine may now only have shadowy recollections of the historical background, through the course of this account of the Graves I have tried to give some indications as to what was going on in and around the region and affecting it. An overall history of the whole region of Aquitaine still remains to be written. The many excellent books about the wines of Bordeaux do not, I think, take into account enough of what caused them to come into being and how economic and other often extraneous matters affected their development. Throughout, I have tried to make the wine of the Graves the hero or heroine of this book but it would have been absurd to ignore the existence of all others. Anyone interested can, with enjoyment, pursue other aspects of this fascinating area and its wines by following up the reading I have been able to do and, if they are even more fortunate, consult additional, possibly undiscovered matter and learn from other writers as yet unknown to me.

THE SCENE
IS SET

Most English and American speakers of what they suppose to be 'English' have heard of the Graves. It's an easy name for even the shyest to pronounce. Yet many wine lovers, even the most seriously interested, might be unable to state where the region is, nor might they be certain about the sort of wine to be found coming from it. Owners of Graves estates have many stories of how audiences at tastings express astonishment at seeing some of the wines of the Graves to be red – when what the customer, even today, expects is a slightly soft and inexpensive white.

As recently as 1950, the pleasant and readable J. D. Scott, in *Vineyards of France*, wrote: 'For some time I felt there was some mystery about Graves. . . . My parents drank it, so it was bound to be all right. My governess referred to it as a white wine suitable for ladies.' Mr Scott with 'the woman of seventeen whom I enormously admired and wanted to impress' searched for Graves on the wine list of wherever he was – and, not finding it 'ordered a bottle of white Bordeaux instead'. He admits that 'I could have been knowledgeable about most other wines, but not very accurately so on the subject of Graves.' He then comments that Graves is 'not truly a dry wine like Chablis or white Hermitage. But it is semi-dry. White Graves can be very good. But the thing to know about the area is that the best wine it produces is red.'

While working on this book I was told by a young member of the U.K. wine trade that, after he had spent time studying in the Gironde, he returned to London where, while he worked for a merchant, the manager of the shop insisted that Graves was a *white* wine – only a white wine. And some years back, a then well-known wine writer who was lunching with me and the owner of one of the great Graves estates that produces both white and red wines, leaned over to ask the host: 'At what stage in the vintage, monsieur, do you decide whether you will make red wines or white?'

As I write, in 1987, the Wine Society in their *News Bulletin* reporting in June about the 1986 clarets doesn't even mention 'Graves' as a separate

23

category in the 'Brief guide to different styles', though this bulletin does include the regions of Bourg and Fronsac, as well as other well-known ones. True, they include Haut Brion in their list of wines offered 'in bond'. But, as will be seen in this book, there are various reasons why the Graves area is either overlooked or ignored by various writers and compilers of wine lists.

Seemingly authoritative books do little to disperse this ignorance; indeed, I needed encouragement, from those both within and outside the wine trade, to venture to study the area for the purposes of this book. There are difficulties not immediately apparent to anyone attempting this type of research: local feelings about the local wines can run high. Perhaps the outsider, such as myself, may be able to select aspects of the subject in which somebody of the region may be too personally involved to see clearly. I hope that my simplifications of various problems may be received with indulgence, more than that accorded to somebody of the area.

The one wine name of the Graves that most will know is Haut Brion. This is because, in the 1855 classification of certain growths of the Gironde, which was prepared by the brokers of Bordeaux, based on the prices likely to be attained by the wines of certain estates – so, among the names of those submitted (not that the brokers always actually tasted the wines!) – Haut Brion was the only Graves included.

To this day, many otherwise serious wine drinkers (including many wine writers in the U.K., U.S.A. and elsewhere) suppose that this 'classification' of the wines, which was not the first to have been drawn up, was based on the quality of the wines at that time, not realising that it was based on what might be paid for the wines. (Cynically, people in some wine-drinking sections of the world might comment 'Plus ça change'.) In fact this is a pathetic error. The history and complexities of the 1855 and subsequent classifications of Bordeaux wines have been admirably set out in the book *The Wines of Bordeaux* (revised edition 1985) by my prickly but respected colleague, Edmund Penning-Rowsell, cited in many of the pages relating to this hereafter.

Anybody in Bordeaux with the time to whisk out from the centre or take an excursion from the airport at Mérignac, can see the Graves – or some of it – a region still, just, under vines. They will see the impeccably maintained estates of Haut Brion and the adjacent La Mission Haut Brion; some may venture further, to La Brède or, even, as far as Langon to treat themselves to a meal at the Restaurant Darroze. Students of wine and members of the wine trade turn off at Portets to Château Rahoul; everyone going south as far as Podensac will notice and should visit the Maison des Vins des Graves on the outskirts of the town, on the main road.

But the Graves is still little-known. The tag in much French writing about it is that it is 'the cradle of Bordeaux wine'. True. Until fairly recent times, the history of Bordeaux, in so far as it involved wine at all, was mainly the history of the Graves. This is why the two cannot be separated. Bordeaux, a journalist once remarked, is a city founded on wine (the film he showed about it at this point was that of a fountain of water!); but Bordeaux is founded on Graves wines – which may astonish those who invest in the 'collectables' of the great Médocs (and Châteaux Pétrus and Cheval Blanc across the river). Yet the Graves is still a beauty asleep in her woods and forests. Even books in French don't always wake the Graves with the proverbial kiss. *Les Vins de Bordeaux*, by J.-R. Roger (published by Cuisine et Vins de France) is infuriatingly undated, but I think that it must have appeared sometime in the 1950s. Although it does have a map of the Graves region, there is a smaller one that gives the impression that the area hardly extends beyond the Sauternais – one has to look closely at the vague demarcation. The same is true of the 1985 edition of Alexis Lichine's *Encyclopedia of Wines & Spirits*, where a map ends just south of La Brède and Beautiran, nor is there much information about the Graves in this otherwise excellent tome. Yet earlier wine writers did know the area and what they said about some of the estates will be quoted later. It's at least something that the 1984 edition of Hugh Johnson's *Wine Atlas* maps the Graves in some detail and mentions a number of estates, growers and makers.

Something should also be said about *Graves de Bordeaux* in the *Le Grand Bernard* French series; author Florence Mothe pluckily puts a dividing line across the map, south of Beautiran and the Château de Mongenan, her ancestral home; we are promised a *Graves des Clairières* volume, which I have not been able to see at time of writing, which will presumably deal with the south of the delimited area.

There is another confusing circumstance. As indicated by the earlier quotation from J. D. Scott, few people up to very recent times have formed any idea of what these wines are like. In the post-World War II period, when export markets began to open up once more, such wines were usually shipped in bulk and bottled in the country of the buyer. They were also cheap. Frequently a white Graves, mentioned only by its generic or regional name, would be the least expensive white wine on a restaurant list and the unworldly and inexperienced diner, tending to like a slightly soft, even a slightly sweet white wine, often enjoyed such anonymous drinks. As wine became more in vogue among a wide range of people, a meek white Graves might be offered by the glass in a pub or in the newly established wine bars, although by the 1950s there was increasing competition, in the U.K. anyway, from Germany's Liebfraumilchs and even more so from the light, dryish white wines coming from Yugoslavia.

Then, for some reason – could it have been the increasing dryness of the dry martini? – there was a growing belief that it was somehow 'better' to drink dry, although the British market continued to bear out the dictum of the late Don Guido Williams, of Jerez, who placidly affirmed 'For the U.K., call it dry and make it sweet.' This is sound sense. Northern countries, where it can be cold and often damp, have enjoyed sweet wines for centuries as did even blessedly sunny southern lands before sugar became cheap. Sweetness, whether it comes from ripe fruit, carefully cultivated, or wine from specially selected grapes, is something to be appreciated: it recalls summer, the ripeness of the fruit – sometimes people forget that a wine grape is a fruit! – puts a smile into the flavour, which lingers uncloyingly on the palate. Sweetness, whether derived from fruit or, as in the past, from honey, was cheering and the black teeth of Queen Elizabeth I were something of a status symbol.

Significantly, such sections of society as had sufficient food to satisfy hunger did not consume the quantities of sweet things that make British dentists, doctors and dietitians lament about the way many of us eat today; the well-to-do in the nineteenth and early twentieth centuries ate more, those who could, drank more, but although sweet wines were esteemed and widely consumed, they were often taken at the beginning of a meal instead of the end, as they usually are now, or as between-times drinks. This sweetness with the 'starter' course doesn't appear to have cut the appetites of the Victorians and Edwardians; also, it should be remembered, the serving of an apéritif before a meal is a recent practice, by no means usual in Britain until the late 1930s or even post-World War II; people visiting France, even in wine regions, may still not invariably be offered a drink before a meal.

So, until quite recently, it was usual at formal dinners to serve a medium-dry or even sweetish white wine at the beginning of the meal and this would often have been a Graves or even a Sauternes or Barsac. There is a menu of a meal in 1937 when the late King George VI and Queen Elizabeth (now the Queen Mother) visited the United States and dined at the White House: this dinner began with oysters accompanied by a big Sauternes; and, in May 1957, a White House dinner for the then President of Vietnam began with foie gras, went on to soup, then featured 'Crab Meat Mornay' with which a Barsac, Château Climens 1942, was served.

But habits were changing in food and drink, even before 1914. Slimness, instead of a 'queenly figure', was healthier – and more practical for active women. As the liking for cocktails spread in the between-wars period, in spite of the Depression, the 'dryness' of the world's most famous mix, the dry martini (after a court case it was adjudged unnecessary to give it a capital letter) became increasingly stressed via more gin; old cocktail recipe books give what would, today, be unacceptable quantities of vermouth in the mix.

Up to 1939 I think that white wines, drunk by themselves, were not in competition with cocktails. Indeed, wine 'by the glass' is a truly recent trend of the last twenty years or so. Champagne was certainly drunk between times, but, as it was never able to be really cheap, it was only a casual tipple for the fairly well-to-do. But when white wines became chic the cult of 'dryness' slurped over onto them and anything that didn't give the impression of pulling the tastebuds off the palate lost out. Prior to the great frost of 1956, which destroyed most of the Chablis vineyard, there were many wines from within the opening-up regions of France that could compete with white Graves as regards dryness – Muscadet, certain Alsace wines, the then inexpensive white Burgundies, such as Pouilly-Fuissé, Mâcon Blanc, even the newcomer Beaujolais Blanc. The slightly languorous fragrance of the Sémillon in the white Graves gave the impression of sweetness, whether or not this promise on the nose was fulfilled on the palate; I can remember several people who would have considered themselves experienced wine drinkers sniffing and turning away from fine white Graves without even tasting.

There is also an economic reason why certain dry white Graves seldom reached the palates of those who would have appreciated them in the 1950s and 1960s: cash flow. As will be described in a later section, certain of the finer white Graves need time – or they did then, for wine-making methods had not altered very much in the pre-1960 period. But the war had left owners and shippers with the need to make money so as to rehabilitate vineyards and update the equipment in wineries. Such older, dry white Graves as were available tended to be shuffled out to whoever would buy – understandably in this difficult epoch. But they were not able to compete with the 'cheapies' from other countries and their makers couldn't give them the necessary time for maturation when they might show their quality, except for the very finest wines – which seldom actually made money for their proprietors anyway, though this may astonish the outsider. White Graves became unfashionable. The cheaper 'little' white Graves were still made without much know-how, sulphured heavily, and their draggle-tailed character was wholly at a disadvantage by the side of the brisker, cleanly made inexpensive whites coming from elsewhere.

Red Graves are, as I say elsewhere, not always wines to enthral the beginner; this is not to say that they are unwelcoming, harsh or slow to reveal themselves, as is fair comment about certain of the wines of the Médoc, such as the St Estèphes or some small-scale Pauillacs. But red Graves, the delight of many lovers of claret, are not obvious wines; those who make them can help them to achieve a certain appeal immediately perceived by the drinker in these days when long-term maturation is a privilege of the wealthy and often otherwise financed estate owner. The 'something' with which the region endows these red wines is subtle, under-stated. Red Graves reveal themselves gradually, unveiling nuances of fragrance and flavour that require informed and experienced selection and adroit handling, in a sympathetic setting, where their delicate charm and underlying firmness, fascinating to the senses and the mind, can be appre-hended. On so many happy occasions it is with the fine red Graves that members of the wine trade who have taught me so much – even those who are themselves owners of estates in the Bordeaux region elsewhere – have luxuriated with these discreetly different clarets.

Indeed, many times I, playing 'the game' of trying to identify wines that have not been named by the host, have been misled by red Graves; the breed and quality many display has caused me to veer, in my pronounce-ments, to many of the finer Pauillacs or, with slightly smaller-scale wines, have supposed a red Graves, with its gravelly under-taste, to have come from 'across the river' and to be a Pomerol. Their spicy, undulating, almost languorous charm is of great delight to me, but this character may not – indeed, it cannot – appeal to drinkers who still look for the reassurance of the 'known names' and may, reasonably, prefer the possibly more familiar wines of the Médoc communes and of St Émilion.

There are, too, so many wines, both white and red, in the Graves.

Some of these are worthy of more consideration than just the *petits vins* of holiday regions. It's not easy to get to know them, though I think that many deserve to be known and better-known – people who go for a label merely indicating that a wine comes from France are, indeed, 'drinking the label' and may be missing something of importance if they neglect wines that are, whether well known or not, definitely French classics.

Graves wines also come from a region of enormous historical interest and, in these price-conscious times, they are, in many instances, still in the category that many of us can afford without wincing. Before I began to study the Graves for the purpose of writing this book I was myself somewhat vague about the wines but I began to be increasingly attracted by this odd, reticent region. Of course, I have not been able to *like* all of them, although I have felt admiration for many and I return to an earlier opinion – Graves wines are not usually for the beginner, even the person who already loves Bordeaux. I would, now, change that assertion a little. Graves wines are not for the insensitive. The wines, like the region, are seldom obvious; they tend to be undramatic, undemanding, gentle – with much that may be revealed to the discriminating. Let this happen. The reward – in a glass – may plead my cause more effectively than any words.

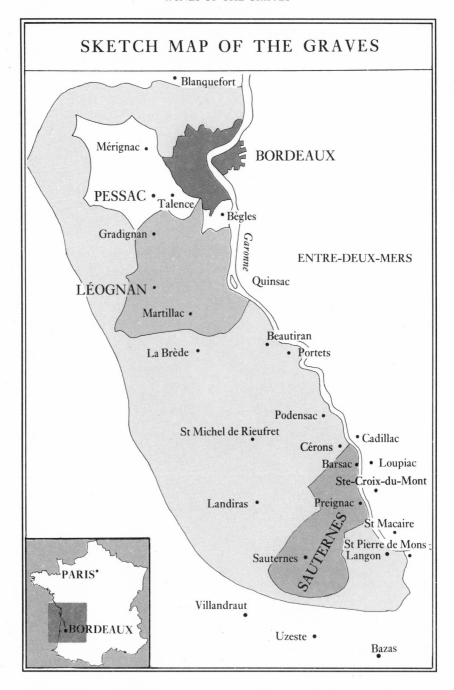

SKETCH MAP OF THE GRAVES

• Blanquefort

Mérignac •

BORDEAUX

PESSAC •
Talence •

• Bègles

Gradignan •

ENTRE-DEUX-MERS

LÉOGNAN •

Quinsac

Garonne

Martillac •

Beautiran
•

La Brède •
• Portets

Podensac •

St Michel de Rieufret
• Cadillac

Cérons •

Barsac • • Loupiac

Ste-Croix-du-Mont

Preignac •

Landiras •
SAUTERNES

St Macaire

St Pierre de Mons

Langon •

Sauternes •

Villandraut
•

PARIS •

Uzeste •

BORDEAUX

Bazas
•

3

WHERE IT IS AND
WHAT IT IS

IT will surprise many, even those who are familiar with Bordeaux and its vineyard, to see, from looking at the demarcated area on the map, the extent of the Graves area. It encompasses the city of Bordeaux itself, sprawls northwards to the Médoc, westwards to the civil and military airports at Mérignac and, to the south, the Landes des Gascogne, and in a great curve up river alongside the River Garonne; it terminates east and south of Langon at, respectively, a little distance from St Pierre de Mons and Mazères. The region is far larger than most people suppose. In fact, the actual *département* of the overall Gironde was not delimited until 1790, when various regions were joined together; these were the Bordeaux region, Périgord, plus the Bazadais and the Agenais, all of which had, before the Revolution, been part of the ancient province of Guyenne (or Guienne). The overall area of what is the Gironde is 1,000,484 ha., making it the largest *département* in France.

To the visitor, perhaps viewing the region from the windows of a train or car, while en route for the Pays Basque or northern Spain, the landscape does not look particularly exciting: flattish (the castles on their spurs of rock are away to the south-west, remote), the occasional big gates leading to some hidden country house. The Sauternais, in the centre, is undulating, with hidden streams and sudden high points of vantage. The land slopes gently to the Garonne, whereas, on the east bank, there are cliffs and outcrops of pale soil. Vegetation tends to be scrubby. The great pine forests, planted in the nineteenth century, only occasionally encroach on the wine region.

Within the vineyards there may be gradual tiltings of the ground but nothing dramatic, as may be seen in the St Émilionnais. The strata below the topsoil have been quiet for a long time, only the occasional variation in the colour of the vines, very slightly lifted or sunken according to the subterranean *croupes*, the little ridges that make so much difference to the individuality of estates, indicates a variation in the terrain.

This is the only French region to take its name from the major part of the soil of which it is composed – the French word *graves* means gravel. This gravel is the small stones, comprising both pebbles and little bits of stones from the river bed of the Garonne and the gravel chips originating in the glaciers of the Pyrenees to the south. Yet few tourists will register the area as particularly gravelly unless they look closely and, in walking in any Bordeaux vineyard, note how many of the locals will pause and, instead of kicking stones and pebbles off the soil, push them back on, among the vines. For stones facilitate drainage, hold the sun's heat, reflect its light. In a vineyard they are usually an asset.

The composition of the Graves terrain is complex. In open places, you may, after a shower of rain, note that certain minute fragments of gravel catch the light and glitter momentarily, although the marl and clay that is mixed with this gravel dull the surface reflections. But it is these minutely shining particles that, as a well-loved radio personality used to say, provide the 'answer that lies in the soil'. For the gravel contains both quartz and quartzite. It was the Marquis de Ségur, the 'Prince des Vignes', owner of – among other estates – Lafite, Latour and Calon-Ségur, who wore iridescent buttons on his waistcoat and, when asked by the French King, Louis XV, what they were, replied nonchalantly 'Oh, – the diamonds from my estate.' (Though this story is also told of the Comte d'Hargicourt, then owner of Château Margaux.) These 'diamonds' were polished quartz and I have been shown many of the stones of various vineyards smoothed into gleaming tones by polishing – one would like to see a designer of modern jewellery make some of them into necklaces and adornments.

What is quartz – and quartzite? Thanks to Imperial College, whose library is an invariably sympathetic help, I will quote some of the definition as given in the *Scientific Encyclopedia of Van Nostrand* (6th edition, 1983): 'The mineral quartz, oxide of the non-metallic element silicon, is the commonest of minerals, and appears in a greater number of forms than any other.... There are two distinct modifications.... It is usual to separate the many kinds of quartz into (1) crystalline or vitreous varieties, actual crystals or vitreous crystalline masses, and (2) cryptocrystalline varieties, mostly compact vitreous sorts, but which may show a crystalline structure under the microscope.' The two sorts have most charming names and colours as, to quote further: 'Crystalline or vitreous: Rock crystal, colorless crystals or masses. Amethyst, clear violet or purple ... Rose quartz ... delicate shades of pink or rose, sometimes red. Citrine or yellow quartz, sometimes called false or Spanish topaz, light to deep yellow. Smoky quartz, smoky brown to almost black, often called cairngorm stone from Cairn-gorm, Scotland. Milky quartz, often showing delicate opalescence . . . Aven-turine quartz . . . Rutilated quartz encloses needle-like prisms of rutile called "flèches d'amour". Other acicular minerals such as actinolite, tourmaline, and epidote, may also be thus enclosed; Cat's Eye shows a peculiar opalescence . . . Tiger's Eye is a siliceous pseudomorph after cro-cidolite of a golden yellow brown color.'

Then, under the cryptocrystalline second category there are 'agate, basanite, bloodstone, carnelian, chalcedony, chert, chrysoprase, flint, helio-trope, jasper, moss agate, onyx, plasma, prose, sard and sardonyx. . . . The word quartz is believed to have been originally of German origin.' Elmer B. Rowley, of Union College, Schenectady, New York, who puts his name to this entry, also mentions the use of quartz in jewellery, its use 'in the ceramic arts', for 'optical and other sorts of scientific instruments, abrasive, scouring, polishing materials, and for refractories'.

Quartzite is defined in the same *Encyclopedia* as: 'A hard, tough, and compact metamorphic rock composed almost wholly of quartz sand grains which have been recrystallised to form a particularly massive siliceous rock. The term is also used for non-metamorphosed quartose sandstones and grits whose elastic grains have been firmly cemented by silica which has grown in optical continuity around each grain.' And, says McGraw-Hill, quartz is 'the principal constituent of sandstone and quartzite and of uncon-solidated sands and gravels'.

This is a bit bleakly intimidating, but it's not impossible to under-stand, although it seems rather remote from the jewel names and associa-tions, such as that of moss agate which, in the Middle Ages, was used to make cups that were supposed to show, by some change of colour, if poison had been put into them with any other liquid. But it's pleasant to think that the soil of many vineyards, including the Graves, is in fact the source of jewels: some of these stones, in polished form, have been prized by many in the past.

The mixed stones of the Graves topsoil also contain some silex and clay. These are good for drainage and, like pebbles, are found in many other wine areas, one can imagine water slithering through them, whereas clay can clog its passage.

The subsoil of the Graves is extremely varied. There are *terrasses* or terraces which lift the land a little higher, endowing the vines planted in them with additional and special nourishment (see fig. 2). Yet this

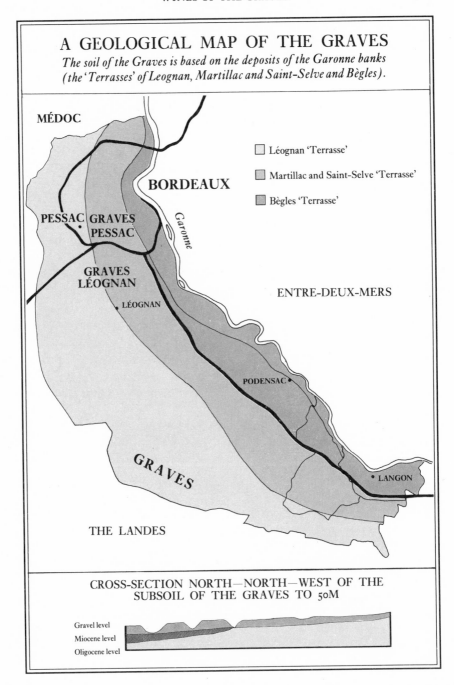

A GEOLOGICAL MAP OF THE GRAVES

The soil of the Graves is based on the deposits of the Garonne banks
(the 'Terrasses' of Leognan, Martillac and Saint-Selve and Bègles).

MÉDOC

BORDEAUX

Léognan 'Terrasse'

Martillac and Saint-Selve 'Terrasse'

Bègles 'Terrasse'

PESSAC GRAVES
PESSAC

Garonne

GRAVES
LÉOGNAN

ENTRE-DEUX-MERS

LÉOGNAN

PODENSAC

GRAVES

LANGON

THE LANDES

CROSS-SECTION NORTH—NORTH—WEST OF THE SUBSOIL OF THE GRAVES TO 50M

Gravel level
Miocene level
Oligocene level

variation might be expected, for the overall Graves area runs for about 50 km north to south, being about 15–20 km wide. Significantly, though, this subsoil may, in places, contain both some iron oxide and that odd substance, 'alios', a type of ironstone, for which the French term is 'crasse de fer'; this alios is apparently found mainly only in the south-west of France and, notably, at Pauillac, which sits on a virtual plateau of the stuff. Is alios also permeable to drainage of water? Writers in the past have wondered and, as yet, no one seems able to give a definite and authoritative answer – it seems an odd element in the soil.

In the important volume on *Le Vignoble girondin* (1947), Germain Lafforgue, Directeur Honoraire des Services Agricoles de la Gironde, makes an interesting point about the regions that are not formed into the *terrasses*, which have substrata, broken up into hollows. The cretaceous substratum of Landiras and Villagrains is apparently special and seems to contain fossils of marine life. Even this section of the Graves is complex. There are several different types of fossil-containing strata, dating from different periods: the sand and marl, some containing fossils of plants, notably at La Brède and at Saucats, and marl with fossilised oysters and chalky sandstone around the Sauternais and chalk and sandstones in the valley of the Ciron. This authority in fact divides the region into 'Aquitanian' and 'Burdigalian' composition, the latter being the sandstone and marl, plus the 'faluns' or chalk enriched with fossils, affecting Haillan, St-Médard-en-Jalles, Mérignac, Pessac, Léognan, Martillac and Saucats. It is a pity that visitors arriving by air cannot pierce the earth to see what lies underneath and affects the region in so much detail, making even this flattish area so varied.

Anyway, to quote further from Lafforgue: 'This is a rather complex mixture, the different constituents varying in their proportions according to quantity and volume – gravel, sand, other elements making up the ground. It is a mantle covering the plateaux and the undulating hillocks between which wind the valleys.' This was written in 1842 by Professor Petit-Lafitte as part of a report, quoted by Lafforgue (my translation). What he has to say about the Graves is still of great significance: after noting that the region is inclined to retain heat and lacks the necessary humidity for other crops, he describes it as 'arid'. But then he continues: 'It seems that the Graves, in other ways so unsuited to general cultivation, is made for vine growing. One might even say that all the factors affecting its formation, its constitution, its situation, the surrounding areas, are united in positively excluding other crops from the area so as establish therein certain produce without parallel, that will never be and never has been equalled, neither in the past nor in the present.

'This arid sand, this impermeable subsoil and these particles of iron that it encloses, all these are what the vine likes. Here its roots like to delve, where they can draw up the precious ingredients that guarantee to its fruit all its wonderful attributes. This polished silex, with its pale colours, is just what is required to reflect the sun's rays, to direct them onto the bunches of grapes and achieve their maturation. These gentle undulations of the ground, the rounded tops of the rises, the slopes hardly perceptible to the eye because they are so adroitly arranged – as it were concealed – these are what enables the sun to kiss and warm the whole surface of the ground, they enable the breezes to blow throughout so as to dissipate the dangerous damp that clings to the earth; finally, the vicinity of the large expanses of water is yet another godsend, for it seems to have been established long since that their proximity too is essential to the production of good wine.' Poetic? Yes – but it's still true!

Anyone trying to grow crops – cereals, roots, greenstuff – or to pasture animals, would not find the Graves ideal terrain. Of course, things *can* be grown, but the land is not rich, even for hardy beasts; in some ways, it seems as if all the elements are on the surface and poultry, rabbits, many small game birds can thrive. But the cow, a choosy feeder and a somewhat delicate animal, is not conspicuous in this part of France; it prefers lush pastureland. Maybe this is one of the reasons why there is no local cheese. Sheep, which have been cultivated for centuries in the Landes, have been valued here for meat and wool rather than milk and the goat, that usually versatile and adaptable animal, is somewhat rare.

Throughout the Graves there are flattish areas where there seem to be no obvious rises and dips in the ground, although, when you look at a field or vineyard planted with vetch, while the ground is being 'rested' and reinvigorated, note some undulations and hillocks, by observing the shading of the foliage. There are also some places where an apparently flat country road suddenly dips and from which no landmark can then be seen. These waves of ground and, within some vineyards, the *croupes* or little ridges or hillocks, are of great importance in the production of fine wine.

It is only quite recently that students of wine have been taught anything about the possible influence of the subsoil in a vineyard – those 'waves' that are often invisible from normal eye-level. Thirty years ago I was taught to look at the angle of a vineyard – its aspect – and also the topsoil, as indicating the type of wine that might be produced from the varieties of vine that might be planted in a particular place. Not much was even hinted at, save by the very few – luckily including my own principal teacher – about the subsoil and those cultivating ground for vines often merely did so because they and their forebears had done so for generations without really knowing why certain plots were better than others.

The enigma that makes an apparently unexciting piece of land capable of producing a crop – grapes – that is extremely varied in quality is something that has provoked speculation for centuries. In 1628 John Locke (1632–1704), the English philosopher, influential in both France and America for his political writings, visited the Graves and, apropos of Haut Brion, commented, 'Why does the width of a ditch separate the reputable wines of the château from the ordinary wines of its neighbour, when, at first sight, the gravelly soil is identical?'

The respected Professor Henri Enjalbert, who holds the Chair of Geography at the University of Bordeaux, has noted that, although an estate's owner can help his land in various ways so as to assist its suitability for vine growing, nevertheless 'If the topography is not favourable from the start, that is, if it is not in the form of steeply-sided hillocks or *croupes*, practically nothing can be done with it. A favourable *terroir* holds its own and only needs attention in minor details. Except for catastrophes, of course, it puts up with all sudden changes in climate because it dries out and drains easily.'

It may surprise a town-dweller to learn about the 'airing' of a piece of land, draining it via the subsoil, so that heavy and persistent rain in the spring and summer can be channelled away and the provision of shelter against such sharp currents of air that may retard satisfactory fruit set and ripening in certain sections of the vineyard, but, now that more is known about vines and vineyards, various man-made devices can assist the natural ones.

Now, as the tap-root of a mature vine will plunge downwards for 15–20 feet or even more, what it encounters below ground and what the roots branching sideways find and from which both draw nourishment is of major importance; the above-ground vegetation takes much from light and water coming down, and the roots derive even more valuable elements from the moisture that is drawn up, by roots channelling downwards and

37

sideways in a variety of subsoils. These subsoils may be watered by or receive drainage from many different types of earth or rock. I have not seen or had time to consult geological studies of vineyards, although I believe these exist and it is possible that, in a perfectly flat vineyard area, scientists can find out whether the subsoil is also consistently flat or, at least, graduated in strata, like layers in a cake and, thereby, they can deduce that the fruit produced above ground and the wine made from it may be the same, whether this fruit comes from one section of the vineyard or from another, at some distance. But, as is now known and understood, in many of the world's great vineyards a mere few yards can make all the difference between fruit that will make good wines and fruit that can make great ones. At least part of this mystery must lie in the subsoil as well as the soil.

In very early times the entire region of Aquitaine was under the sea. This included the whole of the south-west of France. Then, in the Tertiary Age, around 69 million years ago, land rose from the waters. During this period or, rather periods, several of which are named after rocks and with which archaeologists will be familiar, mammals became dominant.

The Pyrenees, as this range was henceforth to be known, were thrust upwards and the topsoil that was deposited upon their flanks and in the foothills was then driven hundreds, even thousands, of miles further away, forced onwards by currents of water that poured down from the mountains. It was as if some giant had flapped the whole upper surface of the land, as someone flaps a blanket when making a bed or agitates a cloth, shaking it free of water in a bath: the sand and gravel from the slopes of the mountains were flung northwards, hurled in a cascade along the flatter ground that was now emerging, the topsoil and quartz coming to rest in what are now the Landes where, though, sand, a lighter element, came first to rest. Further north the remains of this sand, plus gravel and some underlying clay, were impelled towards the Garonne, going as far as to where Bordeaux was to be built, further north into the Médoc, although this then was marshy, hidden ground even when it was not at least partly submerged. The gravelly expanse is sometimes referred to as 'Günz glaciation' which *The Penguin Dictionary of Archaeology* (1972) defines as 'The first major Pleistocene glaciation of the Alps'. The Pleistocene period is the one that corresponds to the last or Great Ice Age when, again according to the *Penguin Dictionary*, ice sheets covered both the Pyrenees and the surrounding land, plus a large section of central France, about 70,000 years before man. As a result of this uprising and shuddering of the earth, several areas of *terrasses* were formed on the left bank of the Garonne; these rose slightly above the surrounding countryside and it is their individual character that makes certain areas in the north of the Graves of major importance. Yet this is only part of the story of the soil, although the upheaving and resettling of the earth folded certain layers below ground that greatly affected plants grown on the surface, especially those that, like the vine, reach deep down for nourishment.

The terrain of the Graves is quite different from that of the right bank of the Garonne; there are more fossil shells there and the composition of the gradual slope of the covering of gravel down towards the river is quite different from that of the banks on the other side. In the Graves, the sand, having been brought in from the west, combines with plateaux of ancient but predominant gravel, the quartz and quartzite seeming to be somewhat dispersed; the alluvial ground appears to be very varied, some of the topsoil seeming to be rather light sand and gravel, with deeper layers of more solid sand and gravel and, within the strata, there are traces of multi-tinted clay on top of what seems to be a stony remnant of a flow of lava in the Pliocene period. Under parts of Léognan, for example, there are patches of *faluns*, a type of petrified sandstone, containing numerous fossilised fish, peculiar to this part of the Graves. It was during the Quaternary period that the lava coating of various sections of the Earth got pushed about and resulted in the projections of the *terrasses*, which are often composed of very varied elements. Subsequent floods, the vanishing of the northern glaciers and, as a result, the rising of the waters and flooding of the lower lands, brought about alluvial silty deposits, combined with those left by the receding salt waters of the ocean.

It is pertinent at this point to quote again from Professor Enjalbert. In a private study of Château Giscours, in the Médoc, he notes that the typical sand of the Landes is black – unsuited to the cultivation of the vine where this black sand covers the gravelly subsoil. In describing the upheaval subsequent to the two tremendous floods about 1,200,000 and 400,000 years before our time, the Professor says that the action of the water, in moving the gravel, destroyed most of the calcareous rocks and those, such as granite, as were likely to rot away. Hence, it is the siliceous rocks that remain – 'quartz, quartzite, touchstones, flints, silex, millstones'. This is apparently true of the sand that is mixed with the gravel, because the finer particles have been carried down to the sea. It is impressive for

39

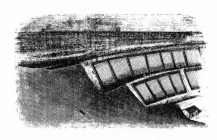

Guyot's suggested layout for a vineyard in the Landes, showing how the sand itself might act as a break against the inroads of the sea. It is interesting to note the steepness of the slopes and the vertical rows of vines (see also p. 157).

the onlooker to learn that there is a variety of different types of 'gravel'.

Professor Enjalbert cites the *galets directeurs* as giving the clue as to what the various sorts of gravel are. These, if somebody could look down on the earlier formation of this part of France from outer space, will demarcate the main courses of the great rivers and it is possible today to trace the subterranean layers where these now lie.

Pyrenean gravel, apparently, is composed of 'fawn-coloured sand, mottled clays and grit which is small and coated with a clay-like substance. This type of gravel is heavy and more suited to the production of white wines than red wines. It can be found in Haut Listrac, at Pape Clément, at Léognan and in Haut Sauternes. . . . The gravel from the Garonne basin was not quite so affected by the invasion of the sand from the Landes . . . this type of gravel [the Professor is here referring to the vineyards of Margaux, where Giscours stands] is composed of pebbles, grit and coarse sand, which have all been washed by the fluvial waters. Furthermore, this type of gravel is "thin" because the particles are both large and because they contain very little clay.' It may be deduced from what the Professor says that, geographically, the Graves is specially favoured and, uniquely, can produce both red and white wines, of top quality, unlike other Bordeaux wine areas.

As Clive Coates has pointed out, the gravels and soils that have mainly formed the Médoc (as well as the vineyards on the east of the Garonne) have come from the Massif Central as well as from the Garonne and are therefore essentially different from the Graves. Of course, some of the Pyrenean upheaval reached the region north of Bordeaux, but this was formed from divers other areas and remained marshy for centuries after the Graves emerged as cultivated or at least cultivatable ground; the complexity of the Médoc's formation at the beginning of time must account at least to a certain extent for the differences in the eventual wines made from vines grown there, as compared with those grown in the Graves.

Geologists may throw up disapproving hands at this inevitably brief and superficial account of what, as I have tried to understand it, has made the Graves so special as a vineyard; at least wine lovers may now appreciate the intricacy of what lies within its earth.

It is still generally accepted that certain sorts of soil are conducive to the cultivation of vines that make certain sorts of wines: gravel, with underlying chalk and, maybe, sand and clay, can nourish this wonderful plant that can make fine reds. Pebbles, limestone or chalk, light sand and gravel – often shimmering as light strikes it – can make white wines of finesse, elegance and crispness. A light-coloured soil will reflect light, which can be of value when the sun does not shine much and, also, when the vines grown produce thick-skinned grapes (such as the Cabernet Sauvignon), that require warmth to ripen them and stress the pigments in the skins that will colour the must; light-toned, pebbly, stony soils can act as night-storage heaters, holding daytime warmth throughout the hours of darkness and reflecting this up onto the bunches of grapes that are sheltered against too much direct, baking sunshine by being suspended below the low-pruned foliage.

The pale pebbles of the Graves, greyish-green, beige, soft pink, purplish-brown, mottled black and tan, some of them clerical grey, some rose-tinted yellow, others assertively slate-coloured with a liquid-like yellow line coiled around them – these are the 'jewels' creating the magic that, even in our scientific time, no mere man has imitated with success in the creation of fine wine. Many of these pebbles are smooth, as the result of millennia of polishing in the earth. Today, millions are hidden beneath the shroud of pavements, asphalt, cobbles, building rubble. But they are there. This earth, as variegated as a stained-glass window, the scales on a fish, the changing lights in a human eye, is Graves.

4

CLIMATE

THIS part of France generally enjoys what is considered to be a 'temperate' climate. The sea is never very distant, nor is the Garonne and there are various little streams running across the area, acting as freshening agents to the land mass. Quite lush vegetation grows along their banks and in the hidden valleys.

It is unfortunate that I cannot cite detailed statistics concerning climate from the past. But instruments lacked precision until comparatively recent times. Since the eighteenth century attempts have been made to observe and measure rainfall and assess the climate, but Germain Lafforgue in *Le Vignoble Girondin* (1947) says firmly that not only were those attempting to make such observations in the past ill-equipped to do so, but often their instruments were badly sited; Professor Petit-Lafitte, for example, who was working from 1848 to 1877, stuck his thermometer up in a training ship, moored in the dampness of the port of Bordeaux, and said later that he ought to have put it somewhere else 'because without doubt the readings were exaggerated, both because of the sogginess of the wood and the nearness of the water'.

Germain Lafforgue gives statistics for the Gironde overall. According to Rayet, the former Director of the Observatory of Bordeaux, who published *Recherches sur le climat de Bordeaux* in 1895, the two major occasions affecting atmospheric pressure are in January and in July. Humidity is usually highest in December and January, when it may be on average 86–87 per cent; in July and August it is around 67 per cent – but, as Lafforgue hastens to say, this can vary a great deal and I would add agreement to that.

Bordeaux temperatures are given as, usually, $-7°$ to $-8°C$ at their lowest (January), rising to 35° in July and August. (But they can go lower and higher.)

In the autumn and winter the prevailing winds in the Gironde are from the east and south-east, in the spring and summer from the west and north-west. As far as rainfall is concerned, this can vary enormously. (The only time I visited Bordeaux and didn't take a mackintosh – in early September – I had to go out with a borrowed umbrella and buy one!) The impression, however, that the whole region is rainy is, as Rayet remarks, mainly conveyed because of the many days in the winter when it drizzles; no wonder many of the Scots and Irish doing business in the Gironde did not complain! But this 'Scotch mist' type of rain does not involve much actual water coming down. October, the latter half of May and the first week of June do seem, however, often to be wet and storms of rain can occur almost at any time, often in June, July, August, less in September, April and May. The point is also made by Lafforgue that, in general, the rainfall tends to be less in the east of the Gironde, across the Garonne.

All these remarks, however, must be taken as generalisations about the whole region. The Graves climate is, as with its soil, somewhat more varied and peculiar.

The Graves can be stuffy, both summer and winter. But there are places with fairly high-sited properties, such as Haut Brion in the north, La Tour de Mons and Magence in the south, among others, where the vineyards benefit by the additional aeration, especially from the winds coming off the ocean to the west, whence their passage is unhindered by any ridges of higher ground in between. This is important, for a vineyard that is too sheltered and enclosed may, if closely planted, be vulnerable to the various diseases that can spread among the vines. The north winds of the winter counteract this to a certain extent, but during the gradual increase of warmth in the middle of the year the grapes are rather more at risk.

Visitors to the Bordeaux region are often surprised that, sometimes for days at a time, the landscape doesn't bask in sunshine; there can be many hours of overcast skies and it may be definitely damp, even if it doesn't actually rain. In high summer the temperature can be high too but, in early autumn, there may be a little light rain, sometimes overnight, which alleviates any excessive dryness on the earth (and, if it comes at the right time, plumps out the grapes and increases the ultimate yield); but there can also be long periods of dryness, over weeks, even months. This can make for 'lean', hard vintages and visitors from many overseas vineyards shake their heads at the veto on irrigation, though there's usually an adequate rainfall if the whole year is taken into consideration. At vintage time it can be really hot. In the winter the cold can be penetrating, without necessarily coinciding with a low temperature – as in the U.K., it's the dampness that can bring the chill into one's bones, just as, on warmer days, it's the humidity that makes one's feet ache.

In most years there are no sudden jumps or falls in temperature, although these can occur. The intense cold of spring 1985, and the snow, as well as the frost which killed many of the plants and shrubs in the gardens of the Médoc (though most of the vines survived) was certainly out of the ordinary. The micro-climates that affect certain plantations of vines are not very marked – as, for example, they are in the irregular landscape of Alsace – although quite often one may be driving down a country road and see rain falling on one side of the track while the other side remains dry.

The Graves enjoys the proximity of the Garonne and the shelter of the land that, on the other side of the river, rises quite sharply, so that wet and any wind from the east seldom afflict the vineyards. And, which is sometimes overlooked, the Graves region is, for the most part, south of Bordeaux and, therefore, south of the other well-known Bordeaux wine areas. Therefore Graves grapes ripen earlier. The vintage here may start and be brought in within days, sometimes even a week or more before the Médoc begins to pick, unless the weather is exceptional throughout the Gironde. This is why, in some years when a vintage in Bordeaux in general may be characterised as 'light' (seldom are there any written-off vintages in these days of informed wine making), Graves wines may be complete, unspoiled by any decline in temperature before full ripeness has developed in the grapes or any onset of heavy rain that may halt or delay picking further to the north; once a vintage is interrupted or suffers days of heavy downpour, many problems can arise and, often, the wines, both those from grapes picked early and those gathered much later, seldom seem to unite wholly satisfactorily after the wine is made and even when the *égalissage* is carried out in the following spring.

Sudden heavy bursts of rain and thunderstorms can occur, even hail, that dreaded fusillade that batters the vines and can strip off the embryonic or ripening grapes. But these storms seem to be localised when they do break and, except for some occurrences in the north of the Graves, there do not seem to be as many disasters affecting the spring 'set' of the flowering vine and the later ripening of the grapes as are recorded sadly elsewhere. Perhaps the pine forests act as some kind of 'blotting paper' to excessively strong western winds and currents of cold air off the Atlantic and, of course, in the proximity of Bordeaux itself, buildings are of some protection.

Enclosed by the Graves proper, the regions of Sauternes and Barsac, cuddled within the larger area, not only look different even to the super-ficially directed eye, but, I should suppose, have markedly different micro-climates. They are perched above most other vineyards but within easy distance of the Garonne from where the mists rise and the *botrytis cinerea*, noble rot, spreads its witheringly benevolent mantle across grapes left on the vines so that, as with Danaë in her tower, a shower of gold – the great golden sweet wines – results. This is all quite different from what growers hope will happen in the Graves, where ordinary grey rot is a plague; true, some white grapes in certain years may receive a touch of the noble rot with which their neighbours are affected, but, even a couple of fields away, the vines and the wines will not be affected.

Throughout the Graves the water table is high. Mostly, cellars are not dug or, if they are, they are not deep, the estates maintaining the *chais* or ground-level wine stores that are usual in most of the Gironde. In some properties that stand on elevated sites on rock, then there may be a true 'cellar' below what is or was a castle. These days modern *chais* may consist of specially designed press- and vat-houses and wine stores, constructed from materials that at once insulate and maintain a beneficent temperature inside, as one sees at Château Fieuzal. Cool, dampish darkness is what wines in bulk and in bottle like, but a *constant* lowish temperature is just as or even more important, so, if this doesn't exist in natural conditions of excavated cellarage or traditional buildings, then enlightened wine makers adapt their practices and draw on the know-how of modern architects and specialist designers.

The possible alteration in the course of the Gulf Stream, about which some uncertainty still exists, may have altered the climate of the British Isles and, I suppose, that of at least parts of the Bordeaux vineyard. Is it also possible, as some people think, that European summers are getting cooler and winters colder? Maybe. But these changes will have taken place and, if they continue, will be taking place over centuries rather than decades.

For the purposes of this book, then, I have assumed that the Graves climate, as it affects the vineyards, is generally as has been described here. What may certainly have affected various specific sites, even whole regions within the area, however, is the changing of the level and the erosion or silting up of the River Garonne. Not only has this affected traffic by water, it will have notably altered the amount of light reflected from the river and the spread of this reflection. Remember that, in distant times, it was the plots of vines along the river banks, the *costes* or *côtes* (slopes) and the *palus* (alluvial river banks) that, throughout the Gironde estuary and up and down the Garonne's course, made the wines that were esteemed above those produced in the land further away from the river. Not that these banks on the Graves side are steep. When, some years ago, the level of the Mosel was altered because of the construction of the canal, the water rose and fears were voiced about the effect on the vineyards, which, in fact, benefited because of more light being reflected on the river banks. Still, various factors have altered and changed the landscape which, in turn, has altered and maybe changed the climate.

Certainly, these days, it is also possible that industrial pollution may have affected the vineyards of the Graves, because of the increased spread of Bordeaux and growth of business; this, even if it does not contaminate, at least causes elements to enter the atmosphere that would not be there naturally. In the flattish landscape, waves of dust and other minute substances may be wafted for large distances around their original 'fall out'. In Chapter 13 the Graves as it is today is considered, but it should be remembered that climate in a contemporary setting can be at least partly shaped by man if not man-made; the 'technopole' or park that some wish to build in about 320 ha. of the A.O.C. vineyard, its boundaries alongside many of the famous estates, cannot but present a major potential change in atmosphere (see fig. 3., p. 168). Even now, segments of such vineyards as have not gone under concrete for ever will have been affected by the city's sprawl and the changes in traffic. Within an area such as the Graves, all this must be taken into account when any appraisal of the local climate is attempted.

HISTORY

5

IN THE VERY BEGINNING

WHEN did man first come to the Graves? It is difficult to be precise. There are traces of Bronze Age remains at Preignac and in a few other places. But although man did inhabit the Gironde in the Palaeolithic era, other traces of human life come late: there seem to be no Neolithic remains, although there are are several that have been identified as Chalcolithic and bronze axes have been found over a fairly wide area. Across the Garonne there are the wonderful prehistoric sites in the Dordogne valley, notably at Lascaux; down in Spain the caves at Altamira likewise bear witness to the early settlements of men and domestic or hunted animals. Though it should be remembered that much of what is now a delectable countryside for holidaymakers was, thousands of years ago, much marshier and unsuited to cultivation or pasturage. The great cave paintings have been preserved at least to a certain extent because their original climate was preserved within them – the dampness keeping the pictorial representations vivid; today, it is the admission of the drier outer atmosphere and the breath of visiting humans that has threatened the caves and their artwork. But certain animals could survive and be hunted by the more adventurous individuals from the early tribes even in regions where life could be only temporarily endured by humans – the cave paintings are records of triumphs achieved in spite of both animal and elemental antagonism.

But the Graves comes mistily out of history with only few artifacts concealed within the gradual undulations of the ground.

The land was then definitely terra firma, bisected by many rivers or rivulets but different from the marshy ground of the Médoc; although the sand of the coast made the west a barren area, the encroachment of this sand was slow.

Yet look at the overall map of the Gironde. Bordeaux stands where it does because, as Camille Jullien, the nineteenth-century historian of the area, said, 'There had to be a city there.' It was the last place along the course of the Garonne where, before the river widened, men and beasts could ford it. (It's astonishing to realise that the first bridge, the Pont de Pierre, was not built until 1822, although Napoleon I had, earlier, wished to construct a wooden bridge.) Early man used rivers and streams as highways, especially for transporting heavy loads, including animals, and Bordeaux was at or in proximity to several waterways. To the south, long before the legend arose of Roland and the Twelve Peers of France defending Roncesvalles against the Saracens, there is an obvious pass across into the Iberian peninsula, where men and beasts could travel without negotiating too many natural hazards. Westwards, there is the Bassin d'Arcachon, bitten out by the sea but nearly enclosed. In the east, tracks as well as rivers came down to the Garonne from what was later to be known as the 'high country' of the hinterland.

For many centuries the story of Bordeaux and that of the Graves have been intricately associated and Bordeaux itself drew so much from the Graves region, in terms of men and women, as well as wine, that I make no apology for telling the story of both the city and the region to the south and west of it; most English-speaking people are unaware of the formative factors of a region that the English crown owned for 299 years, nor do even devotees of claret always associate it with this reticent region of the south-west, where it all began.

But before vines were planted, before the paths followed by pilgrims, scholars, refugees and merchants were beaten onto the map, men came down to the ford which linked what is now the Avenue Thiers in Bordeaux and La Bastide on the opposite bank of the Garonne and they also arrived from the Pyrenees. They were seeking salt. This could be obtained from deposits at the Bassin d'Arcachon and in the small inlets on the Atlantic coast, where the sea would wash into rock pools that later dried and left the glistening debris available for collecting. The Gironde estuary is brown and, doubtless, polluted to some extent today, but in the distant past there must also have been salt deposits along it as well, before the water becomes fresh at the point of entry of the Rivers Garonne and Dordogne – the 'two seas' – that today are the region of the Entre-deux-Mers.

There are many positive attributes of salt and, these days, the scriptural reference to the early disciples being 'the salt of the earth' is unlikely to be understood as the tremendous compliment that it used to be. But primitive man and his animals needed salt for various purposes – as preservative as well as seasoning. Until at least the Middle Ages most animals would be slaughtered at the beginning of winter, because there would be insufficient fodder to supply them; only salt could be used to keep the flesh in an edible condition.

Salt is still used in this way – as with the curing of ham – and maybe its involvement with the hams of the south-west, notably Bayonne, is something very old indeed and may pre-date the practice of smoking meat and fish.

Men and animals seek salt, especially in the heat – to this day, travellers in hot countries are urged to take salt or salt tablets to prevent them becoming dehydrated. Salt 'licks' are frequented by wild animals.

It is not often remembered that roads, tracks or main highways often originated because animals and men wandered through certain places where the going was fairly easy and where water might be available on the way. It is not so long since, in Britain, that geese were walked to London in thousands for the annual Michaelmas Fair and the same sort of thing must have occurred in the wanderings of wild animals, the passage of nomads and that of people going to change their habitations, seek new pastures and, eventually, meet to buy and sell. The earliest people to move within the Graves probably did so only when and where they were driven by necessity – to seek salt or water and for hunting. But gradually, once they had reached the north of the Graves, or crossed from the right bank, the *terrasses*, those slightly raised sections of ground, would have been where they could have settled.

Then there is the tin trade. It's often been stated that the Phoenicians must have brought the first Bordeaux wines, in fact Graves wines, to Britain, because they traded with Cornwall for tin. Yet the copper trade existed even before this. Metal was important for receptacles, for tools as well as for weapons and, in very early times indeed, the copper mines of Cyprus made that island famous and prosperous, for anything that could cut, strike or be indented so as to saw through other substances was precious to early man. The remote eras of history have been named for the iron and the bronze that could cut and kill; man was, first, concerned with survival. Then there are the relics of those who have left us relics in the form of domestic utensils and ornaments, the 'beaker people' (*c.* 2000 BC), those who put bead necklaces and bracelets into their tombs, decorated their pots with 'combed ware' designs and sketched charming representations of animals on the walls of their caves.

Bordeaux was founded by a people about whom scholastic disputes have been and, for all I know, still are being waged. This *fleuve celtique*, as the multi-volumed Bordeaux history describes them, seem to have been

53

composed of a tribe now referred to as the *Biturges vivisques* in the third century BC. The name 'Biturges' apparently means 'kings of the world', but, says the great source book, they are 'a people without history'. They came, they founded the place. That was that.

But the pursuing of any subject can lead to enlightenment in unexpected ways and places. I accepted the statement of the multi-volume history and thought no more about it until I noticed that some of the excellent Italian wines of the Frescobaldi establishment bore the tag: 'Predicato di Biturica.' My friends sent me a note about this unusual term, as follows: 'The Biturges were a people of Gallia Aquitania. They were divided into two tribes, which had their capitals respectively at Bourges and at Bordeaux. They gave their name to the *vitis biturica* which was cultivated in their territory in Roman times. It is not known whether this vine was indigenous or was brought there by the Romans.' Further mention will be made of this vine variety in the section dealing with vines and grapes (p. 181). Yet it is thought improbable that, in this very early period, there would have been vineyards planted in the Graves. The settlement that was to become Bordeaux would have been an unfortified enclosure on the west bank of the Garonne; there would not have been any buildings of importance or size, merely primitive dwellings and, I suppose – but one can only suppose – that there could also have been some large establishments, such as a covered market or places made where people doing business could gather, either near to the ford by the river or where any routes from the south joined the settlement. The river was of major importance but then there would not have been any quaysides or paved paths, only slipways, so that vessels coming from the north or up from the south could moor and take on cargo.

Bordeaux began to grow. Gaul was famous for its wheat, a commodity that was shipped to various ports – the armies of Imperial Rome needed their bread, usually made of *durum*, the hard grain that doesn't go mouldy but, as it gets harder, has to be softened by being soaked in some form of liquid. So, by the first century BC, when Bordeaux had become an entrepôt of some size, with thermal baths and impressive public buildings, wine came up from the south and the hinterland, along what is pleasantly called the *route des amphores*, because of the amphorae which, from their often fragmented traces, have marked the places along the way from Narbonne, Toulouse and Agen by their shards.

Today we tend to think of wine as primarily a pleasant, enjoyable adjunct to civilised living. Then, and for many centuries, it was far more of an essential – a sedative, medicament, disinfectant. The Roman army were issued with a regular wine ration. Maybe people associated some of its beneficent attributes with the semi-magical, semi-hysterical properties resulting from the use of wine in many religious rituals. Any change in the personality of a drinker was often taken to be an indication of a god taking possession of the imbiber.

Casks were in existence even at this early period, but it is the amphorae that enable today's historians to deduce where the wine went. These containers, even those of small size, were used for olives, oil and fruits as well as for liquids; the stoppers were made fast with a type of primitive plaster. Although the amphorae were slightly porous, they seem to have been quite satisfactory as containers; they could be packed on their sides in ships, fitting between the ribs of the hold; they were upended and put into holes in the earth so as to keep their contents cool or, as may be seen in the reconstruction of early wine shops, such as that in Pompeii, they could be propped up in a frame that held them horizontal, ready for use. People who kept stocks of wine in their homes probably had such frames made for the 'special reserves' wines or for use in the dining-room, while the larger vessels were half-buried in the earth of the cellar. When being moved across the land, amphorae could either be wedged against each other on a cart or slung in large-meshed nets on pack animals and, of course, they were also often transported by boats of shallow draught, able to go far up rivers. In fact, transport in the days of Imperial Rome could move with surprising speed: in Julius Caesar's time, the imperial courier would go from Rome to the north coast – the Channel – of France in a week and could reach London within ten days, all the more remarkable when it is realised that the imperial despatches would be carried by a single man, not relays, and that the rider did not, at this time, ride with the aid of stirrups!

A trail of amphorae, all bearing the same seal of their origin and their producer, has been found along the roads to Burdigalia, as Bordeaux was now called. Head of the establishment supplying these quantities of wine was one M. Porci, of Pompeii; some of such consignments may even have been used as ballast and shipped across to Britain. Diodorus of Sicily remarked disapprovingly that 'The natural greed of many Italian merchants causes them to exploit the passion for wine demonstrated by those in Gaul: on the vessels that follow the navigable rivers, on the carts crossing the plains, they send along their wine, from which they gain enormous profits, even to the extent of trading an amphora [of wine] against a slave, so that the buyer frees his servant in order to pay for the drink.'

In view of the demand, it cannot have taken long for those owning property in western Gaul to have decided to plant vineyards and profit by making wine. Roger Dion, the great authority on wine history in France, thinks that as early as the first century BC there was a vineyard in production at Gaillac, on the River Tarn, the wine then coming down by water to Burdigalia, as it continued to do for centuries.

Goods passing through customs posts at Narbonne and Toulouse, however, had to pay duty, so that the Burdigalia price now had to be higher than the buyers expected. Landowners began to have serious ideas about the advantages of laying out vineyards in the south-west, especially after the Roman conquest of Britain; not only did the occupying forces there require more wine than the regular supplies coming up from Italy and, I think, maybe Spain, (which could be shipped through Burdigalia if not direct), but there was another market presenting interesting possibilities – Ireland.

We shall probably never know definitely what were the vine varieties first planted in the Gironde. Where they may have originated is the subject of much learned print. Lucius Junius Moderatus Columella, born in southern Spain and living during the first century BC, wrote much sound practical advice about horticulture, including growing vines. He thought that the vine variety that was planted in the Gironde came from 'very distant regions'. Roger Dion, the historian, thinks that the *Allobrogica*, a strain of vines established in the west of Gaul, suited to resisting cold and frost, should be differentiated from the *Biturca* or *Biturigiaca* planted in the vineyards of Burdigalia. (The section on 'Grapes' (p. 181) has more detail about this.) Roger Dion thinks that the vine he calls *Coculubis* was imported from Spain; certainly the climate of the western regions of the Iberian peninsula might, then, have resembled that of the slightly more northern Gironde and a vine that produced well in one area might do likewise in another, not too far distant.

There are, however, arguments against this: the inhabitants of the Asturias region of northern Spain drank cider and the vineyards do not seem to have been established there until much later. The big Bordeaux history rejects the notion of vines being brought in from the west and the north of Spain in favour of the suggested theories of both Columella and

Pliny the Elder (AD 23–79, author of an encyclopaedic 'Natural History'). Both certainly cite a Spanish vine variety, but one that seems to be somehow different, to which they give the name *basilisca-basilica* and, eventually, *biturica-basilisca*, a variety evolving or seeming to evolve from two types, the one with longish, oval grapes, the other with round grapes. Pliny the Elder (who was killed at the eruption of Vesuvius, calmly noting down what was going on even while the lava fell around – a good journalist!) notes the suitability of this variety, with tiny grapes, resistant to cold and doing well in a poor soil.

One cannot plant a vineyard and expect a prolific yield and satisfactory return on capital outlay within a few years, even with ungrafted vines (which will yield at least some fruit within eighteen months); so the establishing and increased planting of vineyards in the region of Bordeaux is indicative of the feeling of security and prosperity enjoyed at this period of the Roman Empire. A vineyard, runs a saying, is laid out for one's son, the wine is made for one's grandson and even if the vineyard owners of western Gaul didn't always think and plan for the distant future, they had no feeling of uncertainty or awareness of man-made dangers. Burdigalia itself relaxed, neither walled nor fortified; its public buildings were impressive. True, the AD 92 imperial decree of the Roman Emperor Domitian, who wore the purple from AD 81 to 96, required vineyards in Italy and the majority of the Roman provinces to be uprooted and planted with wheat. Yet I have always wondered whether this was as much of a setback to viticulture as it may seem. Those in authority over areas where wine was grown for the use of the Roman army, in various garrisons, were exempt – one had to keep the soldiers loyal – and doubtless many whose private property included vineyards would have asserted that the produce thereof was purely for their own domestic use, to which officials, as a result of being agreeably dined and wined, might henceforth turn a blind eye. The decree, prompted because of the risk of uprisings and riots because of the shortage of bread, was intended to increase the production of wheat – but, the merchant and the landowner of the vineyards within Burdigalia and south of it might have asked irritably, could wheat possibly be grown on land fit only for vines? Certainly not! The peasant farmer is traditionally resistant to change, the tradesman enjoying an income from a commodity in demand resents being deprived of it. The Roman officials were either distant or able to be influenced – 'Come and have a drink and let's forget all this bureaucratic nonsense!' Anyway, Domitian was assassinated in AD 96, the decree revoked by Emperor Probus (AD 276–282) and I doubt whether vast expanses of vineyards had meanwhile been uprooted. In agricultural communities decades tend to take the place of years when time is being considered and, in wine regions, people tend to think in very extended years indeed: 'What my grandfather did' is often, when investigated, something that the speaker's great-grandfather actually did, or even *his* great-grandfather. I don't suppose things were very different even two thousand years ago – there could always have been some cogent reason why a vineyard had not – yet – been uprooted, or why wheat could not – yet – be sown.

Besides, there was then plenty of wheat coming through the port of Burdigalia from the fields of the hinterland across the Garonne. It was being shipped up to the north of France and to Britain. One can imagine a visiting official being shown bales of prime-quality grain, after generous draughts of someone's wine – 'Yes, you see we are doing just as the Emperor required. What a pity that you haven't time to come and inspect the fields – do have just another goblet before you leave!'

The Roman roads brought a variety of people to the settlement on the Garonne: Spaniards, Bretons, Syrians, Greeks, Belgians, Germans, even some British. Initially, the capital of Aquitania – 'land of waters' – had been Saintes, but Burdigalia was growing in importance. Already the lifeblood of the place was wine. Up the Garonne and into the Gironde estuary came the boats loaded with casks and amphorae. In addition to the Romans from Rome who had been sent over to Britain, the British-born subjects of the Empire needed wine and although there were more vineyards in Britain than is sometimes supposed at this time (which makes some think that there must certainly have been a change in climate), the garrisons throughout the British Isles, the cities with their merchants and officials and the well-to-do whose country villas indicate a comfortable life, all needed supplies of wine additional to such alcoholic beverages as could be made in the chillier northern climate. Trading was brisk. It is recorded how a merchant from Trier, an important Roman city, took a consignment of cloth via the Mosel and the Rhine over to England, where he sold it and, having loaded up with china clay, took this down to Burdigalia where he traded his cargo for wine and then sailed north again to sell the wine in Belgium.

About the end of the second century BC Burdigalia became the capital of Aquitania and continued to grow, in size and prosperity. Infuriatingly, there are few records at this time of its emergence to importance. It is possible to imagine some of the life: many citizens had well-appointed villas in the country additional to their town houses and the very early diagrams of the city indicate the civic expansion taking place westwards and to the south (the Graves), rather than north, although, of course, the quaysides did begin to extend in this latter direction along the river, as well as to the south. There were numerous public fountains, and public baths, and water was supplied to private dwellings, for the engineers found it easy to arrange drainage by means of the slopes down to the river – the incline from the centre of Bordeaux down to the quays is still quite steep. Museums have examples of works of art of Roman, Greek, even Celtic origin and private houses were decorated with the work of local artists, many of whom might have worked as itinerants, travelling from place to place where murals, mosaics, ornaments and pieces of furniture would be in demand. The great amphitheatre, the Palais-Gallien, with seating for 15,000, was built; here public spectacles such as gladiatorial contests and, maybe, fights between men and beasts were held; there would have been another theatre as we understand the word, although the remains of that have disappeared. There was an impressive colonnade, the Piliers de Tutelle, presumably part of the temple dedicated to the tutelary deity of the place. Inscriptions on some dedicatory stones include some to 'unknown gods', such as had been remarked on by St Paul at Athens much earlier. The Burdigalians built tombs and funeral stele in a pious fashion, but they seem to have been easy-going as regards religion, the sentiments expressed on many of the stones indicative of an absence of rigidity in the minds of those who wrote them.

Now appear some of the place names. The 'ac' or 'as' suffix to some Latin names develops: Lupus–Lupiacus–Loupiac; Pittus–Pittiacus– Pessac. These names must not be confused with the later suffixes 'ac' and 'oïl' which divided medieval France according to the word that meant 'Yes': the 'langue d'oc' was spoken in the south and the 'langue d'oïl' in the north.

The poet and writer of sharp epigrams, Martial (AD *c.* 40–*c.* 104), who, as a Spaniard, could cast a cool eye on Burdigalia, remarked that it was a bustling, animated place and about this time walls were built around it, often making use of the debris of older structures. It became rectangular, the great amphitheatre and the Tutelle colonnade were left outside the area that could be defended; the ramparts ran from what is now the corner of the Place de la Bourse on the downstream side, up to the Rue de la Vieille Tour, along the Rue des Ramparts to the Place Rohan by the

Cathedral and almost to the river by the Rue du Palais de l'Ombrière. There was an inner fortification in a rectangle from the Place St Pierre almost up to the Rue Ste Cathérine.

Look again at the map. Burdigalia was the only port on the Atlantic coast that was enclosed and that might, at need, be adequately protected. As the Roman Empire slipped into its decline, the roads across the countryside became hazardous; the waterways, less at risk, were thronged with traffic and passengers for it was more difficult to ambush craft on the fast-flowing rivers than to lie in wait for slowly moving carts and possibly unarmed travellers along the highways that were beginning to suffer from lack of maintenance. Vagabonds, including many who had formerly been serfs or slaves, made getting around risky; there were wild men in the Landes and often such savage people formed themselves into armed bands.

In AD 277 Burdigalia was actually sacked by barbarians invading Gaul from the north. Pirates began to establish themselves in the Gironde estuary so, at Blaye, there was an association of lightermen who, at need, were able to block off the river so as to defend the city where, by now, there was a long jetty within the port. The University of Bordeaux had been founded, attracting scholars, professors and students to the city and it does seem strange that so few remnants of the final time of prosperity have survived. However, there were no quarries near Bordeaux then and many monuments and chunks of stone must have been put to a second or third use. Written records are more fragile and easily destroyed or soon rot into nothingness. Now, though, in the third century AD, individual characters begin to emerge in the city of Bordeaux and the surrounding Graves. The old, often unnamed gods are about to give way to the Trinity – and the Roman Empire crumbles as Christianity begins to affect Bordeaux.

6

THE TWILIGHT TIME

FROM THE SACK OF BORDEAUX
TO THE DUCAL DYNASTY

AFTER the sack of Bordeaux in AD 277 reports and records are scattered and sparse. Where *were* those great public buildings of which so few traces remain? Where was the seat of government? Where was the original university? There are only a few contemporary clues; the administration seems to have undergone some reorganisation, in an attempt to rehabilitate the city and to prevent a recurrence of the barbarian attack, but there is no evidence of a regular garrison being established and, certainly, no record of what life in the country was like.

It is the poet Ausonius (AD *c*. 310–*c*. 395) who provides some information, through his verses and letters; he was not only a man of charm and outstanding ability, but also a discriminating and informed lover of food and wine. His family originated in Bazas, but he was born in Bordeaux, where his father was a doctor and where an aunt of his studied medicine at Bordeaux University (the famous School of Salerno was not the sole university to admit women to medical schools!); and one of his uncles was a lawyer in Spain, another in trade, being buried in Britain, at Richborough. The country villa so dear to his heart is a lost site and about eight different places claim to be 'the' one, including the great estate of Château Ausone in St Émilion. But maybe Ausonius had another villa, possibly in the south, for he describes his vines as reflected in the waters of the Garonne, not the Dordogne. Ausonius must have been outstanding, even in an era when only outstanding people are chronicled. Helen Waddell, in *The Wandering Scholars* (1927) mentions that, after studying literature at Toulouse, he held the Chair of Rhetoric at Bordeaux when only twenty-five; then, aged fifty-five, he was called to Rome to tutor the Emperor Valentinian's son, the future Emperor Gratian. In the four years between 376 and 380, Ausonius saw his father, at ninety, honorary prefect of Illyricum, his son and son-in-law proconsuls of Africa, his nephew prefect of Rome: himself praetorian prefect of Gaul, including Spain, Africa and southern Britain as well as France, and in the next year consul'. The liveliness of the mind of those who were born in the Bordeaux region or who at least took it for their native country was manifest early.

Christianity had begun to spread throughout the Gironde. Professor Étienne in his *History of Bordeaux* considers that Ausonius may have been a convert to the new faith, although there is no certainty of this. But his most celebrated pupil, Paulinus of Nola, was a prominent Christian; he flung away a brilliant career, during which he was at one time summoned to Rome to instruct the Emperor Gratian, and, leaving home and family, he went away to serve his God in poverty, leaving Ausonius puzzled and hurt by Paulinus' long absence and silence. The divisive influence of the new faith must have caused many rifts and quarrels among the educated in the outposts of the Empire. (The touching account of Ausonius and Paulinus that is given in Helen Waddell's *The Wandering Scholars* and *Mediaeval Latin Lyrics*, (1929) should be read by anyone trying to make contact with this troubled, remote period.)

Professor Étienne comments that Christianity would have arrived in Bordeaux via the port, where, along with the numerous travellers, new philosophies, theories and scientific discoveries would have entered the south-west. Any boat plying locally would have attracted attention from those ashore; anyone tying up would have had requests for news and information about men and matters; those supervising the keeping of signal bonfires, ready to indicate any danger, would have wanted to hear the latest rumours; and even travellers approaching by foot or on horseback would inevitably have gravitated to the slope down by the river. The original mooring seems to have been where one end of the Pont de Pierre has been built, although no one is likely to be able to go and peer about in the whirl of today's traffic for any evocation of the past just there! Anybody coming over the Garonne by the ford could bring all kinds of news from the 'high country' to the east. Significantly, even at this period, those who crossed over to Bordeaux or traversed the Garonne higher up were said to be 'going to the Romans', which I think may be indicative of how, even when much of Gaul was reverting to wildness and savagery, the south-west of Aquitaine retained some semblance of the former order and civilisation.

A memorial tablet of the third century AD records the name of Domitia, thought to be the first recorded Christian in this region. But there was a great clash of cultures and ideologies, as can occur even in highly educated societies: Urbica, one of the daughters of the most celebrated teacher at the University, was actually stoned to death in one outbreak

62

of violence against the Christians. Bishop Delphin, who had held office in Bordeaux during Ausonius' time, had many serious problems and threats to deal with, one of them concerning Priscillien, Bishop of Ávila, in Spain; this man was preaching a type of heresy associated with asceticism and Delphin presided over a council, held in Bordeaux, that condemned Priscillien, who was taken to Trier and put to death in 385. We know a little about Delphin's activities, because he actually baptised Paulinus of Nola and maintained a correspondence with him; the Christian church at Langon was associated with the Bordeaux diocese and this was near to the burial place of Paulinus' parents, at St Gervais. There is a reference to another 'daughter', that is, a new church, in the same region, because Delphin officiated at the consecration, but the site of this now seems uncertain and it may even have been across the Garonne, perhaps at Ste Croix du Mont.

The building of churches was not only of importance in a religious sense. Now that the former imperial power was crumbling and people needed to be always on the alert against threats and attacks, a church that could, at need, shelter refugees and be barricaded was in more ways than one a type of sanctuary, especially in the flattish region south of Bordeaux where, as yet, there were only a few true castles and forms of fortification. The Graves was as vulnerable now to northern pirates as was the east coast of England, but the northerners, maybe disappointed by the barren land of most of the region and knowing nothing of vineyards, plundered and returned home, instead of settling, as many did, in East Anglia. The northerners were unexpectedly adventurous. In 409 the Vandals swarmed down from the north, overran Aquitaine and got as far as the Spanish frontier, mostly coming overland but also using longships, which would have been able to get down to Bordeaux by the estuary. The barbarians got bolder. In 410 Alaric, King of the Visigoths, sacked Rome and, in 414, attacked Bordeaux. Paulinus of Pella, Ausonius' grandson, attempted to appease the invaders but, like those in England who tried to get the northerners to go away by paying them Danegeld, found that he had the proverbial tiger by the tail and he was forced to flee to Bazas, the home of his family. For a while he then thought of returning to Greece, where he had been born, but travel was no longer as easy to arrange and so he ended his days near Marseilles, in a house perched on a rock, with a small vineyard. His two sons later returned to the Gironde and one of them became the friend and counsellor of the Visigoth King Theodoric I. But Bordeaux had been pillaged and set on fire – the Visigoths were thorough in destruction which is why there are so few surviving records.

Bazas was also besieged but was slightly less vulnerable than Bordeaux. It was the capital of Novempopulania and a city state, with two elevated areas within the main township that could be fortified and defended. Now the whole of Aquitaine was under threat, Saxon pirates descending by sea from the north, Bretons by land from the north-east. Bordeaux was at least now ruled by Theodoric, the first king and a Visigoth, but stable government seemed a thing of the past; the Franks, under King Clovis, invaded Aquitaine, so as, they averred, to drive out the 'foreign' intruders, an old method of putting oneself in the right when undertaking aggression against others. In 498 the Franks defeated the timid King Alaric II and such records as do exist describe little except expeditions traversing the whole of the south-west of France, involving kings and overlords, Visigoths and Merovingians for many years.

The legendary figures of Huon of Bordeaux and the Four Sons of Aymon, supposedly living in this twilight time, are the creations of writers centuries later. Names such as Chilperic, Clotaire, Sigebert, Gontran, Leovigilde and Gondovald make us aware of a great gap between their time and ours.

Two centuries of confusion and battle-clouded events now ensued in the Gironde: was it now – but exactly when? – that Gascony emerged as an independent province and when and under whom did Aquitaine and also Bordeaux get the title of 'duchy'? Between the fifth and the eighth centuries there are records of a mere fifty names of people who lived in Bordeaux and nothing is known about those who may have existed out in the country. The two most common names among these fifty were, for men, Austinde and – significantly – Eyquem; for women there are the exotic sobriquets Isangarde, Entregots, Gardende, Rixende.

There was hardship everywhere. Wolf tracks were noted in the vineyards. (The last wolf is said to have been killed in the Pyrenees as recently as the nineteenth century.) Where wolves originated I do not know but for thousands of years packs of them terrorised parts of Europe and many of the bigger breeds of dog began as guards for men and domestic animals, obviously having wolf blood in their ancestry. In 580 there was a severe earthquake and, in 582, the weather was so intensely cold that wolves came into Bordeaux itself and devoured many of the domestic dogs.

Yet, surprisingly – for survivals are usually surprising and also a tribute to the humans who do survive – vineyards continued to be

cultivated. The religious establishments, although there were not many outside the cities and the actual convents and monasteries in the Pyrenees
in many instances acted as bulwarks against the barbarians and, while they
protected people, the religious also infiltrated a little knowledge into otherwise uncultivated minds. Of course, the church needed wine, both for religious purposes and for medicine; even before the knowledge of distilling
came over the Pyrenees from the Moors, herbs, spices and other ingredients
were combined with wine in a variety of potions by those who treated the sick.

The churchmen and women in the communities of this time
cultivated such vineyards as they had and there are several references to
bishops taking an active part in vineyard work: Paulinus of Pella is credited
with a special method of his own that 'rejuvenated' wines. Wine played
another important part in such social contacts as could be maintained
between the clergy and either other churchmen or the nobility – it made
an ideal present. Alcuin of York (*c.* 735–804), of whom we may be proud
because he was the first European writer on wine (in addition to being
tutor to Charlemagne, his family and the court and writing exquisite verses),
wrote careful notes about a gift of wine he sent (when Abbot of St Martin,
at Tours) to a friend, with instructions as to how it should be handled
en route. Much more of this kind of thing must have been going on. Early
medieval religious settlements might have started by being small, humble
places, with all the inmates, including the superior, having to turn their
hands to husbandry as well as church duties and educating the locals. As
some of these communities prospered, lay workers might be taken on, especially for tasks outside the establishment and such employment may have
possessed some status, as well as often giving those engaged access to educa-
tion and medicine plus the community's resources – fish ponds, market
gardens, pastures and woodland, as well as vineyards.

Increasingly, there are reports of raids and damage done by the
Gascons in the south. The very word 'Gascony' derives from a word meaning an abandoned or devastated area. The early Gascons were savage folk.

Then, at the beginning of the eighth century, the Moors, who had
been occupying the whole of the Iberian peninsula, swept up into France.
The invasions of this period, when territorial rights had continually to be
re-established, make it astonishing that any sort of Christian civilisation
survived. Abd-al-Rahman, the Moors' chief, left some of his forces at Pamplona and went on to attack and sack Bordeaux, then pressing on up to
the Loire after he had defeated Eudes, Duke of Aquitaine – whose two

sons then attempted to set themselves up as overlords in Bordeaux. The tide turned, however, and the Carolingian family from the Meuse with the now nursery-sounding name of Pepin halted the Saracens' advance; one of them, the notable warrior Charles Martel (the word 'marteau' means 'hammer') defeated the invaders and, in 768, Pepin the Short reconquered Aquitaine and took Bordeaux, which Duke Eudes' two sons had unwisely tried to hold against the Franks.

Not that peace could be established. Charles the Great – Charlemagne – went down to Pamplona and Saragossa to attack the 'infidels' and it was while returning that he lost the rearguard of his army, although whether this happened as the 'Song of Roland' recounts, the battle hymn with which Taillefer, William the Conqueror's favourite minstrel, led the Normans into the Battle of Hastings, cannot be definitely asserted. The maternal threat 'If you don't behave, the Moors will get you!' and the belief that Roland's sword was deposited at St Seurin in Bordeaux after his death are essentially folklore but they may also be folk memory. Accounts of the battle in the Pyrenees may have trickled back to the Landes and the Graves. Charlemagne realised that it was essential to maintain a strong province in the south-west and, in 781, Pope Hadrian I (772–795) crowned Charlemagne's son as 'King' of Aquitaine.

It's a pity that nothing survives about vineyards and their progress from this period, because Charlemagne was interested in vines as he was in so many things. It was he who, looking out of his palace on the Rhine, noted that one particular site shed its snow early, so he ordered it to be planted with vines. One of his actions is to have ordered wine to be transported in iron-bound casks, not in skins which must, I have often thought, have frequently imparted an appalling smell and flavour if they had not been properly treated first.

Charlemagne, like many monarchs and rulers, was let down by his progeny and, meanwhile, in the south-west, Gascon ravages continued and the northern pirates became more daring: in 844 the Normans sailed down the Gironde, in 845 killed Sequin II, King of Aquitaine, and besieged Bordeaux in 847. The city tried to resist but the French king, Charles the Bald, was unable to raise the siege and it was burned down in 848, though Charles the Bald did become King of Aquitaine in 855, being succeeded in 867 by Louis the Stammerer. The curious thing about the fire of 848 is that chroniclers cannot agree as to who was responsible.

Battles, pirate raids, the efforts of bishops and archbishops to restore order continue drearily. Meanwhile, though, something of greater and more lasting importance was attracting people from all over Europe to go southwards, taking the famous pilgrim routes to Santiago de Compostela – shrine of St James, the patron of Spain. At this time Santiago was second only to Jerusalem in importance for the devout, Rome coming afterwards. In Jonathan Sumption's scholarly study, *Pilgrimage* (1975), the author implies that Santiago 'was lifted to the front rank of medieval shrines by a combination of shrewd promotion and excellent communications'. For it was easy of access compared with the perils of getting to Jerusalem.

Whether pilgrims en route for Santiago came from eastern or northern France or from the north-west, whether they sailed directly to Spain or disembarked at Bordeaux and went on by foot or in some horse-drawn cart, the majority usually went at least one way through the Graves; there was also a port at Langon by now, for it was there that messengers were known to have arrived as early as 472, sent from Sidonius Appollinarius, son-in-law of the Emperor Avitus and Prefect of Rome, who became Bishop of Clermont Ferrand. The tall spire of St Michel in Bordeaux – 'highest point of the Midi', which region signifies the south-west, not just Provence – wasn't built until the fifteenth century, but it was made so high in order that pilgrims trudging through the Graves might see it and know they were nearing Bordeaux.

The association of Spain and St James the Great, brother of St John, began with a tradition that James had preached the gospel in Spain; after his martyrdom, sometime before AD 44, and the death of Herod Agrippa, who, according to the Acts of the Apostles had him killed 'with a sword', it was said that some faithful Spanish disciples took the body and transported it to Spain, in a marble sarcophagus. While they were sailing along the coast of Portugal, the saint saved the life of a man who, together with his horse, had been carried out to sea – some accounts make him the bridegroom in a wedding party. Anyway, both man and horse surfaced safely, clothes and harness swagged down by scallop shells – hence the emblem carried by pilgrims. St James's body was eventually buried near Santiago and no one knew of its whereabouts until, in 813, it was revealed by the appearance of a bright star, the sounds of an angelic choir – and King Alfonso of León built over the tomb a church which developed into a cathedral.

Even when the Moors attacked Santiago in 997 and burned it, including the church, the tomb remained intact. The Moorish commander rode his horse into the church and tried to make it desecrate the font by having a drink there – but the wretched animal apparently 'burst asunder and died', a moral episode. A monk, praying at the tomb, so impressed the commander that he was not only allowed to continue his intercessions but a guard was mounted there to protect both him and the saint's remains. As H. V. Morton comments in *A Stranger in Spain* (1955), it was a significant event or at least an effective legend: 'That one of the chief Apostles should himself be taking a hand in driving the Infidel out of Spain, and cheering on the struggling little Christian kingdoms of the north, was in those days as important politically and strategically as the explosion of a new kind of . . . bomb today . . . the wise and clever monks of Cluny, who were the keepers of the Western conscience, soon saw that a European main road should be driven across Spain to Santiago, to be thronged with pilgrims from every country, who would form a living bridge with Europe.'

Scallop shells – cockleshells were also sometimes used – indicated that a pilgrim had actually been to Santiago, for they could only be bought there. (A palm branch signified that a pilgrim had been to Jerusalem.) It took about four days to get by ship from England to Corunna if one was lucky. The land route across the west of France to the Pyrenees became known as the 'French Road' in England and I wonder whether some of the odd pipes on which bands of players take part in demonstrations of 'le folklore' today had their origin in the pilgrim staves that were bored with holes so that those who carried them could make cheerful music.

There is an odd survival of pilgrim traditions – or there was, until quite recently – in the building of little 'grottoes' or shrines in London streets, with urchins urging 'Remember the grotto!' and begging for donations. The shells which decorated these 'grottoes' might be oyster shells as well as scallop or cockleshells, but the date when they were put up was 25 July – St James's festival – and the custom dates from the time when medieval people erected such decorations, doubtless then with a figure of the saint in each, to remind people who couldn't manage to go to Santiago at least to honour St James in their prayers.

Henceforth, along the main pilgrim ways, large churches and sometimes special hospices were built, the remains of the hospice at Pons showing the horseshoes imprinted on the entrance walls – upright, so that the luck would not run out – by grateful pilgrims. More practically, Pons gateway has stone slabs on which the bodies of those who had died en route could be laid out before they were brought in for burial. The churches along the 'roads of St James' often have large stone Calvaries and exterior altars in their grounds, so that Mass could be said for the hundreds of pilgrims who could not get into the church itself; the sculptures above the doors are virtual picture-books in stone, as interesting to look at during the services as the decorations and windows inside. Sometimes sections of these churches, such as the porches and side aisles, could afford shelter for pilgrims unable to find lodging for the night: there is just such a commodious porch at Le Nizan, near Roquetaillade, built in the twelfth century, with a commanding view so that any marauders lurking around could have been observed by a lookout. One of the known stopping places for pilgrims was the Priory of Cayac, at Gradignan: 'L'Hospitau de Nostra Dona deu cap dou pont de Cayac', which was the first halt from Bordeaux to Santiago. (This establishment was later used as the headquarters of the Parliamentary forces in the wars of the Fronde and the Duc d'Épernon besieged it.)

In Britain, thanks to our familiarity with the Canterbury pilgrims, we tend to forget the serious hardships and dangers of pilgrims who went further afield. Geoffrey Chaucer, son of a vintner, certainly seems to have known 'Bordeaux town' and travelled comfortably in the company of the nobility whom he served, but many of his fellow countrymen must have blessed him for writing the *Canterbury Tales*, promoting the route to Thomas à Becket's shrine. One can hear the innkeepers, souvenir salesmen and animal hirers: 'Better roads in England, one can speak the language, there's none of that foreign food or dishonest taverners – my dear, it certainly isn't safe there for women and children, and St Thomas probably has a special affection for us English. . . .' Certainly, Dr Andrew Boorde in the fifteenth century is only one of those who feelingly describe the ordeals suffered on many pilgrimages: being robbed by supposedly accredited 'guides', being overcharged for board and lodging and as for the souvenir salesmen . . .

Those who manned the hospices, as well as those catering for the secular accommodation of pilgrims, needed to be capable, cheerful and robust. Some pilgrims were by no means quiet, devout travellers. The Normans in particular got a reputation for being tough customers, loud-talking and the sort of demanding lodgers that the hotel trade detests to this day. Preachers began to denounce self-styled 'pilgrims', who travelled with accompanying retinues 'with bulging purses and trunks of spare clothes, eating succulent food and drinking heady wine'. Somebody might have been ordered to go off on a pilgrimage as a form of penance – it was a convenient means of getting 'difficult' people out of the way for a while – but certainly the better-off pilgrims were not going to deprive themselves of creature comforts and adequate care of their bodies while they journeyed for the benefit of their souls. The truly serious were advised to band together, so as to avoid falling in with unscrupulous racketeers who might pretend to be pilgrims but then, having got the confidence of the holy travellers, would assault and rob them.

The Graves must have seen many thousands of pilgrims making their way south and, probably, exchanging greetings and advice with those returning from Santiago; some tiny hamlets today still retain churches built to cater for such people. Nor would everyone passing through the Graves have always travelled on, or, if they did, they might make a permanent stop on the way back. Maybe some from the harder northern regions found the softer climate pleasing, possibly craftsmen and artisans saw opportunities for remunerative work in a region as yet not likely to provide much competition. Sometimes the appeal of owning a different patch of land may have influenced somebody to settle down. There must have been many who, either falling ill along the way or just finding themselves unable to complete the outward and return journey, simply stopped where they were. And, of course, there would have been some temporary or involuntary stops by people who always enjoyed a wandering life. The Graves may have seemed safer and more attractive than some of the earlier sections of the pilgrim route and, from this time, it became enriched with a valuable and varied range of outsiders, who were to contribute much to its history in the future.

By now the Dukes of Gascony had begun to assume more power. Names such as Sanche-Sanchez, Garsie-Sanche, Sanche-Garsie begin to appear in the scanty historical records and, gradually, it was the Gascons who made themselves masters of Aquitaine too. (Those who visit the estate of Rauzan-Gassies, in Margaux in the Médoc, probably never realise that the 'Gassies' part of its name derives from a version of 'Garcia' or 'Garcie', a family name of this remote time.) But was the Duchy of Gascony freehold territory? This is an important matter for when, much later, the kings of England claimed rights over Aquitaine, it was a debatable point as to how, exactly, they held this section of France in relation to the French crown.

In 1058 Bordeaux – Aquitaine – and Gascony were united. Technically, the ducal overlords held the duchy from the Abbey of St Seurin, in Bordeaux, but, as they were all-powerful, choosing the church dignatories as well as selecting the laymen who had positions of power, this meant very little. The kings of France held their realm from the Abbey of St Denis, where most of them were to be buried – and of which more will be told in the next chapter.

Now begins the rise of a dynasty in Aquitaine that started with a remarkable man and ended with an even more remarkable woman. This dynasty dominated the Graves. It changed the history of England. And it coincided with the beginning of the Bordeaux wine trade as very big business.

7

THE DUKES – AND THE LAST DUCHESS

(ELEANOR OF AQUITAINE)

ONE dynasty dominated Aquitaine in the Middle Ages. It included so many remarkable personalities, was so powerful, had such a lasting effect on the history of both France and England that it is strange that few English-speaking people know much about it. Such fictional accounts as do exist are not only inaccurate but far less interesting and exciting than the truth.

The origins of the Dukes of Aquitaine are somewhat obscure, as is not surprising at this turbulent and scantily chronicled period. But in the eleventh century the then Comté de Bordeaux married into the Sanche family, who were Dukes of Gascony; the women in the history of Aquitaine were no mere chattels, but as active and influential as the men and could succeed to lands in their own right.

These lords of the south-west held Aquitaine and the Comté de Poitou directly from the French king. Whether they also held Gascony, of which they were also dukes, in the same way – as direct vassals – is a matter that resulted in much subsequent argument and conflict, but the possible difference in their tenure should be borne in mind. The territory over which they held sway was vast: it extended from the River Indre in the north down to the Basses-Pyrénées and right over to Burgundy in the east, including the *comtés* of Auvergne, Limoges, Périgord, Angoulême. The Viscounts of Thouars in Poitou were subject to them, so were the seigneurs of Châtellerault and of Lusignan (a member of this last family was to become King of Jerusalem), likewise the lords of Mauléon, Parthenay, Châteauroux, Issoudun in the region of Berry and, in the Limousin, the lords of Turenne and Ventadour. Then there was the specifically Gascon nobility, the overlords of Astarac, Armagnac, Pardiac, Fézensac, all along the hinterland of Guyenne.

No king of France would or could risk a direct conflict with such a mighty vassal. In 1043 there is a mention of a 'Sina' or 'Aina' as being the Comtesse de Bordeaux and of Périgord; she was doubtless of the same temper as her father, the Comte de Périgord who, in an argument with Hugues Capet, remarked briskly 'Who made you a king, then?' using the familiar 'tu'. (Hugues founded the Capetian line, the French royal house 987–1328.)

William I, Duke of Aquitaine, gets tagged as 'the Pious', probably because he founded the gigantic Abbey of Cluny, in September 911, endowing it with much rich surrounding territory. This Benedictine establishment became enormously important and influential as well: independent of temporal authority, it issued orders to numerous kings and, as it was also exempt from the authority of bishops, it even gave advice to popes, who were not always as secure on their thrones as the Abbots of Cluny. In 1145 a former Clairvaux monk became Pope Eugenius III. Clairvaux was another of the Cluny-linked foundations, which were established from Poland to Spain, more than 10,000 monks belonging to them and innumerable lay workers being in their employ. Sir Stephen Runciman (in an address at one of the Aldeburgh Festivals) aptly commented that 'the monks of Cluny were the American Express of the Middle Ages'. As Benedictines, they stressed scholarship as well as the recital of the divine office; they ran schools, assisted the study of the arts and even the sciences, they staffed hospices and hospitals, they ran their estates with great efficiency. Their influence on the history of wine is considerable. Most people know about the work of Dom Pierre Pérignon at Hautvillers in Champagne, which was a Benedictine house. St Benedict in his 'rule' for the Order, had given each religious quite an ample daily wine ration and even when Bernard of Clairvaux (1090–1153) denounced the somewhat magnificent lifestyle of many Benedictines and some of his followers went off to set up a more rigorous rule at Cîteaux, in Burgundy, the Cistercians there still made wine, whether or not they were allowed to drink it.

Dom Justin McCann, in his life of *Saint Benedict* (1938) says, commenting on Benedictine fare: 'Of fasting, while recognising the undoubted austerity of St Benedict's régime, we may point out that, judged by the standard of contemporary monasticism, it is moderate.' His regulations as to the normal amount of food and drink are again austere in our eyes, but generous even to the point of laxity judged by Eastern standards. A sentence that occurs in the chapter on the measure of drink may be quoted as displaying the prudence and discretion of the saint, and also what seems like gentle humour: 'We do indeed read', he says, referring to the *Book of the Sayings*

74

of Eastern Monks, 'that wine is no drink for monks; but, since nowadays monks cannot be persuaded of this, let us at least agree upon this, that we drink temperately and not to satiety. And he allows his disciples a sufficient daily measure of wine.' The reader in modern times should remember that wine was both a disinfectant and a medicament and, especially on journeys, which the Benedictines often took, could be essential when the local water supply was not safe. St Bernard of Clairvaux – of whom much more will be heard in the story of the Aquitaine family – was known for his personal austerity, but although he did impose his individual prohibition about wine on the community at Cîteaux, he could not extend this to the whole Benedictine order.

The influence of the Benedictines on wine is a vast subject, but Desmond Seward says, in *Monks & Wine* (1979), 'the monks of all orders as well as Benedictines seem to have had far less influence on the wines of Bordeaux than they had on those of Champagne, Burgundy or the Loire'. If, by 'influence' he means that no notable innovations in wine making and vine cultivation came from the religious establishments of the Gironde, he is probably correct, but the enormous holdings of the various churches and communities there should not be ignored; they were powerful and significant employers and the wines they made became famous both in France and on export markets.

The power of the Benedictines in the Church and through those of their order as were attached to various courts and consulted by the nobility was as great as that of the Aquitaine ducal house. In both the advice that the monks of Cluny gave out and in their intercessory prayers they were unlikely to have forgotten their first founder and his family, in spite of the problems that Bernard of Clairvaux was to have with the latter. (He deserved canonisation for his endurance of these alone.)

Within the region of Aquitaine the dukes maintained a court of such state that contemporaries found it wholly superior in magnificence to that of the King of France. Some of them even adopted the title *Ducs de toute la monarchie des Aquitaines*. The lands they held were either strategically useful or rich in resources, or, sometimes, both. Great castles began to rise throughout the region and, even in ruins, these are huge, asserting still the power of their owners, who would have lived as well as any in Christendom; no wonder that these people had a high opinion of themselves. 'Opulent Aquitaine,' says a monk, Heriger of Lobbes, 'sweet as nectar, thanks to its vines, strewn with forestland, bulging with fruit and

75

enjoying an abundance of pasture land.' Down the seaboard the ports throve on the Atlantic fish, at Bayonne the regular trade with Spain was augmented by fishing and the town was famous for the fleets it sent out hunting whales. Bordeaux itself was an important port, so were some of the estuary towns, such as Langon, with their local trade in wine, stone from the quarries, wood from the forests, including casks. About this period cultural life also begins to develop. Side by side with the religious establishments, the ruling family were not just coarse warrior types: Duke William V, even when on campaign, would stay up at night reading, like the Emperor Charlemagne, and probably he studied to better effect than Charles the Great, who – though he knew quite a bit about wine – was admitted to be better at reading than writing.

Duke William IX (1071–1127), Count of Poitiers, who joined with Alfonso of Aragon in a campaign against the Saracens, was definitely a 'personality': he was excommunicated for robbing churches and for what Richard Aldington (1892–1962), himself a poet and editor of much romance literature and writer of the 'daring' novel of World War I *Death of a Hero*, refers to as 'general immorality'. William IX was the first of the troubadour poets, something that will surprise many who associate Provence with them (though there is at least one other from the Gironde); one of William's contemporaries is quoted by Aldington (*Fifty Romance Lyric Poems* (1931)) as saying that this Duke was 'one of the most knightly men in the world and one of the greatest deceivers of ladies and a good soldier and a generous man'. It was he who had the likeness of his lady – whether the permanent *maîtresse en titre* or the fancy of the moment – painted on his shield, remarking that, 'Since she has often borne me in her bed, it is fitting I should bear her in battle.' William wrote his verses in the vernacular, somewhat unusual at this time, and Aldington cites his charming lines 'I will make a new song before the wind and the frost come', though he says tantalisingly that some of the other ducal poems are 'extremely free in their speech'.

William IX had a son, later to be Duke William X, by Countess Philippa of Toulouse, but he seems to have got bored with her and, I have not been able to find out exactly how, managed to marry the Countess of Châtellerault, whose name or nickname was, significantly, 'Dangerosa'. This lady had also been married before and, by her first husband, had given birth to a daughter, Anor. The couple married off Anor to young William and, when the first child of this marriage was born in 1122, it was a daughter, who was named Alia-Anor ('another Anor'), or, by mutation Aliénor – or

Eleanor. The son born to William IX and Dangerosa died, their only other child was yet one more girl — the female strain was showing its power. So Aliénor or Eleanor was the greatest matrimonial prize of the Middle Ages, being heiress to William X, her lands extending from the Loire to the Pyrenees and slicing into France across to Burgundy.

No one seems certain where Eleanor was born. Some think her birthplace was in the Landes, some suppose it to have been Bordeaux itself. She was, though, a 'girl of the Graves'. The castle at Talmont, where her mother Anor and her little brother died, has now been almost overwhelmed by the sea.

If we had not heard so much about those remarkable ladies, Queen Elizabeth I and Queen Victoria, we should have certainly heard more about Eleanor, who was as able and as courageous as both — and far more glamorous in both the medieval and the modern senses of this word. Claude Colleer Abbott (in *Early Medieval French Lyrics* (1932)) says, of the poetry of the time, 'among the writing of those poets whose names are music . . . one woman in particular will always be associated . . . no scholar has yet measured the literary influence of her and her family'. True, the Victorian squarson, Sabine Baring-Gould (1834–1924), best known for writing the hymn *Onward Christian soldiers*, but who travelled extensively, including in southern France, writing all the time while his curates toiled, commented prissily that Eleanor had a bad upbringing (she appears to have been at least as well educated as any of her time and her manners seem to have been impeccable). He dismissed her as being 'without religious scruples'. On what he based this judgement I cannot discover and, to readers in the latter part of the twentieth century, she may seem far more sympathetic.

The courtly troubadour poets — who, after all, had to be polite to those who were putting them up — certainly did celebrate her; a popular anonymous verse seems to speak with more warmth than, to my mind, some of the poems addressed to Elizabeth I (were any written to Victoria?) and this, it should be remembered, must have been written after Eleanor's second marriage, and after 1154, when she was in her thirties, no longer a very young woman even by today's standards:

> Were the whole world mine,
> From the Elbe to the Rhine,
> I'd give it all if the Queen of England
> Lay in my arms.

Eleanor was born in 1122. She was in her thirties when 'Queen of England'. Courtly compliments are one thing – the asset that veils a woman with that indefinable asset, charm, is another. Eleanor appears to have had it all her long life.

Duke William X, Eleanor's father, was a turbulent person, even by Aquitaine standards. He seems to have had a running battle with the Church for most of his reign. Bernard, Abbot of Clairvaux, quite a tough personality during his lifetime, was one of the Duke's sterner critics. At one dramatic moment, William, who had been excommunicated – doubtless for oppressing some church organisation – decided to tackle Bernard in person; hearing that the holy man had actually entered his duchy at Parthenay, where he was to say mass, Duke William, obliged to remain outside the sacred precincts, awaited the emergence of the Abbot with his retinue – of armed men. Bernard, to whom a warning was whispered at the altar, grasped the pyx containing the consecrated host and swept down to the church door to confront the Duke. The doorway alone remains. Duke William, doubtless surprised, thereupon fell to the ground in some kind of fit – highly gratifying to the godly. Bernard's church nickname is 'Doctor Mellifluous' – honey tongued – from his powerful preaching, but his recorded remarks, including his bitter opposition to Peter Abelard, tend to be anything but sweet. Whether as the result of this shock or merely because he wanted to get the assurance of assistance of various neighbouring seigneurs in case he required help against the King of France or anyone else, William then set off on a trip to Santiago, at least nominally a pilgrimage. It was, though, a sufficiently long and hazardous journey to cause him to put his affairs in order before he left his duchy.

Though only thirty-eight, he had lived hard and one report says, 'he could hardly satisfy his voracity at one meal'. So, before he left Aquitaine, William appointed King Louis VI of France (referred to as 'the Fat') as guardian to his elder daughter and heiress, Eleanor. Louis had family worries too: his eldest son, Philip, had been thrown from his horse while riding on the banks of the Seine in Paris by a sow rushing between the animal's legs – and the prince died, without recovering consciousness, as a result of the fall. Young Louis, the second son, destined for the Church, had to be prepared to rule and the King was concerned by the threat presented to the smallish and precariously maintained Kingdom of France by a powerful family in Anjou ... who wore a sprig of broom as a badge or identifying symbol and became known as 'Plantagenets', after this plant – *planta genista*.

Bernard of Clairvaux had many problems with this Angevin dynasty and is supposed to have said 'From the Devil they came, to the Devil they will go.' This refers, to the belief that, in former times, the then Count of Anjou married a beautiful woman who always somehow managed to leave mass before the end; four knights arranged to step on her robe, so as to hold her to the spot and, unable to depart because she was pinned to the ground by their feet, she gave a terrible scream at the elevation of the host, flew up into the air and was never seen again — for she was the fairy Mélusine, from whom the family were supposed to inherit both their charm and various other wiles. Not that this seems to have worried the Counts of Anjou at all. One of them, Fulk Nerra — 'the Black' — built numerous castles along the River Loire and established a reputation for energy and ferocity, guidebooks today constantly relating how he galloped from one fortress to another, covering distances that a contemporary rally driver would find challenging.

William X died, in somewhat obscure circumstances, while on his pilgrimage and was buried at the foot of the altar of St James — Santiago de Compostela. King Louis, feeling his own death was near, had already managed to get the Duke's approval of the betrothal of his young son Louis to Eleanor. It was a crafty move to unite France and Aquitaine and the fatherless Eleanor (and her sister, of whom King Louis was also guardian) would have understood the advantages.

Although a great heiress, at the age of fifteen she was not expected to have been able to undertake the ruling of her property single-handed. So, in 1137, she and Louis were married in the Cathedral of St André at Bordeaux and, on their way back to Paris, there was a type of coronation peculiar to the rulers of Aquitaine in the Cathedral of Poitiers. But before the new Duke and Duchess could return to Paris Louis the Fat died and, in spite of the various wise counsellors to whom he bequeathed the care of his son and his kingdom, the King and Queen of France were now two young people — with all the potential problems relating to such.

Events whirled around Eleanor. She gave Bernard of Clairvaux quite as much trouble as her father had done. Her reported statement, 'I thought to have married a man, not a monk', rings regretfully and bitterly down the centuries. There are few remaining places definitely associated with Eleanor, but if you wish to see the sort of castle in which she might have lived as a young woman, it is worth making a detour from the road down to Bordeaux into the *département* of the Creuse. Take the road to a small town called Belabré then, six miles on the road to Lignac, turn right. Here you can see the mighty walls of Château Guillaume, built by Eleanor's father, William X. The moat has dried up, the outer walls have disappeared but, nearer to Poitiers than to Bordeaux, this is still a formidable outpost of the Duchy of Aquitaine; in castles such as this men and women lived a life as civilised as was possible in those turbulent times, listening to and composing music, writing poems, even reading books. Eleanor's one known personal possession – the crystal vase she gave to her husband, Louis VII, on their marriage – is both beautiful and slightly mysterious.

Eleanor put up with Louis for some time. Paris was certainly not Bordeaux, for then many cities in the south would have prided themselves on longer histories and more culture than those of the north, but there were still vineyards within its walls and many poets and minstrels to provide entertainment for the granddaughter of the first troubadour. Louis' adviser, Abbot Suger, seems to have played the part of mediator between the young couple on many occasions, but Bernard of Clairvaux, often commuting between Paris and Burgundy, looked askance at the young Queen; the scandal of Abelard and Héloïse was recent and Bernard was probably not the only churchman to think of women as a nuisance and, even, a malign influence. Unlike Aquitaine, the Kingdom of France was bound by Salic law, which forbade a woman to inherit the crown – hence many machinations by mothers, wives, and mistresses behind the scenes at court. Eleanor, always of an independent spirit, might not have approved of this – she was Duchess of Aquitaine in her own right.

Both King and Queen became involved in civil strife and opposition to the Church early on in their reign. At one time France was under a papal edict – no church services of any kind might be performed. Eventually crown and Church were reconciled and the great Abbey of St Denis, designed to be the burial place of the Kings of France (Denis, Denys, or Dionysius is the patron saint of France), was built and consecrated, an occasion that was also the excuse for much secular junketing. Louis, who seems always to have had bouts of monk-like austerity, gave Eleanor's wedding present to Abbot Suger for the new Abbey and she, although it is said she enjoyed herself at the consecration ceremonies, took the opportunity of asking Bernard of Clairvaux to pray for her to conceive a child.

After seven years of marriage, this was a serious matter. Much today is heard about 'dynasties' but it is difficult to overestimate the significance of the word in a medieval context, when high infant mortality might swiftly

80

deprive a family of the eldest son. Several male children were a safety measure, daughters could be utilised to make marriages allying powerful overlords with each other and, via dowries, joining up estates; even those who didn't marry or lost their partners might enter a powerful monastery or convent, assuring family and friends of their prayers and, often, acting as advisers to the laity. Eleanor's grandmother Philippa, after being forsaken by her husband, went off to the mighty Abbey of Fontevrault, where the Lady Abbess was a noblewoman of very high rank, enjoying a rule as absolute as any queen regnant. Large nurseries were an insurance policy.

So – what was the matter with two healthy young people who didn't have children?

Bernard of Clairvaux was stern with Eleanor – 'Strive for peace', he urged, for the Queen had played quite an active part in the internal wars, on several occasions insisting on her right to various lands – she always stood up for what she thought of as being rightfully her property or belonging to her family. But she seems to have behaved correctly to Bernard and, subsequently, did have a child – a daughter. At least a royal nursery now existed.

Louis and Eleanor then went off on a Crusade, certainly with Bernard's approval. Many nobles went with them, some took their wives and the wives took attendant ladies and maidservants so that quite a social time was had by at least some en route. Numbers of the retinue came from Gascony and the Queen travelled with many baggage wagons – on such a long trip, a woman must have an adequate wardrobe. Eleanor was able to withstand many hardships if these were inevitable, but she enjoyed comfort and beautiful things. There is a charming legend that, 'once upon a time' a magnificent train of nobles came along the road to Jerusalem, led by the 'lady with the golden boot' – even serious historians admit this could have been the Queen of France.

Duke William IX, the troubadour, had also gone crusading and written comically about the hardships. His younger son, a childhood playmate of Eleanor, was now Prince of Antioch so, after a splendid sojourn in Constantinople, the French were greeted at the port of St Simeon by this Prince, Raymond of Poitiers, attractive, courtly, amusing – and a mere eight years older than Eleanor. Some of his courtiers may have already been known to the Queen, for they came from her homeland and spoke *Langue d'oc*. After a time, a 'situation' seems to have arisen.

What did truly happen at Antioch will never be known and the writers of the time are tantalisingly reticent, so it's impossible to be sure whether or not the Queen and the Prince did have more than a polite flirtation; however, Louis and Raymond fell out – some difference about strategy – and the King announced that he was going home, his wife would go with him. Eleanor refused. She intended to stay on, with her own courtiers. Louis insisted – and then the Queen flung at the pious Frenchman the fact that he had no rights over her at all, for they were actually related within the prohibited degrees of consanguinity and their marriage should never have taken place. (I wonder how she had found out – and who had informed her?) But Louis dragged her away and, on the way back to France, they stopped at Tusculum and called on the Pope, asking advice. Yes, the pontiff had to admit, they *were* cousins – nine times removed in civil law, but a deplorable mere four or five times removed in canonical terms. During a period when most of the higher ranks of society must have been related to each other, simply because there were not enough of them to avoid the risk, this sort of thing often provided an easy way out of an unsatisfactory marriage – as witness the English Henry VIII later. Rather oddly, the thinking behind the religious prohibition of human inbreeding – the weakening of stock and the perpetuation of certain diseases – never seems to have been widely understood until recently, so that many of the older European royal families continued to carry the seeds of madness, depravity, deformity and inherited illness up to our own days.

The Pope did his best to soothe the angry young couple, probably saying that he would look into the matter of consanguinity in due course. He personally ushered them into a luxurious bedroom – and Eleanor, always graceful about yielding to the inevitable, conceived a child. It was another girl.

Back in Paris, the Queen seems to have found life dull. Louis was preoccupied with the troublesome Angevin family. Geoffrey, Count of Anjou, had married Matilda, daughter of Henry I of England (the one who 'never smiled again' after his son was drowned in the loss of the White Ship); Matilda was known as 'Matilda Empress', because her first husband had been the Emperor of Germany. So she, Henry I's heir, began to attempt to assert her right to the English throne after her father died, although this claim was challenged by Stephen, Count of Blois, whose mother was a child of William the Conqueror. No Salic law nonsense for the English! The Matilda and Stephen wars caused chaos in England. Geoffrey of Anjou, with the English crown in prospect, made over the Duchy of Normandy, of obvious strategic value, to his eldest son Henry, then only seventeen.

As Abbot Suger had died, Bernard of Clairvaux was the mediator between King Louis and the two men of the Angevin family, when they came to court in Paris, dragging with them an unfortunate vassal who had quarrelled with them and who arrived in chains. 'Beware, Count of Anjou – the measure you mete shall be meted again to you!' thundered Bernard, when the wretched prisoner was subsequently set free. Why this leniency, wondered the courtiers? Had the Queen exerted her charm to soften the hearts of the rumbustious Plantagenets? Certainly she saw them when they were at court – and she noted that young Henry was already quite a man, not handsome, but quick in mind and temper (he had reddish hair), strong, with a sense of humour, possessing a fascination that caused people to have strong feelings of love or dislike about him all his life long.

Count Geoffrey and Henry rode home. At Château-du-Loir Geoffrey went swimming in the river, caught a fever and died. Henry was now in possession of Anjou as well as Normandy – very much a rising man, his mother's claim to England enhancing his potential.

Louis and Eleanor toured Aquitaine in the autumn of 1151. It had been noted that many of the nobility from Eleanor's duchy were replacing the French in positions of authority – she was no mere consort, she ruled her lands. The court spent Christmas at Limoges. Then, at Beaugency on the Loire, a synod called by the Archbishop of Sens annulled the royal marriage though legitimising the two young princesses and Eleanor, who had been quietly working for this – assisted, ironically, by the attitude of Bernard of Clairvaux who by this time definitely wanted to get rid of her as Queen – was free on 21 March – the first day of spring. She rode south, to her own lands, avoiding various lords' ambushes on the way, including one by the Count of Brittany, Henry Plantagenet's sixteen-year-old brother. On 18 May, in Poitiers, Eleanor and Henry were married. He had already sired two children and, in 1153, Eleanor gave him a son. In December 1154, he and Eleanor were crowned King and Queen of England in Westminster Abbey – and she went on giving him sons, plus several daughters. It was not until 1165 that Gerald of Cambridge, wakened in Paris by bells and shouts and cheers, learned from two women carrying torches below his window that 'God has given us an heir – who will cause trouble to your king, Englishman!' Louis had managed an heir at last. His second wife had died after giving birth to yet one more daughter but the third queen, Adela of Champagne, was the mother of Philip Augustus, who indeed was a trouble to the English, preventing the Plantagenets from gaining the French crown.

So the young woman from the Graves, the poet duke's granddaughter, last of the Aquitaine line, founded another dynasty.

The young Plantagenets were known – from their faerie ancestry – as 'the devil's brood'. They inherited their red-haired father's hasty temper. Henry, 'the young king' – because his father crowned him during his own lifetime, always fatal – plotted and warred against the King and died early, lamented by troubadour Bertran de Born. Richard ('*Cœur de Lion*'), Eleanor's favourite, to whom she gave her own duchy in due course, was also fond of troubadours – some said a bit too fond for the begetting of a family – and tournaments, which Henry II would not allow in England; if wars had to be fought, then they should be for real. John, 'Lackland' because he had no territory as a young prince, was as able as his brothers, but was probably what we should now term a manic-depressive. Eleanor's daughters, however, seem less aggressive and one of them, Marie de Champagne, set up one of the famous 'Courts of Love' in Poitiers which Eleanor is known to have attended, in one of the few rooms now existing with which she would have been familiar.

The evocatively named *Salle des Pas Perdus* or waiting-room of the lawcourts is a place whispering with historical associations. Poitiers was one of the important cities of Aquitaine and the great hall, in the former palace, is a huge, light, beautiful room, with some seats running round cut in the stone of the walls, so that 'the weakest might go to the wall' as in old churches. A dais runs across its entire width at one end; this is now backed by fireplaces, added later to facilitate feasting, but the colour and glitter of a twelfth-century aristocratic assembly, as might have been held in Bordeaux or one of the great castles of the Graves, can be easily imagined; it is just as if the former company have just gone out of the doors.

The Courts of Love were in some ways finishing schools for young men and women of noble families. Attending them was similar to 'doing the season'. The young people were made acquainted with music and poetry, instructed in gentle manners and, of course, got to know each other under supervision and might make useful contacts, valuable in the future. Eleanor seems to have been, even as a lady of middle years, still a focus of interest and the songs about her continued to be made.

When Henry II was not subjecting her to a form of 'house arrest'

– which he often did – Eleanor put into force a wide range of practical measures to ensure the peaceful continuation of trade: uniform weights and measures were issued for corn, lengths of cloth and for liquids; coinage was standardised. She founded hospitals, both in England and France and, in 1159, when she was sixty-seven and after Henry's death, she became astonishingly active, collecting Princess Berengaria of Navarre and taking her, via Sicily, to Cyprus to marry Richard I. She visited Rome and when Richard, returning from a wasteful crusade, fell into the hands of the Emperor, Eleanor set about collecting his ransom and herself went off to Cologne to get her son restored to her. She accompanied him on many tours and, when he was dying in 1198, he sent for her to be with him – she travelled down from Fontevrault at top speed. The dates recording her last major tour of Aquitaine show, as one commentator has remarked, not only that she had remarkable stamina for a woman of seventy-seven, but that the roads and general state of communications within her domaines were excellently maintained. Richard's funeral was on 11 April at Fontevrault. On 29 April Eleanor was at Loudun, on 4 May at Poitiers, Montreuil-Bonin on 5 May, then, via Niort, Andilly, La Rochelle, Saint-Jean-d'Angély and Saintes, she arrived at Bordeaux on 1 July – and went on to Soulac on 5 July.

Unlike the rest of France, the south-west had not been ravaged by frequent wars – Eleanor had indeed 'striven for peace'. (Her old critic, Bernard, had died in 1153.) She bestowed charters on many of the towns within her territory and was there in person when the first Mayor of La Rochelle was elected; she made many gifts to religious foundations and restored much wrongly appropriated property. In mid-July 1199 she went to Tours where, in an admirable diplomatic gesture, she did homage to Philip Augustus of France for the lands she personally held from him. If only there were an account of this – the elderly, but graceful lady kneeling before the son of her former husband. But this act ensured that King Philip Augustus could not accuse John 'Lackland' of 'aggression' and when, on 30 July, Eleanor met her son in Rouen, he sealed a covenant with her, granting her Poitou for the rest of her life and saying that she 'shall be Lady not only of all those territories which are ours, but also of ourself and of all our lands and possessions'. After so much travel it is astounding to learn that, in the following winter, off went Eleanor across the Pyrenees to see her last daughter.

She was never to know quiet and, maybe, she throve on action. In

1202 she was besieged at Mirabeau by Arthur of Brittany (the boy portrayed as pathetic by Shakespeare, but in truth a rather unpleasant young man), son John eventually coming to her rescue. Gradually, Normandy was lost to England. In 1204 Rouen and, later, Château Gaillard, Cœur de Lion's 'Saucy castle', that impertinently challenged the French border, fell to Philip Augustus. It was the beginning of the end of English domination over so much of France and it was in that year that Eleanor died.

No one is sure where she departed her eventful life, but she is buried in Fontevrault, to which she had been a generous donor. Henry II, John Lackland and his wife, Isabella of Angoulême are also there, but Eleanor lies beside her favourite son, Richard. Tomb sculptures cannot be assumed to be more than vague likenesses, but Eleanor, her head swathed in the becoming folds of a wimple, has a faint smile on her face and, in her hands, with their gracefully turned wrists, she holds a small book that, as has been pertinently commented, need not be one of devotion. But there is no description of what she looked like, despite a wisp of tradition that she had dark hair and eyes – even though the popularity of blondes was admitted in the Middle Ages. In the cloisters in the Metropolitan Museum of Art in New York there is a capital from a pillar in a church at Langon, possibly carved when Eleanor and Henry visited the Graves after their marriage; a photograph of this, reproduced in Amy Kelly's *Eleanor of Aquitaine and the Four Kings* (1952), shows the Queen's face as having a long, firm nose, wide and deep-cut eye sockets, a square, almost heavy chin and full, sensuous mouth.

Yet there is another supposed sculptured likeness of her – in the Cathedral in Bordeaux. After looking for this on several visits without success, I first saw it in the rainy twilight of a late afternoon; a watery shaft of sunlight lit up a face high above the pulpit which, in fact, is a latish addition to the building and partially obscures the view of anyone looking upwards, which is doubtless why so few have seen what may be a likeness carved by someone who had seen this queen. That first time, in a premature dusk, the pale, slanting light gave the head a curious appearance, suggesting life, the vitality of a personality, behind the eyes, as if someone living wore a mask. The forehead is broad, the features firm, healthy, assertive – 'a very intelligent woman, of a noble line, but of an unstable character', says Gervase of Canterbury, who probably knew her. No soft femininity in this face, although definite allure – that of an assured woman who, all her life, has taken for granted that she is prized not only for what she has but also for what she is.

Under the last Duchess, Aquitaine enjoyed comparative peace, outside the many campaigns going on in other parts of France. Plantations of vines were extended and it was from about this time in the twelfth century onwards that the term 'clairet' comes into frequent use as a term differentiating the light-toned wines of the Gironde from the darker reds that came down from the 'high country' inland and up from Spain, to pass through the port of Bordeaux.

Eleanor spent much time in her own duchy and, when she was there, Henry did not venture to put any restrictions on her, as he often did in England. (With two such strong personalities a clash of temperaments was frequent, though it is denigrating to a great king and outstanding lawmaker that he should be mainly known as the person who clashed with Thomas à Becket. It is even worse that it was a man of the Gironde, Jean Anouilh, who, in his play, has given so many a totally inaccurate account of that section of history.) The Queen would certainly have approved of the way in which, today, the British still say 'claret'. Even the EEC could not enforce a change to 'red Bordeaux' like the rest of the world! 'Clairet' now is a controlled type of wine, not exactly a rosé but pale in colour, and the reds of the region are not 'helped' by the admixture of darker-looking wines from other areas, though it should be noted that, in the past, not only were no restrictions placed on the use of such wines for blending but, as they had to pay dues to the Port of Bordeaux and provided revenue along their routes for those concerned with handling them, their importation was welcome.

Within Bordeaux itself increasing quantities of vines trained on trellises were planted in the twelfth century and they were also grown within the shelter of the city walls, which provided support as well as protection; in the pre-bicycle era such city vineyards would have been easy of access for those working them. A twelfth-century map shows a number of vineyards spreading fan-wise from the walls of Bordeaux, including those of St Laurent d'Escures, St Nicolas de Grave, Barrères and Gratecap, with the vineyard of the Benedictine Abbey of Ste Croix already in production, though not as important as it was later to become. Vineyards were at Mérignac, Eysines, and Talence though, as with Ste Croix, their great prosperity was to be in the future.

It was the comparatively stable life under the rule of the Dukes of Aquitaine and, subsequently, the English crown, that facilitated enormous developments and expansion of vineyards and established a preference for the red wine of the south-west of France in the English export market that remains to this day. True, vines were grown and wine made in England at this time, but, in the palaces of England and Aquitaine, including the court, they would have drunk claret, the wine of Aquitaine. A high proportion of it would have come from the Graves. It is not fanciful to suppose that at least part of the vigour, stamina and vitality of the Aquitaine family and the energy and creativeness of the Plantagenets were due to what they ate – and what they drank. The wine of the Graves is very specially the wine of Eleanor of Aquitaine.

A fourteenth-century Gascon vigneron pruning a vine. The shape of the knife remained the same for six hundred years (Public Records Office).

8

MEDIEVAL WINES

THE END OF
ENGLISH DOMINATION

THERE are many relics of the rule of the English in Aquitaine, although some lie hidden beneath the surface of life today, like strata in rocks. Down in the south there are half-timbered houses evocative of the black-and-white buildings of some of the English Midlands, though some of them are red and cream in France, even a few with the pargeting of East Anglia. In Bayonne Cathedral the arms of England are shown in the roof bosses along the nave. On the quayside of Bordeaux itself there is an enormous gateway, with fat flanking towers – all that now remains of the huge Palais de l'Ombrière, lowering like a wedge on the bank of the Garonne, still referred to as 'The Palace of the Kings of England'. The massive scale of the building is to be deduced from this single entrance. One is told that for over a century the withered right arm of the archer whose bolt struck King Richard I at Châlus was hung up as a grisly memento, like the heads of traitors on spikes on gateways and at the Tower of London.

The whole episode of the end of the 'Lionheart' exemplifies both the high-minded and the hypocritical attitude of many in the Middle Ages. The wretched man, whose father and family had been killed by the English, actually pulled out a spent bolt that was stuck in the wall at Châlus and fired it off at Richard, hitting him in the arm. At first the injury was dismissed – we can hear the 'It's a mere nothing!' of the war-loving recipient – and then the wound became gangrenous; Richard, always his mama's favourite son, sent for her, interviewed the bowman, said he understood the action, forgave the man and died in Eleanor's arms after abjuring everyone to respect his pardoning the assailant. Of course, they did nothing of the kind. Once the King was dead, the unfortunate archer was flayed alive.

From this time on the English hold on Aquitaine was beginning to be tenuous – King Philip Augustus was rising in power. The English nobility realised that they had to show 'firmness' – not always really oppression but hinting at the same – and there were more castles built, indicative of who was in charge. Bordeaux increased in both regal and civic importance. The Kings of England had to keep the locals on their side.

We don't know much about the wines of the time. Records of sales indicate that, essentially, the wine trade has not changed very much: annals include plaintive requests for bills to be paid and at least King John settled some of the accounts outstanding from his brothers' reigns. Exports of wine were becoming increasingly important. Whether or not there was a climatic change in the twelfth century is still argued, but the vineyards known to have existed in the south of England and south Wales could have been severely affected had the Gulf Stream then changed its course; certainly, the great exposed site of the airfield at St Athan, outside Cardiff, a chilly place today, was known to have been an orchard, supplying peaches and similar fruit to the Norman court in London – the climate might then have been milder. So the Bordeaux wine trade now began to be aware of the possibilities of developing export markets, not merely the 'prestige' sales to the court in London. The Bordelais already had established an independence of spirit; now they began to establish *coutumes* and *privilèges* which consisted of charters and exemptions or partial exemptions from various types of taxes and dues. Now their own port began to be known as the 'Port de la Lune' because of the sickle-shaped half-moon curve of the Garonne where the quaysides developed; this was an important differentiation point, marking off the local Bordeaux wines from those of the 'high country' or hinterland, which reached Bordeaux via the rivers, then used as highways for goods. The awareness of the value of the wine developed. Along the west coast of France there were other vineyards – but none were quite the same as the vineyards of the Gironde. Bordeaux wine had for long been an accepted everyday commodity. Now it began to confer prestige and to establish status in any company where it had been bought and where it was served.

Roger Galy, the Bordeaux historian, notes that the term 'graba' or 'Graves' is henceforth used for many of the wines coming from quayside sites – vines may have been grown in odd little plots right down to the edge of the slipways. But the vineyards near to and south of Bordeaux were definitely on gravel, even though some might encroach on the mud of the river banks. The term is certainly relevant in association with the wines shipped from these gravelly slipways. A boat of shallow draught could have taken on a substantial load and gone down, say, to Langon far more swiftly than a consignment travelling by land. We have today forgotten that river transport was often faster and safer than a land route.

What might these medieval wines have been like? They certainly had some quality, beginning to be recognised by those buying them from regions outside the locality and in overseas markets.

In antiquity, wines are divided into white and red, although I think that often they might have been an in-between pinkish-brown or beige, such as one sometimes finds in out-of-the-way places in Europe today, among peasant communities. Here, the grapes, black or white, are all processed or pressed together, the skins of the black grapes releasing their pigment to tint the must and, if the region is hot, the alcohol level will rise, something often viewed with satisfaction by the locals, who appreciate a high-strength drink as a reviver after a day's work.

From very early times, however, it seems that the Graves made wines that were definitely red and definitely white – they could grow both black grapes and white varieties. This would have had a considerable advantage in trading as the market developed outside the immediate locality: the knowledge of what certain grapes could produce in certain soils was beginning to be rediscovered – the Romans had known about it – and this encouraged selective plantings; the religious establishments, many of them in touch with 'sister' houses in other parts of Christian Europe, would have exchanged views of vines and even cuttings as well as other crops. The church needed fair quantities of wine for use in the mass for, until about the twelfth century, the laity received the chalice as well as the consecrated bread or wafer; there were variations and exceptions, as might be expected, isolated communities and those outside vine-growing areas obviously having to make do with whatever form of 'wine' they could get. Strictly, wine intended for consecration should be 'natural', according to regulations that probably originated centuries ago. It could be either red or white. The clergy, together with any religious communities and travelling monks or nuns, plus the ordinary lay men and women, required a fair quantity of wine for the liturgy throughout the year, more at the major festivals and, certainly in the Graves, for the needs of churches along the great pilgrim routes to Santiago – the 'Field of Stars' – in northern Spain. The great abbeys and religious establishments frequently had to entertain important civil as well as religious visitors, and often owned vineyards, but they might sometimes have had to buy in additional supplies.

In the early and middle part of the Middle Ages wine was prized both for what it was and for what it did – medically as well as mystically. From now on, as far as Bordeaux and the Graves was concerned, it was of increasing importance commercially; 'Gascon wines' began to dominate the royal tables in England from the beginning of the thirteenth century onwards; according to André Simon, by 1224 seventy-five per cent of the wine drunk in English royal households came from Bordeaux, the wines of the Rhine and even the Plantagenet's own Anjou being of far less account. The names attached to wines in various records, however, are not always reliable and, as Libourne was also thriving on wine exports, the 'high country' wines going through the Bordeaux region, whether via Bordeaux itself or smaller ports, often were described as 'Bordeaux'. As Penning-Rowsell in *The Wines of Bordeaux* points out, wine was England's largest import; indeed the English Parliament protested at the amount of gold being sent out of the country to pay wine bills. Thus the the amount of 'Bordeaux' imported by England at peak periods in the fourteenth century amounted to a staggering 180,000 hectolitres. The amounts recorded coming into the U.K. in 1985 and 1986 (figures supplied by the French Embassy in London) are:

1985	Bordeaux blanc	81,150 hl.
	Bordeaux rouge	133,083 hl.
1986	Bordeaux blanc	93,706 hl.
	Bordeaux rouge	177,008 hl.

Although I suppose some few discriminating merchants and buyers may have developed preferences for wines of a particular and guaranteed provenance, to most people, even within the Bordeaux region, Bordeaux wine is merely red or white Bordeaux.

Even if the 'Bordeaux' of the fourteenth century did include the 'high country' wines, the bulk of the trade was certainly from within the Bordeaux region. When it is remembered that, in 1985 and 1986, the imports to the entire U.K. of red Bordeaux – now, of course, including the Médoc and various other regions that maybe did not represent a substantial amount of the medieval totals – this fourteenth-century total is still an enormous quantity of wine. It would have gone to a variety of outlets, in addition to the Court and to the major ports; certain important nobles would have bought it, taverns and similar small customers would have taken some. The latter might not have had the chance to buy from other sources. It should also be remembered that, as wine was not laid down at all, customers buying one year would usually – except for some adverse event – buy in the year following.

A reminder of the origin of the word 'claret' is perhaps pertinent here – especially as some people still appear to be confused about it. The *Shorter Oxford English Dictionary* associates it with 'med.L. *claretum*, f. PF *claré*, claret, CLARY', although it does go on to say it was 'used, about 1600, for red wines generally. Now applied to the red wines of Bordeaux.'

The introduction of the word 'clary' is most misleading: clary is a herb (*sclarea*), brought to Britain in 1562, used for various culinary purposes, in brewing and in making 'Clary wine'. But it isn't claret! In case the reader should suppose this to be highly presumptuous on my part, I can point out that the respected *Dictionary* cannot be always up to date and infallible on the legal definitions of certain wines today, as a friend of mine found out when relying rather too much on its sherry entry, and getting into minor trouble with the sherry trade's lawyers. As far as 'claret' in the Bordeaux sense is concerned I have always assumed that it derived from the description 'plus clair' – that is, lighter in colour (applicable to the wines of Bordeaux certainly), than the wines coming both from the hinterland and from the south, where more sunshine would usually release more pigmentation from the skins of the black grapes and result in the must being deeper in colour. Penning-Rowsell quotes Simon, who quotes one Edward Tremaine, as stating that the word was not used specifically for red Bordeaux until 1565. There is also a theory that the term derives from the Latin *vinum clarum*. Today's *clairet*, which may roughly be termed a type of rosé, with its own controls and regulations, is not the same thing. What does seem to be definite is that, as far as the medieval Bordeaux vineyard was concerned, more red or reddish wine then appears to have been in demand – and therefore more was made than white, possibly with the exception of the sweeter white wines; northern export markets certainly would – as indeed they still do – prefer the warmth implied by the colour of a red wine.

The wines made in the Middle Ages would not be acceptable to our palates, if we could summon them for sampling today. Many skills in wine making, many processes and pieces of equipment that are now taken for granted were quite unknown six centuries ago; some might have seemed magic. Many processes and accepted pieces of knowledge common to even the most modest wine makers now, might not have been even guessed at by their grandfathers. Folk habits, family customs, some chance-followed routine originating with the odd piece of advice from a visitor – all these contribute to the finished product, often without those concerned knowing why. It probably cannot be done consciously. Although it is possible to reproduce the sorts of wines that *might* have been made, say, two or three hundred years ago, given the necessary resources, we ourselves cannot assume medieval palates or take ourselves physically back into the skins of the wine makers of the twelfth, thirteenth and fourteenth centuries. The divide between what we can do and what they could do, what they liked and what we prefer, and the accumulation of experience is too great to bridge. For example, the study of yeasts, which began seriously almost within our own time, would have bewildered and astounded pre-Pasteur wine makers in the eighteenth century; then, the ordinary wild yeasts present in the vineyard not only had to begin the process of fermentation but also to continue it, for no helpful injections of stronger strains to finish the work were possible, though maybe some makers did blend in certain other wines to strengthen the young wine, enabling it to finish 'making itself' satisfactorily. Further back, of course, medieval wine makers did not incur the risks of industrial pollution and certain diseases spread rapidly by modern transport. But medieval wines had essentially to be made without the regular use of sprays to disinfect, without extra nourishment, except the manure of domestic animals, and many vines were randomly planted in domestic small-scale plots or, when they were arranged in an orderly way, they might be trained up poles or along trellises, which is not suitable for certain varieties. The works of Columella might have proved enlightening, had these been consulted (see p. 181). Another risk was that of the lazy, careless or simply uninformed peasant worker, whose lack of care might so quickly spoil a large proportion of a crop – in most instances there would not then have existed the know-how to put matters right.

Medieval wine was usually drinkable when first made – when, that is, the first stage of fermentation had taken place, immediately after the vintage. If, though, the often delicious free-run juice that pours away from the piles of freshly picked grapes has started to ferment, one is today cautioned that it may, in quantity, have a slightly aperient action; Shakespeare and others referred to certain wines as 'searching'. As, though, in former times, even those who did have enough to eat usually suffered from some type of malnutrition, constipation was common (holy men in religious communities, often existing mainly on vegetables, seem to have had less trouble with their bowels). So a laxative wine might have been quite a useful thing, if one could plan ahead for its action – Henry II of England is known often to have caused great distress among his courtiers by suddenly deciding to leave wherever they were at a moment's notice, so that 'even those who had taken medicine' had to follow, poor things, longing for rest and somewhere to 'go'.

It should be remembered, though, that right up to the time when wines were understood as perishable commodities and given more informed handling prior to being bottled, a wine shipped to an export market in medieval wines would have been virtually undrinkable according to our ideas. It would have been oxidised, from exposure to the air – casks would not always have been topped up before or immediately after shipment and the racking might have been casual, or non-existent, so that dead yeasts would have remained in the casks, tainting the wine unattractively. The attractive 'selling' descriptions that are attached to wines these days would have been wholly inappropriate in the past – what customers in early times wanted was a fairly acceptable drink, that could be used to accompany food and, in various ways, act as a digestive and disinfectant. Such writers as did mention wine and describe it in former times were usually those able to sample it where it was made – and before it would have deteriorated in the process of keeping.

Even when wine had virtually become vinegar – *vin aigre* – it was much used as a preservative, such as in a marinade, for disinfecting foods as well as keeping them fit to eat. And, as wine contains certain minute quantities of nutrients, such as vitamin B (riboflavin) – if the composition was even vaguely similar to that of wines today – this would have been a useful augmentation to the medieval diet in the winter, when fruit and vegetables would have been scarce and most domestic animals were slaughtered as the cold weather came, because there was insufficient fodder to keep them through the hard period of the year. Wine did have 'tonic' properties. Distilling had spread from the Arab world by the end of the twelfth century and, about 1310, the Catalan, Arnaud de Vilanova, wrote the *Liber de Vinis*, in which, among other things, he advocated the concentrated form of alcohol in the treatment of many illnesses and injuries; in many medieval remedies, herbs, spices, peels, barks and other ingredients are combined with wine and, later, spirits and, as the history of vermouth indicates, such additives could often make palatable a drink that was not easy to enjoy otherwise. In many instances, wine was a more versatile and safer beverage and solution than water.

There were two periods when wine might advantageously be sold and most enjoyed: just after the vintage and again in the spring when the second of the two stages of fermentation would have died down. Then a number of vessels would come down to Bordeaux, to collect supplies of wine; they arrived not only from London and other British ports, but from other northern cities, seeking the warmth and cheer of the beverage. This wine fleet would set sail from Bordeaux between 15 October and 15 November (though this was in the old calendar, so, by today's reckoning, it would have been about ten or eleven days later), according to whether the vintage had been at the usual time or late. While the wine vessels were in the estuary and at Bordeaux, all other activities were subordinated to the trade.

During the period when Aquitaine belonged to the English, any ship collecting wine and bound for London would have a cask poised on the prow and on the poop and these, from each ship, were the 'perks' of the King of England and were delivered free of port and other dues. Once the wine fleet arrived in London the royal *bouteiller* or butler would come down to select whatever the royal household required, before anyone else could put in a tender for the cargo. (There is a well-known Bordeaux family of Bouteillers to this day – just as there are many whose surnames, Gasqueton, de Gasq, Gasc, indicate their Gascon origin of centuries past.) And wherever the steward or butler had the right of selecting wines before anyone else, his rôle was certainly of greater significance than that of a mere 'butler' as we understand the term now.

Camille Jullien, the Bordeaux historian, has remarked that 'even if it was the English who made the fortune of Bordeaux wines, it is also true that Bordeaux wine helped in the creation of the first "marine" '. For the wine fleet began to suffer from the pirates lurking along the west coast of France and in the Channel, so vessels took on board armed men, capable of repelling any attempts to board them and confiscate the valuable cargo. This was the origin of the Royal Navy! For, long before 'the mail must go through', the wine had to be got to the royal table in England. The gigantic casks used for shipping at this time were 'tonnes' or tuns, the majority probably being made from the wood of the forests of the Graves. Each huge barrel would be rolled from the Bordeaux quayside directly into the holds of the waiting ships of the wine fleet, anchored within the port, where the river was deep enough to enable them to stand in close. Each 'tonne' occupied sixty-two cubic feet of space, which is why, to this day, a ship's capacity is measured in terms of 'tonnage', even though the big tonne itself has not been in use for a long, long time. The production of Bordeaux estates is also measured in 'tonneaux' though this, too, is becoming somewhat old-fashioned. (The liquid capacity of a single tonneau is about a hundred cases (a dozen bottles in each case) of approximately 1,200 bottles of wine; see also p. 260.

It was in the medieval period that the people of Bordeaux began to establish themselves as an active, independent and powerful body, often manipulating the French against the English, even while they were themselves nominally subject to the English crown. The Gascons and the well-to-do people of the Graves who had houses in Bordeaux itself became civic-conscious: they organised their own Jurade or governing body. King John used the term 'Jurats' for its members first in about 1206, and this included both the nobility and the merchant bourgeoisie, so that attempts by various monarchs and governors to deprive the Bordelais of their charters and various exemptions from taxes and dues could be resisted both by those who carried swords and those who wielded power via the pen and the account book. Bordeaux enjoyed a considerable revenue from port dues and taxes paid by wines going through the city. In addition, the Jurade strictly enforced regulations that prevented wines from the 'high country' (the hinterland to the east) being shipped before the departure of the official wine fleet, which carried only the wines of the actual Bordeaux region. In those days it was the new, young wines that were attractive to buyers, both in Bordeaux and the various export markets, therefore the Bordelais shrewdly insisted that such wines as came from other areas should not be kept within their city walls; those who dealt in wines other than those of Bordeaux had to keep their wines and do their dealings outside the limits of the city, along the quays. Long-term, however, this had the opposite result from that originally desired, for the great quaysides, extending northwards, became the centre of the Bordeaux wine trade, as they still mostly remain.

'Charterhouse Quay' (the *Quai des Chartrons*), named after a long-vanished Carthusian establishment, now signifies 'wine', just as 'Harley Street' in London signifies 'doctors', or Hatton Garden means diamonds. *Les Chartronnais*, whether or not they still have their places of business on the river, is a collective term for those dealing in wine. Rather oddly, the original Charterhouse, according to Desmond Seward in *Monks and Wine* (1979), was 'founded in 1383 by monks from the chartreuse of Vauclair in the Dordogne, who had fled from English freebooters and who returned to their original home in 1460'. They left a souvenir in the form of the name.

Various kings and governors tried to check the increase of the *privilèges* and *coutumes* enjoyed by the Bordelais and claimed that some, anyway, had never been official. But the locals stood firm – 'It's always been so', they recurrently claimed and, in spite of wars, invasion threats and the complications of politics, nothing succeeded for long in interfering with what 'had always been so'. The Bordelais had the resistance to change – when it so suited them – that is common to many country people.

It should be remembered that Bordeaux and its environs, including the Graves, is not essentially 'French France'. Julius Caesar noted the distinction: 'The Gauls are separated from the Aquitanians by the Garonne.' Early records of the Bordeaux Jurade show that the nobility, minor nobility, bourgeoisie and merchant classes mixed cheerfully together and went on doing so. Their descendants were to be active in the Bordeaux 'Parlement' (see pp. 309–9). People from other countries continued to come in to the 'Port de la Lune' and settle in and around Bordeaux, importing their own traditions, scholarship, ways of thought and social customs, plus their crafts and capabilities; always the Bordelais, whether long-established or recent arrivals, demonstrated a spirit of independence and resourcefulness.

In this stage of their history, when the Graves still dominated much of it, they were greatly concerned with the overall cultivation of the area's vineyard, now that wine exports were proving increasingly remunerative. Yet there were problems. They had to be alert to potentially circumscribing restrictions and oppressive taxes, often imposed by those far away from them; also they needed to be alerted to competition, from nearby and far away. Now it is possible to appraise the development of the Bordeaux wine trade and the concomitant expansions of the Graves in importance.

The influence of Bordeaux at this time was far more than that of a mere central trading point. According to Eleanor Lodge in *Gascony under English Rule* (1926): 'During the Hundred Years War ... the influence she [Bordeaux] had so long exercised through trade was turned into a definite alliance, and Bordeaux became the centre of a confederation of smaller towns, known as "filleules", which imitated her privileges, looked to her for protection and were bound to her as vassals of the English King, their immediate overlord.' These *filleules* included Bazas and Langon which 'were all important for military reasons and for trade. Fortified and strongly situated, they were also centres of the main wine-growing district of Gascony. ... Bordeaux and its *filleules* remained to England when so much was lost at the close of Edward III's reign, and in the fifteenth century formed the last bulwark of her falling fortunes.'

The English complained about the Gascons, the Bordelais complained about the English, both asserting that traders from the two countries

98

were tiresomely difficult about conforming to local regulations and, frequently, that they set up in business and made their homes in areas outside their specially allotted quarters. But the two countries continued to trade. Within the cities of both Bordeaux and London marriages took place between the nobility (very useful to the Gascons who, even when aristocratic, were usually impecunious) and the well-to-do merchants and, in consequence, the interchange of business was considerable. Nationality did not seem to affect public appointments: in 1274 Henry de Galeys became Lord Mayor of London and in 1275 he was also Mayor of Bordeaux.

In 1299 seventy-three vessels, each carrying nineteen tons of wine, arrived in the Port of London from Bordeaux. By 1302 there were six official tasters working in London who were supposed to verify the provenance of the wines (blind tasting certainly under difficulties) and throw away any that they considered bad. High-country wines could not leave Bordeaux before St Martin's Day (11 November) but even the true Bordeaux wines, with the advantage of sailing in the slightly lighter days, were penalised along the way, each one having to pay 'quillage' before being allowed to leave at all. Levies exacted at the Lighthouse of Corduan, a tax levied by the Port of Royan on all ships passing for 'protection' and, in both France and England, the 'gauging' or appraisal of the casks were only some of the impositions that virtually doubled the price of the wine from the time it left Bordeaux. And Graves wines had to get up to Bordeaux in the first place.

True, in 1302 King Edward I of England did renounce his rights to taxes imposed on imports coming to London, but he still kept his *prisa* or *prisage* (the two casks mounted aft and on the poop, see p. 96) and the royal *bouteiller* still had the right of choice before anyone else was allowed to buy. Genuine 'Gascon wines' were considered very smart at the English court, although Peter of Blois wrote that sometimes the most frightful wines were served there – so obviously things could easily go wrong.

The pilgrim routes became more thronged – but goods mostly went by water, both for speed and safety. Bordeaux maintained only a small, ineffectual fleet as such – the armed vessels were intended for protecting the ocean-going groups of ships. In 1304 it was recorded that ships leaving the port of Bordeaux loaded with wine, half of which was Bordeaux wine, were as follows: 40 English, 22 Breton, 10 Norman, 9 Basques, 5 Spanish. The English trade was of prime importance.

The English kings definitely encouraged the wine trade in English ports. In 1338 some Bristol merchants bound for Aquitaine with the royal fleet to pick up wine were accorded royal protection, which was extended to merchants from Lynn, though ships accompanying the fleet had to be equipped with adequate armour and fighting men. André Simon notes a decree of Edward III that is a forerunner of a type of consumer protection, for 'no English merchant nor any of his servants, nor others for them, shall go into Gascony there to abide, nor shall he have any other there dwelling to make bargains or buying of wines by any colour, before the time of vintage, that is to say before that common passage be made to seek wines there; and that none buy or bargain by himself or any other, for any wines, but only in the ports of Bordeaux and Bayonne'. The main trade was to be done only in Bordeaux and the frontier stronghold, Bayonne, because officials there could control dealings. Edward III also prohibited ships from loading up with wine except 'between the Chartrons and Castillon'. This seems quite a long stretch of riverway, but there had been a tendency for ships to load up at the little ports in the north of the Gironde estuary, thus avoiding the payment of Bordeaux port dues and taxes and also shortening the time of the turn round by as much as half a day – advantageous in the season of autumn gales.

André Simon indicates how the wine trade was compulsorily centralised: 'With the exception of the men of Libourne, who were allowed to ship their wines direct to England, all the growers and merchants of Gascony and of the adjoining districts of Agenais, Bazadais, Toulouse, etc., were obliged to send their wine via Bordeaux, where they were made to pay about fifteen shillings per cask as export tax if they were subjects of the English crown and twice or sometimes thrice as much if they were subjects of the King of France; the burgesses of Bordeaux were exempt from all such duty.' The unfairness of this is exemplified when, in October 1308, Jean Ben and Gaillard Ayquem (a name known in the south-west since very early times), both of them from Bazas, 'having shipped by the Swan, of Teignmouth, the one fifty-two and the other thirty casks of wine were made to pay treble fees ... while Arnaud Calhau, rich burgess of Bordeaux, paid none at all for seventy-three casks of wine shipped by the same vessel ... they also had to pay different *péages* or tolls before reaching this port [Bordeaux] and they were even sometimes made to pay a certain fee for the right of sending their wines to Bordeaux'.

Graves producers not Bordeaux citizens were therefore handicapped in getting their wine out of the region although, of course, they could make

100

local sales to the English garrisons there as well as to the religious establishments and churches.

While the great pilgrimages continued, even quite a small hamlet might suddenly find itself with an additional crowd of visitors, who had to be crammed in some kind of shelter – as witness the big porches in many pilgrim churches – provided with some food and drink and, of course, at the major religious festivals, wine was required for the communion of the laity as well as the clergy up to this period.

Everything stopped for the vintage. No church festivals were held while picking was going on – the clergy were probably out in the vineyards with everyone else. Any epidemic, such as the outbreak of plague that killed 12,000 people in 1411, caused serious problems with shortage of labour. But the people of Bordeaux were able to be hospitable: when the English took prisoners, such as happened after Edward III's victory over the French at Poitiers in 1356, victors and vanquished were lavishly entertained in Bordeaux and the Archbishop there was presented with a thirty-five pound cheese by the grateful guests – this probably came from England. The English royal butler would annually purchase between one and two thousand tonneaux of wine and, in addition to London, there were many other English ports, in some of which, such as Southampton, Boston and Hull, there were big seasonal fairs, with quantities of wine on sale. Even the high-country wines, obliged to remain in the Gironde until 11 November, St Martin's Day, would have benefited by the growing demand in Britain for wine – and the Bordelais would have benefited all round.

Wines shipped to England between October and December were described as 'new wines', arriving just after they had been vintaged. By this time the wines shipped in the previous spring or, as sometimes might occur, even a year before, would have usually deteriorated, either by exposure to air or some form of contamination. As the wines became less pleasant to drink, the practice arose of cutting or blending in other wines, often with those that were sweeter (and therefore usually more resistant to ageing as well as being immediately pleasanter to drink), also higher in alcohol – such as might happen with wines from a southern vineyard where the strength would rise as a result of the sunshine – and fuller in flavour, so that these attributes might disguise any thin, even sour taste. A darker colour of a red wine, too, might give the impression of something rounder, more full-bodied – get someone to darken the colour of a light-toned wine and, tasting it blind, see that you do not agree! I have often been caught this way.

It is possible that the word 'bastard' for such blends and semi-compounded drinks, into which a bit of honey and freshly pressed grape juice might have been added, was used as early as this period, although it doesn't get into the *Shorter Oxford English Dictionary* until 1602.

Wines that remained in Bordeaux after December for some reason were racked (pumped off their lees into fresh casks) in the spring; they would be shipped in April and until June, by which time growers would begin to prepare their vineyards and such somewhat primitive wineries and presshouses as were in existence for the coming vintage. Wines of this second shipping were known as wines of *reck*, *reek*, *rec* or *reyck* and, again according to Simon, they were charged less as freight than that exacted from the 'new wines'. It seems odd to us that they were not valued more than the new wines, for, after the end of the fermentation and racking, they might according to our notions have been more palatable to drink. But, we must bear in mind, wines were valued for their freshness then and tastes were accustomed to them; the wines of rack were useful reserves, supposing any of the vessels carrying new wines were lost on the voyage or had had to dump their cargoes. The wines of rack could compensate for this loss to some extent.

The years 1361 and 1362 were poor vintages and it may be assumed that plenty of the high-country wines 'helped' out the short and dreary vintages of the Gironde. In 1363 the weather was terrible: the sea froze and supplies of food for Bordeaux had to be augmented by rations sent over from England. But by 1376 there was a record crop – 23,820 tonneaux were recorded as leaving Bordeaux port and although this high export figure was a record, a substantial tonnage of wine was maintained, even during the various wars, and about 10,000 tonneaux were sent abroad each year. Even when the French managed to capture Budos and much of the Bazadais, the wine trade to England continued.

Meanwhile, Gascons were making a considerable impression in the City of London. The terminology is always somewhat vague and many of them may well have been men of the Graves. English cloth was extremely popular and vast amounts were exported to France – nothing new about English and French visiting each other 'pour le shopping'. In 1214 King John had given the Bordelais an important charter: not only were the wines made from vines belonging to the inhabitants of Bordeaux exempted from all dues, but so also was all the merchandise that they possessed that was lodged in Bordeaux. As the great Bordeaux history comments, 'it was a financial rather than a commercial stratagem', but the Bordelais resisted any attempt to do away with it until in 1776 a royal decree abolished this charter. Wood, stone from the quarries, foodstuffs (such as honey, an important sweetening agent before sugar became cheap), the woad for dyeing, fish, both dried and salted that had been brought up from the south, all gushed from the 'Port de la Lune' once they had been brought to it. The shortage of wheat, for bread, was a perennial problem – as it had been in the days of the Roman Empire – but Bordeaux became an even more prosperous and influential city. True, the wines coming from Poitou, Aunis, Saintonge and consignments from Brittany, La Rochelle and Bayonne, which were shipped directly to English ports, represented competition. The English in England began to feel jealous. All these shippers and traders in wine had a certain standing and enjoyed a protected status when they unloaded their cargoes in England, particularly in the Port of London, where they were (temporarily anyway) able to claim allegiance to the King of England.

What, Londoners wanted to know, about all those Bordeaux merchants, who, by this time, had set up their own wine stores in London? Were they, Londoners asked, English citizens or were they not? Who belonged to what – and more to the point, who paid taxes to whom and where?

Gascons in London were singled out for resentment. Attempts were made to restrict the time within which foreign merchants and wine shippers could remain in London. One can imagine the reactions of the citizenry – 'A decent girl is at risk even in daylight if she goes abroad' and 'They make so much money that the prices soar for honest Englishmen'. For the prosperous Gascons could bid up for English goods which they then might sell elsewhere, instead of just taking them back to their homeland.

The Gascons in fact obtained a charter from the King of England by which they could arrive and stay – anywhere – in England as long as they wished and this agreement included arrangements concerning the 'new wines' as well as the old: two sous were levied on each cask of wine during the forty days after it had been unloaded and, after this payment, it could be sent throughout the Kingdom of England.

Even two centuries later, John Stow's *Survey of London* (see Appendix II) indicates something of the mood of former times; those who brave the traffic today to cross the road to Vintners' Hall are treading on ground somewhat debatable when Aquitaine belonged to England.

Vintry Ward is where the Gascons had their headquarters. From 1364 the Worshipful Company of Vintners had a monopoly of Gascon wines although, according to Anne Crawford's *History of the Vintners' Company* (1977), they subsequently found that the competition from the wines of other countries being exported to England represented a possible serious loss of revenue.

In 1370, the Letterbooks in Guildhall state that, when the 'new wines' arrived, they could not be 'exposed for sale' in any tavern until the stocks of any old wines had been removed. Might this have been because it was feared that the old and perhaps defective wines could contaminate the new wines, or was it simply a means of keeping stocks being turned over briskly? Did innkeepers offer 'Specials' at bargain prices? Nor, it is stated, could the white 'wine of Gascoigne, of La Rochel, of Spain or of any other country . . . be laid in taverns where Rhenish wine is for sale'. Such decrees did ensure that taverners should not be left with unsaleable stocks of wine on their hands, but it also prudently prevented the direct competition of outlets where rival merchants and shippers might attempt to pressurise the keeper of an establishment, or, indeed, even dispute physically about sales and the virtues of their particular wines – in the street or in the tavern itself.

Although Richard II of England, grandson of Edward III and son of the 'Black Prince', is always mentioned with the suffix 'of Bordeaux', it is not known whether he was born in the great Palais de l'Ombrière or whether his mother, 'the Fair Maid of Kent', gave birth in the castle across the Garonne at Lormont. But this was the beginning of the time when the actual rule of the English in Aquitaine was beginning to fade in power. Major changes were coming and these were to affect the Graves more than, perhaps, all the other regions within the Gironde. And another personality emerges from the Graves.

9

THE GASCON POPE

PAPE CLÉMENT

Mᴏʀᴇ details are to be found about Pape Clément, oldest of the great Graves estates, on pp. 285–7. Here it is relevant to give some account of the history of the strange man, scantily described in most accounts, who gave it his name six centuries ago.

The estate of Pape Clément lies beyond Haut Brion, on the Arcachon road, in the midst of houses, little shops and the sort of suburban clutter that grows as a city spreads outwards. When, over a quarter of a century ago, I first went there, everything seemed vaguely dilapidated. The magnificent wine was still as impressive as much older people in the wine trade could recall, though its then owner, Paul Montagne, who had bought the property in 1939, had been hindered in rehabilitating it by World War II and in the between-wars period there had been plans for actually building over the great vineyard, though fortunately these came to nothing.

Today, Pape Clément is trim and impressive – I could hardly recognise it as the same estate I had known earlier. The approach is through wrought-iron gates, via an imposing avenue, with well-kept lawns and formal flower beds. The grey house, vaguely Victorian in its muddled architecture, is topped by one of the pepperpot towers seen on many churches in the Gironde – and on the older part of Château Lafite. Inside, the house is restored, discreetly and with care, looking somewhat impersonal, as it is now used for meetings and conferences.

There is a new *cuvier*, with eighteen new vats. In the *chai* the *barriques* are numbered and dated. The vineyard of twenty-seven hectares is somewhat fragmented, but is no longer handicapped by shortage of funds and lack of equipment; the subtle, alluringly aromatic wine, loved by experienced devotees of claret, maintains its appeal. 'A paradoxical wine', comments Michel Dovaz and most writers mention that Pape Clément takes time – even today, when some classic clarets cannot be given the long maturation of former days and are not, it should be stressed, necessarily less beautiful – it approaches its peak gradually. Many writers have given it less strident publicity than certain other estates' wines – but those who have acquired some knowledge of Pape Clément do not generally need urging to drink it, when they can afford it. Clive Coates described it as 'the most Médocain of all Graves', but I am not sure whether I entirely go along with this – the spicy fruit and 'southern' warmth of Pape Clément in certain satisfactory vintages set it apart from such Médocs as I know well, although my experience is inevitably limited.

For there is as much true mystery here as anywhere in the Graves. Today's visitor, however, may find it impossible to visualise the estate as it was in 1300, when it acquired its papal associations. Bertrand de Goth is one of the three major personalities of the Graves. Eleanor, Duchess of Aquitaine, enjoys a legendary personal glamour and her achievements are remarkable by any standards. Montesquieu, although he seldom reveals himself as frankly as that other great man of Bordeaux, Montaigne, is at least somebody about whom a fair amount is known – from contemporary records as well as from his own writings. But Bertrand de Goth is an enigma, in some ways a tragic hero, a man of great abilities and mighty deeds – with an odd flaw in his character.

The de Goths or Gots were a Gascon family of long standing. Can their name refer to those who, in the distant past, had invaded the region of the south-west from the north? But by the twelfth century they seem to have been as highly civilised as any others, many certainly displaying marked intellectual ability.

It is relevant to note that recurrent references to them – including to Bertrand – as being 'Gascon', indicate how, in medieval times, little difference seems to have been recognised between the Gascons of what is today Gascony, in the south, the inhabitants of the Landes region and the Graves proper, as we understand these regions. The areas were then only sparsely populated, but the overall tagging of those who lived somewhere south of Bordeaux as 'Gascons' is rather like a contemporary reference by an English person to all people living north of the Border in the U.K. as 'Scots'; a Highlander would find this irritating and inaccurate, as would anyone from the offshore islands.

But the word 'Gascons' seems frequently to be used generally for the people of Bordeaux and its environs. Donald M. Frame, in his admirable biography *Montaigne* (1965), cites the subject of his book as being 'a sixteenth-century Bordelais or other Gascon' and he adds a footnote to the effect that he will 'use the terms "Gascon" and "Gascony" . . . as Montaigne did, in their broad sense, to include the people and the large area

– Bordeaux and the Château de Montaigne as well as the deeper south-west – whose usual speech was Gascon, a language almost as close to Spanish as to French. Montaigne did not speak Gascon, but he thought and spoke of himself as a Gascon.' Montaigne, remember, was a man of the sixteenth century, although his family name, Eyquem, had been recorded, in various versions of spelling, many centuries earlier in the annals of Bordeaux. As with all the 'Gasc' variations, noted elsewhere in this history (see p. 202), this name too has survived, although few who know or know of Château-d'Yquem in the Sauternais may associate it with that of Gascons of former times.

Many of us may think of Gascons in general as being garrulous, boastful, adventuring types with long swords and quick tempers and this is certainly an older concept than that of the novels of Alexandre Dumas, where many of us first meet them. Cyrano, Edmond Rostand's long-nosed hero among the 'cadets de Gascogne', came from Bergerac which might seem to be outside the region within which the Gascons who concerned Bordeaux were predominant. There is, too, the region of Béarn, which gave Henri IV, 'le vert galant', to France; also that of the Pays Basque, which has remained straddling the Pyrenees and keeps its special language alive today; these areas confuse the outsider, who is prevented from realising what Gascony was and is.

In medieval times the boundary was certainly loosely defined and, as there was a Gascon accent – even when the speaker was otherwise wholly French – as well as the Gascon language, the influence of the Gascons within this whole area of the south-west must be admitted as being great and long-lasting. It was not until the Gironde came to be a part of France once more, in 1453, that French, rather than Gascon, gradually became the language of Bordeaux and the surrounding countryside. So it is fair to tag Bertrand de Goth as 'Gascon'.

He was probably born in 1305, maybe at Villandraut, although there are some claims, including that by his nephew, the Bishop of Bazas, for his birthplace being Uzeste, where he is buried. Even today, the ruins of the castle at Villandraut dominate the village; the main towers are fat, spreading outwards at their base like trees, shoving their roots into the earth, even though the moat that surrounds the edifice is now dry, humpy with grass growing over many fallen chunks of stone. It has been pointed out to me that not all 'moats' were necessarily intended to surround a fortification with water. In the British Isles the climate would almost certainly have filled up a surrounding depression, but it is reasonable to suppose that elsewhere the ditch around a castle might not have held water – although it would have been useful if it had. In some medieval castles the 'moat' was virtually an extension of a fishpond and, certainly, would have been a drain.

When Bertrand became the spiritual ruler of the western world Villandraut castle received various major additions; there are several Romanesque arches, efficient and imposingly pure in line, and there is said to be a sculptured representation of Pape Clément – with a beard and between two angels – in a tower on the south-west side.

No child growing up at Villandraut could have been unaware of enjoying a privileged position. The inner courtyard of the castle is gigantic. Each one of the huge towers seems to have been provided with its own independent system of heating and sanitation. There must have been at least a hundred or more 'living-in' staff and, in times of wars and rumours of same, many more would have been accommodated in the place. The site is not quite as dominating to the landscape as some of the other castles in the Graves, many of these also belonging to Goth relations, but it is protected by the lie of the land behind much of the building and, when the towers were their original height, they would have made it difficult for any attacker to assault this stronghold.

Although Bertrand was educated as a 'clerk' in the medieval sense and prepared for the Church, he was also trained in knightly exercises; churchmen had gone into battle not long before and, on their travels, were often obliged to live rough and show resource in many practical skills. The young man was obviously brilliant from an early age; trained as a lawyer, he began to rise in the ecclesiastical hierarchy after taking holy orders, thanks in many instances to the influence of various relations already in positions of authority in the Church. His elder brother, Béraud, became Archbishop of Lyons in 1289 and made Bertrand his vicar-general; an uncle, the Bishop of Agen, subsequently became a cardinal and appointed Bertrand a pontifical chaplain. He studied law, both canon and civil, at Orléans and Bologna and in 1295 he became Bishop of St Bertrand de Comminges – that beautiful cloistered establishment. He visited England, negotiating with King Edward I, and also maintained what would now be termed 'good contacts' with Philip the Fair, King of France, who was intent on recovering the province of Guyenne from the English. On all sides he remained popular during his fast rise to power. For five years the great

Benedictine Abbey of Ste Croix in Bordeaux bestowed on him the profits from all its priories, cellars, barns and benefices – he was a rich man from this income alone. Philip of France also rewarded him and, even when Bertrand backed the Pope, Boniface VIII, against the French King, his standing remained high.

Yet it was now that Bertrand was about to play a leading part in a personal drama that is difficult for us to understand today and all the details may probably never come to light. Maybe this was one of the crises in which there is no obvious right and wrong. Yet the action was to end in tragedy. Dante, in the eighth circle of the *Inferno* of the Divine Comedy, puts Bertrand de Goth among the simoniacal popes, who are buried face down, only their feet showing. Yet Dante, too, was active in both political and ecclesiastical negotiations – one might almost say intrigues. He may have been prejudiced.

Bertrand became Archbishop of Bordeaux and, in 1300, received from his brother Béraud the estate that is now Pape Clément. Béraud may have been acting on behalf of several of the immediate de Goth family and have intended this as a joint present by way of congratulation. Pessac was easy of access from the centre of Bordeaux and enjoyed a slightly elevated site, airy, having a ferruginous spring gushing health-giving waters since Gallo–Roman times. According to P.-Joseph Coste in *La Route du vin en Gironde* (1948 edition), the original name of this estate was Sainte Marie de Bel Air and there was an oratory slightly to the north-east of the present château. The name 'Sainte Marie' persisted in references; up to the middle of the nineteenth century the wine casks were inscribed 'Château Sainte Marie Pape Clément'. Clément's house is thought to have been in the Domaine de Forestier, a former property belonging to Sainte Marie and it seems that it was quite unlike Villandraut, although probably of fair size; there is even a tradition that, when Clément was reconstructing it, he called in the painter Giotto to decorate it. The way in which the locals shortened the estate's name indicates that they continued to be proud of the local priest who attained the triple tiara.

It would have taken only about half an hour to ride to Pessac from the Archbishop's Palace in stuffy, low-lying Bordeaux, possibly less if the company had galloped on horseback, instead of using the mules that were often a feature of formal processions by high-ranking clergy. It must have been refreshing to arrive and enjoy the woods around the estate and the vineyard, already laid out and in production. The wines were already of respected quality; the *Vigne de Pape Clément* was used exclusively for the church and its entertaining up until the sequestration of all church property at the French Revolution. Bertrand gave the estate to Cardinal Arnaud de Canteloup (another well-known Gascon name of the period), who succeeded him in the archiepiscopal chair at Bordeaux, and all subsequent archbishops enjoyed the estate as their own – a delightful and profitable 'perk'.

Quarrels about the papacy in the period are complicated. Essentially, King Philip the Fair of France had been utterly against the policies of Pope Boniface VIII, because Boniface had asserted that the power of the papacy was supreme over that of temporal rulers. (Boniface was the first Pope to be put face downwards by Dante in the *Inferno*.) Because the King was not as successful as he hoped to be against this Pope, he tried a campaign of personal denigration and then launched a physical attack, attempting at Agnani to drag Boniface by force into France – though the local citizens prevented this manoeuvre. But a month later Boniface died in the Vatican – 'feared and hated, he could not keep a friend', comments *The Oxford Dictionary of Popes* (1986).

Who was now to be Pope? From 1303 to 1307 the 'weak, peace-loving and scholarly' Benedict XI was Supreme Pontiff. When he died – probably of dysentery, though poison, of course, was rumoured – the problem was acute. I should like to know more about Benedict, for his physician was that remarkable man, Arnaud de Vilanova, pioneer of distillation in the west, himself a Catalan and associate of the poet Ramón Lull. Arnaud belonged to the Franciscan 'Spirituals' and dared to oppose the Pope for attacking them; he went to prison and Benedict died. As a doctor's widow myself I cannot think that Arnaud, a great scientist as well as a true physician, had a hand in the Pope's death – but he may not have been there to cope with the outbreak of illness; this was Benedict's fault. It is never wise to quarrel with someone who can help and cure.

Bertrand de Goth had been observed for some time by King Philip of France. Both may have met when they were students of law at the Sorbonne. When the then Archbishop of Bordeaux attended a synod in Rome despite Philip's disapproval, he found Bordeaux in confusion on his return, the occupying French troops being set upon by the locals, because this was a time when Aquitaine was French rather than English, thanks to the crafty manoeuvrings of the Bordelais. Though Bertrand would not have been materially affected by all this, he was well aware of the advantages of there being peace between England and France – especially for the wine trade. Now came a period when increased business in 'Gascon wines' was something he may have noticed with satisfaction. (If only we knew something about his own Pessac vineyard at this time!)

When the cardinals met to elect a new Pope the French among them included many who had been disgraced by Boniface VIII. Both because of this and because of a natural inclination to back the King of France, they managed to split the vote in conclave and, possibly to his surprise, eventually Bertrand was elected. Was there, it has been suggested, also some sort of bargain between him and Philip? The King wanted a Pope who would be on his side, who would defame Boniface and back France in various ways. Bertrand, very much the rising star in his world, must have found the prospect of being Pope well suited to his great administrative gifts – he was, as everyone admitted, a superb organiser – and the pontificate would be a means whereby he could promote scholarship and help establishments concerned with assisting the poor and needy. Was there, though, a built-in price that had to be paid? Could this be an instance of doing 'the right thing for the wrong reason', the 'greatest treason', as described in T. S. Eliot's drama about St Thomas à Becket (*Murder in the Cathedral*)?

Bertrand was not even in Rome but at Lusignan in Poitou when he heard that he had been elected Pope. In some state, he went slowly down to Bordeaux. The Seneschal of Guyenne found it necessary to recruit some of the Gascon nobility to protect the cortège of the new pontiff and, before Bertrand disembarked on the quay opposite the great Palais de l'Ombrière, large quantities of provisions and wine were sent in. They were needed. Bertrand stayed for a month and his sojourn cost an enormous sum: the Seneschal gave many extravagant entertainments – accompanied by casks of wine – to the new Pope and his entourage; he presented the former Archbishop of Bordeaux with a gold cross and bestowed splendid attire on the eight knights who made up the papal guard of honour. Bertrand announced, at a convened session in the Cathedral, that he would take the name of Clément. He must have devoted considerable thought, as the great Bordeaux history suggests, to what might be done in the handling of the various unruly local nobles – poised between England and France, Bordeaux was more than a place, it was a perennial 'situation' for statesmen.

Clément had asked for only a few of the members of the College of Cardinals to attend him in Bordeaux, his sense of practical administration showing itself in sparing them lengthy journeys and yet more cost to the city, with added problems of accommodation. On 4 September he left and

111

travelled down to pay brief visits to Villandraut, Bazas and Agen, doubtless greeted with much local acclaim. Now he was to be crowned as the head of western Christendom.

Clément V was a diplomat but no puppet. He had intended to be crowned at Vienne, before going on to Rome. At Vienne, still within France, he had hoped to establish a pact of peace between France and England; gracefully he deferred to King Philip's wish that the papal coronation should take place at Lyons and this was arranged for 14 November 1305 in the Church of St Just. King Philip himself was to attend. Clément organised the spectacle as impeccably as anything to which he set his hand. Protocol was meticulously observed. The great 'triple crown', the three-tiered bulgy papal tiara (no longer worn by today's more modest popes) was sent for from Rome; it was so covered with jewels that it seemed to radiate light. This tiara is charged with symbolism: it is, a kind friend in the clergy informs me, first mentioned in the life of Pope Constantine (708–15) and is worn – or was – extra-liturgically. It was first of all a type of Phrygian cap, which will be familiar to many people as the soft, pull-on head-covering worn by many of the French Revolutionary activists and which is shown on representations of 'Marianne', the female figure who symbolises the French Republic. But this simple white cap, indicative of the status of the wearer, became elaborated: a coronet was attached to the lower rim in about the eleventh century, then two 'lappets' or flaps at the back were added in the thirteenth. Pope Boniface VIII added a second coronet, by which he may have meant to show the twofold power of the papal office and then, either under Benedict XI or actually Clément V, a third coronet was added; the tiara was now really big, although apparently it did not get its 'beehive' contours until the fifteenth century. The three sections are thought by some to represent the three 'worlds' over which the wearer holds sway. Popes have had the tiara carried in front of them on occasions when they did not actually wear it.

After the ceremony, the new Pope was to go in procession through the town, King Philip holding the bridle of the magnificently caparisoned mare bearing Clément and, like a humble squire, leading the animal in front of the dignatories of Church and state – though the monarch gave up after a short distance and, giving the bridle to his brother, sat on his own horse, to ride at Clément's side. Crowds thronged the route and, around the Pope, friends and relations, including his brother, Gaillard de Goth, joined in the cheers and rejoicings.

Then, when the processional way took a route steeply downwards, there was a disaster. At one point many spectators had climbed on a wall to get a better view and suddenly the weight of the people caused the stones to give way: there was a thunderous noise, shrieks, the cries of terrified animals and people as the onlookers on the wall tumbled literally on top of the papal and royal train. Pope, King, his brother Charles de Valois and many others were flung to the ground by an avalanche of stones and people, the triple tiara was knocked off Clément's head and rolled into the chaos and confusion on the road, terrified members of the various suites rushed to help but, although the Pope was unharmed and could be dusted down, both King Philip and his brother were hurt and twelve of the immediate retinue were fatally injured, including Gaillard de Goth. The papal crown was retrieved – but a great ruby, one of its finest jewels, had fallen out and was lost for ever. An omen, many must have said (as many did when, at the funeral of Britain's King George V, the cross fell off the imperial state crown on the coffin, as it was borne in procession through London).

Clément had then planned to go on to Rome but, after travelling round the south of France, he eventually settled the papal court at Avignon and began the 'Babylonian exile' as the seventy years during which the papacy was here were sometimes termed. 'He liked Avignon because of the wine!' both the locals and the Bordelais will tell you, but in fact Clément had made a shrewd choice: Avignon didn't come directly under the French crown but actually belonged to the Kings of Naples – a branch of the Angevin family. (The 'Devil's brood' crops up yet again.) Clément would not be too remote from the negotiations he hoped to achieve, as he might have been in Rome and, from this time, his influence spread widely – to England, of course, to Hungary, to Scotland, where he excommunicated Robert the Bruce for murdering 'Red' John Comyn in a church.

Yes, his family had helped him. He helped them. Four of his nephews were made cardinals in 1305 and, of the ten cardinals created then, nine were French. King Philip must have been pleased!

In May 1306 Clément revisited Bordeaux. He was tired after much travelling and, as Pope, his expenses en route were inevitably high. On the way he stayed with the Archbishop of Bourges, who had opposed him and, comment various historians, he probably enjoyed exercising his right to claim hospitality – which obviously had to be somewhat lavish – when

113

visiting someone he didn't like and who didn't like him, but who had to put up with him and the situation. In Bordeaux, however, he was not now wholly popular. Naturally, he stayed in the Archbishop's Palace, but the other dignatories of his suite were lodged in various of the religious houses; lesser followers had to get what accommodation they could – the result being that the locals complained, the city was noisy and turbulent, prices rose, provisions were often scarce.

Clément seems to have been naïvely surprised at the charged atmosphere and spoke of going on to Toulouse, but he became ill with a virulent fever – did they, I have sometimes wondered, have malaria in those days? There are ferocious mosquitoes in Bordeaux, as I can bear witness! He was so ill that his relations, including four cardinals, who watched around him, had to conceal from him the death of another relative, who had been his friend and his Chancellor. He was certainly a man of sensitivity; it is my thought that he was not easily able to understand ulterior motives in others or to support that base intentions might be imputed to himself; there are no indications that the relations he promoted to offices were incompetent or dishonest. He inspired affection and loved his family. He might have been sufficiently innocent to have thought this was enough in his new position but he was not, perhaps, sufficient of a saint to keep quite clear of the machinations involved with much of the diplomatic plans which concerned him.

Once he had recovered, he was carried out to convalesce at the Pessac estate and then went down to Villandraut where he spent Christmas. He had enlarged the local church here and established a collegiate, with several canons. (The church was mainly destroyed in the French Revolution.) Yet around him there was now ceaseless grumbling and intriguing, notably by the Italian clerics, who resented not having direct access to him – for everything went through the hands of yet another relation, Raimond de Goth. Why not? Clément might well have asked – the man was completely trustworthy as far as he knew and there was no suggestion that members of his family were other than efficient, loyal and affectionate (more than could be said of some of the great families of the period). His work was now constantly being interrupted, the demands that were made on him increased. Had he allowed – was he beginning to allow – himself to be corrupted? Here comes the moment of decision.

King Philip wanted to suppress the order of the Knights Templars. They were established in many countries, the names of the Middle Temple and Inner Temple in London perpetuate their occupancy to this day. They owned huge properties, were also bankers – and enormously rich: their influence in Germany, Cyprus, Bologna, Aragon, Castile, Portugal and in England was great . . . and Philip wanted their money. They had been established in Bordeaux in 1158. Clément is said to have tried, in various ways, to restrain the King of France. Yet rumours started to circulate that this order indulged in horrific rites, including Satanism. On 13 October 1307 all the Templars in France were arrested.

At this time their Order numbered about 15,000 and it is at least something to be able to state that other countries did not share in persecuting them although, in some circumstances, they were dispersed. In France, however, there were frightful torturing sessions to make them confess their 'crimes'. The Grand Master of the Templars, who had been summoned back from Cyprus – and had had the courage to come – was burned alive in Paris in 1314. It is said that, as he died, he cried that Clément would meet him at 'the bar of God' within forty days.

The Pope had in fact 'tut-tutted' about the Templars in at least one papal Bull and, in another, much of what had belonged to them was transferred to the Knights Hospitallers of St John of Jerusalem – although King Philip kept all this during his lifetime. Philip was then in exuberant health, but Dante referred to a prophesy that he was one 'who by the tusk will perish' . . .

Whatever the Pope tried to do or refrained from doing about the Templars and although he could consider himself as outside French jurisdiction in Avignon (nominally under Naples), it has to be said that the appalling persecution of the Templars was carried out with his acquiescence, even if not with his sanction. Could he have done anything else? Some of us have seen the discussions of what the Vatican did in World War II about the German crimes against the Jews: opinions are still divided about this as, in some quarters, they still are about Clément and the Templars.

In 1314 he felt wretchedly unwell. He left Avignon, hoping to revisit the gentler countryside of his native Gironde, but on the way he died at Roquemaure, and his body lay in state in the Bishop's Palace while the hastily summoned College of Cardinals began to discuss who should succeed him. For no reason that I can discover, one of Clément's nephews, another Bertrand de Goth, suddenly stormed into the Palace with a crowd of mercenaries, plus a mass of townsfolk; they may well, like the citizens of Bordeaux, have resented the inconvenience and expense to which the gathering of ecclesiastics put the town. Bertrand may have wished to take possession of his uncle's body, the commercial advantages accruing from owning the body of a Pope, even of doubtful holiness, was obvious to civic persons who would thereby benefit from the increase in the subsequent tourist trade.

The uproar was great, ditto the confusion. The body itself was looted and the Palace set on fire, the cardinals barely making their escape. The Italians among them wrote to King Philip that Clément had always treated them with contempt and was now trying – they had doubtless heard about the de Goth family views on the matter, to confine the Church of God to 'a corner of Gascony'. They begged Philip to help them choose a Pope who would not promote and enrich his family at the expense of others – including, it would have been understood, albeit not stated, those who had contrived to elect him. Was it forty days since the Templars' Grand Master had, prophesying, died in flames? Soon enough, anyway. And Philip the Fair, King of France, also died suddenly that year, though it is not certain whether this was as the result of an unknown illness or of an accident – a wild boar upsetting his horse, as a result of which he died of the injuries inflicted 'by the tusk'.

Clément's body was eventually transported to Uzeste although his will, which bequeathed huge sums from the papal treasury, was still being discussed and disputed. The College of Cardinals took two years to elect another pope – Jacques Duèse of Cahors, Pope John XXII. He too promoted his family and gave enormous presents to 'his relatives and compatriots' and although frugal in lifestyle, he did 'accumulate a considerable fortune' so that the very word 'Gascon' must in that time have stood for nepotism and extravagance, even if not a personal indulgence. There were no more Gascons as such in the papal chair, although several Frenchmen did follow Clément.

Five miles out of Villandraut the country road winds through forested land and ascends to Uzeste, on a small plateau. Here Clément's will had stated he wished to be buried, in a church that he had recently enlarged and endowed as a collegiate church, with a 'doyen' or leader and two canons in residence. An important tomb already here was that of Jean de Grailly, which still remains. This man came of a noble family of Savoy and, taking his name from the Pays de Gex, was one of those promoted by Edward I of England, who liked to put his officials in places where they might not be too distracted by family influences and personal loyalties. Jean de Grailly (1278–86) was also Captal de Buch (the word means 'chief officer') and, in 1280, became Seneschal of Gascony.

The campanile of the church dates from a century and a half after Clément's time – and has sometimes acted as a lightning conductor. The exterior of the church is interesting, if one has time to look at it: there are two sundials on the walls, one to tell the canonical hours, and there is an exterior altar, similar to many outside the great pilgrim churches, so that crowds could attend mass in the open or, at times of pestilence, lepers and others considered infectious could be outside but present at any celebration. The lover of Romanesque architecture may regret that Clément lived when Gothic was beginning to be fashionable, but the excesses of the flamboyant style are yet to come; the church has a solid look, its tower and the surrounding pinnacles are pronged with little projections, some of the decorative motifs including vine leaves over the door – 'the True Vine' – and there's a 'cœur flambé', signifying the fire of Divine Love that should possess the soul.

Other external carvings include a bestiary – animals of the night, seemingly malevolent – and a series of symbols indicating how the soul must avoid such sins as, in the passage to the life to come, will weigh down and sink its spirit's bark to be the prey of demons, while, on the spire, a cross is a sign of aspiration and hope. The enthusiastic guide will recount all this and much more about the stone picture-book, carved for the edification of devout who were unable to read. There is the pigeoncot of the collegiate church – the number of pigeons that might be privately kept was, then, regulated according to one's rank and standing – and a 'little doorway' which, one is told, is a feature common to many churches of the period: people not yet baptised had to enter humbly by this way to the church. A nearby spring, today in private property, has a reputation for possessing healing powers. This one appears to have been efficacious for providing adequately abundant milk with which wet-nurses nourished those entrusted to their care; women often plunged their chemises into the holy spring and they then would touch the feet of the Madonna inside the church – which resulted in Uzeste having a business of chemise-making. It is, of course, a very ancient tradition to associate wonder-working waters with a mother goddess or the Virgin as is the use of garments rendered holy by some contact.

Clément had a special devotion to the Madonna of this church and

117

dedicated the statue with his own device and motto 'Tuus sum' ('I am thine'). He extended the previously rather small Romanesque building and the visitor will notice the alternation of Romanesque and Gothic pillars; indeed, the church in its present form was only consecrated in August 1313. The other tomb is of Jean de Grailly, Seneschal of Aquitaine, who received permission from the King of England to establish a chapel there for his family; this tomb is quite fine, in spite – as the guide and guidebook stress – of the damage done by marauding Huguenots, many of whom retreated to seek some kind of refuge in the south-west of France after the Massacre of St Bartholomew (1572), when some of them also sacked the church at Villandraut. Then, in the French Revolution, more damage was done.

In the first despoliation of the church, Clément's corpse was revealed in its rifled sepulchre; his bones were flung onto a bonfire outside though later some were recovered, in fossilised form, and reverently re-interred in the repaired tomb. The statue of the Virgin was discovered in a shrubbery. One curious thing which merits a pause – the Michelin guide only allocates fifteen minutes to the Uzeste church but anyone who encounters the local custodian will be detained by his enthusiasm for far longer – is that, whereas the tomb of Jean de Grailly has been carved with the drapery of his clothes falling as they would have done from a recumbent person, the Italian workmen who made the figure of Clément have shown the drapery of his robes falling as if from someone standing upright. Was the figure at one time standing – or did the workmen misunderstand their instructions?

The jewels that originally decorated the vestments and Clément's tiara were, of course, gouged out; the other rich decorations of the tomb, including the eight columns of jasper and the intricately carved alabaster panels were all smashed or removed, and the jewels and decorations that had been inserted in the Pope's marble gloves and the exquisite vases that surrounded his tomb have also disappeared. Yet the attraction of the Virgin of Uzeste continued in the neighbourhood: a marble plaque records how Our Lady of Uzeste saved the people of Bazas from the plague in 1616. The statue, which has a rather long face and heavy jaw, has been repaired many times, the famous smile somewhat distorted by well-intentioned touchings-up. Many may find the crucifix on the altar, dating from around the fifteenth century, primitive in what, to me, evokes some of the wonders of Catalan art, more pathetic and impressive.

There is an odd continuation of Clément V's work on a commemora-

tive plaque on the wall: on 31 January 1927 Monsignor Hou, one of the
first six Chinese bishops consecrated by Pope Pius XI, celebrated mass
here. It was Clément who, in 1307, admitted China to the Church, sending
envoys to Peking and encouraging the foundation of many convents in
China.

Uzeste is an odd, out-of-the-way place that, in today's quietness,
seems remote from violence, persecutions, civil and ecclesiastical intrigues,
although, if non-religious or staunchly Protestant visitors come, they may
be bewildered, even offended by the fervour that still surrounds the church.
Clément, as worldly success came to him, didn't enjoy much peace and
for many years his bones didn't rest. It is pleasant to remember him by
the great wine that bears his name – plus the crossed keys of St Peter and
the triple crown on its label – though the traveller will have to look for
such bottles in Bazas, Langon or Bordeaux, rather than in the hamlet of
Uzeste. There seems to be a moral here – transient as a wine may be, it
can make a more lasting impression on many of us than a marble tomb.

Pope Clément V wearing the triple tiara with the papal seal (recto left and verso right).

AQUITAINE BECOMES FRENCH

THE END OF ENGLISH RULE IN 1453

Richard II King of England, tagged 'of Bordeaux', was born on the Feast of the Epiphany, 6 January 1367, son of the Black Prince, grandson of King Edward III, his mother being Princess Joan 'the Fair Maid of Kent', a lady who inspired devotion. He was baptised when three days old in the Cathedral of St André and the Bordelais were always fond of 'their' king; they tore to pieces someone supposed to have been one of those who murdered him in prison in 1400. Richard, personally brave, sensitive to the arts and a worker for peace, cannot be the subject of much space here, but what went on during his reign and subsequently is something that affected both the Bordeaux region and the Graves in particular.

It should be remembered that there were no 'British' then. The English, whose rulers mostly spoke French as their first language, who drank French wines and whose trade was so largely involved with their holdings in the south-west of France, thought of Aquitaine as their own by right: 'all of England was stuffed with the booty of France', comments André Maurois about this period. The 1259 Treaty of Paris, between Henry III of England and Louis IX (St Louis) of France, consolidated the presence of the English; the Seneschal of Gascony lived in the Palais de l'Ombrière, the Mayor of Bordeaux was appointed from London. Indeed, in some French books even of the present century, I have found that many authors believed this to have been so – albeit only in theory – until the French Revolution! The Royal Standard of what eventually became Britain bore the fleur-de-lis of France until as recently as 1803.

The Bordelais, piggies in the middle between the two kingdoms, were adroit at taking advantage of the various machinations of the statesmen in the struggles for power, which, of course, were of the greatest importance to the wine trade, and, at that time, the wine trade of Bordeaux was still dominated in many ways by the wines of the Graves.

The French court drank Burgundy – the Duke of Burgundy was a

powerful ally of the Kings of France, richer, with far more extensive territories, the services of top artists, craftsmen, the loyalty of influential
clerics. Could the French King and his nobles be weaned from Burgundy
to drink Bordeaux – and could the English, Scottish, and Irish markets
for Bordeaux be extended? That was the aim of the Bordelais, who always
opted for peace, when trade is simplified and business can be regulated.
Even if the English Kings didn't always pay their wine bills – King John,
like others of his family, left a hefty sum owing and King Henry III paid
off only a small amount of the total – they were customers of undoubted
prestige and merchants could probably press lesser debtors for payment.
The Bordelais wanted to maintain their *privilèges et coutumes*, the various
charters and tax concessions that had been accorded to them over the centuries. They wanted things to go on as before, while, to be on the safe
side, they were diplomatically ingratiating to the French. One can imagine
the veiled overtures: 'We don't want to lose old customers, but sometimes,
we admit, we should like to afford facilities to our – as we may call them
– fellow countrymen. And of course we have no shortage of supplies of
wine, no chance of *our* vineyards not yielding . . . I believe you've had problems with Champagne and Burgundy when Heaven has not been kind?
Shall we submit a few samples?' One has only to read the accounts of trading
to realise that human nature does not alter: the English are informed that,
of course, for ages, they have had first choice of the best wines, but prompt
settlement of accounts would be appreciated. 'Our French customers, we
must inform you, find no difficulty in paying.' To the French, the excuses
for high prices are the demands of the English, 'with whom, of course,
our relationship is special and who would make many difficulties for us
should we change our policy . . .' England and France are adroitly played
off against each other.

The English were beginning to feel uncertain about the slice of France
they thought of as 'theirs'. Edward III and his son, the Black Prince,
defeated the French at Poitiers in 1356 at which battle Sir John Chandos
charged, crying significantly 'St George for Guyenne'. The French King
John and his fourth son, Philip 'le Hardi' (the Bold), Duke of Burgundy,
were as prisoners sumptuously entertained in England at various banquets
when, one may be sure, Graves wines were served, for Bordeaux wines
would have predominated. The old query about how the English held
Aquitaine cropped up, for young Philip smacked the butler's face when
King Edward was served before King John, believing that, as the English

122

held Aquitaine as mere vassals of the King of France, his father, though a prisoner, should have been served first. 'Truly, cousin,' Edward III remarked suavely, 'you are indeed "Philip the Bold".' Matters of protocol, saving or loss of 'face' and arguments as to who sits where are still dividers of men and kingdoms.

Regular 'showing the flag' expeditions by the English into France were now thought of as wise. The Black Prince only got as far as Poitiers on his *grande chevauchée* or excursion. But these cavalcades through the countryside were not merely of military importance. The appalling plague called the Black Death had reached France, Spain, England and Germany by 1348, the decimation this caused resulting in a labour shortage everywhere – and a consequent rise of feeling by many groups of workers that conditions could and should be improved for those who survived. In Florence, in the Low Countries, unrest was rife in the towns; workers sought status with the more powerful officials of the various guilds. The wine organisations, such as the Jurade of St Émilion, founded in 1199 (of which I am extremely proud to be the first woman member), must have looked somewhat warily at their vineyard workers at this time, but, when men and women are caring for living things, plants or animals, it is difficult to abandon or neglect these and, although the larger ecclesiastical holdings may have had a few envious looks cast at them by peasants trying to wring a living from their smallholdings or the plots worked for an overlord, the civic unrest does not seem to have increased throughout the countryside. Wine was virtually a basic commodity and where it could be produced those involved, in the country, could usually manage to go on living and, of course, it was the towns and cities that suffered the greatest losses in the Black Death, as in any epidemic. Some communities perished, but, maybe because of the situation of Bordeaux and the Graves, there does not seem to have been such loss of life as is recorded elsewhere.

In 1373 Richard II's uncle, John of Gaunt, from whom generations of European royalty are descended, made his *grande chevauchée* into France. This was probably a matter of reassurance to the south-west, for, in 1360, the Treaty of Calais had given Normandy back to France. Gaunt, Duke of Lancaster, got to the Dordogne and spent Christmas in Bordeaux, although only half of his force of 15,000 men survived. And, in 1377, the French armies came within twenty miles of Bordeaux, the unfortunate town of La Réole changing hands seventeen times.

The English were having to deal softly with the Bordelais now. The

Jurade de Bordeaux governed there, even the Mayor and the Seneschal of Guyenne not being admitted to the sessions electing its officers; in addition to the 'Jurats', there were thirty 'bourgeois' (often former Jurats), plus 300 council members. So the organisation was a real and practical force.

War up to then, however much it might afflict those of humbler standing and devastate the countryside, was still something of a sport, an occupation suited to the nobility and gentry – which indeed it tended to remain until 1914–18. Chivalry governed many encounters like an earlier version of 'playing the game'; of course, people at the top wanted to win, but, if they lost, their captors would look after them, feast them, put them up while ransoms were raised, often for years. Things were done 'according to the book'. When, in 1389, the French threatened to take Bordeaux, heralds went up to the towers of the city and, after sounding a call, shouted 'Secours de ceux d'Angleterre pour ceux de Bordeaux!' It was impossible to resist and they knew it, just as they knew that the English couldn't or wouldn't come to help them, so, honour satisfied, they opened the gates of the city to the French and doubtless a good time was had by all at the subsequent feastings.

In 1360 Edward III's right to Calais and Ponthieu – relic of former holdings by England in the Loire – had been confirmed by the Treaty of Bretigny. But in England now there was restiveness about paying any sort of 'tribute' to Rome and the activities of the religious reformer Wyclif and his followers also made for uncertainty; when, in 1367 the Black Prince headed a victorious campaign to restore Peter I to the throne of Spain, this must have somewhat reassured the Bordelais about their prospects vis-à-vis the English trade. The Black Prince kept his court 'permanently geared for war' when he was in Bordeaux, according to Gervase Mathew in *The Court of Richard II* (1968) and, when he came back to the city from Spain, apparently he dismounted and entered 'holding hands with his wife and son'. He is said to have entertained 400 people daily at his table in the Palais de l'Ombrière; they would have got through vast quantities of wine. But the rot had set in and Charles V of France declared war on England in 1369. There was a truce in 1381 but, when, after eleven-year-old Richard 'of Bordeaux' came to the throne of England, that country was again restive; the fourteen-year-old Richard quelled Wat Tyler's revolt, but, although he always worked for peace, he never achieved it.

By 1406 the French were besieging Blaye and the Bordelais appealed to England – now Henry IV was king – for help; even if he had murdered

Richard, they hoped he would back them against the French. Before the English could act, however, the Jurats de Bordeaux did: they commandeered the wine fleet, then standing in the river, and peremptorily shot an English captain who imprudently refused to give up his ship. Then they sent fireships into the French fleet, anchored off St Julien, routing it.

Now begins the most active part of the career of the great Archbishop of Bordeaux, Pey Berland. He was the son of a peasant up in the marshy Médoc and, in his lengthy and recurrent negotiations between England and France, he was in some respects an early version of Henry Kissinger; he refused to take sides; indeed, he would not, even under pressure, fight against 'his' king – that of England; he was probably somewhat sustained by the wine of Pape Clément. (What, the Graves growers must have commented, could the soggy Médoc and the overpriced *palus* wines produce of quality comparable to that of the Pessac estate?) The tower that bears his name, alongside the cathedral, indicates how he was esteemed.

In the Agincourt war, Henry V of England, while besieging Harfleur – 'Once more unto the breach' – sent down to Bordeaux for both guns and wine. This was a rather last-chance attempt to regain the English hold over much of France and, when Henry married the French princess Catharine, many must have thought a settlement had been reached – though it was from her marriage, as a widow to Owen Tudor, that the English crown eventually came to Henry VII.

One must, tactfully, mention that most Bordeaux histories play down the English part in these wars – when France is not victorious. (Later, the same thing occurs after the Peninsula War – even a brief visit by Napoleon is recorded in detail, while the Duke of Wellington's visits are almost ignored.) So although the Graves was certainly involved in what was going on at the time, details are scanty.

The Bordelais found that they had not been quite as clever as they had supposed in opening their gates to the French: Charles VII was less indulgent about their *privilèges* than they had expected. He continued levying taxes and eventually they opened their gates again to the English Regent, the Duke of Bedford. It was his sister who was married to the Duke of Burgundy, Philip le Bon (he handed over Jeanne d'Arc to the English), who was tending to side more with England than France. In 1443 the English invaded Maine and Anjou – which they probably still thought of as belonging to them – but, in the south, three French armies threatened Bordeaux, the Seneschal of Guyenne was a prisoner and his royal seal had fallen into French hands. The machinations and negotiations are dispiriting and tedious to sort out.

Pey Berland went off to try to get definite help from England and, before leaving, he rode around Bordeaux and, says an old history, ordered that 'all channels and tunnels' through which the wine came in should be blocked. I take this to mean that he ordered that roads into Bordeaux, which would mainly have been from the Graves, as well as by the ford, should be barred. Pey Berland did this in July, before the vintage, thereby securing such stocks of wine as were already in the city, together with other commodities, but arranging for wine made in the forthcoming months to stay out in the country, not at risk there from whoever took over Bordeaux and also would most likely commandeer any stocks held in the port.

For six weeks Pey Berland disappeared. On 3 October Charles VII took La Réole, only 15 km from Bordeaux, 'liberated' the Entre-deux-Mers, the environs of Dax, the Gers and the Landes, as they were then defined. However, in December Pey Berland came back. He had been heartened by having seen the English fleet drawn up ready to sail at Plymouth.

The subsequent winter was a hard one. Charles VII only escaped in his nightshirt from the house where he was staying in La Réole when it was burned down and he left behind him the sword of St Louis. Understandably, he then retreated. Meanwhile, the weak, pious Henry VI of England married Margaret of Anjou – 'She-wolf of France' as many English called her, daughter of the King of Sicily, overlord of Anjou and Maine. And Charles VII fell in love with Agnes Sorel, whom he loved all his life, although he had not sufficient affection for Jeanne d'Arc to rescue her from the English.

In 1449 the English–French war began again and, in 1450, the English suffered their first defeat for a century and a half in a pitched battle. Fighting took place in the lower Médoc, to the understandable resentment of the wine trade; still, as the export tax on wines other than those of Bordeaux had been lifted, the Bordelais must have felt they had some justification for making overtures to Charles VII. Dunois, Jeanne d'Arc's companion in arms, arrived in the region in 1451 and with a disciplined army took possession of Blaye. Pey Berland still begged for English help, but there was a revolt in Kent and, at the Feast of the Epiphany, the English King and Queen were deprived of dinner, because the local tradesmen refused to supply them until outstanding bills were paid. England was now beginning to be split between the factions of the white and red roses, York and Lancaster.

126

Charles VII compelled Bordeaux to surrender – in the usual chivalrous face-saving way – and went south to take Bayonne until, as Holinshead's *Chronicles* relate: 'In Aquitaine alone the kingdom was losing three Archbishoprics, thirty-four bishoprics, fifteen counties, one hundred and five baronies, a thousand captaineries.'

There was another prolific vintage in the Gironde. The new Seneschal knew little or nothing about wine and, seeing the glut, many people thought to make a killing by making quick purchases of land. Messages were sent to London asking for advice, which did not arrive. The Bordelais found themselves left with huge stocks of wine on their hands – Charles VII and the French court still drank Burgundy – and there were endless problems about who owned what vineyards.

But the English tended to ignore the French in business. They went on appointing officials to posts in Gascony and, often effectively, sending money. Pey Berland, who had now taken an oath to support the King of France, was torn in his allegiance. In October 1452, after Gascons had begged for English help, *le vieux Talbot*, Sir John Talbot, the eighty-year-old Earl of Shrewsbury, landed with an army in the Médoc and advanced on Bordeaux. (There is no authenticated association between him and the estate that bears his name, however.) At first Talbot swept all before him but by the middle of 1453 the French were campaigning hard, less gentlemanly in style, perhaps, than Dunois had been earlier, but with the effective cannon of Commander Jean Bureau augmenting their forces. Castillon, which commanded the Dordogne, was held by them, its strategic value being that it could block supplies coming down to Bordeaux. There are various accounts of what happened then, but Sir John, with his son, began by successfully attacking the Abbey at Castillon; Talbot, like Pey Berland, was supposed to have sworn an oath, when captured years before in Normandy, that he would never fight directly against the French king – a chivalric but ineffectual gesture. The Abbey cellars were broached and Talbot was about to hear mass when he was informed that the French were going to attack; he furiously repulsed the wise man who advised a delay and, in conspicuous scarlet surcoat, with his banner marking him out, he led his forces forward. In fact, it had been a baggage train that had caused the initial alarm but Talbot pressed forward, on to the French stronghold, who were behind a palisade with assembled cannon. He, his son and many of the English nobles were killed in this attack, on 16 July. The monument recording the battle is at the side of the main Bordeaux–Castillon road.

127

Bordeaux was then besieged and, in October, opened its gates to the French, who went on to capture Bénauges and Rions.

Not that the victory was straightforward. There was an epidemic in the French camp. Although the Jurats managed to get Charles VII to spare the lives of twenty of their nobles, they had to pay a huge fine; the English in the city were escorted away by the French, but many of them had already scuttled their ships, so that they now perforce had to stay where they were. In London French merchants were more fortunate and most turned wholly to trade, in which they prospered. Charles VII would apparently have been willing to pay the English to go home and see the last of them but, possibly under pressure from the Jurats, who were well aware of the commercial advantages of the English export trade, some concessions were made to them so that they could continue in business.

Henceforth, though, English merchants coming to buy wine had first to obtain a safe conduct from Soulac; then they had to wear a red cross and deposit any arms they were carrying in what was now a 'foreign country'. They were only allowed to go out from five in the morning until seven at night. Scots, however, were more favoured 'because he [the Scot] hath always been a useful confederate to France against England'. A Scot was allowed to have 'right of pre-emption or first choice of wines in Bordeaux; he is also permitted to carry his ordnance to the very walls of the town'. For, as the French King wrote to the King of Scotland in 1457, 'As for the country of Guienne ... the people of the district are at heart entirely inclined to the English party; wherefore it is more necessary to be watchful over than any other of our lands.'

It was, though, the end of English rule. Charles VII built the Fort du Hà to survey the roads to the south – to the Landes, the Graves and Gascony; the huge Château Trompette, demolished in the Revolution, commanded the port of Bordeaux; the 'Palace of the Kings of England' passed into desuetude and eventually decayed, save for one mighty gate.

Yet wine-trade memories are long and alliances of business can be maintained in spite of kings and wars. England continued to drink Bordeaux wine – especially Graves wine. Buyers arrived in the 'Port de la Lune' every year, every year the wine fleet awaited the rolled-on hogsheads, every year the ports around the English coast received the new vintage; André Simon, as quoted by Penning-Rowsell in *Wines of Bordeaux*, gives the average English imports from Bordeaux as 15,000 tuns at the beginning of the fifteenth century, then they dropped to 8,000 tuns because prices had risen sharply, rose to 50,000 tuns in 1509–18, then fell to 20,000–30,000 tuns, though in the reign of Queen Elizabeth I they were, on average, about 58,000 tuns. But the Bordelais had now to complete with other wines on the English market, also much of the wine trade went through Rouen – which, of course, also handled Burgundy. Attempts were made to promote Graves wines among the French nobility: on 17 February 1525 the Jurats ordered their treasurer to buy '120 tonneaux du meilleur van de Graves', which was to be sent to King François I, the Queen and the royal children. (The reference is from an undated *Aperçu historique sur les vins de Graves*, which seems to have been published in the nineteenth century.) This account says that the hope was that the King would not be too severe on what was still a somewhat restive city, many of whose bourgeois doubtless lamented the 'good old days' of the English. In 1551 the Mayor and Jurats sent a quantity of wine, Graves being specially mentioned, to Anne de Montmorency and the Duc d'Aumale. The Catholic–Protestant conflicts had already begun and, although most of the Bordelais and the officials were Catholics, there were many Protestant communities nearby, notably to the south.

There were bursts of rebellion in Bordeaux: in 1548 rioters rose against the Gabelle or salt tax and many donned the 'English' red cross – the French referred, with some reason, to their 'old enemy', the English. But the ordering of the Bordeaux wine fleet was regulated. In June 1585 the weather was very hot and the marshy lands around Bordeaux, especially to the north, contributed to an outbreak of plague. About 14,000 persons died of this before the end of the year – Michel de Montaigne, at that time Mayor, left for Libourne; he, incidentally, mentions Graves wine, albeit briefly. The plague was so serious that everyone who could left the city and outsiders were forbidden entry, which must greatly have handicapped trade, although I cannot trace any account of how it continued at this difficult time. In 1591 one of the Acts of the English Privy Council says that 'it is credibly reported that certain merchants intend to set out in a very disorderly manner' and, in the same year 'The Council order all who purpose to trade in wine or salt with Rochelle or Bordeaux ... to be ready by the 25th of the month' and also 'A charge of 3s. on the tun of all wines and other merchandise is to be levied on all wines and other merchandise arriving from the ports of Rochelle and Bordeaux at any port in England to cover the cost of waftage for the fleet. These charges fell formerly on the merchants of London, but as the ships of other ports take advantage of the convoy they shall be borne by all', to which was added, 'two suitable merchant ships of those lying in the Thames to be furnished in warlike manner at the charges of the merchants who trade for wines'. A medieval print illustrating some of the 'Anciens Règlements de la Ville de Bordeaux' is headed 'Prohibition for taverners to mix with Graves wines the wine of the Médoc, the Palus and Queyries', suggesting a link with the measures enforced in London forbidding innkeepers to sell more than one kind of wine at one time. The Bordelais were not allowed to 'deceive the public by crying (announcing) . . . wines from other places and growths as Graves wines'.

The affection felt by the English (and, of course, the Scots and Irish) for Bordeaux wines is deep-seated. In February 1584, Anthony Bacon, elder brother of Francis, wrote to one of his family from Bordeaux, 'Being upon the place where the best wine groweth, I have presumed to send you two hogsheads, which indeed would have been more in number, if the bearer could have afforded me more room in his ship.' (Quoted in *Golden Lads* by Daphne du Maurier (1977).)

Now, with the history of Bordeaux and Aquitaine becoming that of the history of France, a new epoch begins for the Graves.

11

'GRAVES' AS DISTINCT FROM 'BORDEAUX'

T HERE was an enormous expansion in the Bordeaux wine trade during
the latter part of the seventeenth century. The region, although always
swift to react, whether to new ideas or against oppressive legislation, then
enjoyed a fair amount of tranquillity. In 1615 Louis XIII married the
Infanta, Anne of Austria, and anyone who was anyone went south. The
city began to develop its own mercantile marine and, although there was
even a movement to establish an independent republic during the Civil
Wars in Britain in the mid-seventeenth century, this was brutally suppressed – Cardinal Mazarin was willing to negotiate with Cromwell but
he did not want a French version of the Lord Protector on his doorstep.
Significantly, the Gironde has always been inclined to some form of
'resistance', even before World War II, as witness the original 'Girondins'
who whipped up the French Revolution; the multi-racial population was
vigorous and innovative.

Long-term, though, the most significant thing that happened in the
Bordelais in the seventeenth century was not the uprisings against Mazarin
during the minority of Louis XIV, the outbreaks of plague (1585, 1604
and 1605), the magnificent visit of Louis XIV in 1660 to marry the Infanta,
Maria Theresa, at St-Jean-de-Luz (where the main cathedral door has
remained reverently blocked up ever since), but a progressive plan of
engineering. The Maréchal d'Ornano and the Archbishop, Cardinal
Sourdis, with the assistance of Dutch and Flemish technicians, carried out
a programme of draining the marshy land, notably in the Médoc. Now
the vineyard area could expand – and now the Graves faced serious
competition.

The Dutch were increasingly doing business with Bordeaux. In 1579
the independent provinces became the united Netherlands and Dutch sea
power and, consequently, trading began to boom. It may have been at this
time that the Dutch cheeses, notably the red-rinded Edam, began as a

commodity brought to the port of Bordeaux in exchange for wine. It is known as 'Hollande' to this day. Dutch merchants began to see the advantages of setting up in business in the port and several established themselves there, notably Jean-Simon Beyerman; in 1620 he founded what is, still, the oldest established Bordeaux shipping house. (The firm joined with a Paris stockbroker in 1825 to buy Haut Brion – see pp. 278–81.)

Up to this time, the Bourg wines as well as those of the *palus* had often been preferred to those of the Médoc; careful regulations protected the local producers – a letter from Henri II in 1550 had stated that, as long as *vin du cru*, coming from true 'bourgeois' of Bordeaux, was available for sale, no one else could trade and, from Michaelmas (29 September) until the following Pentecost (Whitsun), no one except a bourgeois might sell wines in taverns and inns and the wine that such people were allowed to sell had to be of their own production. But by 1647 the prices of Médoc wines, per tonneau, equalled those of the Graves, though both were surpassed by the *palus* wines and also by those of Saint-Macaire, Langon, Bommes, Sauternes, Barsac, Preignac, Pujols and Fargues. What the *palus* wines were like we have no means of knowing, but it is interesting that the south of the Graves and its neighbours were, at this time, producing wines obviously valued for quality and the sweeter wines, of course, for their styles.

From around 1690 the Quai du Bacalan was being built to accommodate the hugely increased trade: the Landes, from which resin had been exported for centuries, now was making tar, this local industry attracting foreign workers. The little ports along the Garonne were busy and trade in certain new commodities, sugar, coffee, indigo, was built up. In the countryside as well as in Bordeaux itself handsome houses, elegantly decorated, notably with wonderful wrought-iron gates and interior decorations, were being built – there are many examples of these in the Graves.

Not that the wine trade was without its problems. After Charles II's restoration to the English throne in 1660, the grumbles of merchants from within the British Isles were vociferous: they were taxed at a high rate, they were not allowed to go out into the country and pick wines on the spot, often they were landed with wines from the hinterland instead of the 'real' Bordeaux they required – and what about the way the Bordeaux shippers indulged in doubtful dealings of many kinds, including the adulteration of their wines? The French retaliated. No one who was not a freeman of Bordeaux was allowed to buy wine direct – business had to be conducted through a broker. In 1667 Colbert inadvertently dealt a blow to the French wine trade because, owing to his protectionist policy, England imposed much heavier duties on French wine – also, it shouldn't be forgotten, the court of the 'Merry Monarch', after the arrival of the exiled Marquis de Sillery, began to revel in the bubbly wine he imported from Champagne.

The tit-for-tat exchanges about wine in particular continued until the reign of William III, 'Dutch Billy', when another event dealt Bordeaux a severe blow (see p. 136). Other export markets had to be sought. Traditional customers could be very difficult to satisfy. André Simon, in his *History of the Wine Trade in England*, says that 'it is very probable that much of the trouble which from time to time arose over the alleged inferior quality of the wines shipped from Bordeaux, was due to the fact that very extensive plantations had been made in the Médoc district at the close of the sixteenth and beginning of the seventeenth centuries. The wines thus made in reclaimed marshes or land formerly devoted to the culture of cereals were, in all probability, inferior to the produce of the older vineyards.' But there is evidence that care was taken to attempt to preserve quality: regulations were backed up by the personal pride of growers. In 1679 the philosopher John Locke (1632–1704), who actually admitted in his *Two Treatises on Government* that people had the right to revolt, visited the Gironde. He commented in '*Observations on the Growth of Vines and Olives*' that 'pigeons' dung and hens' dung they make use of in their vineyards as an improvement that will increase the quantity without injuring the goodness of their wine; but horse dung, or that of any beast, they say, spoils the goodness of their wine'. Did he learn something of viticulture and wine making from Montesquieu (see pp. 307–19)? He wrote that, at vintage time, the grapes must be trodden immediately, 'for they will not keep without spoiling' and mentions that the local priest, who will receive a tithe, does not feel obliged to proclaim one single date for picking – the *ban* or proclamation of the vintage – because 'otherwise it would be impossible to get the pressing done all at one time, due to the quantity of the fruit'. In fact, he was wrong, for in 1620 at Pessac, a man who began to pick on 30 September, before the appointed date, got penalised – he had to donate a 'pipe' of wine to the local hospital. (The official *ban* that year was pronounced on 3 October.)

Records give the usual ups and downs: In 1670 the Graves and Langon were hard hit by spring frosts, very little wine could be made and what was made was of poor quality. In August 1671 the Bordelais suffered from both rain and hail, many vines being totally destroyed. The winter of 1696/7 was a severe one, many vines being frozen and much damage done in the vineyards of Barsac, Graves, Langon and other areas near to the Garonne.

Various forms of 'consumer protection' now began to be manifest, although usually they appear to have protected the producer. By a 1597 decree new wine had to be put into specific casks – those with a capacity of 228 litres (slightly different from today's *barriques*), more than the 225 litres of other casks, and they were slightly heavier because the wood was slightly thicker. Only those authorised could use the special cask. Infringement involved penalties. In 1613 the people of Bazas wanted to use the Bordeaux hogshead, but were forbidden to do so; their casks had to be 195 litres – a difference that would be apparent to the prospective buyer. Anyone who was a genuine citizen of Bordeaux could put wine into a Bordeaux cask, even if it had been produced some distance away; this wine could be brought into Bordeaux and didn't have to pay the dues and taxes levied on other wines, which were heavily taxed, whether they were intended for sale in Bordeaux or to be exported. Bordeaux citizens could keep their wine wherever they liked in the city; other people had to take their wines first to the Quai des Chartrons, where, at the offices of the *Marque du Vin*, each cask received a mark at both ends, a tax having to be paid for this, three-fifths going to the Bordeaux municipality, the rest to those who marked the casks. Such wines could only be kept on the quaysides and in the cellars running between the Esplanade du Château-Trompette and the Rue St-Esprit. Many wines from 'outside' had to pay the maximum tax, some, including the wines of Langon, only paid a proportion of this. In addition, wines from certain regions could not even be brought in for marking and taxing before 11 November, St Martin's Day, and the wines of the 'high country' and the hinterland were not allowed to enter Bordeaux before Christmas. The Bordeaux growers – and those of the Graves would certainly mostly be accredited citizens – had a long start on their potential competitors.

Now, though, there are many instances recorded of the popularity of the Graves wines. André Simon mentions a manuscript in the Paris Bibliothèque Nationale of a Monsieur de Besons who, writing about the trade in Guyenne, says 'there are three regions which are famous as regards the choice of Bordeaux wines, of which high prices can be expected. The most important and the best are the Graves, which area is in the surroundings of the city of Bordeaux.' Another English writer refers to 'our high coloured red wines, called vins de Graves'. In 1612, the landlord of a tavern in Bishopsgate Without, in the City of London, appropriately named 'The Mouth', bought Graves, of which one cask cost £12 a tun and half a cask of 'Graves claret' at £4 a tun. This low price, Simon comments, was 'probably on account of that wine being unsound or otherwise defective'. He includes the well-known reference in Thomas Heywood's play, *The Fair Maid of the West* in 1631, in which a character says that 'sextons love Graves wine'.

Another writer in English, Lewis Roberts, wrote *The Merchant's Map of Commerce* in 1638, to the effect that 'Burdeaux is seated upon the banks of the river Geronde before mentioned, plentifully abounding in those wines, which being White and Claret, are known by the name of this city: here is also near this City the little village of Le Grave, which gives name to these Graves Wines, which we esteem so excellent; and between this town and Tholausa (Toulouse) lie those rich grounds which yield those sweet wines by us known by the names of High Countrey'. The same author, referring to the prohibition on high-country wines being sold before Christmas, says that, in the morning on that day, 'Merchants are more busie in landing their wines, than they are in attending their Mass; that Gaber or Lighter being ever accounted free of Tax and Custom that first setteth her head around when their Mass-Bell ringeth, and then it is lawful for any man for that day to come aboard her and be drunk gratis.' Gervase Markham (1568–1637) gives practical advice for buyers in *The English Huswife*: 'See that your Claret wines be faire coloured and bright as a Ruby, not deep as an Amethyst; for though it may show strength, yet it wanteth neatness; also let it be sweet, as a Rose or a Violet, and in any case let it be short, for if it be long, then in no case meddle with it.' I take the warning to avoid amethyst-coloured red wines to signal that such wines might be a bit too old, neatness is probably what we today would term 'balance', 'sweet' signifies fresh and wholesome and I assume that the admonition to 'let it be short' to mean that the wine should have a clean 'finish' and be neither cloying nor bitter in its after-taste.

Something else affecting the Bordeaux wine trade at this period was the expansion of the trade in *eaux-de-vie* (spirits), of great interest to northern export markets. The ports of Nantes and La Rochelle handled growing amounts of these spirits and, in the Armagnac region, south of the Gironde, many distilleries were set up; even at the Quai des Chartrons there were firms established to distil the wines of the 'sénéchaussée' – Aquitaine – and these spirits also enjoyed exemption from the taxes levied on those coming in from other regions. In fact, the high-country wine business was struggling; in 1637 between 12,000 and 15,000 tonneaux were brought into Bordeaux, but Bordeaux was handling 50,000 tonneaux; the wines from outside were too greatly handicapped, many of the growers, including those who had been also specialising in woad, changed over to other crops, such as tobacco and maize. The plums of the south-west, notably from Agen, acquired fame and so did the salt fish of the south, which appealed to the Bretons as also did Gascon wine.

Then, in 1703, the Methuen Treaty was signed between England and Portugal. This gave certain preferential terms to Portuguese wines coming into the British Isles and it began to be patriotic to drink the Loyal Toast in port. (The Jacobites, in exile after 1688 in France, went on drinking claret and it was often an indication as to where someone's sympathies lay as to what they drank.) But the British still bought Graves – 'Les plus exquises, les plus chers'. Henry Thompson, an English merchant operating from Bordeaux, dealt in grain, spices, plums, *eaux-de-vie* and bought wine from the Graves, the Médoc, Ste Foy, St Émilion and Langon, selling to the Bordelais spices and cloth, brought by him from England and the Low Countries. In his account books for 1647–48, he bought thirty *barriques* of *eaux-de-vie* intended for Middelbourg, forty-seven tonneaux of Graves, fifty tonneaux of Langon wine (unfortunately lost due to a shipwreck), a tonneau of 'vin de Côte', three tonneaux of vinegar (that precious preservative and condiment), ten *barriques* of plums for London, plus *eaux-de-vie* for Nantes and plums for Rouen. The ships taking these cargoes were still quite small; in 1669–70 they held about fifty-four tonneaux if going to London, thirty-six if destined elsewhere; this may have been due to the sandbanks and shallow draft of the estuary. Other craft plying their trade up and down the west coast were small as well.

Now records pick out some of the families that came to prominence at this time, many still active in business today. Who and when among the wine producers had the idea of selling the wine from specific estates? It was a great piece of promotion. One can imagine the English merchant in the export market, prevented from 'buying direct' (i.e. from the grower), nevertheless arranging a type of 'exclusivity' – 'I know the property, the owner's a good friend', which, to this day, often seems to be some kind of guarantee of quality. In the days before labels were used and easily pleased customers could 'drink labels', as some do today, I do not doubt that 'from my special cask', or 'the same wine that is shipped for Lord . . ., I managed to get a small consignment, just one hogshead', appealed to many, if the adroit merchant were pushing a sale. Particularity, something in limited supply, often something rather expensive – these are the ploys of the salesman; probably they were then.

Where were these 'special' wines to come from? Those of the various regions had been sold just as what we should today call 'generics', regional names. Even people who owned estates had not, until now, tried to promote wine from any individual property, apart from Pape Clément, of course, reserved for the clergy anyway. It is some of the great dynasties of Bordeaux that initiated the new trend for estate wines. The most vigorous publicist came from the Graves and the Pontac family.

For much of the following information, I'm indebted to my friend Clive Coates, M.W., whose book *Claret* (1982) is a major achievement. The Pontacs had been established in the Bordeaux region for some time, they owned a fine house in the city and Arnaud de Pontac wasn't merely the owner of Haut Brion, he had estates at Pez, Potensac, and St Estèphe, so that he was in at the start of cultivation of the Médoc vineyards; his holdings included other properties in the Entre-deux-Mers and he seems to have been the owner of much farmland and of forests. At Belin, one of the main roads crossed his land, so that he enjoyed the revenue from tolls exacted from travellers here. His ancestry, according to Clive Coates, can be traced to a Jean de Pontac who, born in 1488, acquired the estate of Haut Brion when he married Jeanne de Belin, daughter of the Mayor of Libourne in 1529. Other writers, however, say that Jean de Pontac bought the estate in 1533, from a Bordeaux merchant of Basque origin.

However, the Pontacs went from strength to strength: Arnaud de Pontac, who died in the early part of the sixteenth century, was a merchant and exporter, owned ships and, like many of his descendants, at one time became Mayor of Bordeaux. His son Jean extended the vineyard at Haut Brion and built what is the château as it appears today; he was a stalwart character, marrying three times, before he died in 1589 at the age of 101.

Jean's son and grandson both became Présidents of the Bordeaux Parlement and then came another Arnaud de Pontac. It was he who sent his son François-Auguste to London in 1666. This was the year of the Great Fire of London, after which rebuilding – and business – was generally brisk. Haut Brion wine was already known and liked there, Samuel Pepys having sampled it at the Royall Oak (a patriotic name, referring to Charles II's hiding in an oak after the Battle of Worcester) in Lombard Street and commenting on 'a sort of French wine, called Ho Bryan, that hath as good and most particular taste that I ever met with'. Diarist John Evelyn (1620–1706) refers to 'discourse with Monsieur Pontac, he gives the names of the wines drunk as Pontaq and O'Brien', thereby causing argument down the centuries as to whether the vineyard could ever possibly have had an Irish name – although, in spite of the special pleading by Irish lawyer Maurice Healy (1887–1943), there really seems no foundation for this theory. Penning-Rowsell, quoting from André Simon's *Bottlescrew Days* (1926), mentions John Hervey, first Earl of Bristol, who bought 'Obrien' in 1705 and Edmund also says that, in a Christie's catalogue, the name is given later as 'Oberon'! 'My Lord Montagu' (of Beaulieu) bought '2 hogshead of Aubryan wine' from 'Rich. Blachford' in 1669. So this was certainly a 'known name' in England, among drinkers who registered what wines were called.

In 1677 the philosopher John Locke went to Haut Brion and described it as being 'a little rise of ground open to the west, in white sand mixed with gravel; scarce fitting to bear anything'. There are many visitors to Bordeaux estates even today, when things have been considerably smartened up, who afterwards express slight disappointment at the absence of picturesque settings, spectacular landscape and 'le folk lore'.

François-Auguste, who may have already been doing business with the owner of the Royall Oak, opened a tavern in London (The Sign of Pontac's Head), which seems to have become fashionable: the wine of Haut-Brion or, simply, Pontac, was mentioned with approval by John Dryden, Daniel Defoe, and Jonathan Swift. A versifier, Richard Ames, who wrote a poem 'The Search after Claret' in 1691, which describes a company going from inn to inn looking for their pet tipple, refers to 'sprightly Pontac'; in some contexts it seems as if this was the term often used to refer in general to Bordeaux wine. John Evelyn was critical of François-Auguste – 'I think I may truly say of him, which was not so truly said of St Paul, that much learning had made him mad', he wrote in 1693, the implication being that François-Auguste was making play with his father's revenues and having a good time, rather than consolidating business, though in 1684 Evelyn noted 'we all dined at Pontack's as usual' and the place is referred to in several contemporary plays, including Congreve's celebrated *Love for Love* (1685).

Because Arnaud de Pontac owned a number of other properties, he could use their wines for topping up casks of Haut Brion if necessary – which it often was because evaporation, in a hot year, could account for a serious loss. There is a most interesting reference cited by Penning-Rowsell in *Wines of Bordeaux* (from the Townshend (Raynham Hall) MSS, for which he thanks Professor J. H. Plumb of Cambridge for supplying). The significant comment is made in 1723 by a merchant writing to the man who looked after the wines of the Prince of Wales, later George II: 'The 4 topping growths of La Tour, Lafite, Châteaux Margaux and Pontac are exceedingly good.' Penning-Rowsell says that the word 'topping' 'of course indicates that they were the top, i.e. first-growth wines'. Although he may indeed be right in this assumption, I admit that I think the implications are different.

True, the word 'topping', according to the *Shorter Oxford English Dictionary*, has the sense of 'very high or superior in position' as early as 1674. But a nineteenth-century definition of 'topping' from the same dictionary as 'That which is put on top of anything to complete it', may well have been in use earlier – and this would suggest that something had indeed been put on top of the wines, so as to improve them. By 1723 many merchants, shippers and proprietors may have been alert to the way in which a little of something additional to the one basic wine of an estate could 'help' it. I wonder whether 'topping' in this context may not in fact mean that the fine wines shipped to the princely cellar were actually intended for 'topping up' less distinguished hogsheads? Even a very small percentage of a superior wine can make an out-of-all-proportion improvement to a cask of something otherwise sound but fairly 'ordinary'. My slight acquaintance with the wine trade has made me aware that, even today when controls are strict and purists tend to be aggressive about 'genuine' wines, it takes a very little of 'something else' to improve a wine that may be perfectly all right, but rather dull – the addition can act like the squeeze of lemon in a sauce, imperceptible but transforming. As wine is made to be enjoyed, I would rather drink a wine I enjoy, meeting my requirements as to quality and predominantly coming from the region that its label purports, than one that I do not – however seemingly 'genuine'. But that is a personal opinion, as is my comment about 'topping'.

The white wines shipped by Pontac were probably drawn from his estates in Blanquefort.

More mentions of specific wines occur in the *London Gazette* regard-

139

ing sales of wine taken as from ships in the Anglo–French war at the turn of the century: 'New French Clarets' are listed and, in 1705, there were '200 hogsheads of Neat Choice New Red Obrian and Pontack Prize-Wines (just landed)', and, two weeks later, '200 hogsheads of New Pontac and Margoos wines' were on offer. The 'Neat Choice' I take to be the then version of the contemporary 'special selection' – this term might look attractive in a list today!

Signs of unrest were beginning to appear in the Gironde. Speculative builders were beginning to buy up property in Bordeaux itself and, except for the very well-to-do, who had extensive private gardens, and the religious establishments with their enclosures, vineyards within the walls disappeared. Louis XIV did not favour Bordeaux – the French court still generally drank Burgundy – and although the appointment of Philip of Anjou as King Philip V of Spain ('The Pyrenees don't exist now!') in 1701 and the 1702 outbreak of war might have adversely affected the Bordelais and the wine trade, they do not seem to have done so. It was, as had been stated, the 1703 Methuen Treaty (see p. 136) that really hurt the French wine trade, not the War of the Spanish Succession. However, the Bordeaux owners and merchants did not seem to be immediately affected; they were enjoying a boom – and seemed unaware of the threats to their trade from other wine-producing countries, and from the rising tide of revolution in their midst.

12

THE BEGINNING OF 'MODERN' WINES

FROM THE EIGHTEENTH CENTURY
TO THE PRESENT DAY

THE eighteenth century is the beginning of the time when Bordeaux wines began to be important in new ways and in new markets. Trade with what are now the British Isles was still developing and also with the 'colonies' of North America that became the United States – the gentry who went there from Britain took with them a love for claret. The French colonisation overseas also ordered substantial amounts of wine. In many of the ports on the west of France, such as Nantes, and notably in Bristol, fortunes were made by luxury goods coming in from the New World, together with the trade in 'ebony' – which was slaves; at least some of this 'black ivory' never came directly to France, however, being exchanged for goods in the Antilles. The 1685 Revocation of the Edict of Nantes by Louis XIV sent many Huguenots to England, to the Cape of Good Hope, and elsewhere – they continued to enjoy Bordeaux wines when and where they were able to worship freely.

Increasingly, vines were being planted. Almost it seems as if the growers in the Bordeaux region – whence the original Girondins came in the Revolution – had a premonition as to what might happen and wanted to increase their holdings as a safety measure. Yet obviously vines were more at risk than many other crops, for, even with ungrafted vinestocks, able to yield earlier than grafted vines, it takes even the ungrafted vine around five years before it will, under the right conditions, yield both steadily and satisfactorily, although it may have borne crops from as early as eighteen months after its planting. Outsiders, unaware of the hazards involved, saw how unwise it might be to join the rush to buy land and put it under vines.

At the beginning of the eighteenth century, the Bordeaux Intendant – the translations 'bursar', 'manager', 'steward' do not really give the term the importance it requires; 'administrator' might be adequate – was one

Claude Boucher (1720–43); he saw all kinds of disadvantages in increasing the area under vines. The big Bordeaux history (Higounet) lists some of his pessimistic forecasts: shortage of grain and meat if land is given up to vineyards; fewer men able to go into the army and navy; too many coopers and fewer farmers and – very important – a drop in revenue because the *bourgeois de Bordeaux*, those comfortable citizens, made wine that was, according to their traditional *privilèges*, exempt from so many taxes.

Boucher does admit that, while in a *'canton appelé le Graves'* excellent wine was produced, nevertheless he deplores that for about ten leagues around Bordeaux, nothing but vineyards were to be seen. Therefore – rather like Domitian (see p. 57) – he proposed to pull up all vines planted since 1709, with the exceptions of the 'Graves du Médoc, des graves de Bordeaux et des Costes' (Côtes).

He wasn't successful and a marginal note made by some wise and cynical reader of his proposal comments, 'This memorandum is inspired by silly ideas and will probably never be put into action.' For all that, Boucher's successor as Intendant, Louis-Urbain, Marquis de Tourny (1743–57) did follow Boucher's policy. After 1725 royal permission was required before vines might be planted; Tourny, famous for enriching Bordeaux by many superb buildings, made investigations into the plantations in the Médoc, where huge areas of land were now going under vines. In 1748 several estate owners were fined and had to have their vines – or some of them – pulled up. In fact, the problem was not peculiar to Bordeaux, because in 1745 it was forbidden to plant any more vines in France (although I wonder whether the wily farmer and the proprietor with 'influence' were strict in obeying this?). Tourny himself had to admit that, in 1756, there were more vines in France than there had been in 1731.

The great religious establishments still owned many vineyards, employing a number of lay workers. Just beyond the centre of Bordeaux you can still see long streets of single-storey, flat, shuttered houses that were, in many instances, the former *échoppes* or places of work of the small tradesmen or workers on the nearby big estates. Alongside the *jalles* or watercourses around Bordeaux, the gravelly land, now drained, was found useful for vines, the *côtes* on the east bank of the Garonne were important vineyards and, to the south and on both sides of the Garonne, much land formerly belonging to feudal overlords had become derelict and was now being planted. As Montesquieu had foreseen (see p. 313), the Médoc was becoming a rival to the Graves and, at La Brède, he probably had more

142

reason to fear the competition, for, unlike the wines of Haut Brion, his wines were not very well known. As a result of this, Montesquieu was one of the first growers to promote his estate wines.

In 1725 there is the first reference to the hierarchy of the great estates, Haut Brion being mentioned among several first growths. In 1730 there is a note about Graves wines – 'the top ones are the growths of Pontac, Lafite and Margo' [*sic*] and later there was a proposal to 'classify' and categorise both the Graves and Médoc wines, the former to include the wines of both Pessac and Mérignac. Were the Bordelais trying to attract the attention of buyers? The value of personal contact, some 'inside' knowledge – 'wines by that name are always reliable' – must have been recognised as important, especially so as the people who actually bought the wines for the wealthy households were usually the stewards, butlers and bailiffs.

If only the Graves growers had grouped themselves into some sort of organisation in the eighteenth century, many problems might have been avoided. Some of the old family names, many seeming to be of Graves origin, now crop up in the Médoc; the estates there possibly had novelty value to potential buyers. One comment by the Abbé Beaurein (writing in 1877 in *Variétés bordelaises*) says of this period that many of the Bordeaux bourgeoisie were now beginning to build houses for themselves in the Médoc. They may have had some notion that it was healthier, or more fashionable; they may have thought it wise to be on the spot to supervise what was going on in the newer plantations of vines.

The wines of the *palus* were not only still popular, but seemed sufficiently robust to travel well, notably to North America. In 1759 Du Hamel de Monceau commented that these wines could be mixed with those of the Graves 'so as to add to the colour without taking away anything of the delicacy'. He also comments that the wines of the *costes* (côtes) were mainly white and were often sold as *vins de primeur*, immediately after the vintage, but he adds that the finest whites were those such as came from the regions of Barsac, Preignac, Langon and Sauternes, noting that these smooth, scented sweet wines got better by long-term cellaring, because, being vintaged late, they could develop, even though at this period they were simply left in wood to do so.

Although the Graves, now apparently split into the *grandes Graves* and *petites Graves* according to Beaurein, were beginning to lose ground to the Médoc, they continued to be of great importance: in 1755 they represented 18.3 per cent of the Bordeaux crop. The Marquis de Ségur, 'Prince des Vignes', owning the estates that are now Lafite, Latour and Mouton (or at least segments of them) plus other properties, was also a proprietor at Bègles, in the Graves. Exports rose and rose; in 1723 exports of wine from Bordeaux represented about 69 per cent of the total produced. But a decline was coming.

One growing business of great significance was that of glass manufacture, especially of bottles. By this time English glass had acquired a great reputation, both for ornamental as well as practical items. Bottles had had to come in to Bordeaux up to now, because although the French glassworks made beautiful objects, there was a special quality about *verre anglais*, which was everywhere admitted and made this glass sought after. Until this time, of course, bottles as such were used as types of decanters or carafes, for putting on the table holding wine drawn from the cask. The well-to-do, such as Samuel Pepys (in the previous century), had had bottles made bearing their own seals or engraved with their initials, into which the wine of their choice could be poured and some taverns also had their own particular sealed or marked bottles. In Britain the use of cork appears to have been known from the sixteenth century as a means of stoppering a bottle, although an inn might use a wedge of wood or a twist of cloth or straw. But bottles of the shape they were then could not be laid on their sides for long-term maturation; if any wine was left in a bottle, it might be 'sealed' by pouring on a few drops of oil (as was done until very recently with flasks of Chianti and other wines intended for short-term consumption). Fine wines put into bottle might have had their corks covered with sealing wax as an additional precaution, but they would have been stood upright.

Exactly when cork first came to Bordeaux I have not been able to discover, but certainly it was during the eighteenth century. The coming and going between France and Spain would have familiarised the use of the bark of the cork oak, *quercus suber*, growing in the Iberian Peninsula; this bark, it was found, was an admirable seal for wine in a bottle. As early as 1723 a glassworks was set up on the Quai des Chartrons by Peter Mitchell of Dublin; more followed – at Bourg, at Libourne and in Bordeaux itself, the factories being powered by coal, which came in from England or from the Aveyron. By 1790 there were five glassworks in the city, turning out 400,000 bottles a year. This glass was able to resist pressure – from inside – it was its quality, plus the rediscovery of the use of cork, that resulted in the evolution of Champagne by Dom Pierre Pérignon.

Why didn't these eighteenth-century glassworks use their superior glass for bungs? Glass bungs and faience bungs exist today, the former quite usual in stoppering the *barriques* during the early days of fermentation, when the bunghole must not be tightly stoppered because of the bubbling up of the 'working' wine giving off carbon dioxide. Bungs made of inert material, such as glass, can be easily disinfected and lifted out when casks have to be topped up. If a wooden bung is used at this stage, which it often is, then it must have a cloth wrapped around it to facilitate removal and the bung and the cloth must be both clean and, at intervals, disinfected. Once the fermentation process – which used to go on for longer in the past than it does today, when time is money and wines are not made so that they require thirty or more years to 'come round' – is finished, then the bung can be driven home and, of course, this must now be a wooden bung, in its cloth, able to be hammered into the cask, which will then be turned to one side, so that the pressure of the wine inside holds the bung in place. If it is then wished to draw off a cask sample, either a tap is inserted in one of the headstaves or else a small hole is bored in one of these, stoppered by a small wooden plug; in order to get wine out, pressure is exerted, usually by means of a claw hammer inserted between the wooden section that lies across the head of the cask and one of the headstaves – this forces out a trickle of wine. People seldom understand that it will not gush forth, but the pressure within is so great that, even if the minute plug is not immediately replaced, there will only be a slight dribble of wine from the hole.

But in the eighteenth century knowledge of bacteria was non-existent. Louis Pasteur (1822–95) did his work a century later. The big change that was first to take place concerned wines in bottle, able to change and develop while the bottle, sealed with cork, lay on its side. The Bordeaux wine trade do not seem immediately to have been much concerned. As H. Warner Allen wrote in *A History of Wine* (1961), 'The ageing of wine in bottle cannot have appeared to them [the Bordeaux growers] as a matter of great moment.' They were more preoccupied with the 'brandied wines' – that is, sherry and port – coming up from the south to export markets; and although the Irish were buying more from Bordeaux, possibly as a gesture because of their adherence to the Stuart cause, demand in England was slackening. Yet the splendid planning and building went on, including the extension of the quays – the Quai du Bacalan was begun in 1690 – and Bordeaux began to have its own fleet to cope with exports. More 'outsiders' arrived, many to become pillars of the Bordeaux wine trade today. From

Hamburg came Jean-Henri Schÿler (1708–76) and Jacques Schröder (1692–1755), to found the firm of Schröder & Schÿler on the Quai des Chartrons in 1739. Thomas Barton came from Ireland and founded his firm in 1755. The arrival of many Jewish families who had been obliged to leave Spain and Portugal was another impetus to vigorous trading. Thomas Jefferson, Minister in France in the last part of the century from the U.S., bought certain fine wines, including the 1787 Lafitte [*sic*], which he stipulated should be bottled at the estate and this was identified among stocks for the President, George Washington, by the initials 'T.J.' and also 'G.W.'

It seems evident that, for the finer wines, Warner Allen is right in his comment: those who wished could have wines put into 'personalised' bottles, but otherwise it seems to have been a matter of scant concern. The Nathaniel Johnston establishment in Bordeaux kept detailed records of shipments and Warner Allen notes that, although some Bordeaux was certainly shipped to Guernsey in bottle, much more would probably have been shipped in bulk to be drunk up quickly; however, Johnston's brother-in-law, in Wimbledon, writes that he proposes to bottle half a dozen from the Lafite 1798 to 'bring out six bottles here to lay by', and in 1808 an Irish Archdeacon ordered for himself and friends '60 dozen of the best Claret in bottles entirely', the reply to this order being 'You mention the Claret to be fit for immediate use. Am I to understand old bottled wine? In that case the order could not be executed, as we only bottle wine when ordered and it must be kept with you till in order for drinking, which might not answer your purpose, and in that case it might be better to send it in wood.' The significance of this comment – and there may well have been earlier undiscovered records relating to the matter – is twofold: the Bordeaux wine makers were still, at the end of the eighteenth century, unable to realise how a fine wine might potentially develop in bottle – should they be able to procure suitable bottles; also, they still kept wines in wood for a much longer time than would be considered suitable today, even when these wines were intended for drinking fairly soon. The 'hat' or debris of stems, skins and, sometimes, stalks, would be left on the surface of the must for several weeks, even six or eight, the tannin being extracted during this waiting period. Then, the wine might remain in cask for four to six years, before it was offered for sale. Filtering, when it was done, might be through a type of straw mat or the wicker of a basket.

During the eighteenth century, the process and practice of selling much wine *sur lie* – that is, drawn straight off the lees in the original *barrique* – seems to have been abandoned, but this change may refer only to the finer wines. Much of what we now know of procedure and treatment comes from the references meticulously compiled in *La Seigneurie et le vignoble de Château Latour* (Fédération Historique du Sud-Ouest, Bordeaux, 1974), to which various authorities have contributed; the routines of this great estate certainly cannot be thought of as standard practice (although I think that the owners of the great estates may well have copied each other if they heard of some success in an adaptation of methods).

In general, if somebody wanted to buy a rather small quantity of wine, they probably took a collection of suitable vessels to the maker or even brought along an old cask into which the wine purchased could be put for transport.

What seems to be fairly usual by now is the topping up of the casks – *ouillage* – which was necessary every week or so and does not always seem to have been done with the identical wine; as is mentioned in the account of Pontac and Haut Brion (see p. 274), if somebody owned several vineyards, a 'second wine', not necessarily even from the same region, might be used for topping up the casks. Because of the long period of maturation in wood, the casks often had to be moved from what might be limited space in *chais* or cellars at their estate or in the shipper's premises in a town; and then they were usually stored in the warehouses at the Chartrons where, of course, a large number could be watched over at a time. Casks had to be regularly 'roused' or stirred up, at intervals, so a number of workers would be kept busy in the *chais*; racking, or pumping the wine off the lees in the casks, had to be done at appointed times each year, although different owners varied in their ideas as to what was ideal procedure.

In addition to the properties owned by the well-to-do, the church holdings, particularly in the Graves, remained considerable. The Carthusians owned the Château de la Marque (now La Louvière) at Léognan; the Benedictines of Sainte Croix, the most influential and opulent establishment, now possessed the big estate of Carbonnieux, at Villenave-d'Ornon; they may have used their Bordeaux premises for longish periods when maturing the wines. The Benedictines seem only to have drunk about one-third of what was usually made in a vintage; they may, together with other religious orders, have exchanged quantities of wines between different establishments of their order. The *Vigne du Pape Clément* is not included in contemporary price lists, although its reputation remained high. It is

147

known that the cooper at Carbonnieux bottled some of his white wine at this time, so, as the Présidents of the Bordeaux Parlement were among the customers of this estate, maybe this 'packaging' was in their honour.

The La Mission Haut Brion estate had been handed over to the Prècheurs de la Mission, usually referred to as 'Lazaristes', an order founded by St Vincent de Paul, in 1634. The brothers were given it in 1664, by the successors of a Jean de Fonteneil, who had been director-general of the Bordeaux clergy. The La Mission wines, though, were sold on the open market and reached high prices, higher than any except the first growths of the Médoc in the eighteenth century. Wine was an important source of income to religious establishments, although in the Gironde there were no foundations comparable to the Hospices de Beaune, or the German foundations at Würzberg, Trier and Bernkastel.

The Graves consisted of a large number of smallholdings, as well as the typical properties, but the owners of these could not do much beyond holding their own in business. In 1780 there were about one hundred farmers registered at Villenave-d'Ornon, with sixty-nine of them owning between them a mere fifty-four hectares; at Cadaujac, in the middle of the eighteenth century, it is estimated that there were then fourteen substantial properties, covering twice the area of land that belonged to seventy smallholders – 139 hectares as against a mere 77. Many of the small farmers were obliged to go and work for the big estates, tending their own land as and when they could, and this circumstance would seem to account for the large numbers of people also registered as engaged in trades relating to wine – for example, coopers and carpenters, in addition to actual workers in the vineyards. The women of these farmers' families were able to do weeding, removing vine cuttings and similar work. Very few owners of plots were able to keep themselves and their families just by living on the sale of the produce of their own holdings.

Although, in the pre-machine age, such workers, both those regularly employed and those engaged from time to time, such as at the vintage, were essential to the running of a moderate to large wine estate, they could seldom manage to increase their own fortunes, nor could they group themselves into a labour force that might have secured overall advantages for them. In some other wine regions the smallholder could often manage on his own, if he could plant other crops in addition to vines and perhaps also keep a few animals; but in the south-west there was little else except the vine. Yet, throughout the year, the peasant was in frequent contact with people – whether clergy or laity – whose lives were far easier than his own. Such circumstances make for great resentment.

Many 'foreign' names now begin to appear in the annals of the Bordeaux wine trade: Johnston, MacCarthy, Skinner, Guestier, Lynch, Barton and Fenwick indicate the English and Irish traffic of trade and there were others, from the German states, as well. With the expansion of trade, some national preferences were beginning to emerge, northern markets and the Bretons liking deep-coloured wines, often fuller in style and somewhat higher in alcohol than straightforward 'Bordeaux'. Many were the 'adjustments' that took place along the Chartrons and indeed, almost up to our own time, it was usual to list even the finest Bordeaux reds under two headings – one *Hermitagé* or 'cut' with either this popular Rhône wine or something from Rioja or Catalonia, plus one 'natural' version. After the War of Independence in North America, consignments of sugar and tobacco were coming in to the Bordeaux ports, although exports of wine were not as yet high to this market. The British business had been hard hit by competition from other countries and the 1703 Methuen Treaty: exports of wine from Bordeaux to England were 1,558 tuns during 1715–19; by 1784–86 they had dropped to 398 tuns. In 1785 French wines in general represented a mere 3 per cent of all the wine that the British were importing – small producers must have been hard hit, as they would have seen prices drop and the Bordeaux *négociants* would not have required such large quantities of wine to make up their blends as in former times.

The satyr-like Duc de Richelieu, when he became the Intendant of the Gironde, did attempt to make Bordeaux wines fashionable at the court, but the tradition of drinking Burgundy was deep rooted. Richelieu's recommendations, including Louis XV in these, may have carried some suggestion that the wines possessed a vaguely 'restorative' property; certainly he himself went on with his sexual marathon until he was well into his eighties.

Arthur Young (1741–1820) travelled extensively in France just before and at the outbreak of the Revolution. He was primarily concerned with reporting on the state of the land and although some of his own ventures in England had been unsuccessful, he became Secretary to the Board of Agriculture and was alert to the problems afflicting the economy of France which, it was thought by many, might affect the British Isles more than in fact they did. Young's editor, Constantia Maxwell, notes how he is aware of the problems of absentee landlords in France, although many were caught between the necessity of being seen at court – which was expensive – and the way in which they were not allowed to engage in trade, so that taxation of their property was necessary, if any maintenance of it and themselves were to be achieved. Young, who often displayed great courage when faced by revolutionary mobs, who often thought he was 'a spy of the Queen', travelled up into the Graves from Auch. In 1787, on 24 August, he observed, 'Many new and good country seats of gentlemen, well built and set off with gardens, plantations etc. These are the effects of the wealth of Bordeaux . . . Reach Langon and drink of its excellent white wine.' The next day, 'Pass through Barsac, famous also for its wines. They are now ploughing with oxen between the rows of the vines, the operation which gave Tull the idea of horse-hoeing corn.' The reference is to Jethro Tull, whose *The New Horse Hoeing Husbandry* had been published in 1731. Young continues, 'Great population and country seats all the way. At Castres the country changes to an uninteresting flat. Arrive at Bordeaux, through a continued village.' (A pity he didn't visit the Château de Mongenan, just outside Portets.) He found the city handsome and impressive, though not the quaysides, which he thought dirty and disordered: 'The mode of living that takes place here among merchants is highly luxurious.' He noted the numerous water mills and the quantities of wine going out of the port; in many contemporary engravings and paintings the quays are ranged with casks, waiting to be rolled into the holds of the ships. Young saw warehouses specialising in English goods, Staffordshire pottery seeming to be very popular, also saddlery; wine, he says 'has increased in its export to England, but not so much as was expected; before the Treaty it was 8,000 tonneaux a year, and it has now risen to 12,000. Brandy has also increased.' This 'Treaty' was the one negotiated between France and England in 1786 which gave, says Miss Maxwell, 'liberty in commerce and navigation. The wines of France were to be admitted into Great Britain on the same terms as those of Portugal.' There had been a huge increase in smuggling – the British do not like being restricted as to what they can buy. Miss Maxwell says that 'in 1785 it was estimated that the quantity of claret imported legally was not equal to half the amount consumed in London alone, and that the brandy legally imported barely equalled a ninth part of the consumption'. French cambric was much worn by the fashionable; Pitt commented in Parliament that the stuff was 'worn openly by every gentleman in the house' (of Commons). English wool was equally popular in France and smuggled in there. But as there were many small ports, notably around Ireland, in addition to Dublin and Cork, and also in Scotland, it is possible that quantities of wine came in despite the Customs, for the value of the exports from Bordeaux rose even though the official quantity declined.

It is only possible to guess at the style of the wines of that time because, although some bottles have survived and I have known those fortunate enough to have tried them, the experience is, naturally enough, somewhat awe-inspiring and even the experienced have difficulty in being critical. I venture to think that such wines as have and do survive probably originally possessed a fairly high proportion of natural grape sugar, which acts as a type of preservative long-term. The Graves reds, enjoying a gentler climate and, often, warmer summers than the Médoc, might have survived today, had only someone buried them or walled up the bottles! Certainly, the Chartronnais must often have been thankful for the wines of the southern Graves to use in blending with the more austere, often thin vintages from elsewhere in the Gironde.

The French Revolution caused most estates, including those belonging to the Church, to be put up for sale to 'the people'. Unfortunately, those who then had the money to buy the properties often lacked the skill to run them; in many instances the new owners were aware of possessing land that could yield top-quality wine, but they had to get this made and to sell it when it came into being. By now, France was surrounded by enemies. Vessels slipping along the west coast often announced that they were destined for 'neutral' ports – but this was a makeshift measure, wholly inadequate for long-term satisfactory trading. Brittany, formerly a good customer for Bordeaux wines, was beginning to replace them by its own cider; the United States, although still enjoying French wines, had begun to drink quantities of Madeira as well. Thomas Jefferson's reference to them is included in the account of Haut Brion.

In *A History of Wine* Warner Allen quotes from the letterbooks of Nathaniel Johnston, whose family and firm are still active in Bordeaux, where it is a little strange to see such 'English' faces in the family portraits on the office walls. In January 1801 Johnston, at that time in Wimbledon, writes to Bordeaux in despair at not being able to find neutral ships because of the 'stoppage of the Danes', which, as Warner Allen points out, was just before the great sea battle of Copenhagen. Johnston says tensely, 'The Americans, I hear, do not yet go to the French Ports as their Treaty with France has not yet come over ratified and I should not be surprised if Jefferson is President – that they should turn against us. GOD HELP US, FOR

WITHOUT IT I FEAR WE SHALL BE SWALLOWED UP.' Yet, as Warner comments, 'It was not until after 1812, after Jefferson's death and Napoleon's fatal invasion of Russia, that the United States declared war on Great Britain.'

Somehow trade went on – in July 1801 Johnston wrote, 'Notwithstanding the War, business has been carried on with France via Guernsey and for Ireland by neutral vessel which are admitted to Entry there coming direct.' Warner Allen continues, 'Trade with the enemy, business as usual ... were the order of the day for the patriotic shippers of Bordeaux in those wars against France.' And 'Between 1729 and 1809 nearly ten times as much French wine was officially imported into this country as between 1699 and 1709 and a great deal more must have been surreptitiously introduced. Quantities of French wine could be blended with Portuguese in Guernsey to gain the advantage of the preferential tariff' (the Methuen Treaty of 1703). And 'Licences were issued at a price for the import through the Channel Islands of French wine and brandy, the Claret Shippers supplementing their wine cargoes with other goods ranging from gloves, lace and prunes' (these would most likely have come from Gascony!) 'to turpentine, verdigris and the juniper berries needed for flavouring gin.' The last three items would also have probably come from the Landes and the Graves.

The turbulence at the turn of the century was entirely adverse to the fortunes of wine growers; freedom without food is not an alluring concept. Napoleon – and his Empress Josephine – came to Bordeaux and, during the war in the Iberian peninsula, generals and staff rushed up and down between Bordeaux and Paris, making their reports; in the late autumn of 1808 Napoleon rode down to Langon and Bayonne, in appallingly wet weather. Accommodation for men on leave and, even more so, for the sick and convalescent, was difficult to find and Jean-Baptiste Lynch, Mayor of Bordeaux, visiting Paris for Napoleon's marriage to Marie Louise of Austria, presented an address begging that peace might be restored – this not apparently being very graciously received by the Emperor.

The Lynch family, originally Irish Catholics, had settled in France and became French in 1710; Jean-Baptiste Lynch, made a *comte* in 1775, concentrated on a political career while his brother ran the Pauillac property and somewhat surprisingly kept it going through the Revolution, the Napoleonic period and the restoration of the Bourbons. Jean-Baptiste was also something of a 'Vicar of Bray' and, as Mayor of Bordeaux, he prudently became *citoyen* rather than *Comte* and, even, according to Clive Coates' researches *Viticulteur*; being Mayor of Bordeaux in 1814, he followed the example of many of his predecessors when Marshal Beresford's army were threatening Bordeaux and, to quote Clive, 'the population understandably somewhat sensitive for the Restoration (not so much of the Monarchy, as of their export markets), *Citoyen* Lynch knew where his duty lay. Tearing off his tricolor, he donned the white Bourbon sash and throwing the keys of Bordeaux at Beresford's feet, he mounted the Tower of St Michel to declaim "Vive le Roi, Vive les Bourbonnais!" . . . Not surprisingly the new Louis promoted him to the Chambre des Pairs, allowing him, following a petition from the inhabitants of Bordeaux, to remain honorary mayor for a further year.' Possibly the only survival of this custom of making proclamations from high towers is at the *Ban des Vendanges* at St Émilion, when the vintage is announced from the top of the Tour du Roi.

Maybe the plain landscape of the Graves, which would have presented few problems to Wellington's army, accustomed to moving at speed in the more difficult regions of Spain and Portugal, was simply not attractive enough to result in many of those engaged in the victorious advance delaying and leaving records of their visit, maybe everyone simply wanted to get on to Bordeaux itself. In February 1814 Wellington crossed the River Adour on rafts made from the pines of the nearby forests; by the end of March, he had forced Marshal Soult into Toulouse and reached 'his last river-line, the Garonne', records Lady Longford in *Wellington: The Years of the Sword* (1969). Here the Iron Duke reconnoitred the bank and, accompanied by only two of his staff, actually encountered a French sentry, who did not recognise him and with whom he had a friendly chat. Although Wellington himself went on to Paris after victory was certain, his troops found Bordeaux much to their liking and Charles Palmer (who gave his name to the Médoc estate he subsequently bought) cannot have been the only one to explore the countryside and settle down. A book written about France just before World War II, *Light and Shade in France*, by Moma Clarke (1939), notes that, while staying in the western Pyrenees the author 'was continually hearing tales of different encounters with the English, from the time of Richard II to that of Wellington's army on its way up from Spain, and one of the sights . . . is . . . where the Duke kept his hounds'. Several of Wellington's staff had packs sent out so that they could hunt during the otherwise 'close season' (for fighting) in the winter, one intrepid M.F.H. actually galloping into the astonished French lines with the cry 'Where my fox goes, so do I!' Descendants of those hounds can still occasionally be heard to give tongue there – I have seen a shabby animal suddenly throw up his muzzle and utter the unmistakable cry. Moma Clarke also recorded that there are many legends of 'English gold' hidden in various places and 'not far from Orthez, where Wellington met Marshal Soult, there is a little colony of golden-haired people with blue eyes ... the descendants of our gilded English soldiers'. In June 1814 Wellington bade an official goodbye to his forces at Bordeaux, where they embarked for England, much to the distress, apparently, of the female camp followers who were not allowed to accompany them.

By 1815 and Waterloo, says Warner Allen, 'bottled vintage wines had definitely established themselves'. The 'Comet Year' of 1811 – comets are traditionally supposed to mean that the vintage will be good – was already recorded for Lafite; there are even notes made by men still alive who have sampled the early nineteenth-century vintages of this wine and found them far from faded. The Graves, with its older tradition of making fine wine, seems to have fallen somewhat out of fashion, although André Jullien, whose *Topographie de tous les vignobles connus* first appeared in 1816 (there were several subsequent editions), gives a description of Haut Brion together with the other first growths. He says that: 'Les vins de ce cru ont plus d'étoffe, de corps et de spiritueux que les précédens, une sève plus riche en arôme, mais moins de bouquet: l'âpreté qui characterise tous les vins de Bordeaux est plus prononcée dans ceux-ci, et ils ont besoin d'être conservés six à sept ans en tonneaux avant de parvenir à leur maturité, tandis que ceux des trois premiers crus sont potables au bout de cinq ans.' (My translation: The wines of this growth are more substantial, both in body and in alcohol, than the former ones [Lafite, Latour and Château Margaux], and they have a richer, stronger aroma – but less bouquet; the harshness that is typical of all Bordeaux wines is more pronounced in these and they have to be kept for six or seven years in wood before they attain their maturity, whereas those of the three first-mentioned are drinkable after five years.) Is this at least one strong reason why shippers and merchants trying to revive trade after the Napoleonic wars concentrated on the wines that seemed to have more immediate, agreeable appeal and that took less time to 'come round' than the great Haut Brion, which generalisation may also have been applied to many other Graves? The necessity for adequate cash flow and a quick turnover is nothing new in the wine trade and certainly even the foremost estate owners needed the wherewithal to repair often neglected properties, engage skilled workers and

154

attempt to revive or create trade, particularly in export markets.

Wine exports had fallen away during the Napoleonic blockade of Britain; the various fleets manoeuvring in the war prevented the continuation of the trade via the small ships that had been taking wine from the south-west to smuggle in to the Channel Islands and other northern ports. Britain was still drinking Graves, however. In the display of bottle or decanter labels at Vintners' Hall in London – still in Vintry Ward – there is a silver one bearing the words *Vin de Grave* (*sic*) which dates from 1809. But Bordeaux was accustomed to the vicissitudes of the market and exports of 70,000 tonneaux are recorded after 1814. (This total wasn't exceeded until 1849.) There were big vintages in 1840 and 1841 and the Bordeaux shippers had difficulties on their hands because of the industrialists and manufacturers in the north and east of France – now beginning to be of great importance – who were keen on establishing a system of tariffs, whereas the Bordelais, obviously, were set on maintaining free trade.

There's an odd postscript to what happened after 1815 in the archives of Longwood House on St Helena, where Napoleon died in 1821, attended to the last by some of his more faithful friends. Sir Hudson Lowe, the governor for part of the time, for whom Napoleon conceived a violent dislike, received a letter of instruction about 'the providing and shipping of wines, groceries and other articles necessary for supply of Bonaparte's table – particularly French wines of which there is reason to believe the consumption will be unusually great'. In *Slow Boats Home* (1985) Gavin Young, visiting the island, noted that the sum mentioned was £2,445.10s. per annum and that the wines were particularised as 'Wines, clarets, graves, champagnes and madeira.' Napoleon, understandably, was nothing of a gourmet or a wine lover, but either his suite or the long-suffering governor may have been – and Graves is the only specified claret.

The growers, at least some of whom were those who had bought up wine estates after the sequestration of the properties at the Revolution, were much freer to operate, in some ways, than they had been in the former days when there were some controls; in 1789 all the *privilèges* and tax exemptions and concessions had been abolished, so that it was now every man for himself. A comment in the *Journal d'agriculture practique* in 1844 mentions the uprooting of classic wine varieties, the uninformed treatment of certain vines – many of these now being planted in rich soils, suitable for other crops. And, more than this and at a time when it seems as if half the Médoc estates were up for sale, the vineyards were being savagely

155

exploited at the expense of quality – the anonymous writer says that, in a fine-wine vineyard, only about 20 hl are usually made from 30 ha, whereas in many properties as much as 200 hl were being made from a mere 30 ha of vines.

In *Histoire de la vigne et du vin en France des origines au 19e siècle* (1959), Professor Roger Dion expatiates on the way in which, at this time, there was quite a savage difference of opinion between the owners of the superior estates, some of whom were returned nobility or at least people who had some knowledge of wine making from the past, and the stubborn peasant, who simply sought to make money. He quotes from a man in one of Balzac's novels, who jeers: '. . . these gentry sell, in a good year, what makes them about four hundred francs per arpent [a measure of land], whereas from only twenty casks, sold at thirty francs each, I make six hundred! Who's the fool? Quality, quality! What's quality to me? Let the noble gentlemen keep their quality – for me, quality's cash.'

By the middle of the nineteenth century trade was more stable and, although the oidium hit the vineyards in 1853, the immediate result was merely to send up the prices. Napoleon III, according to Pierre Vital *Les Vielles Vignes de Notre France* (1956), had observed the 'liberal ideas' of the British during his stay in England and he applied some of these to the alleviation of duties on foodstuffs; in 1860 he made a treaty with Britain that brought the cramping regulations to an end. The 1862 total of both wine and *eaux-de-vie* from the Gironde being exported reached 600,000 hl annually and was over the million mark by 1870.

Charles de Lorbac, in a series of books on *Les Richesses gastronomiques de la France*, wrote a section 'Vins de Graves des environs de Bordeaux', which was published in 1866. Some of his comments are worth noting, especially his comment that, though unfortunately the Graves has recently suffered severe set-backs, the wines, although less *bouquetés* than the Médocs, are full, complete, fleshy and possessing much liveliness. De Lorbac refers to Wilhelm Franck's 1824 comment that they can last for as long as twenty years. De Lorbac also stresses that Graves wines take more time to come round than the Médocs and must have plenty of time in bottle, though he admits that all Graves cannot attain the quality of Haut Brion – obviously not. He remarks on the great variety of soils and would like to know more in detail about them – what is underneath the subsoil? Are there two types of alios – friable and solid?

Commenting that the fragrance of a wine derives specially from the grape variety, he reports, after mentioning the Cabernet Sauvignon, that whereas the Médoc vines are pruned low and planted in parallel lines, so that they can be worked by a plough, the majority of Graves vines are trained high and worked by the *pioche* (the tool still in use for turning earth and for minor excavations even underground in stone. But because workers are now scarce, de Lorbac hopes that this method of cultivation will give way to the more straightforward, modern methods. For it is the Graves in particular that is suffering from the move of the peasants to the town and this makes all the equipment and requisites for daily routine even dearer to those who remain in the country. Many old vines have been destroyed but, now, more suitably selected varieties have been introduced and are planted in sections instead of haphazardly. Yet the attack of oidium had been terrible – no more Graves on sale because there was none available – though the good vintages of 1864 and 1865 somewhat made up for the appalling period 1854–64. The use of sulphur and the devoted work of both estate owners and official bodies may now enable formerly devastated and fallow lands to regain their reputation for fine wines. (Alas, worse, in the form of the phylloxera, was to come, but this de Lorbac didn't known when he wrote.)

Phylloxera hit the Bordeaux vineyards soon after de Lorbac's book. In 1881 there was a phylloxera congress in Bordeaux to discuss methods of dealing with it, according to George Ordish in his masterly book *The Great Wine Blight* (1987). It was established that the aphis could not live in sandy soils and experiments were reported in the 1870s of plantations being made in sand near to the Atlantic, the sea water even penetrating the sand; another discovery was that siliceous sands, to the extent of 60 per cent, were more suitable for vines than 'shell sands'. 'Vines', comments George Ordish, 'throve in most sands except those having too much sea salt. In spite of the presence of the pest in the area vines were growing well in the Gascony Landes. . . . Sands are usually poor soils, and if fertilised with compost and farmyard manure can be much improved. This altered their nature, it was found, and, as the organic matter in the soil increased, rendered the vines liable to attack by the pest. In other words the soils were ceasing to be sandy. Chemical fertilisers were not so dangerous in this respect. . . . Another disadvantage was exposure to storms and the blowing in of salty spray from the sea, which burnt the vine foliage.' It was because of this discovery that the aphis couldn't live in sand or, of course, in flooded or partially flooded vineyards that caused a revival of vine plantations on the Garonne banks, many of these having been allowed to fall into desuetude in the earlier oidium plague. And, as Pierre Vital remarks, the efforts to try anything that would enable threatened vineyards to keep producing resulted in all kinds of hybrid vines being planted – at least they usually yielded something, of no matter of what quality – and, alas, producers took to using artificial colouring matter, blending regardless and adding alcohol to weakly constituted wines. By the time the controls of wine making and naming were instituted at the beginning of the twentieth century, notably the 'Capus Law' of 1909, forerunner of the formation of the A.O.C. regulations, much harm had been done, many reputations damaged and a serious loss of traditional quality was noted in many otherwise formerly fine wine vineyards where, by this time, at least the grafting of classic vines onto resistant American rootstocks had saved the vineyards.

The damage had been severe. Pierre Vital notes that, in 1852 the area under vines was 143,000 ha, but only 133,000 ha in 1952 – although it is fair to say that the latter figure must still be considered to a certain extent as the aftermath of World War II and the inevitable deprivations, loss of trade and shortage of capital. Production, however, had gone up – in 1952 it was 4,500,000 hl as compared with the 1852 1,500,000; it was essential, therefore, that controls should be tightened to protect both the fine-wine traditions and the reputations of many estates now suffering from the casual or misleading nomenclature still far too frequent.

Charles Quittanson, writing a preface to a facsimile reprint of André Jullien's book *Topographie de tous les vignobles connus* in 1985, quotes Adrien Berget, who, in *Les Vins de France* (1900), pointed out that, long-term, it was a combination of the changed hands of the great estates and the coming of the railways that essentially revived viticulture and viniculture in France. If new owners had not felt the necessity to explore new methods, there might have been a decline in many properties, content to live on their traditions. If, in the middle and later nineteenth century, communications had not been speeded up, many vineyards might have died forever – and there are many that, in our time, are remote from the main highways but have been buried under the urban sprawl of Bordeaux.

André Jullien, in his account of red Graves and the hugely increased traffic at the port of Pauillac, cites the light, crisp, agreeable dry white wines 'the best coming from the communes of Blanquefort, Eysines, Talence, le Taillan and, above all, those of Villenave d'Ornan' and he concludes by mentioning the wines of the south-west of the region where, in the 'cantons of Podensac and Langon there are excellent sweet wines, known as Barsac, Sauternes, Bommes, etc.' It was to take a long time before any sharp dividing line was drawn between the sweet and the dry wines within the overall Graves area.

Today, the building of the autoroute to Toulouse and the south and the great roads around Bordeaux itself enable traffic to speed towards Spain and, within the Graves, for the properties to enjoy receiving visitors who can avoid the hustle of the main highway. Estates look trim, signs, even if not always easy to follow, are in evidence, guidebooks indicate the 'monuments historiques' and, among the restaurants and little hotels, there is a pleasant absence of chichi, although it is obvious that the area is arousing itself from the resigned and often dilapidated condition of thirty years ago. The Graves is still a somewhat hidden region – but sending out signs that it is worth exploring, even and mainly via the wines that are increasingly being listed.

Two nineteenth-century tools: pruning knife (left) recalling the shape of the fourteenth-century knife shown on page 88, and a bident (right) used for breaking up the earth prior to planting the vines.

THE WINES

13

THE GRAVES
VINEYARD TODAY

THE Graves region is in shape rather like a long glove, flung down onto the map of the Gironde. It crinkles into folds just north of Bordeaux, then gathers into a crumpled shape not unlike a hand, around Langon in the south. It is about 50 km in length and varies in width from about 15 to 20 km.

DEMARCATION

In former times, as will have been noted from earlier sections of this book, the Graves region was often associated with that of the – then – lesser-known Médoc; it also extended into the Landes. The northern boundary was vaguely at the Jalle de Blanquefort. As defined by Galet (*Cépages et vignobles de France*, 1958–62) the area as shown of the Graves vineyard on a 1714 map extended from the Jalle de Blanquefort down to the Bazadais (around Bazas); the finer red wines were said to come from the north, around Bordeaux, the best whites from the south. These last are mentioned as being produced from the communes of Podensac, Cérons, Illats, Pujols, Landiras. Then there were the *Petites Landes*, the area between the River Garonne and northwest of the Graves proper. The most respected wines come from Villenave-d'Ornon, Arbanats, Virelade, Podensac, Cérons, Illats.

Yet the exact demarcation of the region has only quite recently been established. In the 1920s, for example, the owner of several estates was prohibited from using the name 'Graves' for certain of his wines and the official boundaries of the Graves were only set, at Podensac, in 1924, the limitation being confirmed in 1935.

THE ORGANISATIONS

The official organisations, which have become of increasing importance with the years, are, first, the Syndicat Viticole des Graves et Graves Supérieures. This was set up in 1904, its aims being to promote the wines of the Graves, to protect what later was defined by the A.O.C. regulations, to advise growers and publicise the achievements of those engaged in vine growing and wine making and also to formulate a marketing programme. The headquarters of this organisation is the Maison des Vins de Graves at Podensac, first set up as early as 1799, the Podensac building established in 1982. This surprisingly early date – coincidental with the French Revolution – is significant: the Graves was 'the' region for quality Bordeaux wines (with only a few exceptions), up to the turn of the eighteenth and nineteenth centuries. The proud past traditions were assumed by growers as of right. True, the few great estates were already well established, but it is nevertheless right to remember that the many other producers had thought about grouping themselves officially really early – many must have been proposing such an organisation before the upheaval of the Revolution. The St Émilion vineyard was also of considerable antiquity, but it was the Graves that, influential for centuries in the export trade for Bordeaux wines, maybe because of its aristocratic proprietors, maybe because of the traces of associations with various markets overseas and, I like to suggest, the tenacity of those who for so long have been making wine in an otherwise somewhat challenging countryside, established such an organisation.

Président of the Maison des Vins de Graves today is Monsieur Pierre Guignard, who is also in charge of wine making at Château Roquetaillade; he is supported by other vigorous members of the Syndicat. The building at Podensac was established in 1982 and is a good example of a small older house being adapted and extended to serve the Syndicat today: the *chais* and conference rooms are modern and well designed, conferences and seminars are frequently held and tastings arranged; even members of the public who are interested in wine can visit the premises, be advised on where to go and be provided with the first-rate maps and local brochure.

The Union des Crus Classés des Graves was founded in 1960; its headquarters is the Maison des Vins, the imposing building at 1 cours du XXX juillet, in the centre of Bordeaux. The Président is Tony Perrin, much respected for his overall work on behalf of the Union as well as his own achievements in the production of fine wine (see p. 263).

THE SHRINKING VINEYARD

The Union des Crus Classés de Graves, which accounts for about 25 per cent of the whole surface area of the A.O.C. 'Graves', yields about one-quarter of the total amount registered under this A.O.C., but accounts for around 50 per cent of its value. This, of course, is because all the classed growths are included.

The Syndicat Viticole des Graves Pessac et Léognan was created in 1980. It extends through the communes of Talence, Pessac, Mérignac, Léognan, Canéjean, Gradignan, Martillac, Cadaujac, Villenave-d'Ornon, St-Médard-d'Eyrans. It replaces the former Syndicat Viticole des Hautes Graves de Bordeaux, which was set up in 1964, and aimed at protecting the greatly extended A.O.C. 'Graves' and succeeding the Syndicat des Graves de Bordeaux, which was established at Léognan in 1904. The work of these bodies has been, throughout, to promote and protect the specific A.O.C. 'Graves' and particularly to 'obtain an identity for the region in the form of A.O.C.s of the locality similar to those of the Médoc'. It will be obvious that, for some while, work has been progressing towards this end. Obviously it is of importance for the producers to establish a differentiation of this kind, but although interest in and knowledge of wine is increasing throughout the world and 'news' of official changes is sure of notice, it has to be noted that some authorities, viewing the situation from the outside and having export markets in mind, are inclined to deprecate this change which, they think, may confuse the buying public who, for the most part, are not really acquainted with the significance of the various appellations anyway. The Syndicat Viticole des Graves Pessac et Léognan represents 55 *crus*, an area under vines of about 900 ha, with an annual production of approximately 35,000 hectolitres. About 75 per cent of the annual earnings from their wines are accounted for by exports.

The area under vines is less today than in the past: 1,498 ha white wine (about 47 per cent); 1,695 ha red wine (about 53 per cent).

In 1874 there were about 10,000 ha under vines. The table overleaf, taken from the 1986 edition of 'Féret' (*Bordeaux et ses vins*, 13th edition), shows the decrease in the properties of various centres listed in previous editions of this 'Bible of Bordeaux' from the beginning of the twentieth century:

	1908	1949	1969	1981
Gradignan	31	11	5	1
Mérignac	30	5	3	1
Pessac	37	16	6	4
Talence	21	10	5	3
Léognan	66	26	19	19
Martillac	21	15	16	10
Cadaujac	30	18	11	6
Villenave-d'Ornon	51	21	7	5
	287	122	72	49

There are various reasons why this decline has occurred. First, of course, the spread of the city of Bordeaux itself; until fairly recently it was not always possible to 'build high' and although it now is, there are numerous aesthetic and social reasons why this type of building may not be allowed to proliferate without restrictions. There is still a 'flight from the land', the younger generations of families formerly content to live at least in country towns or villages now seek the city, where there is a greater range of diversions as well as occupations that at least seem to be more secure than agricultural work, at risk still from the vagaries of the elements. Children must go to school, women who would previously have remained at home go out to work, the immediacy of resources such as medical care, domestic equipment, leisure facilities, and the diversions of urban life have greatly affected many regions of France, including the Graves. People live longer, infant mortality has been reduced, human beings have a right to enjoy so much more than was possible even in the fairly recent past. So there are more people – and they must have places to live and in which to work. The fact that an increasing interest in conservation and the study of country life and natural things has increased in recent times, so that there is genuine appreciation of regional characteristics and stress on regional traditions of all kinds, not only in wine and food, is one of the contradictory elements in such areas as the Graves of today. But once buildings have taken over from farmland, pasture and vines, it is unlikely that there can ever be much of a revival of what once was there in the earth.

The Graves survived invasions, wars, sequestration of many properties and in the nineteenth century two major vine diseases, oidium and

166

phylloxera. But even during such times there was a demand for wine, especially the wine of Bordeaux. When some of the most important export markets ran out of money almost overnight and the national economy suffered in consequence, it must have seemed to those who were attempting to revive vineyards after the appalling losses of World War I that, with shortage of labour and the beginning of many ways of life totally different from anything known to wine drinkers before 1914, it was impossible to hope to continue. The immediate post-war vintages in the Gironde were variable: 1919 a hot year, 1921 great for Yquem but elsewhere ..., 1923 charming, pretty clarets but would they last?, 1924 some fine red Graves but not immediately appealing. 1925, 1926, 1927 – forget them. 1928 – well, some members of the wine trade still wonder whether wines of this year, like those of 1870, will ever come round. In 1929 the world Depression caused many who had previously been able to make a passable living from their vineyards to abandon them – it is one of the ironies of life that the 1929 clarets were of remarkable quality, for those who were able to make them well and keep them properly. But some growers simply could not hold on.

Then there was the necessity for constructing an airport at Mérignac, which, with the growth of air traffic and the size of commercial planes, has had to be extended, in addition to the military air base nearby. A glance at the table opposite will show how many vineyards have gone under the tarmac here. In 1956 the majority of the vineyards of France were hit by devastating frost, not in some instances as severe as that of the winter of 1985, but in those days the post-war rehabilitation was barely finished and the technical and scientific resources were not as they are today. Gradually inroads have been made into what was an important vineyard area, so that in the Graves around Bordeaux – Pessac and Léognan – 350 châteaux and 5,000 ha of vines are definitely under threat from the urban sprawl. A group of growers, most of them young, have, in recent years, managed to resist this lava-like tide; in 1970 the Pessac and Léognan vineyard area was down to 550 ha, but the efforts of what is now the Syndicat Viticole des Graves Pessac et Léognan have managed to extend the area to 850 ha and it is their aim to revive it to the 1937 size of 1,500 ha. This would seem hopeful, although progress in the world of wine is necessarily slow.

GRAVES LÉOGNAN:
A VINEYARD IN DANGER
VINEYARDS TO THE NORTH OF THE ZAD TECHNOPOLE

Legend:

1 under vines
2 A.O.C. area
3 Areas with wine growing potential
4 Urbanised zones
5 A.O.C. zones under threat of urbanisation
6 Protected forest areas
7 Boundary of the technopole
8 Boundary of the ZAD
9 Boundary of wine-growing region Graves Léognan
10 Agricultural and forest areas

THE 'TECHNOPOLE'

A new threat has recently appeared. This is the proposal to establish a 'technopole' in the Graves Léognan area – a huge set of installations known as 'Armines', intended for 'research and development of industrial processes, created by the School of Mines'. If work goes ahead, not only will 320 ha. of vineyard land be invaded and taken over, but, as the Association pour la Sauvegarde des Graves de Bordeaux point out, the social life and local ecology would be distorted and affected forever. At the time of writing it is such a matter of moment, the situation changing constantly, that further comment is not possible. These who oppose the 'technopole' indicate several other possible sites that would not affect established vineyard land or historic and residential areas (see fig. 4). It is to be hoped that they will be listened to. Reference to fig. 3 will indicate the way in which the proposed installations will nudge into the heart of the Graves de Bordeaux – remembering, of course, that the possible pollution from even the most modern establishments of this type can affect the surroundings as much as the actual occupation of the land.

There are, at the time of writing (1987), about 600 growers in the region, 351 estates, throughout the 3,000 hectares under vines. The estimated capacity for 1987 is as follows: Graves blanc: 55,841,55 hl; Graves Supérieures blanc (sweet white): 26,870,62 hl.; Graves rouge: 105,135,57 hl.

THE A.O.C.s

The A.O.C. 'Graves' was created in 1937 for both red wines and dry white wines. In 1939 the sweet whites were defined as 'Graves Supérieures'. There was the classification of 1953 and then of 1959 (see p. 241). Towards the end of 1987 two new A.O.C.s – 'Pessac' and 'Léognan' – have come into existence, additional to the three A.O.C. 'Graves': Graves rouge; Graves blanc (sec); Graves Supérieures (moelleux).

The communes from which these wines come are 44 in number: Arbanats; Ayguemortes-lès-Graves; Beautiran; Bègles; Bordeaux; Budos; Cabanac et Villagrains; Cadaujac; Canéjan; Castres; Girondes; Cérons; Cestas; Eysines; Gradignan; Guillos; Illats; Isle Saint Georges; La Brède; Landiras; Langon; Le Haillan; Léogeats; Léognan; Martignas; Martillac; Mazères; Mérignac; Pessac; Podensac; Portets; Pujols-sur-Ciron; Roaillan;

PROPOSED ALTERNATIVE SITES
FOR THE ZAD TECHNOPOLE

SITE DE
St AUBIN
DE MÉDOC

LE VERDON

HAUT-MÉDOC

GARONNE

PARIS

LACANAU

N215

GRAVES

NORD

MÉRIGNAC

BORDEAUX

ENTRE
DEUX
MERS

SITE
DE PESSAC

SITE
ARCACHON-
LA TESTE

N250

A63

N10

GRAVES
PESSAC

GRAVES-
LÉOGNAN

CÔTES
DE
BORDEAUX

N113

TOULOUSE

ARCACHON

ZAD
TECHNOPOLE

SITE DE
CESTAS

BAYONNE

GRAVES

SITE
DU BARP

St Jean-d'Illac (anciennement dénommé Illac); St- Médard-d'Eyrans; St Michel-de-Rieufret; St Morillon; St Pardon-de-Conques; St Pierre-de-Mons; St Selve; Saucats; Talence; Toulenne; Villenave-d'Ornon; Virelade.

On 6 July 1984 there was a decree whereby the wine regions of certain areas can add 'Pessac' or 'Léognan' after the word 'Graves', if the wines are made in the following communes. To have 'Pessac' the area of production must be in the communes of Mérignac, Pessac or Talence. To have 'Léognan' the area must be in the communes of Cadaujac, Gradignan, Léognan, Martillac, St-Médard-d'Eyrans or Villenave-d'Ornon.

The new A.O.C.s will confirm these two regional mentions, while doing away with the prefix 'Graves' for wines made in and subsequent to the 1987 vintage (see the official Décrets Appendices V and VI).

The specific *crus* of Pessac and Léognan, at the time of writing are listed below, in alphabetical order: the classed growths are further described on pages 262–88 and marked here with an asterisk:

Ch. Bardins (Graves Léognan): Cadaujac; owner Christian de Bernardy de Sigoyer
Production: 15,000 bottles red, 1,200 bottles white
Ch. Baret (Graves Léognan): Villenave-d'Ornon; owner Sté Civile Ch. Baret
Production: 48,000 bottles red, 36,000 bottles white
*__Ch. Bouscaut__ (Graves Léognan); Cadaujac
Ch. Brown (Graves Léognan): Léognan; owner Jean-Claude Bonnel
Production: 45,000 bottles red
*__Ch. Carbonnieux__ (Graves Léognan): Léognan
*__Chevalier, Domaine de__ (Graves Léognan): Léognan
*__Ch. Couhins__ (Graves Léognan): Villenave-d'Ornon
*__Ch. Couhins-Lurton__ (Graves Léognan): Villenave-d'Ornon
Ch. de Cruzeau (Graves Léognan): St-Médard-d'Eyrans; owner André Lurton
Production: 200,000 bottles red, 60,000 bottles white
Ch. Ferran (Graves Léognan): Martillac; owner Hervé Béraud-Sudreau
Production: 20,000 bottles red, 25,000 bottles white
*__Ch. de Fieuzal__ (Graves Léognan): Léognan
Ch. de France (Graves Léognan): Léognan; owner Bernard Thomassin
Production: 160,000 bottles red, white wine vineyard recently laid out again

Ch. Gazin (Graves Léognan): Léognan; owner Sté Fourès-Michotte
Production: 60,000 bottles red

Grandmaison, Domaine de (Graves Léognan): Léognan; owner Jean Bouquier
Production: 66,000 bottles red, 15,000 bottles white

Hannetot-Grandmaison, Domaine de (Graves Léognan): Léognan; owner Mme Beaumartin
Production: 15,600 bottles red

*****Ch. Haut Bailly** (Graves Léognan): Léognan

Ch. Haut Bergey (Graves Léognan): Léognan; owner J. Deschamps
Production: 85,000 bottles red

*****Ch. Haut Brion** (Graves Pessac): Pessac

Ch. Haut-Gardère (Graves Léognan): Léognan; owner Bernadette Lesineau
Production: 100,000 bottles red, 12,000 bottles white

Ch. Haut-Nouchet (Graves Léognan): Martillac; owner Lucien Lurton
Production: red wine vineyard being replanted, 24,000 bottles white

Ch. Haut Ponteil Bergey (Graves Léognan): Léognan; owners Alain and Francine Plantade
Production: 12,000 bottles red

Ch. La Garde (Graves Léognan): Martillac; owner Louis Eschenauer
Production: 250,000 bottles red, 35,000 bottles white

Ch. La Louvière (Graves Léognan): Léognan; owner André Lurton
Production: 200,000 bottles red, 60,000 bottles white

*****Ch. La Mission Haut Brion** (Graves Pessac): Talence; owner Domaine Clarence Dillon S.A.

Ch. Larrivet Haut Brion (Graves Léognan): Léognan; owner SNC Ch. Larrivet Haut-Brion
Production: about 100,000 bottles red, 12,000 bottles white

*****Ch. La Tour Haut Brion** (Graves Pessac): Talence; owner Domaine Clarence Dillon

Ch. La Tour Léognan (Graves Léognan): Léognan; owner Sté Civile des Grandes Graves
Production: about 30 tonneaux red, 15 tonneaux white

*****Ch. La Tour Martillac** (Graves Léognan): Martillac; owner G.F.A. du Château La Tour Martillac

*****Ch. Laville Haut Brion** (Graves Pessac): Talence; owner Domaine Clarence Dillon S.A.

Ch. Le Pape (Graves Léognan): Léognan; owner G.F.A. du Château
Le Pape
Production: 20,000 bottles red

Ch. Le Sartre (Graves Léognan): Léognan; owner G.F.A. du Château
Le Sartre
Production: 25,000 bottles red, 25,000 bottles white

Ch. Les Carmes Haut Brion (Graves Pessac): Pessac; owner Héritiers
Chantecaille
Production: 18,000 bottles red

Ch. Malartic-Lagravière (Graves Léognan): Léognan; owner G.F.A.
Marly-Ridoret

Ch. Olivier (Graves Léognan): Léognan; owner M. de Bethmann

Petit Bourdieu, Domaine de (Graves Léognan): Léognan; owner André
Pointet
Production: 3,000 bottles red

Ch. Pape Clément (Graves Pessac): Pessac; owner Montagne et Cie

Ch. Pique Caillou (Graves Pessac): Mérignac; owner S.C.I. Château
Pique Caillou
Production: 90,000 bottles red

Ch. Pontac Monplaisir (Graves Léognan): Villenave-d'Ornon; owner
Jean Maufras
Production: 45 tonneaux red, 27 tonneaux white

Ch. de Richemorin (Graves Léognan): Martillac; owner André Lurton
Production: 190,000 bottles red, 35,000 bottles white

Ch. de Rouillac (Graves Léognan): Canéjean; owner P. Sarthou
Production: 20,000 bottles red

Ch. Smith Haut Lafitte (Graves Léognan): Martillac; owner Louis
Eschenauer

The musts, prior to any enrichment, should contain at least 170 g.
of sugar for the red wines, 187 g. for the whites.

Alcoholic strength is as follows:	Minimum	Maximum
Red wines	10°	13.5°
Dry whites	11°	13.5°
Sweet whites (moelleux)	12°	No maximum degree

The limitation of the *rendement* or amount of wine made in the vineyard area is officially set at a maximum of 40 hectolitres per hectare.

There has been a change in production in recent years. As has been mentioned, the northern part of the region is primarily devoted to red wine, the central and southern areas tending to make more white, but since 1962 more red wine has been and is being made: in 1945 there was a proportion of 2 to 1 of white wine; in 1961 the proportion had altered, so that it was 4 to 1. Today it is about 1 to 1. The change may be due to the fact that, until quite recently, the white wines were, except at the highest quality levels, unable to compete in export markets with wines available in low- and medium-priced ranges coming onto major markets from many other countries of the world; the appeal of 'claret', however, the red wine of Bordeaux, was maintained and increased. It has yet to be seen whether some of the new methods of making good-quality dry and dryish white wine will affect the overall current trend.

Vintages – in hectolitres

	1980	1981	1982	1983	1984	1985	1986
Graves blanc	25 551	22 469	64 043	43 202	48 708	48 814	60 415
Graves supérieures	21 714	12 356	20 100	25 953	19 434	14 516	28 822
Graves rouge	62 098	66 469	100 869	94 868	60 073	98 585	132 303
Total	109 363	101 294	185 012	164 023	128 215	161 915	221 540

It is pertinent to indicate some of the changes that are, at the time of writing, affecting some of the vineyards of the world and may be introduced by some Graves growers. Mention will be made of new methods of vinification (see pp. 213–6), some of which may have been adopted within the Graves by the time this book appears – the *macération préfermentaire* would seem already to be influencing some of the growers.

There is currently a move in some other regions to make 'organic' wines. It appears that there are various groups within this movement, with differing requirements as to what is done to produce the approved wine; however, I think that this is still something very much in its infancy, established vineyards perhaps owing more than new ones to the past, the precautionary measures taken against certain pests and diseases varying according to area and to the grapes involved, the treatment of the vineyard depending on the availability of suitable manures. To date, I have only been able to sample a few wines made 'organically' and although some have been pleasant and good, as wines, some have not! It is therefore unwise to pronounce, although it would seem sensible to use preventive products to keep vines healthy; wine cannot be appraised in quite the same way as fruit and vegetables and the freshness (or otherwise) of these does seem to affect their flavour quite as much as the presence or absence of the products the 'organic farmers' do not use. Of great importance in wine making is the selection of suitable 'clones' or strains within the variety of the vine that may best flourish in a particular place. Clonal selection, also the choice of suitable *portes greffes*, the vinestocks that take the graft, is another factor that can make an enormous difference to a vineyard and its wine. These matters, however, like the details of vineyard layout, variations in pruning and winery design, are more the concern of the specialist and in any event the effect of work on them makes anything between hard covers date very speedily.

MACHINES IN THE VINEYARD

What has made a great change in the appearance of many vineyards, however, is the use of various mechanical appliances: the tractor is commonplace today and the huge ones that straddle the rows perform in a short time tasks that, previously, required hours and days of manual labour. The mechanical harvester is a more recent introduction: not only can it pick off the ripe grapes far faster than human hands – not always easy to engage just when they are required – but the grower who has one can wait, without risk, until plots of grapes are perfectly ripe, something of major importance in making good wine but not always possible when vintagers have to be allocated to different sections of the vineyard, while the sky is scanned for any sign of a change in the weather. Of course, a machine is costly and, in the Bordeaux vineyard, it is not possible for one to work all night, as in many southern hemisphere vineyards, because of the heavy night dews, but the machine can work longer hours than human beings, and even though it requires skilful operation, if a vineyard is all in one piece instead of in various different *parcelles*, it will pay for itself in a surprisingly short time. It has already been established that wines made from machine-gathered grapes are in no way inferior to those picked by hand, provided that the

175

skins of the varieties are not so thin that there is a risk of them splitting and fermentation starting before they can be brought to the winery.

The change that the use of mechanical harvesters will effect is socio-economic. For centuries the Graves has, in the autumn, been invaded by bands of men and women arriving from the south, sometimes generation after generation going to the same property, also itinerant students hoping to earn enough to make a working holiday profitable. The traces such people have left over a thousand years or more have been enriching in language, customs, foodstuffs and recipes and, of course, in the children often conceived in the carefree rejoicings accompanying the harvest. Although it is impressive to see a machine prowl through a vineyard and the fruit arrive in prime condition, at the winery (it can even be crushed in the vineyard by some machines), there will henceforth be a change in local life. (In Champagne the use of mechanical harvesters is still forbidden – and the pickers come down from the industrial north to be housed in the special *vendangeoirs*, but how long can this continue?) Changes must take place. In 1876 Dr Jules Guyot, who is immortalised by the *taille Guyot*, the method of pruning and training now followed in so many classic vineyards, studied the south-west of France and urged that the vines should be trained low and that the 'gigantesque et horrible charrue, traînée par deux bœufs gros comme des éléphants' should be abandoned in favour of a single ox or horse – this was a radical alteration on a par with the tractor and the mechanical harvester of today – and the pruning-by-machine device which I believe may follow.

Rearrangements of the vineyards and readjustments of the regulations will accompany these changes – change is inevitable and can be beneficial as well as imposing an alteration in approach and attitude on those already adept in the practices of growing vines and making wine. The wise among them will accept that this must happen.

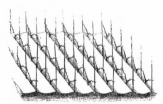 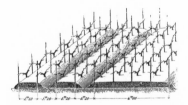

Guyot's observations of nineteenth-century planting methods showing (left) how the vines were built up with soil in double rows and (right) an apparently unsatisfactory method of training.

14

THE VINES

WINE begins with grapes. Wine makers throughout the world agree that, unless the quality of the fruit picked at vintage time is good, no skill or treatment can make the wine superior. If the grapes appropriate to the site of the vineyard are correctly chosen, grown and cared for, then great as well as good wines are able to come into being, although sometimes they do, even now, seem to achieve this triumph by a combination of luck and chance as well as skill, care and investment.

THE MARKET'S DILEMMA

It should be borne in mind that, these days, the technicians who literally fly in and out of certain wine regions may affect what is produced there in a way that the serious – sometimes solemn – lover of wine may not suspect. Wine makers and those who advise them, within the interchange of knowledge and experience that characterises the wine trade, must make a commodity that can be sold – and, when possible, sold in huge quantities, to such recently established markets as the great supermarket chains, whose buyers have at least some notion as to the type of wine their customers are likely to buy. Technicians in wine are well aware that many wines in the cheap- and medium-priced ranges should, ideally, appeal without startling or affronting the drinker, even though the more experienced drinker may find such wines bland, even insipid. The technician can make such wines almost anywhere; the marketing men can go out and sell them almost anywhere, backed up by the advertising campaigns. Yet, often, along the line of getting a wine to a wide public, the regional character of many wines may be banked down, even lost, so that it may not be easy to distinguish the wine of one region, even of one country, from that of another when 'light, medium dry whites' or 'medium reds' are submitted to a jury of tasters.

This is where the growers of the Graves are faced with a dilemma, shared by many throughout the world of wine. They enjoy an established name, an historic tradition, they can look back on centuries of making wines that a number of export markets have liked and re-ordered. What do they do today? Should they concentrate on making quantity, or attempt to retain not only quality but quality in association with the regional style? Should they make wines that are easy to sell quickly – anywhere, to anyone, or dare they make wines that need knowledgeable salesmen to promote them, for intelligent and sensible drinkers to enjoy – and buy a second time? It has been cynically remarked that a wine able to rival all the best-selling brands now marketed would be white, low in alcohol so able to be quaffed in quantity, with a vaguely agreeable smell, a flavour that verges on sweet but ends with a touch of sharpness so as to convince the superficially attentive drinker that it is 'dry'. I cannot disagree. Many people drink wine not for the pleasure it gives them, but for the sake of drinking, being seen to drink and for the effect it may have on them. Alas! Think of this when somebody inveighs against a wine that falls short of what the critic expected – the maker is producing something to *sell*; he may have a family, an overdraft and immediate problems that get in the way of the creation of a fine wine – that is unlikely to make a major profit anyway.

It might be expected that the area of the Graves, extended as it is, would grow a variety of grapes. Plantations of both the black and white varieties do not appear to have been radically changed for the past century and a half, although some varieties have not been much replanted since the phylloxera plague of the late nineteenth and early twentieth centuries. The study of what vines were planted in particular regions is complicated by the circumstance that many have 'local' names, or nicknames. Ampelography, the study of vines, has resulted in the authorities discovering that some varieties thought to be quite on their own are in fact related to or even regional versions of established varieties. Germain Lafforgue in *Le Vignoble Girodin* (1947) gives a list of synonyms, of which those varieties of vines used in the Gironde in general and the Graves in particular are given in appendix III. It must be realised that, in the past, neighbour would give vine cuttings to neighbour; travellers, especially in a region at as much of a cross-roads as the Graves, would have brought cuttings or sent them to interested friends; the scholars who went between the great religious houses before the French Revolution would certainly have packed plants, including vines, for their opposite numbers in other establishments; and the interested layman abroad would have noted and maybe snipped off a shoot for replanting in his vineyard at home. The name of the vine variety would have been of secondary importance: sometimes it might have simply been tagged with that of the place from which it was supposed to have come, sometimes it got a name because of what its fruit was like. The botanists came comparatively late on this scene and, for the vigneron, what the vine cutting produced was of far more importance than what it was called.

THE VINEYARDS

How the Gironde vineyards first came into being is difficult to know – maybe we can never be definite. A purely domestic plot of vines that might combine plants giving fruit with a trellis or arbour, for shelter from the sun, is something that, as drawings from ancient Egypt show, was an adjunct to civilised living, as enjoyed by the reasonably well-to-do, from early times. The enclosures of many of the early religious establishments were not extensive and probably the layout was dictated by the area available that might be devoted to vines rather than to other crops.

The Romans, however, did plant vines in rows. At St Émilion one can still see the lines of stone, rather like elongated plant holders, that they used to receive the vines in neat array. The Romans, of course, enjoyed the services of slaves or freemen throughout the year; tending the vines is something that can be a full-time occupation, requiring informed care. It is perhaps a legacy of Roman occupation that, by the early Middle Ages, vines in the Bordeaux region were cultivated in more methodically arranged plantations than elsewhere. Definitely they were planted in rows. The words *régas*, *arregges* and *arrégailles* (meaning rows) recur in documents of the period, states Pierre Vital in *Les Vieilles Vignes de notre France* (1956). In other regions of France vineyards seem to have been planted haphazardly, individual vines only being uprooted when they died or had ceased to yield. Vineyards in these early times may have been more like the vegetable plots or allotments of householders today, with clumps of different things planted together; the produce of such plantations would mainly have been intended for immediate domestic use rather than for sale. Inside the walls of cities vines were planted, often up against the city walls, therefore often irregularly arranged, although in the enclosures of gardens in religious holdings they might be trellised. Whether the owner of a vineyard could afford to buy vinestocks from someone having more vines than required for immediate use, or whether these had to be grown from slips, it is difficult to know.

What is relevant is that an ungrafted vine can, usually, yield some fruit within eighteen months of taking root, so that any prunings, even of 'sports' and shoots, would not usually have been difficult to obtain in a vine-growing area.

What must have been realised quite early on, even by the inexperienced, is that a vineyard planted in rows can be more efficiently tended than a series of vines planted without any order. Drainage can be organised when plants are arranged side by side, weeding and hoeing and ploughing can be systematically carried out and a check kept on what has been done and what is still to do. If an animal pulls a plough, it is easier to guide it in a straight line, if an employee is paid by the amount achieved, it is easier to see how much he or she has finished. Picking can be methodically organised and supervised when harvest time comes.

Unfortunately, such pictorial representations of vineyards as do exist from medieval times do not provide much information as to the detailed layout and arrangement of vineyards. At least I have not been able to discover any evidence to the contrary that it was in Aquitania that the planting of vines in straight lines was pioneered. The antiquity of the Graves vineyards is such that the Romans may have established their ruler-like rows of vines just as they did their ruler-like roads and that in this region or, at least, that of the Aquitanian vineyard anyway, the planting of vines in rows on a large scale was first established in France.

Today, of course, the use of machines dictate other changes in vineyard layout. For many years now tractors have been progressively in use, to turn the ground, to spray the vines, to pull the carts that hold the fruit picked at vintage time. Their activities, straddling the rows of vines, have more recently been augmented by that of the mechanical harvester, and it cannot be long before the pruning machine is also introduced. All this means that the space between the rows of vines and the height to which they are trained must be able to accommodate the machine. The clusters of red roses planted at the ends of the rows of vines are a pretty Bordeaux tradition said to have grown up for several reasons – to make the horses drawing the ploughs and harrows turn right round at the ends of the rows instead of cutting the corner, to prevent schoolchildren nipping off the grapes on the outside of the vineyards and, more likely, to show any sign of certain vine diseases, which roses pick up quickly – just as, in the past, those going into coal mines would take canaries because the birds would be swift to react against any cut-off in the oxygen.

But the vineyard owners who, centuries ago, decided to train their orderly rows of vines either in clumpy bushes or along strings were making as decisive an alteration in vine cultivation as those who buy or hire mechanical harvesters today – following the change from man to horse-drawn tools between the rows. Such changes are not always easy to pinpoint by dates, but they have come – and they will come.

THE GRAPES

My friend and colleague Jancis Robinson, M.W., in her impressive book *Vines, Grapes and Wines* (1986), mentions that it was at the 'end of the 18th century' that the white-grape varieties were mostly pulled up from the majority of Médoc and many Graves estates. Well, demand dictated supply and whether or not the Médoc could have made fine white wine, we shall probably not have the chance to find out – the Graves can, did and does, in addition to its fine and good reds.

Today, the authorised vine varieties that may be planted in the Graves are as follows: for red wines, Merlot, Cabernet Franc, Cabernet Sauvignon and, of lesser significance these days, Malbec and Petit Verdot; and for white wines, Sémillon, Sauvignon Blanc and Muscadelle. Some description of these vines and the type of wine they can produce will be included later, but the history of the varieties planted in the Graves is of interest – not only is it quite long, but the way in which 'different' varieties often turn out to be different local pronunciations or variations of the same vine emerges when one studies the contemporary accounts.

Montesquieu's son, Jean-Baptiste de Secondat, wrote a *Mémoire sur la culture de la vigne en Guyenne* in 1785 and in this he gives references to many grape varieties that I have found difficult to trace today – they may indeed have existed, but could have been local names, in the patois, of some classic varieties. Here there is an interesting reference in Émile de Perceval's *Montesquieu et la vigne* (1935), where the author thinks that the 'vidure' or 'biture' is in fact a vine mentioned by both Pliny and Columella – the *biturica*. Here my friends in Italy, notably Leonardo de Frescobaldi, have contributed the following, quoting from Lucius Junius Moderatus Columella, in *De re rustica* (Book III, iii, 19–20): '... vines of the second quality, which can be recommended for their growth and fruit-fulness, such as the Bituric and the Basilica, the smaller of which the

Spaniards call "coccolubis" – both of them by far the closest to the very best; for their wine stands long keeping and attains some degree of excellence with age. And in fact they surpass in productiveness all that I have mentioned above, and also in hardiness, for they withstand storms and rain with the greatest fortitude, they have a good amount of juice and do not fail in lean ground. They endure cold better than wetness, and wetness better than dryness, and yet they are not bothered by heat.' Though Columella adds that 'there are besides many sorts of vines of which we can relate neither the number nor the names with assurance . . . neighbouring regions disagree and call the same wines by different names'.

So, given that the Biturges, a people of Aquitania in Gaul, consisted of two tribes, one with its capital in Bourges, the other in Bordeaux, it is reasonable that they should have given their name to *vitis Biturica*, cultivated in their territory in Roman times, although it is not known whether this was an indigenous variety or was brought to Gaul by the Romans.

And, comment my friends, 'of course nobody really knows whether Biturica and Cabernet Sauvignon are the same grape or not – but at least there is a plausible case'. The Predicato di Biturica, as planted in the hills of the Nipozzano estate in Pelago, east of Florence, gives Cabernet Sauvignon and Sangiovetru as the two grape varieties; it cites 10–20 years' longevity of the wines, and refers to the 'Biturica' of Pliny which is 'sometimes known as the "Vigne dure" or hard vine'. Synonyms for the Cabernet Sauvignon include Carmenet and Cavernet and the Massoulet, which Jean-Baptiste de Secondat describes as 'the grape without a defect'. The local names are given by Émile de Perceval in *Montesquieu et la vigne* as Bouchet (St Émilion), Petit Fer (Libourne), Graput (Ste-Bazeille) and, here and there, Moza, Moustère, Cahors, Quercy, adding – he is quoting from Petit-Lafitte (*La Vigne dans le Bordelais*, 1868) – that, in the Graves, this vine makes a wine 'of brilliant, glowing colour . . . elegant, delicate, full, fair, smooth, with a marked bouquet, and which is ready to drink and lasts for a fair time'.

There would seem to have been many supposedly different varieties in the eighteenth and early nineteenth centuries, for de Perceval states that the Abbé Bellet, writing in 1730 about his *Voyage en Guyenne* – names forty different varieties. Jean-Baptiste de Secondat apparently mentions forty-six different ones; de Percevel names the 'Malbeck or Côte Rouge', also the Balouzat and, among the white grapes, the Musquelle, which is also mentioned as Muscadet (somewhat improbably), the 'Blanc Doux' for the sweet wines, the Pruéras or Prunelat, all of which, de Perceval says, were still cultivated at La Brède, though I doubt that a wine detective would find them there today. Others listed include the Mêlier (? Meunier), Malvoisie, Auvernat (a sweet grape) and the 'plebeian' Enragéat – this being the Folle Blanche, not in favour at La Brède.

Even from this quite recent study it would seem that this is a matter of 'You pays your money and takes your choice'. In the seventeenth and eighteenth centuries the local name for a vine might vary almost from village to village, especially in fairly isolated communities; such things were not always written down – as with 'manners' today, those who knew, knew, by inherited knowledge. Speech, as pronounced by different people, can vary sounds of words and spellings enormously.

In trying to work out what vines were planted in particular places, it must also be remembered that, in the past, both black and white grapes would often have been planted side by side – vines would be replaced one by one, rather than being uprooted and replanted in lines or sections of the vineyard – and the wine would be made with the whole of the mixed-up fruit, gathered and pressed as and when convenient. This is how the Burgundy 'Passe-tous-Grains' is made; the expression signifies that all the grapes (*grains*) are processed (*passés*) together. This is of special relevance in a region such as the Graves, where both red and white wines were and are made.

Grapes intended for wine making should, certainly and ideally, be picked when each section of the vineyard and each variety of grape is perfectly ripe. But in a smallish vineyard it would have been usual to pick when most of the fruit seemed ripe – and also when the pickers were available. It is a matter of great responsibility to those who direct the vintagers in a vineyard such as any in Bordeaux today, or anywhere else where the micro-climates can affect ripening of the grapes, because several days may elapse before the fruit of one small section is ready after the grapes of an almost adjacent plot have been gathered. Much careful directional harvesting is essential here – one cannot send a band of pickers or a machine simply to take off the grapes of one even medium-sized vineyard all at one time; a day, a few days can mean a great difference in the ripeness of the fruit, whether the grapes are black or white.

So, I think that it is very probable that, in the past, many of the small overall Graves properties (and other vineyards) might have been

183

harvested as, when, and how the owners were able to do so. Just as there might have been white and black grapes planted together, so there might have been different varieties of both black and white grapes within the same property – and all would have been picked and put into the press in one operation. It must have happened in many regions; I have had pinkish-greyish-yellowish wines made by this sort of mixing from the backyard vineyards of friends and café owners in many Mediterranean countries.

This is what many old-style wines, including those of the Graves, must have been like: there would have been no stress on colour in many instances, if both black and white grapes were involved; there would certainly have been no aim at limpidity before there was some knowledge of clarification and filtering – and many small-scale growers wouldn't have bothered centuries ago. The highish alcoholic strength of some of these wines in past times might have been an asset – a reviving drink to the worker, who might be almost toothless, probably had bad breath and suffered from various forms of malnutrition, but who needed the 'quick lift' that his descendants may now take in spirit form. Such drinkers would not have been much concerned with the star brightness of the wine, or the fragrance – which can be inhibited by the too high alcohol produced in many hot vineyards.

In 1876 the great Dr Jules Guyot (whose work on vines has commemorated his name by the 'taille Guyot', the method of pruning and training he evolved) completed his *Étude des vignobles de France*. He states that, in the Gironde, it is the red wines that are of prime importance, although he mentions 'the King of wines in this country, Château Yquem'. It is a personal notion of my own that, in the time before sugar was cheap, the great sweet white wines were primarily prized for their opulent lusciousness and red wines conveyed to the drinker an idea of warmth, endorsed, as it often would have been, by the fruit manifest in them. Drinkers in cool, cold, damp regions (and the Gironde can be all these) would have enjoyed drinking something red, as well as something white and sweet.

Dr Guyot says that the Graves is planted with the same grape varieties as the Médoc for black grapes: Cabernet Sauvignon, Carmenère, Cabernet Franc, Petit Verdot, Merlot and Malbec. He also mentions that, in the Graves, the 'carbenets sont désignés sous le nom de vidure, grosse, petite, sauvignonne'. This 'vidure', says Jancis Robinson in *Vines, Grapes and Wines* (1986), had been noted in both forms as early as 1736 by the Abbé Bellet around Cadillac (only just across the Garonne from the Graves) and she adds that this *vigne dure* is the tough-wooded Cabernet (Sauvignon). Pierre Andrieu in a *Petite Histoire de Bordeaux et son vignoble* (1952) repeats the belief that the 'bidure' or 'vidure' grape that the Abbé Breton, Cardinal Richelieu's Intendant, took to be planted in the Loire in the seventeenth century among other Bordeaux samples and the one that proved successful, was the 'Cabernet' and he goes on to assume that it must be linked with the *vitis biturica* of Roman times, citing Roaldès (1519–89) and one Elie Vinet, whom I cannot trace, who think that this vine variety went to Italy and Rome from Bordeaux, its homeland, not the other way round. Andrieu assumes that this 'Cabernet' was the Cabernet Sauvignon; but as it is now known that the 'Cabernet' of the Loire, nicknamed 'le bon Breton', in fact is the Cabernet Franc, I hesitate to take this statement for gospel. I do not think that the Cabernet Sauvignon flourishes in the sharper, cooler atmosphere of the Loire, whereas the Cabernet Franc, given even a little kindness by the sun, can and does in the soils of that vineyard. Red Loire wines made from the 'Breton' are different from young Cabernet Sauvignons, as has been demonstrated by the owner of Château de Pez, in the Médoc, who annually vinifies a small amount of each of the claret grapes of his vineyard separately, so that students can sample them.

Now comes a most interesting diversion, relevant to the Cabernet. It bears on what I have later to cite about this variety, so the reader will, I trust, have patience. Guyot, writing in 1876, spells Cabernet Sauvignon 'carbenet-sauvignon' and he says that it gets its suffix because it is so similar in appearance to the Sauvignon Blanc that, until the grapes turn colour, it is not possible to distinguish between the two, either by leaf formation or the shape of the grape cluster. In her wonderful English translation of Dr Pierre Galet's great work on wines, Lucie T. Morton (*A Practical Ampelography*, 1979) says, 'We tend to be wine and grape knowledgeable, but vine ignorant' and, in stressing that 'ampelography is fun', she mentions how Galet's method of measuring and codifying leaf structure enables identification of vine varieties to be made easier. Lucie Morton's work makes it both easier and fun for me, the outsider, to attempt some study of grape varieties.

Guyot's spelling is significant. In the nineteenth century pronunciation was different from that of today – in English, the obvious survival is that of the word 'off' being sounded still by many of the older upper classes as 'orf', and 'gone' as 'gorn'. So, in French, with 'Cabernet'. Many of my friends in the wine trade in the various southern hemisphere countries

I have visited, pronounce this word 'Carbonet', whereas, in Europe, we say it with a short 'a'. The lingering of the 'r' sound, as in 'Paul Maul', 'shopping maul', which would have been usual in the eighteenth and nineteenth centuries to our British ancestors, remains there – in England, we say 'Pall Mall' with the short 'a' and 'shopping mall'; again significantly, even further back, the place name came from the game 'Pell Mell', the vowel sounds being pinched, which echoes the 'refeenment' of the days when young ladies were instructed to shape their mouths around 'prunes and prisms' – perhaps to ensure that, when they lost the teeth at the sides of their faces, their enunciation was not impaired.

Guyot refers to the Cabernet Franc as the 'franc-carbonet' and he adds to the list of black grape varieties that of *cruchinet*. This I cannot identify, although it may be the *crujillon*, a synonym of the Carignan, according to Jancis Robinson. Another slight confusion appears to exist concerning one of the synonyms for this grape. Dr Galet gives the following: 'Breton, Bouchy, Véron, Carmenet, Gros Bouchet.' But, in the same work, he gives the list of synonyms for the Cabernet Sauvignon as 'Petit-Cabernet, Vidure, Petite-Vidure, Bouchet'. I certainly dare not query such an authority, but, in using Gros Bouchet for the Cabernet Franc, I have had experienced wine trade friends stop me with a correction; in the St Émilionnais the grape is certainly often mentioned quite simply as 'Bouchet' or 'Bouschet'; synonyms for the Cabernet Sauvignon seem rarer. What I venture to suggest is that certainly Dr Galet is correct – the full name for the one-time-used synonym for the Cabernet Franc *is* Gros Bouchet, but – and this is an important qualification – it is shortened to 'Bouchet' when the more usual words are not used. It may be that the term Bouchet has survived, in shortened form, for a grape that does not enjoy the world-wide renown of the Cabernet Sauvignon. After all, most of us will refer casually to 'Cabernet' when it can be taken for granted that we are mentioning the Cabernet Sauvignon – if we meant otherwise, we would particularise. So it may be that the full form of the synonym for the Cabernet Franc is indeed Gros Bouchet, but the first word has been dropped in most wine talk, just as the qualifying 'Sauvignon' is dropped when the context of the speech or writing makes it perfectly clear that only 'the' Cabernet is meant.

But the list of vines is extensive and Germain Lafforgue surveys the scene, starting in 1841 with Comte Odart's list, in which there are the following: Cabernet, Carmenère, Verdot, Merlot, Malbec or Cot de Bordeaux, Tarney, Coulant.

The 'second rank' of vines is: Cauny, Hourca or Roumien, Grosse Mérille or Bordelais (in Agen). In the category 'to be viewed with suspicion' there are: Petite Parde or Gascon de l'Orléannais, Pelaouille or Pénouille, Gros Cruchinet. For the white wines, Odart's list is: Blanc Sémillon, Sauvignon (Surin, Fié-Blanc, Fumé de la Nièvre), Sauvignon à gros grains, Musquette (Raisinotte, Muscadet Doux), Blanc-Doux or Douce-Blanche. He then adds that he will not comment on the Rochalin, the Verdot, the Pruéras or Chalosse 'which are not thought of as making a special contribution to the quality of the wine'.

Lafforgue then gives the list of Petit-Lafitte, as in *La Vigne dans le Bordelais* (1868). Here, Petit-Lafitte divides the types of vines into what he refers to as 'Basic varieties' and 'Complementary varieties'. I am giving this in full, because it cites some varieties that are, to us, rather unexpected in this particular region:

Basic cépages:

Vignes rouges de Graves	Cabernet ou Vidure
Vignes rouges de Côtes	Malbec
Vignes rouges de Palus	Verdot
Vignes blanches de Graves	Sauvignon
Vignes blanches de Côtes	Sémillon
Vignes blanches de Plateaux	Enrageat

I take the 'Plateaux' to be the slightly elevated flattish vineyards to the west of the 'terrasses', away from the river.

The *cépages de complement* are as follows:

Vignes rouges	Merlot, Mancin, Tarney-Coulant, Teinturier, Syrah, Massoulet
Vignes blanches	Rochalin, Muscadelle, Blanc-Doux, Pruéras, Blanc-Auba, Massoulet

Lafforgue notes the appearance of the Syrah, 'ou plant d'Hermitage', which he says was brought into the Médoc by Monsieur Destournel [*sic*]. It then seems to have been planted quite soon after in the Graves also, then in vineyards on the right bank of the Garonne, as a variety able to assist others rather than to dominate the particular plantation.

In this context it is interesting to cite the findings of Clive Coates, who has traced the *encépagement* of Haut Bailly in the 1890s, when the aftermath of the phylloxera had led to the grafting of national vinestocks onto aphis-resistant North American roots; the owner of Haut Bailly, how-ever, was absolutely against grafting (see p. 271) and the proportions of the vineyard were as follows at the end of the nineteenth century, all on their own roots: one-twelfth each of Merlot, Malbec, Petit Verdot, Cabernet Franc and Carmenère (an old variety only recently again per-mitted), the remainder being planted with Cabernet Sauvignon. It is true that, in former times, even during my memories of certain classic Bordeaux vineyards, a greater number of vine varieties seem to have been planted than is usual in most estates today. It is possible that the greater knowledge of how to protect and care for the vines, the use of mechanical appliances and the vastly extended experience of wine making have resulted in the choice of the few effective varieties rather than the many – some of which must have survived from former days and the retention of which could have been justified by their being kept in the vineyard 'to be on the safe side'. Myself, I think it is the great strides that have been made in clonal selection, the choice of the exactly appropriate strain for a particular site that have whittled down the vine varieties; if one selected clone will perform admirably in all but the most adverse circumstances, in an equally carefully selected plot, then this does away with the need for diversification of the vineyard with other varieties. But, it should never be forgotten, Bordeaux wines are usually composed of different varieties of grapes and I do not think that this will ever radically change, even if regulations permitted.

HISTORIC PLAGUES

It was the 1850s attack of oidium that was both serious in the short and long term; proprietors began to wonder whether certain established vine varieties were able to withstand this powdery mildew. This plague is often referred to as *oidium tuckeri*, after John Tucker, gardener to a Mr John Slater of Margate, where it was first noticed, according to George Ordish's masterly book *The Great Wine Blight* (1972). Powdery mildew spread rapidly through the French vineyards, although, in the Palace of Versailles, the greenhouses were safeguarded by a lime-sulphur spray, known as 'Eau Grison', after its inventor, who was in charge of the establishments. It was not possible to use this particular form of preventive on a large scale, but dusting with sulphur was practicable and indeed, according to George Ordish, a 'M. Marés ... found that sulphuring both increased the set of the fruit and led to an earlier harvest'.

When the statistics of the *département* of the Gironde were published by Cocks and Féret in 1874, the proportions of different varieties planted show that, from now on, the known varieties are those that still dominate the vineyards. Here are the figures as they affect the Graves:

Canton de Blanquefort: Cabernet 2/3, Merlot and Malbec 1/3
Canton de Pessac: Cabernet 1/2, Merlot and Malbec 1/2
Canton de La Brède: Cabernet 2/3, Merlot and Malbec 1/3

For the Petites Graves:

Canton de La Brède: Malbec 4/5, Verdot, Merlot, Cabernet, etc., 1/5
Canton de Podensac: Malbec 2/3, Merlot, Lardotte, etc., 1/3

For the Bazadais:

Grapput 1/2, Malbec 1/4, Mancin, etc., 1/4

For the white wines, the proportions are:

Grands Graves de Bordeaux: Sauvignon 2/3, Sémillon 1/3
Région de Cérons: Sémillon 3/4, Sauvignon and Courbin 1/4
Région de Budos: Sémillon 3/4, Sauvignon and Johanisberg 1/4 [*sic*]

In the Petites Graves:

Canton de Podensac: Sémillon 2/3, Cépages divers 1/3
Canton de La Brède: Sémillon 1/3, Enragéat 2/3

For the *ordinaires*, the Enragéat and the Jurançon Blanc are given as in the Réolais and Bazadais, the Enragéat being of much greater importance.

Then, though, there was the attack by the aphis, *phylloxera vastatrix*. Here, the sandy soil of the Graves was a great safeguard – the aphis cannot live in sand; but in the Côtes the devastation was horrific and many vineyards had to be pulled up, some of them never to be revived. Some hybrid vines were planted in the Entre-deux-Mers by proprietors desperate to get some sort of crop but, once the safeguard provided by the grafting of national vines onto American rootstocks was understood, these varieties either disappeared or, in certain instances, were themselves used as rootstocks. Féret lists the different vines, as quoted by G. Bord, in *Les Variations*

189

de l'encépagement dans le vignoble bordelais (1932) as follows: Red wines: Basic vines: Malbec, Cabernet (ses variétés), Merlot, Verdot (ses variétés), Syrah.

Vines for *vins communs*: Pignon (Pardotte, Tripet, Boulignon), Petite Chalosse noire, Mancin, Amaraye, Hourcat or Balouzet, Grapuut (Boucharès), Pénouille (Pelaouille), Cruchinet (Doux-Same, Chaussé), Teinturier, Fer (Béquignol), Massoutet (Pinot de Bourgogne), Mancin colon, Bouton Blanc or St-Macaire, Jurançon or Arrivet, plus other varieties now beginning to disappear.

White wines: Fine varieties: Sémillon, Sauvignon, Muscadelle.

Heavy croppers: Enrageat.

Secondary varieties: Blanc Auba, Blanc Doux, Blanc Verdet, Pruéras or Prunelat, Blanquette, Rochalin or Blayais.

For additional information about some of these little-known varieties, I have given some synonyms see Appendix III.

Pierre Andrieu, in his *Petite Histoire de Bordeaux et son vignoble* (1952), devotes one section to an 1827 guide, of which he gives the name as *Guide conducteur de l'étranger à Bordeaux*, with no further details. But what he extracts from this is of some interest, apropos of grapes: 'There is the Carmenet, the Carmenère, the Malbeck, the Petit and Gros Verdot, the Merlot, the Massoulet.' The comment on the Merlot is that it gets its name because the blackbirds (merles) relish its juiciness. Other varieties 'produce fruit that is, to a greater or lesser degree, pleasant to the taste, but the wine they make is of poor quality. It is useful, however, to know what they are, so as not to confuse them with those [the classic and approved varieties] just mentioned and not to allow oneself to be influenced by the sweetness of the juice.'

Andrieu then lists – from the 1827 guide – the following: Mancin, a big black grape; Teinturier, which makes a weak, sharp, bitter wine. (The Teinturier is one of the few wine grapes to have coloured juice, pinkish-red, but, as far as I know it is not used for any of the finer wines of France these days.) Then there are mentioned the Pelouille, with the note 'floppy, colourless wine'; the Petite Chalosse noire, the Cruchinet and the Cioutat which, says Andrieu, used formerly to be known as 'Persillade' because its leaves were somewhat similar to parsley. This type of parsley, however, would have been the larger-leaved variety, sometimes seen in the Mediterranean, not the tightly leaved British type.

It is strange to see included some names associated today with

190

vineyards distant from those of the Gironde: I think that in many instances a small quantity of some southern vine variety might have been introduced to give colour and firm fruitiness to the more delicate vines of the locality. The long list of names is somewhat similar to that of the varieties planted in the Rhône valley, or in the port region of Portugal, where many different vines, sometimes both of white and red varieties, were until very recently being used and may legally be included to this day.

If a vine takes root or is satisfactorily grafted and then bears adequately, no farmer is going to pull it up merely because it is slightly different from those planted around it; in the first instance, a vine that has died or had to be uprooted because of disease may be replaced by whatever is immediately available, and somebody may have a few 'samples' with which to experiment for, in spite of the strictness of regulations and controls today, there cannot be an authority on vines personally inspecting every single plant in a vineyard.

Lafforgue also makes the point that, these days, it is important to select vines that will be able to bear satisfactorily and make the sort of wine that is currently in demand in the market; as he says – writing just before 1947 – 'no one can now leave wines five, six or more years in cask; three years at most is the time they can wait in wood'. So, he continues, there has been a decline in the use of vines that make big, solid wines that need ideal weather conditions and take their time about maturing. And this, he says, is why both the Petit Verdot and Gros Verdot have almost disappeared from the Graves vineyards, why the Cabernet Sauvignon has taken over much of the rôle of the Cabernet Franc in the Médoc and why the Carmenère has been eliminated. The Sémillon and Sauvignon remain, for making fine white wines, the first-named asserting its importance over that of the second, with its too low yield. In view of the rush to plant Sauvignon in subsequent years, in an attempt to capture the market for the newly fashionable light dry white wines, this is a significant remark.

WHAT CONTRIBUTION THE GRAPES MAKE

In describing vines and the type of wine that each makes, what is of importance? Most Bordeaux wines are blends – blends of the different varieties of grapes grown in the vineyard and blends of the different plots that make up that vineyard, which may consist of *parcelles* of land separated from each other – and, in consequence, each having a slightly individual micro-climate, a particular aspect, a special *croupe* or ridge, some peculiarity of the subsoil. There may, near by, be a wood, a pond, a river or stream that will affect the atmosphere or, far off, a break in some hills through which a channel of air will reach a particular plot at a certain time of day. Then there are the regulations governing Appellation d'Origine Contrôlée – even a few yards of one vineyard may be, strictly, outside the official boundary – everything else may appear to be the same but the wine cannot bear the relevant A.O.C. when made. (Anomalies of this sort do still occur, although many are being ironed out.)

Nomenclature is far more important than drinkers in export markets often realise. The more precise the place name, the more elevated in status – and higher in the ranks of the A.O.C.s – will the wine be and, in conse-quence, it can command a higher price. It is not merely a loss of prestige that is involved if a wine is declassified by its owner – such an action will cost him a great deal of money, which may need to be put back into the vineyard or winery. Yet there are still instances where a conscientious pro-prietor will reject certain vattings as unworthy of bearing the estate label of the *grand vin*; the rejected wine may be sold under another of the registered names belonging to the property, or it may simply be labelled as a 'generic' – that is, under its area name. In view of the splitting up of the Graves regions, such as Graves de Pessac and Graves de Léognan (see p. 250) now about to leave off the prefix 'Graves', this extension of precise nomenclature will become of increasing importance.

It is, therefore, difficult to go into much detail about the possible wine that may be made in the different areas of a fairly extensive vineyard from several different grape varieties. Of course, if the proportion of, say, Merlot is predominant in one set of plantings, then that estate's wine will usually be characterised by the attributes of the Merlot. But certain grape varieties do not always achieve optimum ripeness every year and this too must be taken into account. One section of a vineyard may suffer from adverse weather conditions, one particular plot may be planted with fairly young vines, each set of circumstances resulting in a slight variation in the wine that is made as compared with the wine that the grower thought it was going to be possible to make that year. This, of course, is part of the fascination of claret.

TASTING DESCRIPTIONS

Then there are the words with which a description of a physical set of sensations is attempted. These too vary. For example, when I have been speaking to audiences in the southern hemisphere, I have sometimes been asked to explain what I mean when I refer to the 'gooseberry' flavour of certain Sauvignons – as the gooseberry does not grow all over the world! I am at a loss when friends on the other side of the world ask if I do not associate certain wines and grape varieties with, say, guavas, papaya or mangoes – I lack the automatic evocation of such fruits, which to me are still 'exotic', not eaten every day. There is the difference in the words used by one generation compared with those used by another: some of my young colleagues among the wine writers will use terms such as 'rubbery', 'yeasty', 'biscuity', 'peppery', which would never occur to me when I am attempting to describe bouquet or flavour – these words are terms of praise for many colleagues, to me they would only be used pejoratively! In addition, those of us fortunate in being able to use another language fairly fluently are continually coming up against the problem of trying to translate something that can only be said in one way, in one set of foreign words: How can one render the term 'un vin fin' in English? And, always, language is changing, so that a word immediately understood within one set of people may puzzle another group.

So, in attempting some description of what the grapes involved with the making of Graves wines contribute, it should be stressed that the best way to register them is to taste them and make up one's own mind. I would also suggest that the chapter 'What are the Wines Like?' may be of help here. Many lovers of Bordeaux wines will tend to start an appraisal of any by evoking their particular favourites – which may be the wines of the Médoc or St Émilion; few will have had their first experiences of Bordeaux via the wines of the Graves, because, as even estate owners in other regions of the Gironde admit, the Graves are not often 'beginners' wines, they are too subtle, too reserved and their appeal is not always immediate and definite.

A PERSONAL VIEW OF THE DIFFERENT VINES OF THE GRAVES

In thinking of the contribution of the various vines, it may be helpful to reflect briefly on the place and the climate of the region again: there is a southern softness, an aromatic underlying whiff in the bouquet of even the most assertive wines, a touch of the delicacy bestowed by the gravel, these and many other factors affecting the fruit of the vines and likely to change them in what they do to the wines made from them.

With the black grapes, the pigments in their skins are lured out by the action of the sun, so that many red Graves are very dark toned when young, even in otherwise 'light' years. Here, in admittedly personal terms, are my notes about the grapes of the Graves, which should be read in the context of where they are grown.

BLACK GRAPES

Cabernet Sauvignon

This is one of the best-known black grapes in the world, enjoying so much popularity at the present time that I am tempted to say its cultivation is something of a cult. Jancis Robinson in *Vines, Grapes and Wines* (1986) pertinently comments – from her age group (which is half that of mine) – 'Do so many of us worship it because it is inherently the best red grape variety in the world, or simply because it happens to be the principal ingredient in the most widely available fine red wine, claret?' Her knowledge of North American wines is so vast compared with mine that any disagreement may smack of asperity, but I must admit I do not 'worship' the Cabernet Sauvignon. Nor do I like – however much I may admire – wines with too high a proportion of this variety in them (with a notable exception mentioned later). I find that, whereas the Cabernet Sauvignon is certainly the backbone of claret, its very commanding quality can, if allowed to predominate, result in aggressiveness, demanding attention instead of attracting it by charm and allure; 'straight' Cabernet Sauvignon wines I find difficult to enjoy, to luxuriate in drinking; some exceptions are those small-scale wines made with a proportion of *macération carbonique* wine in them but also and, significantly, wines coming from ungrafted vinestocks, as still exist in some regions of the New World and where the soft, but powerful

194

depth and 'bloom' of the wine makes one understand how our ancestors loved the pre-phylloxera clarets.

The discreet use of the Cabernet Sauvignon is what I love in certain fine red Graves. When very young these tough-skinned grapes can produce hard, almost bitter, mouth-puckering samples. Jancis quotes a Californian statement that 'Cabernet Sauvignon is a wine for people who like to sleep on the ground, play rugby, climb mountains, eat Brussels sprouts and do other things in which some punishment is part of the pleasure.' Dear me. It is the power in the Cabernet Sauvignon that endows so many wines with nobility – but I do not think they need to punch me in the palate to convince me of their quality. Wines I love to drink may be demanding – they are not punishing. Dexter Galet in *Cépages et vignobles de France* (1958) describes the Cabernet Sauvignon as a vigorous variety, susceptible to powdery mildew, but a small producer. D. P. Pongrácz (*Practical Viticulture*, 1978), a great and much-missed authority, mentions that this variety is, though, resistant to rot, except when there is a great deal of rain. The rainfall in the Graves can be heavy, but the Cabernet Sauvignon can sustain much of it. The bunch of grapes is smallish and winged, the berries cluster quite tightly, the leaves are sectionally separated, virtually cut out.

Wines made with a predominance of the Cabernet Sauvignon are usually markedly coloured and tannic – hence the longevity of many. Some people remark on a whiff and flavour of blackcurrants in some of them and I can certainly understand this, although, when I have been tasting the fine red Graves, the emergence of the Cabernet Sauvignon is often so concentrated and pungent that, instead of 'blackcurrant', my tasting notes often read *cassis* – the blackcurrant liqueur (for which Burgundy is famous).

Many people note a 'spicy' bouquet and flavour in red Graves – this I think may also derive from the Cabernet Sauvignon when very ripe; it opens out and seems to give off what some of my Bordeaux friends describe as 'acacia' – the warm aroma that is redolent of more spice and fat than in other regions. There is a firm but multi-layered 'feel' to the wine that I associate with the Graves.

The former method of allowing the 'cap' or 'hat' of the debris of pressed grapes, stems, stalks and skins to remain in contact with the must for several weeks has now changed: the period has had to be shortened to days, at most a week in many instances. The wine maker must adjust the contribution made by the other grapes in the blend so that, to make fine red Graves, the wine can unfurl itself rewardingly, against the backing of the Cabernet Sauvignon. There is the additional contribution of the wood – the cask – which (to my mind) is somewhat exaggerated in wines made to please the wealthy drinkers of the New World. But behind even the most delicate fine red Graves there is the Cabernet Sauvignon, wooded, with the strata of smells and flavours that are delicately enticing. In my view, it gives of itself more gently in the red Graves and, sometimes and in the right vintages, more rewardingly than in non-French vineyards.

Cabernet Franc

This is now a widely planted black grape, often, I think, giving of its best when planted alone (but not in the Gironde), as in some of the red wines of the Loire. Few Britons like these, because of their crispness and acidity. In a year when the grapes have enjoyed a fair amount of sunshine, not necessarily downright heat, they are delicious.

In wines where they contribute to the blend, the Cabernet Franc grapes provide what I usually describe as a 'leafy freshness', a zip and lift to the wine's flavour additional to the touch of 'green' in the bouquet. Plantations are in fact currently being reduced in the top Graves estates, as may be seen by the proportions cited by them. Some people say they find a whiff of raspberries in the Cabernet Franc. Its freshness is one of its charms. It seems, sometimes, to come underneath the Cabernet Sauvignon with a soubrette-like perkiness, a fresh zest – lightening the initial impression of a fine wine.

This is a fairly vigorous variety, though it is susceptible to powdery mildew, but it seems to do quite well in even fairly heavy soils, such as those of the clay in many of the river-bank vineyards. The wines it makes tend to come round fairly early for drinking, but it does not deteriorate or drag them down when it is used in a blend. It usually ripens about a couple of weeks before the Cabernet Sauvignon, so it is useful when pickers have to be programmed for work around the vineyard. The leaves of the Cabernet Franc are not quite as heavily indented as those of the Cabernet Sauvignon and the bunch of grapes, often seemingly fatter and looser, is long and not as tightly clustered.

Merlot

This is a black grape, although there is also a Merlot Blanc (of which I know nothing). It is supposed to get its name from *merle* – blackbird –

196

but this arguable. What is definite is that this is the only one of the claret grapes on which the pickers sometimes slake their thirst – the other varieties are too thick-skinned and sharp in juice.

The Merlot has marked charm and to certain clarets it gives a tightly packed bouquet, like a posy of tiny flowers, with a follow-on of a gentle fruitiness. The concentrated bouquet is something that is pronounced in many great clarets but I have to say, from admittedly limited experience, that, when the Merlot is used on its own in other vineyards, the fragrance can make it seem top-heavy, the flavour tending to be unbalanced because of the lack of tautening acidity and crispness, the lasting impression being of a wine that is overblown, heavy rather than tantalising on the palate, sometimes short.

In the great Graves reds the beautiful languorous Merlot fragrance emerges with elegant charm – nothing overwhelming, everything velvety. The scent of the Merlot seems to be apparent in the red wines of this region in a very soft, lingering way, slithering underneath the Cabernets.

The Merlot ripens early and is susceptible to both downy mildew and rot, so that, in certain vintages, it suffers severely and its absence, in the wines of some estates where it usually makes a pronounced contribution, can radically alter the overall style, making such clarets oddly untypical of their expected character. As the Merlot cannot resist damage from rain, it tends to be the first black grape to be harvested.

The leaves are indented, though not as penetratingly as in the Cabernet Sauvignon; the cluster is longish, the grapes held loosely together, sometimes with a wing to the bunch.

Malbec

This is sometimes known as the Cot or the Auxerrois and possibly the most famous wine it now makes is the 'black wine' of Cahors, where some plantations are supposed to be a century old and where, presumably, the grafts were done immediately after the discovery that the American root-stocks resist the aphis.

Malbec is grown in other parts of France and was perhaps more widely planted in the Gironde in former times. It is another early ripener – this would have been of greater importance in days before there were mechanical devices facilitating pressing, so that grapes ripening early on at vintage time could keep workers engaged before the later pickings came to the presshouse. Malbec seems often a victim of *coulure*, the disease that makes the berries drop off the cluster and it also appears to be vulnerable to rot and to downy mildew. Its contribution to a blend would seem to be fruitiness, colour and a certain amount of tannin. The leaf is hardly indented at all and the cluster is a loose one. It is difficult to be precise about the Malbec, but its presence in some of the Graves should not be forgotten.

Petit Verdot

Although this variety has seldom been planted in large quantities in the Gironde, it is often valued for the crispness, acidity and taut, brisk style that it can provide in a blend. Once I heard it described by a grower as being like the odd squeeze of lemon in a sauce – providing a 'lift' that might not otherwise be there. It has a disadvantage, though, because it ripens very late and, therefore, can be adversely affected by any wet and cold that may change the climate after the bulk of the picking has been done. Is the word 'Vidure' related to 'Verdot'? This is something that the etymologists must tell us. Is it a 'strong vine' – the *vigne dure*? May it have been confused in early times with Cabernet Sauvignon? I cannot say.

WHITE GRAPES

Sémillon

This is a very interesting variety. It is grown in many other wine regions of the world and, in Australia, is confusingly known as 'Hunter River Riesling' in the Hunter Valley in New South Wales. It seems to have been planted in parts of the Bordeaux vineyard for centuries and, according to Jancis Robinson in *Vines, Grapes and Wines*, is the second most widely planted grape in France – the first being – surprisingly – the Ugni Blanc. In the Sauternais and Barsac regions it is of enormous importance, because it can develop the 'noble rot' (*botrytis cinerea*) when conditions are right, so that the opulent sweet wines of the Sauternes and Barsac regions can be made. Jancis makes the important point that in certain vineyards enjoying world fame, such as Château Yquem, there would appear to have been developed specific individual clones of this variety. Indeed, the wines it makes can vary enormously in style: recently I tasted a New Zealand Sémillon not intended to be a sweet wine and, together with a number of other experienced tasters, would have thought it some version of the Sauvignon Blanc!

The Sémillon has sometimes been criticised for having too obvious a fragrance and for making wines that can be rather sloppily sweet, tending to flabbiness and lacking definition. During the post-World War II period, when attempts were being made to bring white Bordeaux wines into line with the demand for assertive, dry whites, the Sémillon fell out of favour, its bouquet being its enemy because people sniffing this in a white wine decided, often without tasting, that the wine would inevitably be 'sweet'. However, my friend the Australian Welshman, Len Evans, recently gave a tasting of Australian Sémillons and demonstrated that, with a certain amount of bottle age and, of course, in a correctly made wine, the grape seems to shed its 'puppyfat' sweetness and is transformed into something aristocratic and distinctive; he stressed that the wines of this type need time, often as much as ten years, and this is borne out by the longevity of some of the great white Graves, their delicacy and firmness combining with the grace that makes them memorable. And just before writing this, in 1987, I was present at a dinner when the 'R', the dry white wine of Château Rieussec, was served, vintage 1985: it had, Baron Eric de Rothschild informed the company, 60 per cent Sémillon and, he added, it needed time – it certainly did, for the charm was as yet hidden, the wine, straightforwardly agreeable, had not yet begun to show what the Sémillon can do.

The grape seems a vigorous one, though in damp and humid conditions it may develop 'ignoble rot'. The leaf is slightly indented, the cluster quite long, the berries packed fairly tightly, and winged.

Sauvignon Blanc

This grape has a variety of other names, the most famous being the 'Blanc Fumé' of the upper Loire and, more recently the – to me – idiotic 'Fumé Blanc' version used in many New World wineries, where its name is supposed to appeal to the public. There are various grapes that are said to be related, including some that are now known not to be related at all, but the Sauvignon Blanc is extremely important today now and becoming more so.

Used alone, in suitable conditions, it makes a direct, crisp wine that often gets tagged with the adjective 'green'. Some of my young colleagues use the expression 'cat's pee' about this grape, but as far as I'm concerned, it's the Müller-Thurgau that evokes 'cat's piss', the Sauvignon Blanc says 'gooseberry'. Most interestingly, Jancis Robinson points out that, between 1968 and 1979, 'more than half the Sauvignon vines planted in the Gironde were uprooted, leaving just 2,400 hectares'. This was the time when 'dryness' was of paramount interest for the drinkers of white wines, but I do not think that the public was quite fair to many white Bordeaux; the lack of crispness in many instances was the result of the drinker receiving an impression of sogginess, which I suppose could have been the way they were made and the length of time they were, then, still kept in wood. Once control of fermentation was fully understood and the use of stainless steel or other inert substances was appreciated for the vats – many small-scale whites may never go into wood at all these days – then the lightness and freshness the public wanted could be produced.

If anyone wants to know what good but old-style white Bordeaux (not the wines of the top properties) used to be like, try the 'Bellaterra' wooded white of my friend Miguel Torres Jnr. This he makes in Chile where he produces another in accordance with modern methods and stainless steel vats; it is wholly Sauvignon (and there are no grafted vines at all in Chile) but when he put it on the Chilean market, it was so unlike the traditionally made local wines that he made 'Bellaterra' as well; it is not sweet and is impeccably made, but it has the soft, mouth-filling style that many white Graves used to have – and it is curious that it is 'Bellaterra' that the U.K. provincial public enjoy, not caring always for the intense, taut, dry-finishing wines to which many U.K. drinkers have become accustomed. Again I quote from Jancis Robinson, 'The Sémillon gives guts and longevity, the Sauvignon Blanc aroma and *nervosité.*'

The sudden enthusiasm for the Sauvignon influenced one experimental plantation in the Graves which is described in Appendix IV. This was the now discontinued dry white wine, La Tour Alain, named for the then head of Sichel & Co. It attracted some attention as 'the only wholly dry white Graves', but many people, registering its flowery bouquet, were so sure that this was the prelude to a sweetish wine that they shied off. The more recent extension of knowledge of both grapes and wine making have changed the situation once again; though I will venture to say that wines made wholly from the Sauvignon in the Gironde do seem to be slightly fatter and softer than the steely Sauvignons produced in more northern vineyards. Graves Sauvignons, if 100 per cent, have, in my admittedly restricted sampling, a lack of inner character; pleasant drinks, but without much interest to them. Similarly, certain 100 per cent Sauvignons from California have often seemed lacking in bouquet – maybe because of their somewhat high degree of alcohol – and however carefully other Sauvignons have been made by my southern hemisphere friends, I think that they often lack the 'snap' of Sauvignons from cool vineyards – the few that have seemed successful to me have combined this fresh, 'green' style with an assertive format, quite unlike the wines from warmer areas. The 'cold steel' of a fine Sauvignon doesn't emerge in a soft climate.

Professor Galet in *Cépages et vignobles de France* says that the Sauvignon Blanc is sensitive to powdery mildew and black rot, but is fairly resistant to downy mildew and *botrytis*. It is pretty vigorous and comes early to maturity, but it is subject to *coulure*. The leaf is fairly indented and the cluster is compact. When the grapes are fully ripe they often acquire a golden tinge.

Muscadelle

Despite its name and despite the fragrance associated with it, this is not a member of the great Muscat grape family (see below), nor has it anything to do with Muscadet in spite of some writers in the past assuming a relationship. But it is definitely, sometimes confusingly, aromatic. In certain regions of the southern hemisphere it is used to make dessert wines and sweet table wines, when it can attain true quality and refinement. In the Bordeaux region, it contributes a touch of intense fragrance to certain white wines, plus a very slightly 'raisiny' back taste; this last is more obvious in Muscadelle wines made elsewhere but, if a white Graves is adroitly made, this attribute can stress the overall character very pleasantly.

Its leaves are slightly indented, the cluster is large and loose, the grapes when fully ripe being slightly speckled on their greyish-pink skins.

Thanks to Jancis Robinson's book, I can now list some of the synonyms that she has discovered for the classic grapes of today – among which there are some associations with the odd names of the past. Here, in a brief form, are some of them:

The Petit Verdot: Carmelin; Gros Verdot: Verdot-Colon, Plant de Palus; Carmenère: Carmenelle, Cabarnelle, Grande Vidure, Grand Carmenet; Poulsard: one of these versions is Peloussard – I wonder if that can be related to the Pelouille?

Jancis lists the Grand Noir de la Calmette, with its synonyms Grand Noir and Teinturier and mentions that a number of other Teinturiers are

201

planted still, 'including the father of them all, Petit Bouschet'. Muscadelle: Musquette, Muscadet Doux – and many others. Mauzac Blanc: Maussac, Mauza, Mousac – and others, which makes me wonder whether this variety, too, may not be another version of another older name. She also lists the Petit and Gros Manseng, which I think must be the 'Mancin' of former lists, and the Camaraket of Béarn and the Palougue, both of which may have been known earlier, to judge by the sound of their names, as much as the spelling – the curious way in which Gascons are supposed to put 'ng' on the ends of words that finish in 'n' and, to this day, the south-west accent that reverberates somewhat though the nose can account for many versions of what may be only a few names.

These, then, are the Graves grapes. But it is up to the person who lays out the vineyard to determine the proportions in which the varieties should be planted; once again, though, it should be remembered that different strains of the same grape variety may be developed, thanks to clonal selection, and that these may, in the future, make a tremendous effect in the vineyards of the Graves.

Further to the section on Sauvignon Blanc (p. 199), Appendix IV gives details of the evolution of a dry white Bordeaux, in advance of its time. Whatever clones were used to make this wine will probably never now be known, but the fact that the wine was made at all as early as the 1950s shows the way in which wine makers are always looking to the future.

In Germain Lafforgue's *Le Vignoble girondin* (1947) there is a long list of synonyms of grape varieties used in the Gironde, which I have extracted as having particular relevance to vine names that may be encountered by those able to pursue further research in this aspect of the subject. It will be noted that many of the names vary according to what may have been the local pronunciation of the words (see Appendix III).

15

THE WINE

Dᴇᴛᴀɪʟs of how a classic wine is made can vary, according to the resources of the winery and the knowledge and aims of the person in charge. Compliance with the regulations still enables considerable variations to take place: the arrangements and plantations of the vines have been mentioned, the equipment available and the advice of consultants must be taken into account. The traditions and potential of each property will also be different, even from those of neighbouring estates. The experience of those engaged in the day-by-day running of the vineyard must naturally be weighed, together with the wishes of the overall owner or the board of directors, plus their associates, also the theories of the consultant oenologist – a person of increasing importance these days. Finally, a great deal depends on the markets that are chiefly concerned and, ultimately, the funds that are available.

It will also be appreciated that, although members of the wine trade are generous in exchanging news of discoveries, experiments and fresh products, reticences, even secrets, must often be maintained. The person outside the trade and, certainly, the competitor within it, may guess at what a certain proprietor does to achieve outstanding success – they may seldom know for sure. This is understandable. Indeed, the rôle of the consultant oenologist must often be to spread information without abusing the confidence placed in him or her by a variety of different wineries. So I myself tend to be wary of any disclosures of 'what makes Château X so unusual'; sometimes this type of 'secret' can be a pretty story, sometimes it is a piece of semi-nonsensical technical jargon. If an owner can reveal some of the character and procedures whereby his wine is brought into being, this merits acceptance – it is unwise and, certainly, discourteous, to attempt to investigate further and probably quite pointless. In giving an account of the principal estates of the Graves I have, of course, included such details of wine making as the owners or their associates gave me. I have not attempted to do more – and, it is worth stressing, even by the time this text appears in print, some modifications or alterations in procedures may well have taken place.

THE RED WINES

These are made according to the usual Bordeaux methods. I am repeating the account of what happens, so that anybody visiting an estate may know what the various pieces of equipment are and how the wine is handled.

The grapes are brought to the *cuverie* or vathouse as soon as possible after they have been picked; if they are left, piled up, in what may be a fairly high temperature at vintage time, then a type of undesirable fermentation may start up as the pressure of the heaped-up fruit may break the grapeskins and cause the juice to begin to run.

The grapes arrive according to the variety being picked – some varieties ripening before others, as has been stated – and also according to the sections of the vineyard where the pickers or a machine have been organised to work. The grapes then are 'pressed' on being received at the winery. This term, however, is misleading: the huge beam presses and mighty screw presses one may see in museums are now things of the past. The word 'crushed' is perhaps more accurate. What occurs is that the containers of grapes are tipped into a large hopper, through the base of which passes an Archimedes screw – a never-ending spiral. The speed of this can be adjusted so that grapes with specially tough skins can receive more pressure as they are squashed by the action of the screw. The Cabernet Sauvignon, for example, has a fairly tough skin and, in a very dry year, the skins of other grapes can be thick also.

Sometimes this crushing or squashing by the fruit passing along the constantly turning screw is the only form of 'pressing' the grapes receive. They may, though, also be subjected to a preliminary treatment before they drop onto the screw, by means of a device called a *fouloir égrappoir*: this looks like a whirling drum with a spike on it; the grapes drop onto the drum, the stems and stalks are clawed off and put to one side. The fruit, by this time partly crushed, drops down onto the turning screw. Then the pulp proceeds into the fermentation vat, where the process of fermentation will start. Some vats are wood, some stainless steel, some of various types of material that can be kept scrupulously clean – for the risk of infection is great at this stage of wine making.

The stems and stalks that may have been whirled off earlier can be added to the contents of the vat – the *cuvée* – according to whether the wine maker considers that they can contribute to the ultimate wine by means of the substances, notably tannin, that they contain. There will be, in every

204

vatting, a mass of skins, pips and general debris of stalks and stems. This, which is known as the 'hat' (*chapeau*), will rise to the surface where it will sit; according to the wine maker, this hat may, at intervals, be pushed down into the juice, or else the juice will be 'pumped over', or, sometimes, a type of grid is put over the hat so as to keep it at least partially submerged in the juice. The effect of contact by the skins with the juice during this first period of fermentation, when the contents of the vat heat up considerably and bubble, is to extract the various substances from the general debris that makes up the hat; in the past, the hat might stay on the vat for several weeks, resulting in a wine so high in tannins and acids that it would require many years of maturation in wood to become ready to enjoy as a drink, but this is no longer done. A hat may remain on a vat, in contact with the wine, for a period that may vary from only a few days to up to two or three weeks, depending on what the wine maker is aiming at and, additionally, what the wine of this particular vintage may do, for there is still considerable extraction from the debris.

As the fermentation starts and the yeasts act on the sugar in the juice, the temperature of the contents of the vat will rise and must be carefully watched; if it goes up too high or drops too low, the yeasts will cease to work. This is why cooling devices of various kinds are now routine equipment in most cuveries, so that the fermentation can progress steadily, without interruption, with controls exercised throughout: a top temperature of about 25°C is usual for Bordeaux rouge, 30°C for a classed growth. Again, the use of certain specific yeast strains is now recognised as of prime importance; see the reference to the work of Peter Vinding-Diers in this respect (p. 213), also to the innovations of M. Dubourdieu (p. 214) which have shown the value of skin contact for a longer time, this *sur lie* procedure being conducive to an additional richness of flavour.

The stems and stalks of the grapes earlier put aside may be squeezed in a type of press that rather resembles a meat press; this extracts what may be a harsh, hard liquid which is sometimes added to the *grand vin* in certain years to augment the juice if and as the wine maker thinks this advisable.

Once the first part of the fermentation process is finished, the bubbling and warmth in the vat die down and, as the cooler weather comes, the yeasts cease working. The contents of the vat will then be run off and, with fine wine, destined for maturation in wood, they go into the Bordeaux *barriques*, although at this stage each is still the product of one single grape variety; the *égalissage*, or putting together of the different wines in cask after they are made, takes place in the spring following the vintage. After any secondary fermentation takes place, the wine, having being 'mixed' or combined in a vat for the *égalissage*, goes back into 'small wood', i.e. the *barriques*, and is then racked or pumped off its lees, the deposit in the bottom of the cask, into a fresh cask.

The malolactic fermentation takes place after the first fermentation and before the second stage of the overall process; the effect of the changing of malic acid into lactic acid is to reduce what might seem to be too much acidity (which is why, in certain other vineyards, the 'malo' is suppressed because the aim is to accentuate the acidity in what could often be a flabby wine). The malolactic fermentation always takes place in Bordeaux but, with white wines, it is not essential and depends on the type of year and, of course, the decision of the maker.

The wine undergoes several rackings, the number of times racking is done depending on the wine maker. The wine may go first into new wood – casks that have never been used before – or into casks that have already been in use for the maturation of the estate's wine. The contribution of the cask to wine is significant, but the cost of a *barrique* is so high that only the wealthy estates can afford to put all the vintage into new wood. Also, a wine may not always require this type of cask maturation and some-times it can develop perfectly in a cask that has previously been in use. Or the wine may be given a period in new wood and then moved on, to an older cask, according to what the wine maker thinks it may find beneficial – or what casks are available. The subject of 'wooding' is vast and complex: the use of 'large wood' – casks bigger than *barriques* – is sometimes involved with fine red wines. And sometimes wines do not go into *barriques* at all, maturing satisfactorily in vats, which may be of wood, like the fermentation vats, or of stainless steel or other materials – for many of the small-scale wines, the use of *barriques* would be an extravagance that could not be justi-fied by the price the wine might fetch. It must be emphasised that the 'wooding' of wines is very much a matter of the personal opinions of the maker – and of the markets for the particular wine. Some of these like wines that are noticeably wooded, others do not. Anyone familiar with the wines of the southern hemisphere and California will be aware of the dif-ferences of opinion about this stage in the production of fine wine and, too, of the astonishing knowledge of the origin of virtually every stave in a cask! Different cask makers can have surprisingly different influences on wine. I must admit that I am not as aware as my friends in the New World of many of these nuances – and I remember the puzzled reply of one French wine maker to the query 'Where do you get your wood?', which was 'From the forest'. New World wine makers would be able to specify the particular forest (for casks for wine must be of a certain type of close-grained wood), the preliminary maturation of the wood and the maker of the cask! Myself, I have a feeling that our European nonchalance on this subject is perhaps due to the dampness in which most of the classic wines in this continent are made and matured – it is just possible that damp oak is damp oak, contributing in general but not differentiating very much in its particular shades of flavour to the wine for which it acts as a cradle. There are two major cask producers in France and those experienced in tasting a variety of wines (perhaps most notably, white Burgundies) can describe the differences in the character bestowed by the cask to the wine. To me this is something that, when it is pointed out, I can apprehend – but I do not pick it out primarily. Differences do exist but I do posit that they may emerge more in the wines that are subsequently matured in the drier – not necessarily hotter – atmosphere of the southern hemisphere.

It should be stressed again that, although the contact of the hat with the juice is now a week or ten days, whereas in former times it might have been several weeks, the wines of those earlier days would then often have remained in wood for three or four years. Because the grapes were usually picked then when less ripe than would be insisted on today, the resulting wine did require a longer period in wood and, because of the maceration taking place for a longer time, the wines were more tannic; this element, holding the wine together for a long life, was, of course, able to affect the wine during its time in cask, because of the exposure to the air. Today, with the pressures of 'cash flow' in the estates even of millionaire owners, a wine, whether in wood or in vat, will usually be considered ready to go to the bottling line after eighteen months or two years. Today, people are not ready or able to wait many years before sampling a wine they want to buy for drinking or, perhaps, lay down for a mere decade or so instead of far longer. But in my talks with those who have been able to try wines made in the older style and from my experience of such elderly masterpieces, I have concluded that it is not fair to assume that wines made, as once, for very long-term maturation are other than 'different' from those made to come round sooner. Indeed, so many more wines are good drinking as they are made today that it would be foolish to generalise: wines that survived in former times would, I suggest, have been exceptional anyway.

At the end of their first year in cask, red wines are 'fined'. The fining agent is often egg-whites – ideally from free-range hens – but other substances, such as isinglass, may be used. They are all albuminous (one editor for whom I wrote an article was horrified at the mention of ox-blood – 'Suppose the wine drinker were a vegetarian?'). These fining agents put an opposite electrostatic charge into the wine, so that particles in suspension within it are attracted to the fining agent and eventually sink down to the bottom of the cask or vessel used to contain the wine. (Until comparatively recently the rôle of a fining agent was described as being something like a net, to spread out and catch and drag down the particles, but this is not so.)

During the first year of the wine's life the bungs on the *barriques* are loosely in place on the upper side of the cask and, in the first stages of the development, the continuation of the fermentation will bubble up to force its way past the bung and stain the 'waists' of the casks in this overflow. The claret-coloured band around each *barrique* gives a pleasant overall impression, but it is an indication of the wine 'working'.

In a property of any size, the wines of the first year are kept in a separate *chai* from those of the second and when a vintage is moved into the second-year *chai*, the bungs are driven home hard and the casks turned, so that the bungs are to one side. Henceforth, any samples that are required from the second-year wines must be drawn by means of a tap or spigot, or by a very small hole, plugged with a minute wooden stopper, which will release some wine if pressure is exerted on the cask head – usually by inserting a lever (often the clawhead of a mallet) between the crosspiece on the head of the cask and one of the staves, which forces out some wine. It usually surprises people that, once the small plug of wood is removed, there is no gush of wine, but in fact the pressure within the cask prevents this occurring and only a trickle will escape even if the hole is not at once replugged.

If the wine spends only a short time in wood, or is matured wholly in a large vessel, such as a vat, then, of course, it can still be racked off its lees into another container and, if a sample is required, this can be drawn off by a tap at the base. Vats of this type should not be confused with the fermentation vats; they can be cylindrical, but are often rectangular. They vary in size, though many are large. Such containers may also be used for blending and storage, as they are closed. To avoid possible confusion, it should be pointed out that a fermentation vat can, in due course, also be used as a maturation vat and for any *égalissage*, and the wine may also go into the same vat for fining or prior to bottling; there is no rigidity about this procedure and, of course, much depends on the space, the financial resources available and, ultimately, on the individual wine maker, who will have evolved definite ideas as to both what is ideal and what may be practicable and affordable. (I have gone into some detail about vats, *barriques* and general containing vessels, because they do vary from property to property and the basic notion of lines of *barriques*, taking the wine direct from the fermentation vats, is by no means apparent everywhere. Much depends on the size of the property, the resources of the winery and the traditions and practices of the maker.)

When the wine is bottled depends on the decision of the maker. According to the way the vintage has turned out, the wine may be bottled slightly sooner or slightly later, but with the red wines eighteen months to two years is a fairly general period.

The decision is also conditioned by the 'wooding' or other maturation of what has been made. Obviously, no estate wants to have to cope with bottling at the busiest period of the year – the vintage – and, as August is the great holiday month in France, labour is not abundant at that time either, so bottling may take place earlier in the summer or once vintage activities are virtually concluded. This, again, depends on the resources available, also whether the wine is to be bottled at the property or if it is to be sent elsewhere, in bulk, for handling either by a shipper in Bordeaux or even being shipped or dispatched in bulk to a purchaser elsewhere in France or in another country. The finest red wines, of course, are estate-bottled and mechanisation has speeded up this process, which might, in former days, take place whenever people were free to do it – not always a good thing for wine waiting about in cask in the meantime. Indeed, weeks, even months might elapse between the start of bottling and its completion, the wine altering, not always for the best, the while. August and vintage time can also be very hot, not suitable for bottling.

The 'wooding' of wines, previously described, is another thing that varies from property to property. The sight of ranks of new casks, awaiting the next vintage, is impressive and something that arouses much pride in the owner or members of the establishment. But, quite apart from the expense, some wines are not destined to spend all their time in new wood, although far more new wood is usually involved in this region today than in the past. The present-day wooding does, in many instances, involve a proportion of new wood annually, but the wine spends less time in it – it is going to be bottled earlier. Treatments involved, such as fining and filtration prior to bottling, are now subject both to expert advice and to the knowledge of what such treatments will do to the wine – until comparatively recently many practices were sometimes inclined to be a matter of tradition or be carried out when opportunity offered and the workers involved happened to be available. It may astonish many to learn that, as recently as the early 1980s, only the very finest estates – Haut Brion, Laville Haut Brion, Domaine de Chevalier – used new wood for maturation. But nowadays, with the incentive of the revision of the classification (see p. 233) in prospect, but not yet having taken place, many estates have made use of it since 1983. Of course, as well as adding to the cost, wooding of this sort can add enormously to the value of the wine: my friend Clive Coates is firm that any revised classification should only include wines aged in oak, for, he says in this context, 'No wine not matured in wood can be more than pleasant, good even – but it cannot be a true grand vin.' He comments that the selection of the source of the wood is more important than many lay drinkers would suppose: Allier wood endows the wine it holds with refinement, Nevers gives it a more robust style, so it depends what the maker wants to achieve. Among the estates now using new wood must be included all the existing classed growths, plus such progressive and important properties as those directed by Pierre Coste (see p. 217), the Lurton estates, Rahoul, Roquetaillade-la-Grange and an increasing number of others.

As has been mentioned, the debris – stalks, stems, pips and so on – may be pressed and added to the *grand vin* if the maker thinks a slight augmentation of the elements squeezed out will help a particular vintage. Or these pressings may be added to the final squeezings of the grapes, which often go to make the wine destined for domestic consumption on the property, quite separate from the *grand vin*. Some of this final debris may go to a distillery for making into industrial alcohol (distillation is not carried on by estates these days), or, in the form of the *râpe*, compressed claret-coloured cake-like material, it may be used as manure for the vineyard – no waste!

Throughout the making of the wine, the various authorities who exercise controls will be in touch with those on the spot at the vineyard and in the *cuverie*. Statistics are kept, analyses recurrently taken. There is nothing haphazard about the production of even a modestly priced red Graves these days. The details of the cork – the increasing cost of corks vies with the rising price of casks as a perennial topic – the design and information given on the label, the capsule, any strip label or back label are all subject to controls. The colour of the glass of the bottle likewise – brownish for red wines, the shade only varying a little within the permitted tones. If you find an old bottle you may be surprised not only at the apparent simplicity of the label (which may or may not be 'designed' at all) but at the weight of the bottle; if this is a hand-blown bottle, it will be much heavier than a moulded bottle and the punt will be deeper. Such bottles and the elderly wines they contain are rarities now.

THE WHITE WINES

The dry or moderately dry wines are made essentially in the same way as the reds. Or they were. The awareness of the need for crisp dry whites has radically altered what many producers now do for, as will have been understood from some of the opinions previously quoted in this book, the dry whites of the Graves are or were no longer wholly in line with the commercial requirements of export markets conditioned by lighter, friskier whites, certainly as far as the medium-priced and cheaper wines are now able to be retailed.

Before detailing some of the modifications of white wine making, it is practical to give a rough idea of how the wines were and, to some extent are, made. But the remainder of this section should be read and borne in mind while the basic method is being described. The experiments with a longer period of time being allowed for the wine to remain *sur lie* are still continuing. What is beginning to be appreciated – of great importance in view of the extending of plantations of Sémillon today – is that, as Pierre Coste stresses (p. 218), the state of ripeness of the grapes for white wines, often a haphazardly considered matter in the past, is able to endow the resulting wine with a notably increased amount of flavour and character. Both white grapes and red or black ones will accentuate in acidity as well as sugar and this acidity, which is tartaric (not malic), can make all the difference between an adequate wine and a fine one.

The grapes do not, after crushing, go through any period of skin contact and indeed there is no obvious need for them to do so, for the

211

skins of white grapes will not impart any colouring matter to the must. Sometimes a process known as *débourbage* – which may be translated as 'cleaning up' – is used. This involves the freshly pressed juice being put into a vat with a certain proportion of sulphur dioxide – SO_2 – for approximately twenty-four hours. This removes all solids in the ultimate wine and also acts as a preventive against premature oxidation (the contact with the air that causes white wines to darken in tone and often become aged before their time). The 'press' used for most white wines and, sometimes, for certain types of red wines, is the horizontal type: slatted cylinders, fitted inside with loops of chains, are filled with the grapes. Then, as the cylinders revolve, the grapes are flung against the sides of the cylinder as the cylinder turns, the chains break up the fruit and the juice runs out between the slats into a type of drain underneath. It can then be directed into vat or cask as required and, subsequently, also into vat or cask once the initial stages of fermentation have been completed. The bottling usually takes place earlier than for red wines, the whites in the 'small-scale' category often being bottled in the spring and early summer after their vintage.

All this, the traditional method of wine making, can result in agreeable white wines but, as producers have been finding out for some years, these wines may seem out of key, old-fashioned, to palates in export markets and even in other parts of France – where Alsace wines are increasingly sold for aperitif and casual drinking, as well as with food. Leaving aside the use of the white grapes, Sémillon and Sauvignon Blanc, which has been previously mentioned (pp. 198–201), even discarding the use of 'wooding' for white wines made in this region – which inevitably involves additional capital outlay, scrupulous care and surveillance throughout – the result has been often found to lack the particular traits of crispness, lightness, elegance and fruit plus fragrance with which producers of white wines in other French regions and in other countries can woo the palates of the extending market for inexpensive table wines. The finest white wines of the Graves are, without question, in a category apart; but they are not produced in large quantities, they are inevitably expensive and they appeal to an educated and discriminating section of the public, not to the mass market. This is why the major changes in the history of wine making in the Graves have taken and, certainly, are taking place even as I write, with the production of the white wines, notably those in the lower price ranges.

It is only possible here to indicate some of these changes and only in a non-technical way. But indubitably the white Graves, which are the

212

most important of all the dry white wines of Bordeaux and which have played a major part in the history of the region's wines, are being subjected to alterations that will affect white wines of many other wine areas.

NEW METHODS

One small example is the way in which Peter Vinding-Diers, at Château Rahoul, has evolved a system that is a variation on the process known as *triage* or special selection of the grapes. The berries, de-stemmed and de-stalked, pass over a moving band and, on this, those that are slightly heavier than others are detoured off to the side and channelled separately away from the others. These grapes will be heavier because, within them, the concentration of sugar will be high and they can be separated before they go into the fermentation vat. (This, it must be noted, does not affect the selection of 'nobly rotten' grapes, affected by the action of *botrytis cinerea* for the making of the great sweet wines of Sauternes and Barsac, which must actually be picked separately, as each berry ripens and develops the rot on its skin.) The result of the *triage* enables white wines of a certain type to be made that possess a more definite, intense character and can usually last longer in bottle than those put into the fermentation vat without any sort of surveillance and selection.

Then there is a method known as *macération préfermentaire*, which my friend Clive Coates M.W. described in the magazine *Wine & Spirit* (November 1984). This has already been brought into use in other regions of France, but it was pioneered in the Bordeaux area by the estate of Doisy-Daëne, where M. Pierre Dubourdieu has been experimenting; this property in Barsac makes both dry and sweet wines and, according to Edmund Penning-Rowsell in *The Wines of Bordeaux*, the vineyard from which the dry wine comes is composed of 60 per cent Sauvignon Blanc, 20 per cent Sémillon and 20 per cent Riesling. But the grapes alone do not account for the major difference in the character of the dry wine.

As Clive Coates points out, the process of *macération préfermentaire* has been copied from the Muscadet area, where it is accepted that white wine can benefit by being allowed to rest on the skins of the grapes – *sur lie*, or on the lees. The aromas and flavours that are peculiar to each grape variety are, Clive Coates states, 'essentially situated within the skin of the grape itself, rather than within the flesh'. But, if the grapes are not in prime condition when picked, the skins may also convey to the wine disagreeable odours and flavours, which is why, until recently, it has been deemed advisable to take the must or juice away from any skin contact as soon as possible. The clusters or bunches of grapes are not de-stalked and 'the final *jus de presse* is normally discarded or used separately for inferior wine'.

However, a winery today is far more advanced in equipment and the maintenance of hygiene than it was even twenty or thirty years ago; the 'controlled fermentation', by which is signified the maintenance of the desired temperature of the must in the fermentation vat, so that the fermentation proceeds steadily, without interruption or sharp rises and falls in the temperature of the juice, is something that enables what might, in earlier days, have been worrying periods during the vintage, now to be avoided. As Clive Coates notes, if it is possible to obtain fruit that is both completely ripe and absolutely healthy, is it advantageous to achieve separation of skins and juice as quickly as possible, given that the flavour of the ultimate wine is apparently due to a great extent to the elements in those skins? Was it, perhaps, possible to adapt a red-wine method of vinification to white wines, since the various procedures involving skin contact were numerous and varied?

Pierre Dubourdieu began tests with the Oenology department of Bordeaux University in 1981: Sauvignon grapes were de-stalked and lightly crushed, then pumped into an *autovidante cuve*, plus some SO_2 and pectinase, to prevent oxidation. Maceration was allowed to take place at 20°C for twelve hours, then the free-run juice was drawn off, the pulp pressed and the *jus de presse* added to the juice prior to conducting *débourbage* and getting on with the fermentation in the usual way. The results of this showed that by comparison with wine made from Sauvignon grapes in the traditional manner – that is, getting the pulp off the skins as soon as possible – the wine made by the *macération préfermentaire* method demonstrates a Sauvignon aroma and flavour that is more definite and typical of the Sauvignon grape. The importance of this is obvious to anyone who has read the account (p. 200) of the sudden rush to plant this variety – and then to pull it up in favour of the Sémillon. I will add that, from what are admittedly only a few tastings of the dry Doisy-Daëne made in this way, the wine does possess a weight and complexity that are quite surprising. Certainly dry, it has a warmth and rotundity that, to me, is indicative of the area, which is temperate, even warm, with a length and multistranded set of flavours that in Clive Coates's description evoke 'passion fruit ... also ... apricot, nuts and even ... raspberries'. I would not go quite so far into detail, but there is a tautness and clean back taste that is tempting.

This *macération préfermentaire* has apparently been copied and developed in Bergerac, where the owner of Châteaux Belingard and du Chayne, M. Laurent de Boisredon, allows the maceration to go on for 12–18 hours at 12° before conducting the juice away; it is significant that he also centrifuges the must, which eliminates nearly all the wild yeasts and apparently necessitates the addition of *saccharomyces cerevisae*, so as to let the fermentation go on. The wine in Bergerac is then left for two or three weeks on its lees so that, as in the Muscadet region, the wine can 'feed off the dead yeast cells and in this way become richer and fatter'. It is then racked and goes into stainless steel vats, but is not filtered or fined until bottling is to take place.

The procedure at Doisy-Daëne is that the grapes are de-stalked and left to macerate for twenty-four hours, receiving a light sulphuring to avoid oxidation; about 90 per cent of juice apparently flows off before the pressing begins and this process need not be either fierce or prolonged. In order to precipitate the 'gross lees' the must is cooled to 0°C and centrifuged, before being combined with the free-run juice. After the fermentation is finished, the wine is again cooled, down to −3°C, centrifuged to get rid of the yeast cells and 'also to get added richness out of them because the yeasts are artificially autolysed, before being ejected. This process in addition removes the oxidase enzymes which cause white wine to turn brown with age. As the wine is still full of CO_2 there is no danger of oxidation.'

Other properties, both in the Graves and in nearby regions, have also begun to experiment with this *macération préfermentaire* procedure, varying it, of course, from property to property; in the tastings of such wines as I have had, the zip and freshness plus fruit of the result seems to justify the change from traditional methods. The innovative work that has been done will, I think, show its influence on many wines in the future.

Although this may seem light years removed from the procedures traditional in making white wines, such as those for which the Graves has been renowned over the centuries, it does not, in fact, involve techniques or equipment that are unknown to most wine makers or not available in the majority of wineries. The importance is that the subtle elements that differentiate the character of one grape variety from another are mainly to be found in the skins of the grapes which, handled in a certain way and processed with care, can make a far more substantial contribution to the ultimate wine in terms of both immediate appeal and long-term retention of prime quality. The material from which the wine is made and with which its character is established is available – the grapes; now that more is known about the growing and handling of them, the possibilities for the augmented subtleties of the wine would seem to be considerable.

The demand of the market, and the competition, must always be considered, especially in the lower price ranges, where the bulk trade is done. In the seventeenth and eighteenth centuries, the Dutch were important buyers of Graves wines, because they wanted the light, dry whites for which the region was already well known. Today, the requirements can vary considerably between the main export markets – the United States, for example, preferring a slightly wooded character even in the cheap wines, the U.K. liking the clean, straight, stainless-steel-vatted style of the medium dry whites that sell in vast quantities. The Graves has a natural following among French drinkers, because its wines are so different from the very dry whites of parts of the Loire and the others based on the Chenin Blanc; the aromatic white Rhônes, too, are not immediate competitors – but the various whites of Alsace can be, because they are, like dry white Graves, suitable drinks as aperitifs, in between times and also with certain foods. All these preferences and possibilities have to be taken into account when a change is effected in wine making, so that the expense involved and the subsequent publicity that is necessary may be justified. It will be interesting to see whether *macération préfermentaire* wines make a marked impact on customers and, too, whether they maintain this alongside the cleanly made but more traditional white wines of the Graves. White Burgundies, made from the Chardonnay and the Aligoté, are totally different – and increasingly expensive. But too much 'tradition' makes dull little white Graves.

THE ROLE OF THE OENOLOGIST

Even a few years ago it would not have been routine for the owner or wine maker at an estate seemingly in satisfactory condition to make regular use of a consultant oenologist. Now it is with pride that many properties, in detailing their organisation, include the name of the authority who is their consultant. This is as inevitable today as it is for a doctor in general practice to refer a patient to one of the specialists known to him, who will be up to date in the latest discoveries and treatments involved with a particular malady or deficiency. No one individual could keep abreast of all that is happening in the world of wine; no single person could employ the resources of the huge laboratories, testing stations and nursery plantations, be aware of the developments in various chemical treatments and maintain contact with the rapid evolution of what is involved with clonal selection.

Each wine region and each wine-growing country has its centres for research, its training schools and refresher courses and knowledge is shared between many. For the grower, the oenologist will not only be able to keep up to date with a variety of trends – in what is happening in other vineyards and what may be likely to happen because of various economic factors – but he or she will, by being involved with the practical application of what may have been largely experimental work, be able to adjust and adapt theory to practice. In addition to the special skills involved, much discretion has likewise to be brought into play, because the consultant may know the details of what is going on at one estate – whether for good or bad – and can, in general terms, use this knowledge in advising other growers, while avoiding particularisation to the disadvantage of any.

Two of the very big 'names' that are used in the revitalising or reconstruction of vineyards in the Bordeaux region are those of Professor Pascal Ribereau-Guyon and Professor Émile Peynaud. It would seem, from a very cursory notion I have been able to glean, that both are activated by different views and opinions, which would be quite natural and the work of both has won the respect of many, even if each has his special partisans. But one name in the Graves attracts affectionate mentions, as well as respect from all sides – that of Pierre Coste.

Monsieur Coste is a *négociant en vins* at Langon, highly qualified during his activities there since 1950, member of numerous learned associations and recipient of a considerable array of awards. More – he is an enthusiast and highly articulate, a well-educated man, about the wines of his beloved Graves. A 1984 study concerning the Graves vineyard of the past, present and future is that of a precise student of words: in commenting on the great estates of Pessac, Talence, and Mérignac, he says – if I translate him adequately – 'The wines are notable for an immediate maturity, with a full-bodied character, tannin and substance, low acidity and a bouquet so "original" [I might substitute 'unexpected'] that it may sometimes bewilder the beginner-drinker. This evokes [the words] soot, tar, ink, peaches, fruit stones, juniper, incense, fur … the amazing thing is that this cocktail of smells makes up one of the greatest wines of the world.' He notes the tremendous differences in certain of the estates, even when these are virtual neighbours, but he realises that the bourgeois growths, however individual they may be, cannot attain the *singularité* that warrants the creation of a different A.O.C. for them. (The forthcoming new A.O.C.s were not envisaged at the time of his writing this.)

What M. Coste stresses, in such of his work as I have been privileged to read in French, is the qualities that correctly made and matured white wines can give to the drinker. Here he is insistent on basic quality, being, in this respect, similar to a physician who prevents an illness attacking or affecting the human being: white wines do not have the protection of tannin, like the reds, and it is no good trying to put a fault right in a white wine once it has been allowed to attack the wine – nor is it advisable to achieve a neutrality, a sterility, a loss of individuality in a wine that may, technically, be 'all right'. The emphasis on perfect ripeness of the grapes is referred to again and again; the fruit, in prime condition, must get to the press without delay or damage. The processes involved with handling it must be careful, gentle – M. Coste refers to M. Dubourdieu admitting that, even with all the requisite equipment, some stages of this pressing cannot be hastened. Fermentation must proceed slowly. The vats must be scrupulously clean, the wine must, throughout, be vigilantly observed so that, oddly enough, it is virtually 'sterile' but in fact is all the more 'living' on account of all its attributes to do with the aromas and properties of the fruit being brought to the fore. Then, once in bottle, the wine will have the opportunity to develop, expand – and live much longer than is usually expected for a white wine.

The dynamism, years of experience and, above all, the enthusiastic way in which M. Coste foresees the future as bright for the once-lagging and flagging small-scale white Graves has already done much to spur on growers not only to take advantage of modern knowledge and equipment, but to keep a balance in making their wines, so that these, while appealing to an increasingly demanding and informed public, retain their individuality and display their considerable pleasing attributes.

16

WHAT ARE
THE WINES LIKE?

THERE is a recurrent and insoluble problem about wine writing. Is it possible to describe wines so that the reader can gain some idea as to what they taste like? To translate one set of experiences, mainly sensual but including certain cerebral impressions, into written words is difficult anyway. With wines it is hazardous. At least, if a lecturer is discussing wines with an audience there are the constants: the speaker and the listeners are there, the wines are present. The occasion is *now*. Even if many of the audience are unreceptive, even if the speaker is inadequate to the occasion, even if some of the wines are unexpectedly less attractive, everything is happening at one time. Contact can be made with the wines, the tasters, the lecturer.

The written word, though, is far more ephemeral than the spoken phrase where wines are concerned. Within hours, days, tasters may differ about the same wines on which they previously agreed, but an article, a book, even a recorded talk cannot isolate a tasting experience. The wine itself may have changed; the taster may bring to the experience a mass of knowledge, prejudices, personal preferences – the author of the words on paper or on record may have no clear notion of this, and often no control of the circumstances in which the wine is tasted. Writers for newspapers and magazines must aim at being understood by both the beginner and the experienced – meanwhile, the wine, subject of what is being written, may have altered; although such wine articles do not always linger in the mind as long as their authors hope, there is the added hazard of words in a book being referred to again and again, sometimes over years, during which both the wine under discussion and the reader of the text (and certainly the author) will have undergone radical changes.

A warning should be given about writings on wine that are able to be categorised as 'historic', even 'definitive'. This often occurs in connection with well-known names in writing, for the glamour of the author brushes off, sometimes as authoritative, onto the text (especially by a good writer) and the reader, maybe half a century or more away from when the words were set down, goes on accepting them without question. But it is useless, in fact ridiculous, to go on giving advice about certain 'known names' in wine by 'respected names' in wine writing when what was written was set down half a century or so ago, possibly about wines tasted years before that and when the readers are primarily concerned with buying their next bottle from a supermarket or, maybe, venturing into a purchase from a merchant established within the past twenty years. (And did the much respected writers *really* know more than an agreeable superficiality about the wines in the first place? I do not think that many writers prior to 1939 were informed to the extent that many of those writing today seem to be – though my predecessors in wine writing often wrote elegantly and charmingly.)

Wines and writing about wines cannot remain, like bees fossilised in amber, static. Indeed, one of the pleasures of wine is that it provides the 'joy as it flies', the delight being no less real for being as transient as a flower. But, of course, it is of interest to know what serious wine lovers have recorded about wines of the past, as long as we do not directly associate what they thought then with what we may think now.

There is also the generation gap in wine writing. I admit, I am baffled by the adjectives 'peppery' (I don't like pepper), 'biscuity' (what sort of biscuit? – the term is lacking in precision), 'rubbery' (it would to me suggest something pejorative – neutral plastic piping temporarily repaired by something of rubber, imparting an alien flavour to the wine). Yet these are terms of praise frequently used by many of my younger colleagues. They use jargon and slang that I neither understand nor would associate with certain taste experiences. They are not wrong. I hope they do not think I am! But the difference in the use of tasting terminology exists also between British English and the 'English' used in other English-speaking countries.

It must be stressed and repeatedly stressed that it is extremely difficult to differentiate between what is good – which the taster may not personally find appealing – and what is liked. Considerable experience and continual alertness to impressions and attempts at precision in translating them into words are necessary in doing this. The taster is also conditioned by individual requirements: whether appraising wines to buy purely for personal use, or in order to report on behalf of others, to lay down wines for the future, maybe to place large orders for the supply of major retail outlets – these, even subconsciously, inevitably affect the taster's attitude to the wines. There are, too, the impressions registered when tasting young wines, which are usually different from those made by the same wines when fully mature and ready to drink. Many inexperienced drinkers experience disappointment when, on entering a tasting room or a *chai*, they are given a glass of something that seems wholly remote from anything they can imagine themselves enjoying or even respecting. The study of potential in wines is tantalisingly difficult. However, I think that the lay taster, considering buying wine purely for personal pleasure (and ignoring the possibility of 'investment'), should try to note what it is that makes certain wines so sought-after; aggressive marketing and lavish promotion will not ensure a world-wide reputation and justify the high price paid for some wines – the taster should try to register what it is, in certain wines, that makes them praised, whether for long-term laying-down or for short-term consumption.

It is as unwise to overpraise wines as to denigrate them. Something may go wrong, whether with the costly or the cheap. Not all can appeal to the majority of drinkers. Also, some commentators criticise or even condemn medium-range wines that do not – because they cannot – provide the profound and detailed pleasure of certain great classics. So, I think, that it is a waste of space to try to provide detailed descriptions of wines that the reader may not know – may not ever experience.

But it is of some interest to see what adequately authoritative writers have written in the past about certain estates and vintages, even though tasting notes cannot be 'definitive' (the expression implies there is no more to be said) and, as one may gather from the dates of these notes, their samplings have been done in different places and over varying lengths of time. Wines change and can surprise even those who know them well, from when they are in their first stages of maturation to what they do when in bottle. It can, of course, be interesting to know what an owner or a broker says, when one is on the spot – but are such comments to be accepted as gospel? Perish the thought! If every reader of wine comments accepted the verdict of a few 'experts' – a word never used, as far as I am concerned, except sarcastically, for we are all beginners, none of us 'experts' – then the prices of certain wines would soar, those of others would sink and the auction rooms would have even more fine wines in which to trade, rather than ordinary customers be able to buy wine to enjoy drinking.

So I have not attempted lengthy descriptions of the wines of specific estates. This sort of writing may well be out of date by the time a book is published! Some generalisations are possible: for example, a vineyard where, for some years, there has been a preponderance of Merlot will be different from one where the Cabernet Sauvignon has dominated certain traditions existing over the years. Any changes due to rebuilding, alterations in the style of wine making followed, extensions to the winery, changes in ownership and direction may be indicated, but the reader and the taster must taste and form their own conclusions.

Generalisations about vintages are not easy as far as the Graves region is concerned, because of the size and the north/south extent of the area. A micro-climate may provide definite but unexpected exceptions to an over-all estimate of the climate of a particular area; changes, such as building – from Bordeaux in the north – construction of the autoroute, clearances of woods, any large-scale building operations, may all alter the statements the writer may have been prepared to make about a particular segment of terrain.

Those who read vintage reports on the Bordeaux area should bear in mind that, unless it is specified otherwise, these will usually refer mainly to the Médoc. Sometimes even the commentator may not be aware of how much this is so. But the Médoc is neither the Graves nor the 'across the river' vineyards and, within the Graves, vintage conditions may be different and the results markedly so. No other area within the Bordeaux vineyard and, indeed, few other regions of France produces such substantial quantities of fine wines both red and white, many of them made at the same estate; in some properties the white wines may be assumed usually to have the advantage over the reds, in some it is the other way round. Here, the Graves is far more akin to some of the New World wine properties, where fine reds and fine whites are made under the same ownership.

Yet, of course, a vintage that favours the production of white wines may not equally favour reds – the two require certain differences in climate and conditioning, however adroitly they may be made within the same property, even within the same set of buildings comprising the *cuvier*.

Finally, something that I must reiterate: growers and merchants agree with me that the wines of the Graves, both red and white, are not usually those that can be easily appreciated and understood by the novice in wine drinking. Some, of course, do make an immediate appeal – but this is not like the appeal of, say, many of the St Émilion or Pomerol or St Julien wines. Graves wines do not proclaim their superiority from the first sniff, yet it is this subtle style, well-bred reserve and underlying refinement that, to those who have been able to gain some experience of Bordeaux wines, can both astonish and please: the whites are notable for the way they can develop, the reds possess an individuality and charm that provide great pleasure as well as intellectual satisfaction. Both need to be approached with an open mind and explored without any thought that they may resemble others of the Bordeaux classics; they are not 'like' these, although most of us have mistaken them for others in blind tastings.

In the forthcoming pages, I give some of my own general impressions of Graves wines, white and red. Subsequently, I have selected some extracts from other writers, a few of them going a little back in history, because it is of interest to see what the nineteenth-century writers thought, some showing views of drinkers throughout the middle of the twentieth century whose opinions were not moulded by what their forebears had found in the wines and, also, those of contemporary writers for whom I have respect, even when I am not able to agree with them. The reader, who will also, I trust, be a taster, must make up his or her own mind. It is possibly helpful to indicate why some of the wines may fall short of what I have thought they might attain in quality. Even some of the great estates can show vintages and even wines that fall short of expectation; people who 'drink the label' may not notice or care, but it is worth bearing in mind that wines, like people, do not always realise their full potential. Throughout, I have tried to differentiate between wines that are smaller in scale and attainment than those bearing the great names, but this is not to say that such wines can contribute less in quality and pleasure than the more important and impressive ones.

DRY WHITE GRAVES

As regards colour, the dry white are pale, with what I usually think of as a 'lemony' tone colour. With age they darken, but nowadays only the slightly sweet versions have a tinge of gold to them, for care is taken by the makers that such wines do not give the impression to the drinker of being 'rich' – i.e. sweet. The finer whites have a delicate shaded range of tones, again veering always to the pale shades, deepening to a hint of gilt in the heart of the wine. 'Silvergilt' might be a description, or, occasionally, that of old, well-cleaned bronze, where the colour has assumed almost a liquid appearance.

Small-scale dry white Graves of definite character can provide

223

immediate pleasure, for casual drinking as well as with food. At their best, they have a moderate, fresh fragrance, which leads on to a straightforward, slightly full flavour, combining a definite, almost crisp dryness, with a suggestion of underlying softness. They should finish cleanly. Some attain length, leaving the palate toned-up and pleased.

The finest white Graves are, or can be, so different from this as, sometimes, to give the impression that they are the wines of a different region! Their pronounced, assertive bouquet may initially seem cool and fresh, but then wafts along, to unfurl a series of fragrances, varying from the slight steeliness of the Sauvignon Blanc to the softer firmness, warmth and honeyed allure as the Sémillon makes its presence felt. The complexity of this type of bouquet is very beguiling.

Then, as the wine makes its impression on the palate, the essential dryness is maintained, but the body of the wine is marked and important; given some age, fine dry white Graves can be very big in stature and, as the Sémillon takes over from the Sauvignon, the shape of the wine is pulled together, intensified, remaining taut and intense, but gaining in power while maintaining its original elegance. The dry finish has overtones of softness, without ever verging on the sweet and the cleanliness of a great wine in this category will astonish anyone expecting a decline in the after-taste, which is usually definite, lengthy, aristocratic to the last whisk of flavour.

Unfortunately, there are still some of the *petits vins* in the dry white category that are far too *petit*: they prove dull, flat beverages, lacking in bouquet, a fault common to many slovenly made wines and that should not appear in wines above the 'ordinary' ranks. If there is an initial attack of an aroma, it can convey a sogginess and the taste is nondescript – few would be able to trace the locality of the wine or the grapes within it. Sometimes, too, wines that even their makers have hoped might attain finer quality may disappoint by being unbalanced: an apparently definite bouquet may trail away, the wine leave only an indeterminate impression on the palate and finish abruptly, almost sharply, without grace. If you encounter such a wine, give it the benefit of the doubt – and try it again at some other time and, maybe, from some other retail source. And certainly reappraise it after an interval, when any prejudices may be abandoned or forgotten.

SLIGHTLY SWEETER WHITE GRAVES

Sometimes these give the impression of being or about to be sweeter than they finish – and, for the sensitive drinker, they can be a revelation. It is always possible for even a modest wine to 'turn round in the mouth' and this is the type of Graves that may do so. The colour need not be a definite guide to sweetness or dryness although, of course, it can indicate some age. The initial whiff of fragrance can be full, it should not be merely sweet or just a waft of something sugary, but rather an indication of warmth and slight softness. The impact on the palate can be straightforward but, after an almost crisp initial sensation, it can become moderately full and fruity, though never too much to be unbalanced or a wine unsuited to serving with food. (If a bone-dry aperitif wine has not been served before a meal, then this is the sort of very slightly sweet white that can charm preprandially and go on to sustain its impact with sensitively selected first courses that are not too strident in taste.)

SMALL-SCALE RED GRAVES

Those from the southern part of the region must, if possible, be appraised as being different from those in the middle of the Graves vineyard and, certainly, from those in the north, near to Bordeaux. It should be understood that, even if some millionaire bought an estate, poured money into it and employed the services of renowned wine makers and technicians regardless, that estate would be unlikely soon to rival or surpass those of the established reputations, notably those in the north. Wine growers and wine makers have to think in decades. Certain of the processes of nature cannot be speeded up, even in this technically orientated age. The maturity of a vineyard is requisite for the production of certain quality and, as many marketing departments seem unable to understand, it is not possible to churn out wine year after year, obtaining better results (but who decides they are 'better'?) with each vintage.

Anyone who, today, sees a red Graves from a possibly as yet unknown listed estate, stands a very good chance of getting a reasonably priced wine agreeably typical of both the Graves region and the overall Bordeaux vineyard; it will be well made, so as to give pleasure to the drinker and, even if it cannot improve dramatically with long-term keeping, it can

225

develop pleasingly in bottle.

There is a place for small-scale wines in every wine region – one cannot frequently and casually quaff a great growth, which requires discrimination in choice and informed care in handling. The smaller-scale wines also need serving with care, but they may be chosen for drinking on a variety of occasions, casual and semi-formal, to accompany a variety of foods, and they do not demand a great deal of concentration and attention from the drinker. This is what they are intended for. If, sometimes, one provides additional enjoyment, to the mind as well as the senses, this is a pleasure and should be a reminder to note the progress of what is being made at the particular property involved.

However well they are kept, small-scale wines have shorter lives and are usually ready to drink before the 'big stuff'. In the red Graves, it is usually pleasant to note the fairly deep colour most of them possess, a definite shade of blackcurrant juice. The bouquet is moderately assertive, somewhat aromatic, with the occasional whiff of spice. On the palate the fruit is usually initially noticeable, the red Graves have what I term a 'plump' rounded style; one squeezes the wine in the mouth. Then there is often a slightly drier flavour and aroma, as the wine leaves the palate. When the vintage is somewhat thin, lacking in body, there can be a touch of harshness and, from this type of year, the red Graves do not show to advantage without some form of food – they seem to crave for something to round them out on the palate.

FINE RED GRAVES

The variety of colours, aromas, flavours is very great among the top wines of this region. Many compare them continually with the wines of the Médoc, but, although I have some knowledge of the latter, I find I do not do so – the finest red Graves are neither better nor inferior to the Médocs, but *different*. Sometimes, as we all do, I have confused a great red Graves with a Médoc and then I am feeling around in Pauillac, or, occasionally, in Pomerol, because the touch of firmness, verging on hardness, underlying the main flavour seems, to me, often difficult to distinguish from the gravelliness of the Graves (and there is a streak of gravel in the Pomerol vineyard too). It is significant that many authorities on Médoc wines, including numerous estate owners, have a particular liking for the great red Graves – maybe because they are indeed essentially different. The colour at the outset can be very dark indeed – 'black plum' is what I sometimes note. The bouquet has evoked many adjectives, including spiciness, acacia and, often, blackcurrant or cassis (the blackcurrant liqueur). In many years there may be an aroma of warmth, almost exotic, very charming and alluring.

On the palate the individuality of the particular estate will, of course, predominate, but most of these wines are what I often describe as close-packed in texture, which makes them fascinating to discuss. The fruit some-times appears very intense, notably in the young wines, but underneath there is always the lightness, elegance and firmness of the gravel below the more obvious top tastes. Years ago I used to think that I could register an underlying cool, stony flavour, as when one sucks a pebble, but although this still can be traced in certain wines, the greater reds have a concentration, almost a sweetness that forms a layer over this dryness.

They trail gracefully away, like many fine clarets, often with an addi-tional whiff of spiciness – which sometimes seems like nutmeg to me – in the after-taste. With age, the elegant charm emerges gratifyingly. Great red Graves can be big wines without being 'meaty' or overwhelmingly sub-stantial; this, perhaps, is another of the attributes that make them elusive for the beginner to appreciate, but it is a characteristic that makes them excellent partners for simple but subtly flavoured foods and for meat and poultry dishes where the ingredients are of the finest.

Wines in the lower ranges of the red Graves that do not, for various reasons, justify the foregoing praise, may, in my experience, give an impres-sion of plainness; there may be a whiff of something in the bouquet that does not lead on to anything else – promise, not performance and, even, a vulgarity. Sometimes I have noted too great an emphasis on the Cabernet Sauvignon, which I personally tend to find hard, even aggressive unless the wine is very carefully made. Among the 'little' red Graves, the impres-sion I usually get when these are less successful is that they lack fruit – as this can be one of the great charms of the region's wines, anything sug-gesting leanness or stringiness is undesirable. Unfortunately, some wines are, still, just dull. There is also a flat, heavy, almost earthy taste which I do not think should be there – it suggests a vineyard on a clay soil, not gravel. A too short finish is another failing sometimes. Makers can produce admirable small-scale wines in the Graves but not all of them have yet been able to learn from the experience of others and make the most use of the resources of modern technology. Understandably, some of those concerned with the finer wines exercise caution, but occasionally this seems to have been carried to an extreme and results in a wine that lacks plumpness and fruit.

In general, both white and red Graves seem most successful when the makers have been content to let the wines 'do their own thing' and have not attempted to over-stress the soft, rotund opulence that can be so alluring in the reds but which, if exaggerated, can result in earthiness and coarseness. The white wines should be neither shrill, bone-dry characterless tipples, nor heavy beverages, lacking in the *nervosité* resulting from a correct balance of acidity and fruit. Too much obvious wood, too great an attempt at 'modernity' via crispness, too much emphasis on the Cabernet Sauvignon and the initial impression that the wine may make – these are traits that the affectionate outsider can, I trust, mention without giving offence, but which it is only for those immediately involved to correct. It is pointless to make a cheap commercially acceptable wine that might come from anywhere – I have noticed this trend in certain low-price Riojas and Italian white and red wines, when technology, urged on by marketing expertise, takes over from informed wine making and observance of traditions, while being mindful of progress in both vineyard and winery. In suggesting some of the defects that may be encountered in Graves wines my attention has been to alert the reader to basing any critical comment on what is good, in all ranges, whether the wine is liked or not, and to adopt a positive approach. It is always so easy to denounce what may seem 'bad', though quite often an attitude to wine that has benefited from a perspective and affectionate interest in the whole subject can not only detect the defect but also the reason why it may have come to the fore in a particular example. The quality that, hardly noticed, may lurk within the wine can then be sought out.

Of course, these remarks about Graves wines are generally true when applied to the wines of many other regions. The appraisal of all wines is subject to certain procedures accepted as guides. With a wine region enjoying the history and great traditions of the Graves, however, the approach should, I think, be open-minded but reinforced by all the experience and knowledge that it is possible to bring to the study of the wines. There are some magnificent wines, there are some that are currently perhaps not as good as they might be. Just as it is right to admire the former, so it is wise to watch and reserve judgement on the latter.

In the following extracts, arranged chronologically, it should be remembered that the wines being described would, in many instances, have been made differently from the wines of today. The writers, too, may have adopted a different attitude – more general and eloquent – than the widely experienced and often technically qualified contemporary wine writers. Some of the latter are members of the wine trade, which also conditions their reactions.

Vins de Graves by Charles de Lorbac (1866). (My translation.)
Less fragrant than the wines of the Médoc, those of the Graves are generous or, in Bordeaux jargon, full-flavoured, ample, fleshy, able to be kept for a long while and possessing much vivaciousness. Already, in 1824, in the first edition of the treatise on the Gironde wines, W. Franck thought that 'The delicate Graves wines are, usually, both higher in alcohol and deeper in colour than those of the Médoc, although the latter tend to be preferred for their bouquet and their taste.' The life of Graves wines is amazing – often when twenty years old they have lost nothing of their prime quality.

Claret and the White Wines of Bordeaux by Maurice Healy (1934)
When one excludes the Sauternes, it is fair to say that the white wines of Bordeaux are as far beneath the white wines of Burgundy as the average red wines of Burgundy are below the average red wines of Bordeaux. I cannot understand how so much good land, well suited to the growing of a red wine, should be given up to this white stuff.

Natural Red Wines by H. Warner Allen (1951)
The Graves wines are remarkable for their brilliant colour, their breed and a certain austere majesty in their finesse. They are generally more impressive than the Médocs, but to my mind they just lack an indefinable delicacy of charm, an elusive magic, no doubt a very tiny, almost imponderable quality, but none the less so attractive, which is the exclusive property of the Médoc Clarets. They cannot quite equal the balance of Médoc at its best, but they are apt to be fuller-bodied and at their finest excel in dignity and splendour. They are rather awe-inspiring than lovable. Mr Healy, with this taste for Burgundy, inclines towards Graves as the great wine. It is the less noticeable difference of soil that makes Médoc such silky, gracious wine, and

red Graves such noble warriors – the distinction always seeming to me like that between glossy and matt prints of photographs.

It is usually said that the Graves wines are longer lived and, in *The Wines of France* I repeated this common judgement. Further experience makes me doubt whether it is well-founded. The pre-phylloxera Haut-Brions certainly run with their rivals of the first growths, but I know of no conspicuous instances in which the less famous Graves growths have outlived their opposite numbers in the Médoc.... There are certain years, usually not the greatest, when the Graves wines in general show more successful vintages than the Médoc; 1914 and 1923 are cases in point, and the Saint-Émilions not infrequently follow their lead.

White Wines and Cognac by H. Warner Allen (1952)

A word must be said as to the white wines of Graves, which, if they are not overloaded with sulphur and glycerine, may be dry, distinguished and pleasantly perfumed. There are no great white Graves that can be compared with such red Graves as Haut Brion or Pape Clément, though there are some outstanding growths; and the greater part of the white wine drunk from this district consists of wines blended from various vineyards.

Guide to the Wines and Vineyards of France by Alexis Lichine (revised edition, 1986)

... the best of the Graves and the best of the Médocs will have recognisably similar features, but they are by no means twins. If the Médocs ... are more feminine and delicate, the Graves have more body, a distinct character and a pleasing earthiness.

The Wine Book by Jancis Robinson (1979)

Red Graves are noticeably different from Médoc in their texture which is to some 'stoney', to others 'sandy', and when young they are perhaps less fruity than their counterparts from the Médoc ... the very best dry white Bordeaux comes from the Graves region and can be heaven, full-bodied dry wines that are capable of ageing and of standing up to rich food.

The Great Vintage Wine Book by Michael Broadbent M.W. (1980)

White Graves vary from almost bone dry to medium dry. The best keep well; the very best need bottle-age – the longer the better. The style depends on the balance of Sémillon and Sauvignon Blanc. The former, more yellow, soft and buttery (always reminds me of lanolin) on the nose and broader on the palate, gives it its main Graves character; the Sauvignon Blanc, a crisper, fruitier, more acidic grape, gives it its refreshing quality. I probably stand alone in deploring the overuse of this grape and the smart modern wine making which is turning so many Bordeaux whites into pale imitations of Sancerre, but perhaps they *are* an improvement on the carelessly-made, flabby and over-sulphured Graves and near-Graves of the past.

The Wines of Bordeaux by Edmund Penning-Rowsell (5th edition, 1985)

The sale of red Graves, even that of some of the classified growths, has never been easy, with the result, of course, that the vineyards have not been so well looked after, the wine not so well made, as would have been the case if the financial return had been better. In recent years however this has to some extent changed.

Wine Factfinder and Taste Guide by Oz Clarke (1985)

The description 'earthy' which is often applied is a fair one for many of the wines, because there is an indistinct, dry backbone to the fruit which stops them being razor-sharp in their flavour definitions as the great Médocs often are. Yet they do often have the blackcurrant and cedar flavours of the Médoc, as well as having a little of the full, plummy roundness of Pomerol. For blind winetasters they are an endless tease, and frequently the rule followed is – if it seems like a Médoc but not quite, and yet seems like Pomerol, but not quite – plump for Graves. . . . There has been a rush to uproot Sémillon and replant with the more fashionable Sauvignon, but with a couple of exceptions like Malartic-Lagravière and Couhins-Lurton, Sauvignon doesn't perform at its best by itself in Bordeaux, often giving a rather muddy, tough wine. Sémillon, on the other hand, is well suited to the area, and gives a big, round wine, slightly creamy but with a lovely aroma of fresh apples which is very exciting. Ideally, the two should be blended with Sémillon the dominant variety. White Graves is still often a dull wine, but if it is fermented at a low temperature, and if new oak barrels are used ... the result is a wonderful soft, nutty, dry white, often going honeyed and smoky as it ages.

Great Bordeaux Wines by James Seely (1986)
Red Graves varies in style with the differing soil types and *encépagements* of its widespread area; it is possibly more Médocain in style than anything else, especially in the northern, gravelly vineyards of Talence and Pessac.... White Graves, to the uninitiated, equates with indifferent quality, medium-dry wine produced in large quantities.... The super, delicate dry white with its marvellous ageing quality that is made at the Grand Cru properties, both northern and southern, is quite a different ball-game.

Bordeaux, the Definitive Guide by Robert Parker (1986)
The top whites of this region are rare and expensive, and in a few cases capable of rivalling the finest white wines produced in France.... However, the greatest wines of Graves are its red wines.... For the great red wines of Graves, their personality traits are quite individualistic and unique, and not difficult to decipher when tasted blind in a tasting with Médoc wines. While top wines such as Haut Brion and La Mission Haut Brion differ considerably in style, they do share a rich, earthy, almost tobacco-scented character, which seems to taste like a blend of a great St Émilion from the 'graves' section of that appellation, and a great Pauillac, with a toasted, smoky component added for additional complexity.

The Académie du Vin Guide to French Wines by Steven Spurrier (1986)
The white, with almost no demi-sec made these days, is at its finest in the north, where certain *crus classés* make an extremely fine wine that is a little understated at first and repays ageing, while the wines south of Léognan can be elegant and fruity, but are less interesting and may be drunk young. Red Graves have the same clean, dense fruit as a Médoc, a similar austerity when young and a soft charm with sometimes a hint of roses in the bouquet. They are perhaps less striking than the grand Médocs, come round a little earlier, but are their equal in finesse.

17

CLASSIFICATION

THE 'MOST DELICATE' QUESTION

THE significance and the implications of this word 'classification' as related to the wines of Bordeaux is not as widely understood as might be expected, even among those who are devoted to the wines. The term *cru classé* or 'classed growth' is, unfortunately, not precisely defined – although most Bordeaux lovers understand what they mean when they use the phrase. Even some books are vague on the subject – for there is far more behind the term than the famous 1855 classification, to which many only refer. For anyone concerned with the Graves wines the subject of classification or, as it might also be termed, categorisation, is a sensitive one: at the time of writing a major change may soon be introduced in the local legislation. So it seems wise to clarify what the term means and how it is used today.

From early times vineyards in the south-west of France were subject to strict controls. In his *Petite Histoire de Bordeaux et son vignoble*, Pierre Andrieu (1952) notes that everything planted by smallholders – fruits as well as vines – was subject to the approval of the overall owner, whether an overlord or the local civic authority. In 1898 historian Roger Grand pointed out that permission to undertake cultivation on any specific site had been subject to the landlord – whoever this might be – receiving a type of tithe or royalty; this could vary from as little as one-eighth to as much as one-half of the resultant harvest, although the more usual proportion was between one-quarter and one-third. The landlord was entitled to survey the plantation and, if it were allowed to deteriorate, he could, in theory, eject the tenant; this, however, was something that did not – because it could not – apply to a vineyard, which had to be kept going indefinitely and might vary, in both yield and appearance, from year to year.

There is a record of how, in December 1419, Arnold Arros, who held some plots of land in the Graves from the Chapter of Saint Seurin in Bordeaux wanted to pull up all the wheat and other crops in his holdings and devote the entire area to vines. Arros didn't bind himself to observe the official *ban* or proclamation as to when the vintage might start, but he did agree to the 'royalties' that were required of him and engaged himself to call in the official *gardes-vignes* when he wished to begin picking. These *gardes-vignes* are the ancestors of today's inspectors and, says a contemporary account, were types of policemen who were also instructors, sent by the landlord to oversee the harvest, both so that there should be no risk of a tenant defrauding his landlord and, also, so that, if there should be some problem occurring at the time, they could advise and help the small-holder. Throughout the centuries the *gardes-vignes* were employed and, by 1766, there are mentions of *gardes-femmes* – were these ladies officials or merely employees of the landlord sent round to keep an eye on what went on at vintage time?

It is significant, in view of the importance in today's economy of even quite small-scale vineyard owners, to realise that, in the past, the *vigneron* was not just a mere peasant farmer; he had more status. The controls exercised over vineyards were, of course, also applied to their owners or tenants, but the position of anyone actively running even a small vineyard was of substance, he was not a mere serf. The *gardes-vignes* had to be fed while engaged in their work and their rations were specified: bread, wine, eggs and cheese, or else bread, wine, beef or goat meat; sometimes they seem to have preferred to be paid in money and then, presumably, they brought their own picnic lunch. It is a forerunner of the admirable *cuisines des vendangeurs* where the pickers and, sometimes, favoured house guests eat at vintage time these days.

Other officials engaged in the world of wine were the *Courretiers* or *courtiers*, a term translated nowadays as 'brokers'. Theirs, too, is an ancient rôle, likewise subject to controls. As early as 1414 a decree prohibited them from taking any samples of wine – anybody who was found doing so was to be beaten. This was doubtless to prevent them asking for endless 'samples', which they would either have used up themselves or offered for re-sale. They came into prominence as an organisation after the departure of the English and when, in 1554, a stern order was given forbidding any English from coming to the Gironde to buy wine and from circulating in the vineyards independently; then the *courtiers* gained enormously in importance and influence for, says a sixteenth-century writer, they were 'mainly established to escort the English in the Graves' and most of them spoke English. (By this time the English wine buyer might have been rusty when speaking Gascon or even French.) The way in which the Bordelais kept protective controls over their wine was detailed – in 1662 they even forbade any brewing of beer in the region, for fear that this might cause a drop in wine consumption!

So it will be appreciated that the tradition of 'arranging' the wines into different categories, regulating each of these and regulating the adaptations and evolutions of the controls, is nothing new. The overall organisation of the great Bordeaux vineyard, notably the Graves, is impressive, detailed, with a long history, worked out over many centuries. So, before the reader attempts to understand what is happening today about the classification and associated regulations, it is wise to clear the mind of previous thoughts on the subject – and to remember that *un cru classé* is not the same thing as a 'classy growth'. (Incidentally, the use of the circumflex accent on *cru*, seen in some past English writings on the subject, is not correct for the word employed in this context. The noun *cru* should not be confused with the past participle of the verb *croître* – to grow, although it is easy to see why this often occurs.)

The *Shorter Oxford English Dictionary* defines 'Classification' as '1. The action of classifying. 2. The result of classifying; a systematic distribution or arrangement in a class or classes 1794.' *Collins English Dictionary* gives what may be a more definite description – 'Systematic placement in categories.' The translation of *classé* is, of course, 'classed' – but the word 'class' in English today has overtones of at least implied quality, superiority, in one way or another; used by itself, the term is of praise – if anything pejorative is intended, there will be a prefix, e.g. low class. Because it can sometimes be helpful to evolve a precise understanding of a term by translating it, I suggest that the word 'category' and 'categorisation' can have more immediacy in certain contexts than 'classed'.

Here, only the wines of the Graves are being considered, but the overall history of the various classifications of the wines of the different regions of Bordeaux, as admirably documented in Edmund Penning-Rowsell's book *The Wines of Bordeaux* (1985), should be referred to. The classed growths of Bordeaux are of prime importance to those who, these days, make fine wine a commodity for investment rather than drinking – or, even, for bequeathing to one's heirs – and there is not much space devoted in even the specialist publications on wine in the United States to non-classified wines, when someone writes about 'collectables'. I have to admit an intense dislike of those who flaunt the great names of wines as status symbols and also of those who buy only for future profit rather than drinking – to me, this is like trading in flesh. It takes the fun, the social pleasure and the often humbling experience of wine discoveries out of the occupation which, to me, can be serious, but should never be solemn.

It cannot be denied, however, that anyone who sees the terms 'classed growth', *cru classé*, 'classified growth' on a label will have their attention tweaked towards feeling that, somehow, this so-described wine must have something that puts it above others. This is bound to affect those who consult wine articles advising on 'What to buy', if such words are repeated in the copy. Yet people who see these words on a wine's label may, quite reasonably, suppose that, if the phrase is augmented by 'second growth', 'third growth' or *premier grand cru classé*, these relate directly to established opinion as to the quality of the wine; it is logical to think that a wine that is in some way rated 'first' is somehow 'better' than one rated 'second' or 'third'.

The influential American writer Robert Parker has permitted his publishers to print the description 'the definitive guide' on his book *Bordeaux* (1986). As 'definitive' has the dictionary meaning 'the final word', I hope that this is not true. But Mr Parker also confuses categories within a classification and seems to assume that they relate directly and currently to quality. Many, within and without the wine trade, have attempted personal 'classification' of Bordeaux (and, even, Burgundy) wines, arousing fury in those concerned and wry amusement in others. Such personal categorisations must be merely personal, transient, conditioned by the character or experience of those who compose them. For example, Robert Parker, in writing about the red Graves, puts in his assessment – not, please note, classification – La Mission Haut Brion as 'outstanding'; then he places Haut Brion, as 'excellent', then La Tour Haut Brion, and only then come Domaine de Chevalier, Haut Bailly, Pape Clément and La Louvière, together with other well-known properties, including some that are officially 'classed growths'.

Every wine lover is entitled to his or her opinion as to what is 'top', 'great', 'fine' and so on. Many like to have their drinking and buying guided this way. But what has this to do with 'classification' in the defined significance of the word?

As early as 1647 the Jurade de Bordeaux, with the aim of establishing the prices of the wines, made out a list of seventeen sub-regions within the overall vineyard, all of which were then known to make good wine.

The Graves was at the top of this list. In Penning-Rowsell's account the author states that 'some sort of classification existed by the mid-eighteenth century is shown by the fact that there was a fixed scale of prices for all the growths in each class, with an equal step between each'. He mentions a reference by André Simon in *Bottlescrew Days* (1926) in which there are cited three main categories of red wine – 'The first comprises the growths of Pontac, Lafitte, and Château de Margo.' Then there are listed many 'second-class growths', both these categories being exported to various countries, the English buying a large proportion of the wines in the first group, the wines in the third category going to northern France and then the *Palus* wines, which were not 'classified'. In the middle of the eighteenth century two reports were prepared by the Bordeaux Chamber of Commerce the parishes where the wines of Bordeaux are made and their different prices. Pontac – Haut Brion – was included in this with its high price, equal to other 'first growths' as we know them today. Penning-Rowsell notes that, with other growths of the Graves in this rating, the 'low prices for the Graves demonstrate their comparative obscurity in the eighteenth century'.

Clive Coates M.W., in No. 34 of his personal and meticulously researched bulletin *The Vine*, gives a list cited from Professor Pijassou's *Le Médoc* from the archives of Tastet and Lawton, established in 1740; Pijassou 'has established a classification based on the average prices in livres tournois per tonneau en primeur from 1741–74'. Head of this list is Haut Brion, and Clive adds that, although he doesn't know whether Tastet and Lawton dealt in Graves wines, 'the absence of any other Graves is significant. The explanation is perhaps that the next three top estates after Haut Brion which remain today were all in ecclesiastical hands: La Mission Haut Brion, Pape Clément and Carbonnieux. The other main Léognan properties: Chevalier, Haut Bailly, Malartic-Lagravière and de Fieuzal, were not constituted until the 19th century.' He refers to the 1762 sale of Carbonnieux wines (see p. 263) but 'This, however, could have been a white wine.' My own comment on the Tastet and Lawton list is that the 'Pontac', which comes in sixteenth place and to which there is a bracketed query after 'Margaux', might have been a blend of the wines from the Pontac properties. The use of other wines under the same proprietorship, often made in the same winery as the *grand vin* and matured in the same place, makes it still debatable whether such a wine is entitled to stand on its own, whether at least some of it may be used as a 'topping wine' (see p. 139) or whether it is a blend and/or brand produced under the aegis of a reputable establishment, possibly enjoying the vicarious advantages of its kinship to a more famous name.

Clive mentions my dear friend, the late Ronald Barton, as having supplied him with classifications dated 1824 and 1927, which, respectively, are the same as the Simon classification previously cited and the classification of Wilhelm Franck's first edition.

A classification made in 1767 gave the prices according to the communes, the red Graves and the Médoc wines being divided into three categories. The wines coming into the 'first' section of these classifications were owned by well-to-do families, many of whose members belonged to the Bordeaux Parlement. Naturally, they would have said, their wines were of fine quality – they got the top prices, didn't they? In the period before long-term maturation in bottle and in the absence of detailed tasting notes, quality was, understandably, equated with price. The 'noblesse de bouchon' would also have assumed that their particular wines were fine wines as a matter of course – and gratifyingly remunerative when put on sale.

As far as the Graves wines were concerned, this 1767 classification divided them into the following categories:

Graves rouges
1er *crus*: Pessac, Mérignac; 2ème: Talence, Loignan [*sic*], Gradignan, Caudeyrans, Begles [*sic*]; 3ème: Poudensac [*sic*], Virelade, Portets, Castres, Arbanats, Beautiran, Aiguemortes, Eyran, Cadaujac, Le Bouscat, Canéjean, Eysines

Graves blanches
Barsac, Preignac, Longon, Sauternes, Cerons [*sic*], Bommes, Pujols, Blanquefort, Gradignan, Poudensac [*sic*]

In May 1787 Thomas Jefferson, the U.S. Commissioner and Minister in France, went to Bordeaux and recorded various purchases of estates 'of first quality'; he bought and sent to a relation back home six dozen 'of what is the very best Bordeaux wine. It is of the vineyard of Obrion, one of the four established there as the very best, and it is of the vintage of 1784, the only very fine one since the year 1779.' (More about Haut Brion is to be found on pp 272–8.)

In 1824 Wilhelm Franck wrote a *Traité sur les vins du Médoc* and, as it is thought that, certainly up to this time, the Graves and the Médoc were thought of as a single vineyard region, it is significant that the Graves parishes of Pessac, Mérignac, Caudéran, Taillan, Blanquefort, Léognan and Gradignan are listed here: Haut Brion is listed as a Pessac first growth, then come La Mission, Savignac, two third growths and three fourth growths. The white wines Franck lists are Haut-Preignac, Haut Barsac, Sauternes, fetching high prices in 1825, less in 1826; after these Franck lists Bas Preignac, Bas Barsac and, finally, Cérons, Ste-Croix, Dumont [*sic*], Loupiac, and St-Pey, Langon, Fargues, Virelade, Landiras and others. Franck was well aware of the difficulties in his *Traité*. It was in the preamble to the second edition (1845) that he notes, 'Now we arrive at the most delicate section of our work.' Though Haut Brion was not only then rated with the first growths (Lafite, Latour, Margaux) but the price was also equal to that of Château Margaux, although Lafite was higher. Franck 'classified' the wines – as Clive Coates comments, 'This was the last important independent list before the "official" assessment of 1855' – and then he added 'Bon Bourgeois' as another category. But this did not include any Graves.

Penning-Rowsell observes that this statement is still true, 'for while there are many who say that the classification is irrelevant, meaningless or outdated, it is a factor still to be taken into consideration in any survey of Bordeaux . . . it still counts for something'.

As will have been seen, it was always the prices of the wines, maintained and likely to be maintained, that originally determined the 'classing' or categorisation. In a classification of some sort made in 1848 La Mission Haut Brion was rated a 'second fourth', a category that eventually became the fifth. In 1855, what is now 'the' classification was made.

This was prepared for the Exposition Universelle, in Paris, made by the brokers of Bordeaux and then approved by the Bordeaux Chamber of Commerce. Again, it was based on prices that the wines were likely to attain and, for various reasons, some since-famous estates were not included: some had been broken up at the time of the Revolution and not rehabilitated, others had gone through difficulties that, at least for a while, affected both the quality of the wines and the demand for them, certainly in the 1848 'year of revolutions'. Some wines were not even tasted by those compiling the list! But the white wines of Sauternes and Barsac were classified and so were sixty red wines of the Médoc and the red Graves, Haut Brion.

Penning-Rowsell comments that the inclusion of the latter might be due to the 'old boy network' among the Chartronnais, but I think that it would have been simply impossible to leave out Haut Brion, already famous in export markets, owing much to the past work of the Pontacs in general in Bordeaux – and, of course, maintaining a price on the same level as the sought-after growths of the Médoc.

The English, still retaining their love of claret, had commented on the classification system before 1855. In *A History of Ancient and Modern Wines* in 1824, the author, A. L. Henderson, divides his list into five sections, according to price. By 1862, T. G. Shaw, in *Wine, the Vine and the Cellar* and Charles Tovey, in *Wine and Wine Countries*, both devote a fair amount of space to the 1855 classification. Shaw, who was concerned with the practicalities of wine making and the care of wine once made, comments, 'It would be much better if no names were mentioned, as they are rarely to be relied upon, and often mislead; for, not infrequently, what are considered second growths prove superior in some years to those of high repute.' He also comments, 'The Vins de Graves are also favourites, though not equal to the Médocs.' Tovey quotes extensively from a Monsieur Rabache, of Bordeaux, who had written *A Key to the thorough knowledge of the Vineyards and Wines of Bordeaux*, and he remarks admiringly, 'We have met with nothing equal to this work for truthfulness and care in compilation' and he says that Rabache's text is 'the most recent and intelligible of all similar publications', after respectfully naming 'M. Julien, Count Chaptal, M. Guestier'.

Rabache says that 'If our forefathers were less advanced than we are in knowledge of the sciences, they were perhaps better observers . . . our ancestors very wisely observed that the produce of the vine was not alike in every place, and that, even in a village, wines of different qualities were produced. They also remarked that the wines produced by the same proprietor on a particular soil were every year of qualities, relatively either superior or inferior to others. They therefore found it necessary to classify the vineyards according to the quality of the wines regularly produced by each particular plot of ground. Hence the distinction of crûs [*sic*], or growths.' Rabache, too, notes that it is possible to have a first-growth wine that is made from inferior fruit or simply has been badly handled, whereas when 'a second or a third growth has been made in perfection in all respects, the inferior growth will produce a wine superior to that of the superior estate. This is one of the reasons why very few wine merchants sell their wines by number 1, 2, 3, 4, instead of naming the growth. Another reason is that, sometimes, wines of peculiar growths are ordered of a merchant, who, having none of them, in order not to own it, prefers sending No. 1 or 2, which may be this, that, or the other.'

It is pertinent here to insert Rabache's comment, quoted by Tovey, that 'The Grave [sic] White Wines have never been classified, but the Château Carbonnieux, at Villenave d'Ornon, is celebrated for a particular séve (sap) [sic], and bouquet which makes it resemble Rhenish Wine. The other growths do not deserve any particular notice.'

Although wine commentators fairly point out the importance of not accepting the 1855 classification as an ultimate verdict on quality, it is obvious that the name of an estate that is classed or categorised as 'second' or 'third' will, in the minds of most potential purchasers, seem to be at least likely to be higher in quality than an estate marked 'fourth' or 'fifth'. Not many people will weigh up the different regions that may be involved, nor will they always be aware of the variable climatic conditions that may, in a particular year, affect one wine adversely or favourably against another. Yet it is, I think, impossible to pin down fine wines into rigid categories, just as it is impossible to say of a human being that, because of coming from such a family, being educated in a particular place, trained in a certain way, achieving material success, he or she *ought* to be superior or inferior to anyone else. And, when appraising wines, some personal preferences must often blur any attempt at an objective assessment. It is to be noted, too, that it is not obligatory for an estate to specify its classification on the label of the wine. Some do, some don't.

The history of Bordeaux classifications must, here, be restricted to those that concern the Graves. In 1943 the then Vichy Government of France ordered another attempt at classification to be made of Bordeaux wines and many of the great red Graves were now included. They were classified in 1953 as follows:

Pessac
Ch. Haut Brion
Ch. Pape Clément
Talence
Ch. La Mission Haut Brion
Ch. Latour Haut Brion

Martillac
Ch. La Tour Martillac
Ch. Smith-Haut-Lafitte
Cadaujac
Ch. Bouscaut
Léognan
Ch. Haut Bailly
Ch. Carbonnieux
Domaine de Chevalier
Ch. Fieuzal
Ch. Olivier
Ch. Malartic-Lagravière
This classification was confirmed in 1959. It will be noted that the wines
are not sub-divided into categories but solely by their regions.

The white wines were classified in 1959:
Léognan
Ch. Carbonnieux
Domaine de Chevalier
Ch. Olivier
Ch. Malartic-Lagravière
Cadaujac
Ch. Bouscaut
Martillac
Ch. La Tour Martillac
Talence
Ch. Laville Haut Brion
Villenave-d'Ornon
Ch. Couhins
Pessac
Ch. Haut Brion
Haut Brion Blanc was not included in this classification at the request of
the proprietor.

From time to time suggestions for reclassifying the wines of various sections
of the Bordeaux vineyard are put forward; Alexis Lichine boldly attempted
this in 1959 – and discussion is still animated about his proposals! His
wish to revise the 1855 was practical – he has pointed out the way in which
estates classed as second, third and so on, are at a disadvantage and he

proposed categories of: *Crus Hors Classe, Crus Exceptionnels, Grands Crus, Crus Supérieurs, Bons Crus*. But as yet such a major change has not been made, although it is my opinion that some alterations in the existing scheme of things may very well involve the Graves, which is such a diverse region in so many ways, with previously virtually unknown properties now evolving both quality and the sort of individuality that can excite interest in export markets.

A pertinent comment by my young colleague, Oz Clarke (in *Webster's Wine Guide, 1988*, Webster/Mitchell Beazley), should be regularly recalled to those obsessed with the authority or otherwise of the 1855 classification. He says, 'An interesting point to note is that the *wine name* was classified, *not* the vineyard it came from. Some of the vineyards that make up a wine are now completely different . . . yet, because the "brand name", expressed as "Château" this or that, got into the lists, the level of classification remains.' The splitting up of sections of a vineyard that might come into the owner's possession by marriage or purchase could mean – in some instances it probably still does mean – that an 'estate' is composed of several different sections of land, some of which may be quite separate and even distant from others, including the 'house', château or simply the winery. Plans of vineyards of a century ago show considerable parcelling out. Although it is obviously advantageous to have a property all in one piece, marked off from its neighbours or the surrounding countryside, there can be instances when one holding is particularly valuable – and it doesn't matter to the owner that it may be apart from the main holding. There is at least one instance in the Médoc when the name of a classed growth disappeared for some years; another famous classed growth in fact owned some of the territory that had previously been the other vineyard, but did not make the wine. Some short time ago the name and the sections of what had been the former vineyard were bought by yet another proprietor, who will, I suppose, now begin to produce wine fully entitled to bear a once-famous name. One cannot, however, surround every estate with a neat wall or fence and there still exist strips of vineyard belonging to the owner of a *very* great estate that are actually in another commune! The regulations are 'adjusted' to enable such anomalies to be ironed out, but it must be stressed that it is the *name* of an estate that was classified in 1855, not every square metre of a particular section of vineyard.

Recently, I have even heard suggestions that it would be easier for the general public to understand the concept of classification if all Bordeaux wines were put into one huge classification anyway. Somebody has, I believe, put forward the notion that a classification of *all the wines of France* should be attempted.... This sort of thing should, in my opinion, come rather low in the priorities of those who wish to increase the love and knowledge of wine. Would anyone be able to compile or read such a list?

But, in order to understand what has motivated classifications of wines, it is fair to sketch some of the initial difficulties that face anybody trying to 'tidy up' or simplify the numerous existing lists, for the overall benefit of the lover of wine.

In beginning to 'classify' or categorise, the following are matters to ponder: should an estate that is all in one piece be compared with another consisting of different plots, some of them widely separated? (This bears on other aspects of wine legislation also.) Is it possible to categorise wines that, quite legally, may bear the same area name but may have been made from sections of a vineyard split between numerous owners? (As happens in a number of regions.) Can any categorisation differentiate between the wines grown or at least supervised by a single estate owner and made in his winery, and those composed from wines purchased from an assortment of growers and also 'finished wines' made by other makers, for the purpose of blending? (This, too, happens in many regions.) What about wines made from grapes grown on a specific estate, the property of one firm or owner, and those put out under the same firm's label that have been made from 'contract grapes', bought in from another plot – albeit within the same defined region? There are many instances of this happening in France and elsewhere.

Then, how can one category or 'class' be named without another one seeming of lesser quality? Is there any point in sticking the tag 'Outstanding' on one list of wines, when other sections in this classification may be headed 'Remarkable' or 'Fascinating'? Of course, I am writing somewhat facetiously, but one should remember W. S. Gilbert – 'When everyone is somebodee, Then no one's anybody!' Myself, I am for classifying wines that have established reputations – and, thereby, have secured markets within which a particular price level can usually be attained. But how could anyone indicate to the novice drinker what shades of enjoyment would be implied by 'On occasions outstanding, but sometimes disappoints', or 'Generally sound, if somewhat unexciting'? For these judgments one must consult the wine merchant, or, even, the more informed wine writer.

When, in 1985, during the St Émilion classification, the *Grands Crus*

(Ausone and Cheval Blanc) were separated from the *Premiers Crus* (which last numbered ten and have since become nine), it was felt that the situation of the Graves' classification might also be considered and possibly revised. However, as usually happens when someone wishes to define and write down a commodity that is variable, difficulties began to proliferate.

From being privileged to have frank conversations with some of the authorities concerned, I am quite convinced that all have attempted to re-assess the wines of the Graves as dispassionately as possible. Tastings are blind; judges – with high qualifications plus reputations for being strict – are carefully chosen; no proprietors may take part in the tastings. This admirable procedure means that at least a set of categories relating to quality may eventually be worked out – but what must be the responsibilities of the judges when it is remembered that their verdicts will have an important, maybe adverse, effect on the prices that these wines may fetch once the results of such tastings are published? Remember that, when judges from outside a wine region are brought in to share in the marking and overall appraisal, the outsiders often mark far more severely than the 'locals'; some-one with a perspective of wines other than those under consideration may, indeed must, have a different set of standards from somebody having been accustomed to the particular wines for a lifetime, finding them dear, under-standing certain defects, thrilled by some triumphant results. But, again, who is to be considered finally 'authoritative'? The local, with deeper understanding of the wines, or the outsider, with a notion as to the sort of competition the wines may meet elsewhere and the preferences of a public open-minded about style and, certainly, price?

In the Graves, the classification problem is complicated because, in some instances, one plot of land categorised as a 'classed growth' may be worth more, in terms of what it is and what it may yield in volume of wine, than its neighbour; but changes may occur more rapidly than in the past and it may be found that the terrain previously supposed to be inferior, merely suffered from insufficient investment and knowledge and, quite within a short time, may subsequently rival the ostensibly superior neighbour.

What about the regulations on what constitutes an 'estate'? Here, the complexities of what happens in Burgundy, with growers, *domaines*, and the *négoce*, are repeated with a Bordeaux accent. Ideally, when the word 'estate' is used, the wine should come solely from that estate – frag-mented and parcelled around though it may sometimes be – and then be made in the *cuvier* or winery of that estate and nowhere else. But some proprietors, even of certain classed growths, may own an estate where they have not built a winery; the wine they make may be made near by, under their supervision, or in the press-house of another property they own, admirably equipped, in both instances the technological advantages being obvious, especially when the distance between the 'estate' or vineyard and that of the winery is negligible. But is the resulting wine truly 'estate made' and 'estate bottled'?

There is also the delicate matter that, sometimes, certain properties may find that from one estate there are not sufficient grapes to make up the necessary *rendement* or yield in terms of wine; if this should happen – for no one can foresee exactly what will occur in one micro-climate possibly only several hundred yards away from another that is totally different – then it is admitted that, certainly until fairly recently, estate owners may have made use of the grapes or the wine from other properties that they own, as happened in the past, albeit from different 'estates'. Naturally, no proprietor wants the quality of a wine already proud of an established reputation to decline and it would no longer be possible for somebody in the Graves to send down a load of grapes or several containers of wine from, say, St Estèphe, as Monsieur Pontac probably did. But suppose there are near by up and coming vineyards, under the same ownership and enjoying the same advisers and the expense-regardless equipment, gracing the winery of an estate bearing a respected name? Should the grapes from such plots be refused entry to the major *cuverie*? Should it be impossible to satisfy the queue of customers for a *grand vin* simply because the fixing of the *rendement* or official yield of hectolitres per hectare has been reduced – a very large question posing problems in many regions of France these days – so that maybe the quantity available will drop and people get tired of asking for something that they can never be sure of obtaining? Or is it sensible for an owner to make use of grapes in the same region, from another property that he owns and that will anyway be made into wine under his or his oenologist's supervision? After all, the owner of a vineyard with an established reputation is not usually willing obviously to sacrifice quality for quantity (although it has been known in the past).

In Alexis Lichine's *Guide to the Wines and Vineyards of France* (revised edition, 1986) the author makes a significant point about the singularity of the situation in the Graves vis-à-vis classification: compared with the Médoc, St Émilion and Pomerol, the Graves, he states, has only a fairly small number of châteaux in relation to the land under vines: 'In the entire Médoc, nearly 30 per cent of the vineyards are held by top classified châteaux, all of which bottle the wine themselves and sell it under the individual, well-recognised château label. This is in striking contrast to the Graves, where classified châteaux hold just over 10 per cent of the 2,400 hectares ... of vineyards. The rest of the vast vineyard area is given over to small properties, most of which produce white wine, sold either under a lesser château name or to Bordeaux shippers, who, in turn, market it as generic "Graves".'

This comment leads on to one to do with marketing. Many of the well-known estates in the Médoc and other regions of the Bordeaux vineyard either will sell their estate wines to the shippers in various markets or, in certain circumstances, will grant such a shipper an 'exclusivity', so that he can buy the whole crop (or a large proportion of it) and portion out his supply to other shippers acting as wholesalers, or else sell direct to merchants – who, of course, may in many instances themselves be shippers as well. With the most famous and sought-after estates a type of quota system is often involved so that the wine may be fairly apportioned and not swamp one export market while depriving another. Some years ago there was an example of this when, to the fury of the owner of a world-famous growth, the head of an up-and-coming retail chain, who would not ordinarily have been allocated any of the great wine direct, managed to depute several other regular purchasers, sure of getting some of the wine, to 'sell on' some of their allowance for offering via his retail chain; he was using the magnificent wine as a type of very superior 'loss leader', selling it at a fair but not preposterously high price, so that wine-wise customers rushed into the retail shops to get some Château X. This not only brought into the shop people who might not have thought of buying wine there and who probably bought other wines while they were in this outlet, but the 'bargain' attracted enormous publicity, of the 'even at a seemingly cut price shop, you can get the very top growths ...' type. Hesitant shoppers were, understandably, lured in, feeling that the finest wines were not stocked only by intimidating merchants. But today all arrangements as to who gets how much, where it goes and what, subsequently, may happen are closely surveyed.

Many of the smaller Graves properties will sell their wines directly onto the Bordeaux market to brokers, who will then sell it to their various customers, both within France and overseas. This can be exasperating to the visitor who 'discovers' some charming but modest wine and then finds that even the producer does not keep track of where it is available retail once he has sold it. Sometimes the producer may be able to name certain 'prestigious' customers, such as famous restaurants or, even, a particular well-established merchant, but this need not mean that the enthusiast can be sure of finding the 'new' wine in these outlets all the time or even frequently.

My dear friend, David Peppercorn M.W., gives an interesting example of this sort of procedure when in his admirable book *Bordeaux* (1982) he comments, in the section devoted to that very fine property, La Louvière: 'Apart from the wine sold under the La Louvière label, various other names are used in conjunction with the château name; they are mostly exclusivities of various *négociants*. The names are: Le Vieux-Moulin, Clos-du-Roy, La Haute Marnière, La Tourette, Le Pin-Franc, La Haut-Gravière, Coucheroy, Les Agunelles and Les Lions.' Note the phrase 'in conjunction with': there is no suggestion of any wines that are not specifically Château La Louvière being sold *as* the estate's wine; association with a fine, respected and widely known estate, though, can be helpful both to vendor and buyer.

So, if there is to be a new classification, then much rethinking must take place as to the definition of an 'estate' and any possible associated sources of wine and where this wine is made. There must be some decision about what happens where an estate does not possess cellars for maturation. There must certainly be some clear thinking about the permitted *rendement* or yield that may sometimes exceed the official yield in hectolitres per hectare permitted by the authorities; this type of wine can, often, be a bargain for customers who patronise an experienced merchant and who are not mere 'label drinkers': as a portion of a wine may have had to be 'declassified' – and at an early date after the vintage, too early, say many growers, for them to know whether they should declassify unsuccessful *cuvées* of the *grand vin* anyway – it will suffer both having to bear a less 'known' name and perhaps be regarded with less enjoyment and respect by the more ignorant members of the public. (Or should more of the famous estates make 'second wines', as some already do?)

THE SIGNIFICANCE OF THE A.O.C.s

The public, even the many intelligent drinkers, cannot easily grasp the implications and requirements of the A.O.C. regulations any more than they can understand the significance of 'classification' and the differently categorised growths. I have just been unsuccessfully trying to convince the wine buyer of an otherwise respected London club that he is wholly mistaken in supposing that 'They just blend in anything they want to, in order to fill out the quantity.' For those who do want to understand, I therefore include some remarks about the A.O.C.s here. It will save time that might be involved in looking up the basics in some other book. It should be stressed, however, that the Appellations d'Origine Contrôlées have a different purpose and are totally different in practical application from the question of classification. They do, however, affect all the fine wine vineyards and currently are much to the fore in the Graves. They may, in the near future, become even more relevant to understanding this area.

First of all the actual name – it means 'Controlled source of origin'. The term A.O.C. is not directly related to the quality of any wine bearing these letters or words on its label but, by implication, all the fine wines of France do possess A.O.C.s. The details of each A.O.C. vary and they are continually being revised in all the regions where they exist. In general terms the A.O.C. stipulates: the exact defined area of the vineyard; the vines that are permitted to be grown, plus the way that they are cultivated and pruned; the minimum alcoholic content of the finished wine; the amount, in hectolitres per hectare, that the specific A.O.C. vineyard is allowed to make. All these things are, overall, intended to let the consumer know in some detail what to expect from a bottle of wine, also to protect established traditions and prevent exploitation of a vineyard so that the quality goes down.

As people do not always appreciate, there are A.O.C.s that fit inside each other, like Chinese boxes. In the Bordeaux region, for example, the lowest of the whole series will be 'Bordeaux' and then, progressively, through *Bordeaux Supérieur* to specific areas and, finally, to the communes or parishes within these areas. The more specific the A.O.C. the more the wine is likely to be fine: Château Lafite-Rothschild, for example, is A.O.C. Pauillac, but it is also a Médoc, a Bordeaux (and certainly *supérieur*). People who complain that they have bought a 'Château La Tour' or 'Latour de . . .' for a modest price and demand to know how some merchant dare charge a high one for a 'Château Latour' have not looked at the A.O.C.; there are about seventy-seven estates entitled to be called 'Château La Tour, Latour, La Tour de . . .' from various regions within the Bordeaux vineyard. But there is only one Château Latour that is A.O.C. Pauillac – the great first growth.

In addition to nomenclature, there is *rendement*, and here terms can be confusing: if the amount of wine made, for perfectly good reasons, including the variations in the weather, exceeds the amount specified by the A.O.C., then, even if it comes from the same vineyard and is made in the *chais* of the *grand vin*, it has to be 'declassified', a term that both is and is not directly involved with the 'classification' system. For example, a St Julien estate might declassify some of its wine to A.O.C. 'Haut-Médoc' or even lower down the scale; it can choose to do this, of course, if there should be a *cuvée* (vatting) that for some reason does not attain the quality of the other varieties of the *grand vin*. The thing to remember is that the regulations controlling the wine ease up slightly with each subsequent declassification.

Up to now, however, the Graves has only had 'Graves' and 'Graves Supérieures' as its two A.O.C.s and if, for any reason, a wine has to be declassified, it will go down to 'Bordeaux Supérieur' and thence to 'Bordeaux'.

In the autumn of 1987 two new A.O.C.s were made, 'Pessac' and 'Léognan', a logical follow-on of the 1984 regulations allowing these two regions to put 'Graves de Pessac' and 'Graves de Léognan' on their labels – if they so wished. On 9 September 1987 a new A.O.C. Pessac-Léognan was established, the *Décret* authorising this being given in full in Appendix VI. It is, of course, a major change and some respected estate owners who have expressed their views to me think it will augment the regional publicity in a valuable way and stress the wines of Pessac-Léognan as individual in style, in the same sort of way that has long since been established with the commune names of the Médoc. Writers such as Florence Mothe refer to the northern region of the Graves as 'Graves de Bordeaux', the term 'Graves de Portets' is also in use and I am informed that a forthcoming book is to deal with the 'Graves des Clarières', the south of the region. The present is a time of transition and those who see the changes occur in the grouping and in the legislation affecting the wines will have to bear in mind a number of factors. Note that the new A.O.C. Pessac-Léognan applies only to red or white wines from the following ten communes:

Cadaujac, Canéjean, Gradignan, Léognan, Martillac, Mérignac, Pessac, St-Médard-d'Eyrans, Talence, Villenave-d'Ornon. Vine varieties are, for white wines: Sémillon, Sauvignon, Muscadelle; for reds: Merlot, Cabernet Franc, Cabernet Sauvignon, Cot (or Malbec), Petit Verdot, Carmenère. The last-named variety used to be widely planted in both the Graves and Médoc prior to the twin plagues of oidium and phylloxera in the nineteenth century, but it is apparently subject to *coulure* (when the grapes drop off before becoming fully ripe).

I have only a very few times sampled wines in which there was known to be a proportion of Carmenère but these experiences confirm the supposition that the variety added depth and colour. According to Jancis Robinson in *Grapes, Wines and Vines* (1986) synonyms for the Carmenère include Carmenelle, Cabarnelle, Grande Vidure, Grande Carmenet, Carbouet. It is easy to imagine how some of these versions of its name could have been confused, in speech or writing, with one of the Cabernets. To comply with the new A.O.C. regulations, the red wines Pessac-Léognan must contain 25 per cent Cabernet Sauvignon and the white wines 25 per cent Sauvignon, the latter being thought by some to be rather high in view of the way in which the Sémillon has proved its worth in recent times. Other details, dealing with the musts, age of vines, method of pruning and density of planting are all given in the *Décret*; the natural alcoholic content must be 10 per cent in the finished wine, the *rendement* is a little lower than that for wines A.O.C. Graves.

Wines of the 1986 vintage which have already been sold may, if they comply with the regulations, be labelled with the new A.O.C., though they must previously be checked and it is appreciated that, when made in 1986, they would not have been subject to the stipulations concerning the *rendement*. As far as the classed growths are concerned, the label description *Cru classé des Graves* may henceforth be used instead of the phrases *Vin de Graves* or *Grand vin de Graves*, if the new A.O.C. requirements have been met. As long ago as 1964 growers hoping for a new A.O.C. 'Haut Graves' were disappointed. By dropping the overall regional term 'Graves' in the new appellation, they may feel that an accolade has been bestowed and progress towards prestige has been made. What will the customer think? Only time – and sales – can indicate results.

People do, naturally, buy wines by name – whether these are 'known' or a novelty; so the naming, the categorisation and the relevant regulations are perhaps more 'topical' for the Graves than for anywhere else in the

Bordeaux vineyard. There is the minor point that the 'Graves de Vayres' area, in the Entre-deux-Mers, is nothing at all to do with the Graves proper, although it is situated on a smallish outcrop of gravel; it is seldom listed in the U.K. and production is not large – but still, the existence of another name slightly similar to that of the subject of this book does reinforce my personal opinion that it would be helpful to the promotion and knowledge of Graves wines if some more names would differentiate between the sections of this extensive region – and provide more interest than just the one single word.

The problem facing the growers is very much one of our times: interest in wine is widespread, but export markets can be swayed by fashion and may be fickle in what they demand. If an attempt is made at reclassification, this will make news – for a short time. Producers will be confronted with difficulties concerning prices as well as *'le standing'* (prestige); certain properties, especially the many in the south, where quite recent improvements in quality are due to dedicated and informed owners, will need to publicise wines even within France and certainly on export markets. How can such up-and-coming growths justify claims to 'going up higher' if there is a change in the classification? May the answer lie, as some growers seem to think, in an adaptation of what happened in St Émilion in 1984? The number of St Émilion A.O.C.s was then reduced from four to two – St Émilion and St Émilion *Grand Cru*, properties previously entered as *Premier Grand Cru Classé* and *Grand Cru Classé* were added to the overall section *Grand Cru*. In addition, each one of the classed growths here had to agree formally that its delimited vineyard area should not be augmented or added to within the forthcoming decade, so that the classification could stand. Penning-Rowsell notes drily, 'This prevents an estate from acquiring another property and adding its produce to the amount declared from the authorised classified vineyard, a practice not unknown in the Médoc.'

The work of the Institut National des Appellations d'Origine (INAO) works, like a ripple from a stone thrown into a pond, outwards and affects all producers. The inspector will arrive, at some time between January and May, to check on everything that is taking place at the vineyard, note the *rendement*, any alterations in progress and so on. In the Graves he may arrive in mid-December, or perhaps not come until the June following the vintage, for, reasonably enough, only so much can be done in a day; but wine, wine making and what is taking place within the vineyard are changing all the time, even imperceptibly.

The date of the vintage is subject to controls – but not rigidly; the hundred days usual between the flowering of the vine and the start of picking does not vary much, but it can vary somewhat, both because of the variations in the climates of certain plots and the rate of ripening of different grape varieties. Officially, the *Préfecture* will declare when picking may start, a beginning being made with the dry white wine vineyards and grapes, the black grapes being picked from about five days later and onwards and, finally, the grapes for the sweeter whites. The grape varieties may vary considerably in the ripening, also being substantially affected by the *portes greffes* (the aphis-resistant vinestocks onto which they are grafted), which nowadays are carefully selected and chosen according to site as well as vine variety. They influence and can contribute more than was formerly supposed – and, certainly, more than I was ever taught thirty-five years ago!

Realistically, it can only be the grower, the owner, the person in charge at the vineyard who makes the decision when to start picking. 'We can't put a policeman behind every vine!' one highly placed authority told me and the French, pragmatic at all times, accept that, in the production of a commodity as individual and personal as wine, it is the individuals who must put themselves, like their vines, at risk – and for them to make up their minds.

There is, obviously, a great difference between the north and the south of the Graves – and do the long-established, well-known estates in the north *need* any change in classification or the A.O.C.s? Their wines are already renowned. It is the *terrasses* that make virtual islands of some properties and they feel, fairly enough, that, as they are already accepted as 'special', their individuality is able to be noted by their estates' names. It is not that they are secure – no fine wine estate can ever truly think it is, until scientists can control the weather! – but they are established. In the Médoc, some fine estates not in the more famous communes merely get the A.O.C. 'Haut Médoc', such as the beautiful Château La Lagune, at Ludon: does this seem a source of great dissatisfaction? Will the A.O.C.s 'Pessac' and 'Léognan' add greatly to the renown of Haut Brion, or Domaine de Chevalier? Maybe not – but, for those entrusted with the regional promotion and, I assume, the proprietors of other estates less famous as yet, the changed 'tags' on the labels may make an advantageous difference, as wine lovers seek 'new' wines that are nevertheless within classic and famous vineyards.

For estates in the centre and south of the Graves the way in which the question of possible reclassification is intertwined with that of the A.O.C.s makes the whole subject more complicated and, to those involved, it must be recurrently irritating. Any rearrangement, with additions, of the classification may enable many to hope for higher selling prices for wines that are to be 'classed growths' and, long-term, to bring such individual wines to the attention of customers who might not otherwise seek them out or think of them as important growths. Whenever the question of classification crops up, it must be said that there will always be some properties that have not only tried harder, but succeeded more than others – wines are no more equal than human beings in achievement – and I suppose it is up to the owners of such oncoming estates to decide whether it is of supreme importance for them to be classified – when, as has occurred within other regions of Bordeaux, certain estates can sell their wines at prices equal to or even above those of many 'famous names'. (The Pomerol wines have never been classified – but Château Pétrus achieves the price and the renown of the first growths these days.) To Monsieur André Lurton and his brother Lucien, making outstanding white wines and most promising fine reds from the great and elegant estate of La Louvière and their other properties, does it matter – or does it matter very much about this business of classification? Money is being poured into this outstanding property, so that its potential would seem to be at least that of certain of the *crus classés*, where, as can happen, financial resources are not always as large and, perhaps, quality may have inevitably slipped a little. Before leaving this delicate matter, it is wise to take thought.

Classification began and, to a certain extent, still begins with price. In many instances, nowadays, price is equated with quality. But the two may not always coincide. This is where the sense and the sensitivities of the individual drinker and buyer of wine must be especially alert where the wines of the Graves are appraised. A drinker who does not just 'drink the label' but who expects a wine that is outstanding as regards price, reputation or place in any classification; always to be a memorable drink, is bound to be disappointed at one time or another. There are some very fine wines in the Graves; there are excellent wines as yet categorised (by me personally) as 'small-scale'; there are even a few wines each having the aura of a great reputation, costing a great deal of money that, if the drinker is both honest and moderately experienced, scarcely justify the price of the bottle. Yet the same wine, even in the next vintage, may be a glory on the palate.

We do not yet know enough about the Graves, this 'cradle of Bordeaux' and, at the time of writing, so much is changing that it is impossible to risk generalising in detail. This is one of the excitements of wine, another of the true 'mysteries' that make it unwise only to go by the letter of the law or the categories of any classification – or, even, to be hesitant about risking what may be a gorgeous experience in wine drinking, even if, as yet, the particular wine has not been highly placed in print.

THE CÉRONS REGION

A separate note about this is, I think, justified, because some may remember, as I do, that Cérons was, until fairly recently, regarded as a separate region for white wines; I can recall that they were sometimes likened to small-scale Barsacs, for they were sweetish, but finishing dry and lightweight. 'No legal delimitation has been required to fix the boundaries', says Pierre Célestin in *Les Appellations d'Origine Bordelaises*, published in 1932. For many years the properties within Cérons, whether actual estates or plots of vines, were usually owned by growers in Cérons itself, in Podensac and some in the parish of Illats.

As Féret in the 1986 English edition points out, the Cérons region is similar in appearance, soil and subsoil, to that of the Graves. With the demand for red wines and dryish whites on the increase, many of the local growers, therefore, have been producing red wines which can bear the A.O.C. 'Graves' and dry whites which can bear the A.O.C.s 'Graves', 'Graves Supérieures', or actually 'Cérons'. Certainly the bulk of the wines are white – Féret estimates about 80 per cent – and the A.O.C. 'Cérons' today is applied to approximately 575 hectares under white wine vines, 22 hectares under black grapes.

Those who like everything to be put in writing and subject to categorisation should note how the overlap of which is what in Cérons can be confusing to the ordinary customer and drinker. Essentially, for the white wines, the requirements are the same for grapes as for the Graves in general, so is the yield; the musts have to contain at least 212 grammes per litre of natural sugar. After fermentation, the wines must attain at least 12.5 per centage of alcohol by volume (Gay-Lussac).

For the sweet whites, specific requirements apply, as they do for the sweet whites of Sainte-Croix-du-Mont and also Loupiac. Essentially, these regulations control the yield per hectare and the A.O.C. that the wine is subsequently allowed to bear and, of course, also control any treatment; but whether the wine gets the apparently superior A.O.C. 'Cérons' (or any of the others making sweet whites) or is simply able to bear the A.O.C. 'Bordeaux', is a very complicated business and, as far as Cérons is concerned, small-scale growers may certainly not suppose it to be worth their while.

What should be remembered is that, whereas the Cérons whites may bear the A.O.C.s Cérons, Graves Supérieures or Graves, the red wines may *only* bear the A.O.C. Graves. This applies also to the wines of Illats, also Podensac, where both white wines – sometimes sweet – and red wines are also made.

18

THE ESTATES

IT would have taken a far longer time than most authors have at their disposal and – taking into account the hospitable traditions of the region – greater endurance than I could apportion over even a generous period, to taste, much less to visit, even the majority of the 351 estates that compose the Graves. Indeed, even citing the basic facts and figures need not be a 100 per cent accurate guide. A friend of mine quoted an estate owner in the Bordelais; he stated that it was useless even attempting to be exact about the proportions of different vines planted within a vineyard – of course, there were times when sections would be lying fallow, others when replanting had taken place but the vines were young, at other times a section, albeit small, might have suffered damage or disease of some sort, reducing the proportion of grapes that would otherwise have been expected to yield. New techniques of vine growing and wine making are introduced . . . one variety changes somewhat . . . the provisory statements are infinite.

And – how much information does the reader require – and how much does he truly need? By the time this book is read some properties will have been able to indulge in much rebuilding, markets may have been created for others by merchants outside France who have 'discovered' wines that are 'new', a vogue or fashion may have arisen for certain estates' wines that have evolved somewhat differently from what might previously have been expected. Has one estate been able to follow up their success in vintage x with something equally outstanding in vintage y?

I do not, I admit, think that tasting notes between hard covers are always helpful to the eventual reader of the book; who thought what about which depends on when and where the wine was tasted. So, if a prospective buyer wants to see the progress of Château X, the wise thing is to remain in touch with a merchant who will either have bought it at the opening price or have been able to taste it throughout its maturation; this individual, with whom the possible buyer should be in sympathy, will have formed his opinions and should be able to advise both the private customer, whose preferences may be known, and the trade buyer – either for restaurants or some catering establishment or syndicate – so that the requirements of both may be satisfied. As to the person who considers wine, a perishable commodity, as something in which to 'invest', quite apart from ever intending to drink it, I will say little. People who deal in 'collectables' of this sort shunt fine wines in and out of the salerooms until such bottles can only achieve fame if the price they eventually attain makes headlines, rather than the enjoyment they may give to the drinker. It is no longer possible for beginners in wine today to go out and, albeit at some cost, treat themselves and fellow enthusiasts to a bottle of fine Bordeaux, as once I could. I hope that the suppliers of such wines to those who thus trade in them – their ancestors would doubtless have been speculating in flesh – will screw every sou out of such customers as they can. But fortunately we can still, notably in the Graves, turn to wines that are not yet 'collectables' but that can demonstrate many of the attributes of fine Graves in lesser-known and affordable ranges.

In the following pages, therefore, I have thought it wise not to give detailed tasting notes, but to attempt some indication of the styles of some of the wines that I have been able to get to know. Anyone is entitled to disagree.

Each vineyard has a personality. Sometimes, certain estates get their individuality more from the *régisseur* or, even, the *maître de chai* than from the owner. When a dynasty of those wholly involved with the production of an estate wine can supervise its evolution from generation to generation, the result can be fascinating: contributions from inherited know-how and personal experience match the qualifications of the younger technical expert but, sometimes, somebody quite outside the whole scene can, in some way, twitch up a good but ordinary wine to notable status. There are many stories to tell about vineyards and, in the future, someone may add to this tapestry of events, quietly creating new traditions.

ARRANGEMENT

The classified, and some non-classified growths are dealt with in this section. A list of non-classified growths is given in Appendix VII. This is not to say that the latter are less worthy of note, but many of them may not be as easily available to readers in export markets as the majority of the 'known names' of the classified growths. I admit that I hope I may live to see some more subdivisions created within the Graves, so that wine lovers outside France may come to appreciate and enjoy the wines of areas that, as yet, are somewhat submerged in the generic area term.

In expressing a few personal opinions about the classed growths, I have allowed myself to be, occasionally, critical. The Graves region makes wines that are so varied in style and, sometimes, unequal, from year to year, in quality, that this has seemed to be fair comment – although I do not (unlike many who write about wine today) think that it is useful to the reader to have an author expend precious chunks of texts on what is disliked and why it is 'bad', at least to the writer; absence of comment seems wiser, and, of course, no author can have sufficient experience of a range of wines all at one time so as to comment dispassionately as well as personally.

There are other limitations. The wine trade is endlessly generous – but there are few writers on wine who are, as it were, continually awash in fine wines of superlative vintages. There are several world-famous Bordeaux growths that I may have tasted or drunk only a few times – at least two that I cannot remember having had the chance to try for many years! For research, such as when writing this book, I naturally try to attend as many relevant tastings as possible – and otherwise go out and buy what is on sale, trying to sample wines such as the reader may do, drawing on the resources of such retail outlets as are available, of all types. Special trade tastings and pre-auction tastings of 'finest' and 'rarest' do provide opportunities for sampling certain wines in a series of vintages – but what I thought about some of them several years ago and what they might taste like now may not always seem helpful to the reader who may be looking at this chapter several years hence.

Besides, especially in the Graves, there are many discoveries now to be made, about methods as well as wines. Some properties begin to rise in interest and increase in quality, others may go through a rather static period, some seem to have a dull or even indifferent phase – which last it doesn't seem helpful to pick out. Suddenly, a wine that has up to now been unknown can produce both enjoyment and quality, at a much lower price than might have been expected. This is the sort of thing that makes the Graves such a worthwhile area for exploration.

NON-CLASSIFIED GROWTHS

Where it has been possible, I have added some notes about such properties as I have been able to try and about which I have managed to gain additional information. Generalisations are risky and, as all but the wine snob will admit, there are wines for casual drinking as well as those about which one wishes to think, in addition to those that are imposing, worthy of detailed discussion. Here, there is one caveat: those who make wines do, understandably, love them and also think of them as good, even 'the best'; they cannot easily see their cherished 'children' in the perspective of the drinker who has the wide selection of wines of the world available to him, as is the fortunate situation of most wine lovers in the U.K. A 'little' Graves may be as good as it is possible for it to be; this is not the same thing as saying that it is almost or very nearly on a par with, say, La Mission Haut Brion or Domaine de Chevalier in an outstanding year – the kinship of the Graves is extensive rather than close and a shared A.O.C. can be misleading, as I have earlier suggested.

Even though a detailed survey of all the estates in the Graves is, as will have been understood, impossible for one mere human being, there are some properties that are specially interesting. There are pleasant stories concerning some, about others major contributions have been and are being made to wine history in the region; it has also been possible for me to gain some detailed knowledge of a few others. Although anyone exploring in this important wine area will be able to add to the information given here, it has seemed right to me to incorporate such additional particulars as I have been able to find out.

If anything in this book makes the reader try different Graves wines, the writer's efforts will have been justified. They cannot, always, result in memorable experiences, but they may frequently increase both experience and enjoyment.

A NOTE ABOUT CAPACITY

The potential or usual amount of wine that is produced at a Bordeaux estate is generally expressed in terms of tonneaux, each tonneau consisting of approximately four *barriques bordelaises* or the hogsheads of the region. This measure, deriving from the old 'tonne' or 'tun', which was 252 gallons, the huge cask occupying 60 cubic feet in the hold of a ship, hence the measuring of a vessel's capacity in 'tuns', is today about 214–223 litres per tonneau, or 47–49 gallons (U.K.). The tonneau, therefore, represents approximately 100 cases of wine, each case containing 12 bottles of the 'standard' 75 cl. capacity.

Some 'historic' measurements of capacity may be useful if the reader is consulting old documents – though these may not be reliable! The fourteenth-century *barrique* was about 200 litres; the pipe was about 400 litres – and therefore 2 barriques; a tonneau was supposed to be 2 pipes.

The *Shorter Oxford English Dictionary* gives the definition of 'pipe' as: 'A large cask with its contents (wine, beer, cider, beef, fish, etc.), or as a measure of capacity, equivalent to half a tun, or 2 hogsheads, or 4 barrels, i.e. usu. containing 105 imperial gallons. Sometimes identified with BUTT.' The same source gives 'Butt' as 'A cask for wine, ale, etc., holding from 108 to 140 gallons. Later, a measure of capacity = 2 hogsheads, i.e. usually in ale measure 108 gallons, in wine measure 126 gallons.'

In recent years, when fine wine is shipped in bottle and, therefore, in cases of a dozen bottles each, rather than in bulk to be bottled in the export market buying it, the classed growths of the Graves, all of which bottle their wines at the property, together with some other growths, may express their usual amount of wine produced in terms of *caisses* or cases or in bottles. This is often easier for the non-wine-trade reader to understand. But it should be stressed that the figures stated represent the *usual* amount of wine that the estate has at its disposal for sale; they may not represent the total amount of wine produced, or not what is made every year. There are several reasons why these statistics vary. The owner or owners of the estate – they may include a number of directors who are, to a certain extent, 'sleeping partners' – may, according to what has been agreed between them, take a certain quantity of wine into their personal reserves. The whole crop, in difficult years, may be sorted out according to the various *cuvées* or vattings, one or more of which may be judged unworthy of bearing the estate label as the *grand vin* and, therefore, be declassified. In some estates there may be a 'second wine' (as the Château Bahans of Haut Brion) which may be made from the young vines or vattings that, for some good reason, are not incorporated with the *grand vin*. Maybe, in some years, there has been a climatic disaster and if, for various reasons, major replanting has had to be undertaken, wine made from vines suffering from this may be put out under the label of the second wine and often proves a bargain to the percipient and knowledgeable buyer.

There is also the possibility that, in certain years, the official *rendement* or yield has been, for perfectly good reasons, exceeded (see pp. 246–52). Some wine may then have to be declassified, go down one step, as it were, in the A.O.C. staircase; it cannot bear the label of the great property – but it is another bargain that the merchant may recommend to customers who are not mere drinkers of labels and names.

For the purposes of this book I have given the yield in tonneaux or, where it has been given to me, in cases and bottles as well. The two do not and cannot be exactly equated – at what point does the person bottling off from a *barrique* close the tap? There may, in some years, be a lot of deposit in the cask. In others, the wine may run star bright almost down to the dregs. Hence the varying amount.

These days it is unlikely that no wine at all will be made, even in an otherwise very poor year, but a major drop in yield can occur. Likewise, an unexpectedly large crop may be produced.

There is another possibility. Land that is legally within the limits of the appropriate A.O.C. may be acquired by a grower, so that a property can be extended – and the amount of wine made under the estate's name may be greater than that stated in the statistics issued before the extension. This is something that can only be checked against the month by month and year by year figures which will be available from the various trade organisations and, of course, the properties concerned.

To the best of my knowledge, the figures quoted hereafter were officially correct at the time of writing.

Because of the alteration in the A.O.C.s of the region (see p. 249), Appendix VII gives the most recent particulars of these at the time that this book went to press.

The classed growths are given in alphabetical order but, after Haut Brion, I have put La Mission Haut Brion, La Tour Haut Brion and Laville Haut Brion because these now comprise one estate for ownership.

The non-classified growths begin with La Louvière and the important Vignobles André Lurton; then there are mentions, albeit brief, of such properties as I have been able to get to know a little. The final property is that of Rahoul, because of the significant contribution made to the Graves by the then administrator, who is one of the dedicatees of this book.

THE CLASSED GROWTHS

CHÂTEAU BOUSCAUT (CADAUJAC)
Owner Société Anonyme du Château Bouscaut. Director, Lucien Lurton
Vineyard
32 hectares *vignes rouges*
  50% Merlot

35% Cabernet Sauvignon
15% Cabernet Franc

10 hectares *vignes blanches*
   60% Sémillon
   40% Sauvignon

Production
   140 t. red (13,000 cases) (180,000 bottles)
   30 t. white (3,000 cases) (75,000 bottles)

This is an impressively sited property that the traveller down the RN 113 will see from the road to the south. The pleasant eighteenth-century building has been carefully restored after a fire in the 1960s and its overall layout makes it most attractive to view. At one time a group of Americans bought it and wisely brought in Jean-Bernard Delmas, of Haut Brion, to attend to the rehabilitation of the vineyard and winery. Then, in 1980, it was sold to Lucien Lurton, whom James Seely refers to as the present-day *Prince des Vignes*, with some accuracy, for he also owns Brane-Cantenac, Durfort-Vivens, Desmirail, Villegeorge and, in Barsac, Château Climens.

In the past the Bouscaut wines have won many awards and now the investment in the estate by several owners has made it a source of reliable classic Graves. My admittedly limited experience of both the red and the white wines inclines me to think that, to my taste, the whites are more exciting, sensitive, combining delicacy with breeding, the red wines perhaps not being quite as interesting up to the present when I have tried them, although remaining firm and sound. The red wines remain in wood for about eighteen months, about one-quarter of the *barriques* being replaced annually. The white wine is fermented in stainless steel and subsequently goes into wood for about six months.

CHÂTEAU CARBONNIEUX (LÉOGNAN)
Owner The Société des Grandes Graves. Director, Antony Perrin
Vineyard
38 hectares *vignes rouges*
   60% Cabernet Sauvignon
   30% Merlot

7% Cabernet Franc
2% Malbec
1% Petit Verdot

35 hectares *vignes blanches*
  66% Sauvignon
  34% Sémillon

Production
  140 t. red (15,000 cases) (220,000 bottles)
  120 t. white (15,000 cases) (210,000 bottles)

The red wines remain in wood from eighteen to twenty-four months, according to the type of vintage, the whites – which are among the very first to be vintaged in the Bordeaux region – go into new wood for three months or thereabouts. About a quarter of the casks used for the red wines are renewed annually.

This is both a historic and very beautiful property, situated on a slightly elevated set of ridges up above the valley of the 'Eau Blanche' stream. It has been under vines since the thirteenth century, when it belonged to a Ramon Carbonnieux, and the house itself dates from around 1380. The du Ferron family were subsequent owners, influential in Bordeaux affairs, and they kept it until 1740 when they sold it to the Benedictines of the Abbey of Sainte Croix, one of the more important religious establishments and considerable landowners. There has always been a certain attraction exerted by the wines (and spirits) produced under the auspices of religious foundations and the sales of Carbonnieux increased markedly among the local nobility and gentry. This part of the Graves had, up to this time, concentrated on making red wine, but the Benedictines began to plant vines for making white wine as well, which achieved fame in export markets as well as locally. It was now that the legend associated with this wine came into being. A beautiful Bordelaise, travelling on board a ship that was attacked by Turkish pirates, was captured and sold into slavery, the chief eunuch buying her for the Sultan's harem. (In fact this actually happened to Aimée Dubucq de Rivery, cousin of Josephine, Napoleon's first wife, as she was voyaging from Nantes to Martinique, and her astonishing life is told by Lesley Blanch in *The Wilder Shores of Love* (1954).) The heroine

264

of the legend became the Sultan's favourite, on whom he lavished anything she desired – and she informed him that it was essential, if she were to preserve her beauty and good spirits, that she should be supplied with her favourite 'mineral water', the white wine of Carbonnieux. Varying versions state either that the Sultan knew quite well that the 'mineral water' was actually wine and arranged for consignments to be sent, or that he naïvely commented that he wondered why Christians should want to drink wine at all, when they might enjoy 'mineral water' of such fine quality.

After the Revolution, Carbonnieux was bought by Elie Bouchereau, who was in charge of finances in south-west France, and his family ran it and maintained its reputation until 1887. After this it passed through several owners but in 1956 was bought by Marc Perrin, a *pied noir* from Algeria, whose family had been making wine there from the middle of the nineteenth century. The contribution that many of the *pieds noirs* have made to French wines is considerable – theirs has often been the 'shot in the arm' that an established region may need from time to time. In this instance, Marc Perrin was fortunate because, in 1962, the French had to leave Algeria.

Marc Perrin died in 1982 and his son, Tony, who had worked alongside his father, runs the estate today, as well as exercising much influence overall in the region. As James Seely comments, 'Carbonnieux is a jewel among the Graves', and the family are devoted to the place, maintaining it with impeccable taste so that the fame of its wine is balanced by the beauty of the establishment. This is in plan like an 'E' minus the middle stroke, the dwelling quarters being on one side, the administration and the large *chai* on the other; extensions and renovations are progressively in hand.

Carbonnieux white wines, like several others among the great white Graves, are particularly attractive and I have always loved them; sensitive, fragrant, capable of having surprisingly long lives for whites. The reds tend to be full in style and, as with many fine Graves, have accentuated fruitiness, they are mouth-filling; perhaps they do not always attain the great delicacy and finesse of the whites, but they are agreeable, impressive Graves.

DOMAINE DE CHEVALIER (LÉOGNAN)
Owner The Société Civile du Domaine de Chevalier. Directors, Claude Ricard, Olivier Bernard

Vineyard

15 hectares *vignes rouges*
  65% Cabernet Sauvignon
  30% Merlot
   5% Cabernet Franc

3 hectares *vignes blanches*
  70% Sauvignon
  30% Sémillon

Production
  50 t. red (5,000 cases) (60,000 bottles)
   6 t. dry white (800 cases) (9,600 bottles)
  (All bottled at the estate; released only after two years.)

This remarkable estate is a true 'belle au bois dormant', for the entire plantation of vines is, all together, hidden within a forest although quite near to Léognan. The pines surrounding it make it seem remote from everything else, acting as a real enclosure and, of course, a windbreak. The soil is real Graves gravel, but apparently there are undulations below ground – those slight variations that can make such great differences in the wine from this type of vineyard. Clive Coates in *The Wines of Bordeaux* says that the subsoil is 'clay-iron'.

The original vineyard was laid down as quite a small plantation in about 1770, by a man whose name, Cibaley, acquired an 'h' and, from Chibaley, became Chevalier. The wine made there began to get a reputation for quality but, no one seems to know why, at the beginning of the nineteenth century, the vines were pulled up and the plantation reforested. However, in 1865 it was bought by Jean Ricard, whose father owned Haut Bailly and who had purchased several estates. Jean Ricard started the vineyard again – his surname is, rightly, famous in Bordeaux wine history. Jean's son-in-law then took it, Gabriel Beaumartin. A dealer in timber he apparently adored the estate – it arouses affection in all its owners – and not only was he able to supply timber for the casks, but the workers in his mills were a convenient labour force at vintage time. After Beaumartin's death in 1942 the estate was taken over by another Jean Ricard, grandson of the first one, and his son, Claude, took over in 1948.

266

The remarkable character of Claude Ricard – an outstanding concert pianist and a considerable athlete – would be intimidating were he not also a personality of a charm exceptional even among the charming members of the wine trade. In wine, he is a perfectionist, whisking around the vineyard on his green bicycle, supervising, literally, the progress and eventual picking of every bunch of grapes on the vines. The vintagers obviously share his enthusiasm; here is no aloof proprietor, descending from an imposing mansion, but the boss who gets his hands and his boots dirty with the best of them, when he darts out from the low-lying white house, where the rooms are informal and friendly, everything in them seeming to have been put there because somebody liked and wanted them around. Claude Ricard will rush to play the piano, even while fortunate guests sip the exquisite white wine and luncheon waits – but never spoils. Outside, he will encourage the older vintagers, many of whose families have been picking at Domaine de Chevalier for generations, and the less experienced workers draw his attention to individual bunches of grapes before venturing to use their shears – he will suggest a day or two longer for one cluster to ripen more; looking at another, he will tell the man or woman to go ahead; he studies the carefully filled baskets with an eye alert to even one imperfect berry.

The white wines are fermented in cask for three to four weeks. The red wines are aged mostly in new wood, but care is taken so that their natural aromas are not overwhelmed by the oak of the cask – Domaine de Chevalier is not a wine for drinkers who enjoy obvious 'wooding', it is too delicate, too finely balanced.

Claude Ricard said he would retire in 1988. That would be his fortieth vintage. In 1983 the property was bought by the Bernards, a distilling family, and Olivier Bernard, who now runs the estate, has inherited the same devotion and implacable perfectionism that seems to have inspired all its owners. His knowledge of wines combines enthusiasm for his own with a not always usual perspective on other wines, both of different regions of France and of the world.

For those who love them, the Domaine de Chevalier wines are exasperatingly difficult to describe. The really tiny production, especially of the white wine, may make bottles from this estate out of the range of many a wishful buyer, for prices are inevitably high. Domaine de Chevalier is totally lacking in what a French-speaker might describe as 'le grand flan-flan', there is no voguishness about the wine, it is too refined, too discreetly subtle to appeal to those who, understandably, like their Graves to be somewhat obvious, with initial appeal. Yet I admit to a prejudice and a predilection – the 1937 white wine was the first great white Graves I ever drank and which I still remember. Subsequent samplings – never, alas, many! – have confirmed my opinion that this is not only a 'grand vin' but one to share only with the discriminating; it is a wonder to those who are willing to let it talk to them.

The white wines are so extraordinary that it would be worth while presenting a bottle to anybody saying scornful things about dry white Graves. They should, though, be given time to age gracefully to their prime. The reds, likewise, need time; those that I have been able to taste in their youth are *nerveux*, tending to hold themselves back even when, in certain vintages, they are very much of a style that gets my tasting note 'smiling wine'; they evolve their real charm gently, with the years, revealing shades of fragrance and flavour that require leisurely appraisal and no previous notions about red Graves, venturing to an impressive maturity. Not, maybe, wines for the absolute beginner, definitely not for partnering too robustly flavoured foods. But what intricately constructed charmers!

CHÂTEAU COUHINS (VILLENAVE-D'ORNON)

Owner I.N.R.A.

Vineyard

About 10 hectares

Vignes rouges

    45% Cabernet Sauvignon

    34% Merlot

    18% Cabernet Franc

    3% Petit Verdot

Vignes blanches

    82% Sauvignon Blanc

    18% Sémillon

Production

    40,000 bottles red

    12,000 bottles white

Château Couhins-Lurton (Villenave-d'Ornon)
Owner André Lurton
Vineyard 6 hectares 100% Sauvignon Blanc
Production 25,000 bottles

There are two estates here, created from what was previously one. It was owned by the Gasqueton-Hanappier families and, in recent years, was divided after the death of some of the members.

Château Couhins, a classed growth for white wine, is an all-in-one-piece vineyard and now belongs to the Institut National de la Recherche Agronomique – hence the initials I.N.R.A. The Ministry of Agriculture is the overall owner.

Château Couhins-Lurton, also a classed growth for white wine, is now owned by André Lurton, who was tenant of the estate first from Mme Gasqueton, then from I.N.R.A. The small house is pretty, very much in French provincial style and I remember with pleasure the *rosé* wine that the Gasqueton family used to make there. Other old wines made at Couhins had a particularly delightful bouquet, almost a scented fragrance, and could age attractively. The minute property apparently stands at the highest point of Villenave-d'Ornon and is said to have both the soil and subsoil especially propitious for the production of white wines. As the Lurton family is particularly gifted for these wines, there would appear to be a bright future for the estate. The wine goes into new wood, is bottled about ten months after being vintaged and then has some further maturation at the estate.

CHÂTEAU DE FIEUZAL (LÉOGNAN)
Owner S.A. Ch. de Fieuzal. Director, G. Gribelin
Vineyard
35 hectares
Vignes rouges
   60% Cabernet Sauvignon
   30% Merlot
   5% Cabernet Franc
   4% Petit Verdot
   1% Malbec

Vignes blanches
60% Sauvignon
40% Sémillon

Production
150,000 bottles red
16,000 bottles white

This is a fairly old estate, which at one time belonged to the La Rochefoucauld family. It was bought by Abel Ricard in 1893. It is unpretentious in its approaches – until you note the tremendous amount of building that is going on at the present time, the glistening new paint, the smell of fresh wood and the opening of the earth around the modern installations. De Fieuzal used to command high prices and it sold its wines to the Vatican in 1893 for the pleasure of Pope Leo XIII. But the property suffered from the circumstance of being much neglected in World War II, until Abel Ricard's daughter's husband, Erik Bocke, a Swede who was in theatrical management, came back from Morocco, and began to revive the estate; thanks to him, it was in much better condition when he sold it to the present management, whose activities are now galvanised by the energetic and enthusiastic technical director, Monsieur Dupuy.

The old house has been demolished and the new *chai* is impeccable in layout, cleanliness and equipment. 'Old' may often appear picturesque, but it is not always synonymous with the production of fine wine and these days De Fieuzal is run by perfectionists. For example, the wood used for the *barriques* has to be split by hand, not sawn, and must be aged in the open before it receives the wine – new wood for the new wine, a luxury not every estate can manage. Nor does Monsieur Dupuy believe in standing the casks on scantling – the props on which they rest – that is above gravel: these *barriques* are so arranged that, underneath them, there are channels that are swilled down for absolute cleanliness at least once a week. Nor does De Fieuzal make use of the *barriques de transport*, the reinforced casks that these days are seldom used for shipping wine – because this is bottled at the estate – but can be utilised for keeping wine; De Fieuzal's *chais* contain only the traditional casks used in the Bordelais for maturation.

It is true that money alone cannot ensure the production of a fine wine – but it can assist the wine to realise its potential. De Fieuzal merits more attention in the U.K. than, up to now, it seems to have received. The white wine can be full and very *bouqueté*, a definite, pleasing mouthful.

270

Such red wines as I have been able to try have been impressive, markedly fruity, with both depth and length, attractive as well as elegant drinks.

CHÂTEAU HAUT BAILLY (LÉOGNAN)
Owner S.C.I. Sanders. Director, Jean Sanders
Vineyard
25 hectares *vignes rouges*
   60% Cabernet Sauvignon
   30% Merlot
   10% Cabernet Franc

Production
   100 t. (120,000 bottles)

This is a fairly recent arrival among the fine Graves. It seems to have been divided off from various vineyards around it in about 1840, when it belonged to the important Ricard family. It then seems to have passed to various owners, including a somewhat eccentric proprietor, Alcide Bellot de Minières, who set himself resolutely against the practice of grafting the threatened vines onto phylloxera-resistant American rootstocks. He was obsessional in this and many ways and was known for swilling out the *barriques* just prior to the vintage with old Cognac; the dregs that remained from the spirit would certainly have affected the incoming new wine and, I must add, it is not entirely unknown, even these days, for casks to be rinsed with something other than wine – thereby adding a little 'extra' to the character that many customers have found highly enjoyable.

Bellot de Minières was certainly respected for his ability, Haut Bailly was much in demand on the market, prices soaring, and his contemporaries nicknamed him *le roi des vignerons*. He died at Haut Bailly in 1906 and the estate passed to another well-known authority on Bordeaux wines – Frantz Malvesin, who wrote *Histoire de la vigne et du vin en Aquitaine*, published in 1919. Malvesin appears to have continued the 'no grafting' policy, but began to pasteurise the Haut Bailly wines, something that seemed initially successful, enabling bottling to take place as early as a mere eight months after the vintage. However, a pasteurised wine is a mummified wine and, after Malvesin died in 1923, this practice was discontinued.

Paul Beaumartin was the next owner of Haut Bailly, himself related

271

to the proprietor of Domaine de Chevalier, but he had problems – financial ones – and, in the 1930s, the estate and its wines declined and after Beaumartin's death the then owners showed little interest in the property. In 1955 Haut Bailly was bought by Daniel Sanders, a Belgian who, in World War I, had convalesced in Bordeaux, become fascinated by the region and married the daughter of a local merchant. He was impressed by the 1945 vintage and bought the estate, already having property in the region. Haut Bailly is today run by his son.

The quality of Haut Bailly – the potential of which Daniel Sanders realised – has risen steadily in recent years. The vineyard is all in one piece, the soil and subsoil, where gravel and pebbles abound, representing as much as 50 per cent of the terrain in one plot alongside the château. Even a quick glance shows the preponderance of gravel here. Those concerned with the estate are proud of its special position and properties. The alios, on which much of the vineyard sits, holds water and prevents the vine roots plunging very deeply into the earth; my friend Clive Coates comments that this prevents the soil from becoming acid and, likewise, the wine.

There are plantations of vines that are old for a modern vineyard: in 1984 some of them, as many as 40 per cent, were thought to be more than twenty years old, 30 per cent more than fifteen years old, with as high a proportion as 20 per cent being as old as fifty years, with the remainder of the plants being younger vines. As is known and admitted, old vines may not yield as much in quantity, but they can bestow quality in the form of a soft, billowing fragrance, leading up to a fullish flavour, providing much charm as well as firmness. My first experience of Haut Bailly was of the 1929, which I drank in the early 1960s, impressive and possessing much 'allure'. On the somewhat few occasions since when I have been able to sample and drink Haut Bailly, I have been able to register a well-balanced as well as a very correctly made wine, demonstrating the fruit as well as the spicy bouquet of good red Graves plus, in certain vintages, assertiveness and length. I have found that some French writers describe Haut Bailly as *féminin*, which I do not understand – charm, fine proportions, discreet authority are not exclusively masculine or feminine!

The second wine of this property is known as 'La Parde de Haut Bailly'.

CHÂTEAU HAUT BRION (PESSAC)

Owner Domaine Clarence Dillon. Directors-general, the Duc and Duchesse de Mouchy. Director, J. B. Delmas

Vineyard

42 hectares *vignes rouges*
  55% Cabernet Sauvignon
  25% Merlot
  20% Cabernet Franc

  4 hectares *vignes blanches*
  50% Sauvignon Blanc
  50% Sémillon

Production
  120 t. red (150,000 bottles)
    8 t. white (9,600 bottles)

The most surprising thing about this property is that there is not already an entire book devoted to it, its wines and its history! It is only possible to give a few morsels of these. It is world famous and its wines have maintained their reputation; sales attract enormous publicity – and soaring prices.

It is a very old estate. The word 'Brion' is said to be local dialect for 'gravel'. It seems to have been owned by a Jean de Ségur, another notable Bordeaux surname, as early as 1509, although, as 'Aubrion', it appears in records of the previous century. But it was in 1525 that Jean de Pontac, already prominent in civic activities in Bordeaux, married Jeanne de Bellon, daughter of the Mayor of Libourne, part of whose dowry was Haut Brion. The Pontac family seem to have been founded by an Arnaud de Pontac, whose death seems to have occurred about 1518; but the family tree is complicated by the fact that Jean de Pontac married three times – the last when he was seventy-six – and after having fathered fifteen children, died when he was 101 years old. He had served under five kings of France – six, if one counts Henri IV, who Jean, a fervent Catholic, always opposed – and he was supposedly the richest man in Bordeaux. It was Jean's fourth son, Bishop of Bazas, who inherited the estate, although not the house, and it was Jean's grandson, Geoffrey, who eventually took over the estate, his uncle the bishop bequeathing it to him. This man left Haut Brion to his son, Arnaud III, and his town house, the Maison Daurade. His wealth, his civic works and his influence were immense, yet he retained his interest in wine. It was his son who was sent to England to promote the wines of 'Pontac' and of Haut Brion. (An account of the activities of François-Auguste may be read on pp. 137–8).

Unfortunately, François-Auguste accumulated more debts than he could pay when he inherited the estate. His sisters married quite well, one married Jean-Denis d'Aulède, who was the proprietor of Château Margaux at that time, another married Jean-Baptiste de la Tresne, later a marquis; it was Thérèse d'Aulède de Lestonnac (see p. 280 with the association with La Mission Haut Brion) and a nephew, Louis-Amand de la Tresne, who split the great estate between them.

The success of Haut Brion in London is also recorded elsewhere (pp. 137–8). The 1707 *London Gazette* announced the sale of '. . . new French prized Clarets upon the gross lea and lately landed, being of the growths of Laffit, Margouze and Latour . . . plus 200 *barriques* of new French Obrian claret, taken and condemned at prize out of the ship Liberty'. Quite a haul!

According to Haut Brion's elegant handbook, it had become usual to bottle the wine at the estate by the middle of the eighteenth century, although definite orders seem to have been required before this was undertaken. '"Topping up" was done with new wine and the "drawing off" of the wine from its barrels . . . was done twice a year. The beneficial contact of the wine with the tannin in the wood led Viallon [the *maître de chai*] to keep the wine in barrels for eight years or more.'

It was at this time, just before the outbreak of the Revolution, that some of the most interesting papers come into the Haut Brion archives. For in 1787 Thomas Jefferson, in Paris, ordered the Honorary American Consul in Bordeaux, John Bondfield, to buy a barrel of Haut Brion; on being informed that only six casks were available anyway, Jefferson was told that Bondfield 'offered him 600 pounds for one of his *barriques* but he refused. I ought to get two cases from the first hogshead that he draws off. It is very much exaggerated to pay three pounds a bottle for a wine bought directly from the estate, but this vintage has such a reputation that those who have it are getting those prices.' One has to comment 'Plus ça change', but the reference to 'cases' is also of interest at this date.

Jefferson himself visited Haut Brion in May 1787 and commented on the soil which 'consists of sand in which there is an almost equal quantity of round gravel or little stones, and a little silt as in the soil of the Médoc'. A meticulous observer, he recorded details of vines and vineyards wherever he travelled and, the day after his visit, he wrote to a friend in Virginia,

'I cannot deny myself the pleasure of asking you to participate in a parcel of wine. It is of the vineyard of Obrion, one of the four established as the very best, and it is of the vintage 1784.' He wrote to Bondfield that Haut Brion 'is a wine of the first rank and seems to please the American palate more than all the others that I have been able to taste in France'. Not only did Jefferson serve it when he was President of the United States, but Washington, Madison and Monroe also offered it at the White House.

One of the d'Aulède daughters married a Count Jean-François de Fumel, one of the descendants of François-Auguste, bringing him two-thirds of Haut Brion, and it was this man's eldest son, Louis, who inherited the great estate, although the Marquis de la Tresne retained a small portion of it until 1840. It was Louis's son, Joseph, who made many improvements to the property, creating a pair of parks, the smaller of which still exists, an orangery and many buildings adjacent to the château itself. Joseph, who had become Governor of Guyenne, was a philanthropist on a large scale: he gave the huge fortress of the Château Trompette, in Bordeaux, of which he was governor, to the people of the city and had his gold plate melted down to relieve the hardship caused by bad harvests, in acknowledgement of which he was publicly thanked and made Mayor of Bordeaux – which did not prevent him and his daughter being guillotined in 1794. Only days afterwards, the head of the tribunal who had condemned them was himself arrested and executed.

The great estate did get back into the hands of the family, but, understandably, they left France and sold the property to Talleyrand in 1801. Although this remarkable diplomat kept it only for four years, he certainly made use of the wines which, accompanied by his great chef, Carême, went to the Congress of Vienna where so many schemes and manoeuvres of statesmanship took place during the lavish entertainments.

Subsequently, Haut Brion passed through various hands and, at the beginning of the nineteenth century, seems to have gone through a period of unpopularity.

Wilhelm Franck thought the vineyard was over-manured; he also suggested that the wine needed six or seven years in wood before being bottled, which would have put it at a disadvantage by comparison with wines that needed less time in cask. The estate had several owners and eventually the portion that had belonged to the La Tresne family was bought by a banker, Larrieu, who made many improvements, so that the whole vineyard was again united. It was as well that it was in good hands,

275

for the great vine plagues of the nineteenth century afflicted Haut Brion in spite of its selection as a first growth in the 1855 classification: according to the estate's brochure, the harvests from 1851 to 1854 and from 1881 to 1884 'were scarcely a fifth of normal'.

After the Larrieu ownership, some of the park had to be sold for building but, in 1933, the American financier Clarence Dillon came into the Gironde, with the idea of buying a property and, in 1934, purchased Haut Brion.

Clarence Dillon apparently inspected several top estates and there is a pleasant, though unsubstantiated story to the effect that, having seen Château Margaux, he was about to go to Cheval Blanc, with a view to buying that, but the weather was so cold that, even with a rug bought en route, he decided to opt for Haut Brion, as being nearer to Bordeaux – and warmth. It was Clarence Dillon's nephew, Seymour Weller, who, having become a French citizen, directed the property during World War II, when the house became a rest home for *Luftwaffe* pilots – it had originally been equipped as a field hospital. The *régisseur* was Georges Delmas, of a famous Bordeaux family, whose son, Jean, took over in 1961, continuing the tradition of fine wine making – and who was actually born at Haut Brion.

Clarence Dillon's son, Douglas, became the U.S. Ambassador to Paris in 1953 and his daughter, Joan, married H.R.H. Prince Charles of Luxembourg – he, being a Prince de Bourbon, was one of the descendants of Henri IV. On his death, in 1977, she married the Duc de Mouchy, one of whose ancestors had been an eighteenth-century governor of Guyenne. She had succeeded her cousin, Seymour Weller, as President of Haut Brion in 1975 and the Duc and Duchesse de Mouchy run the property today. Clarence Dillon died in 1979, aged ninety-six, having seen his glorious estate regain all its quality and fame.

The establishment is magnificent – there is no other word. Visitors may feel overwhelmed by the minutely groomed vineyard, the imposing buildings, the palatial winery; walking through the aisles of vats and casks, one brushes their sleek sides with awe, viewing the spotless floor – from which one could cheerfully eat a meal! – and enjoying the vistas of the lawns and flowerbeds, manicured into elegant trimness, it is impossible to believe that this basilica of claret can actually produce a wine worthy of its setting. Yet the red Haut Brion does not let down the awe-struck taster: 'elegant ... balanced, distinguished' comments Clive Coates and he, like most writers on claret, remarks that it is quite different in style from La

276

Mission. Some of my friends find Haut Brion akin to certain of the greater Médocs . . . Well, the higher one goes, in the echelons of tasting, the more the differences and subtleties emerge. I myself do not find Haut Brion red wines, such as I have had the good fortune to sample, really more than cousins of the Médocs: I cannot agree with the adjectives 'soft, with delicate, flowery aromas'. Opulent, although discreetly so, yes – subtly imposing, the beautiful assertiveness of the two Cabernets being gently underlined by the presence of the Merlot. But this is a real 'grand seigneur', it doesn't bother to be impressive, it lets the drinker find out how impressive it is, taking its time, indulging in a gentle crescendo of its bouquet to the nose and thereby informing the palate that something 'important' is in the offing. The flavour builds up from this introduction. I do not endorse the adjective 'bricky' that one of my younger colleagues uses, because this has connotations of coarseness that are out of place here, but I see that the term may have derived from the tinge of earthiness – in the fresh, almost wet smell and substance that can be so gratifying, even when this great wine has to conflict with other aromas and tastes, as in restaurants. Monsieur Delmas says that it is this hint of soil that should 'dominate the grape, though when the grape dominates the soil a less good wine is made'. Here is a wine from the soil of the Graves that seems its apogee. If anyone cannot give their heart to it they must give it their homage. For it is unquestionably great.

The white wine, which, as has been stated, was not submitted for the more recent classification (p. 242) is one that I have not tasted often enough to feel that I may risk a generalisation. It is certainly quite different from the 'neighbour across the road' white wine, and has registered with me as straightforward, cleanly finished and definite.

The 'second wine' of Haut Brion is Château Bahans. This was, until fairly recently, a non-vintage blend which I found enjoyable and 'classic' Graves on several occasions. Monsieur Delmas, one of the pioneers of clonal selection, has made important progress in this as well as with the *grand vin* and, in the late 1970s, the quality of the wine made with the acquired knowledge of the particular clones began to be so good that, from the 1982 vintage, a date was put onto Bahans; the abundant and good vintages of the early 1980s were conducive to this and most of the production today is a vintage wine although, of course, it is up to the makers to decide whether any non-vintage shall also be made. The pronunciation of the name, incidentally, seems to vary: I myself have known it to be given as 'By-once', with the final 's' sounded and this has come from fluent French speakers.

277

The sounding of many final consonants – such as Portets, Illats – is peculiar to the south-west of France; it is sometimes suggested that it is a relic of English occupation, although probably only an etymologist could be definite about this. The twang and tendency to put an 'ng' sound onto the end of many words in this part of France (as in *demain*) was noticed by Henry James in *A Little Tour in France*, which was published in 1882, although he doesn't write much about Bordeaux (except that it was impossible to get decent claret there and that no bottles for drinking were open at an exhibition being held!), but he ascribes the tendency to further south, in the region of Toulouse.

CHÂTEAU LA MISSION HAUT BRION (TALENCE)
CHÂTEAU LA TOUR HAUT BRION (TALENCE)
CHÂTEAU LAVILLE HAUT BRION (TALENCE)

Owner Domaines Clarence Dillon. Director, J. B. Delmas
Vineyards
La Mission
20 hectares *vignes rouges*
   60% Cabernet Sauvignon
   20% Cabernet Franc
   20% Merlot

La Tour Haut Brion
 6 hectares *vignes rouges*
   70% Cabernet Sauvignon
   15% Cabernet Franc
   15% Merlot

Laville Haut Brion
 6 hectares *vignes blanches*
   60% Sémillon
   40% Sauvignon Blanc

Production
   La Mission 84,000 bottles
   La Tour About 18,000 bottles
   Laville 20 t.

This is an astonishing trio of estates. La Mission itself is picturesque and full of interesting things and the wines of the three present a gamut of

278

fine white and red Graves, distinguished and world famous. As, from 1983, the properties have belonged to the estate 'across the road' – for Haut Brion is exactly that – the united vineyards represent an imposing complex, within the sprawl of suburban Bordeaux. Originally, it is possible that the La Mission estate formed part of the Haut Brion vineyard and the La Mission vines in fact extend on both sides of the road from Bordeaux out to Arcachon, so that one segment is actually in Pessac.

The first reference to La Mission is in 1630, when Dame Olive de Lestonnac, widow of one Antoine de Gourgue, made it the subject of a bequest. Her husband was the first president of the Parliament of Guyenne and obviously the property was substantial – the will refers to a 'grand chay cuvier garni d'une fouloire en pierre de taille' and with several plots of vines, given in 'journeaux', the measurement relating to the amount of work that could be done in a day. James Seely in *Great Bordeaux Wines* (1986) says the total extent was about 13 hectares. The will also mentions that the land adjoins some of the property of Monsieur de Pontac. Dame Olive's family obviously were not in favour of her gift to the Director-General of the Priests of the Clergy of Bordeaux, because the estate wasn't handed over until 1664. In 1682 the bequest was made over to the 'Prêcheurs de la Mission', who were usually referred to as 'Lazarists', as they had been founded by St Vincent de Paul in Paris and had their head-quarters at St Lazare. The 'missions' of the brotherhood were aimed at isolated country communities and they built a chapel at La Mission, which from 1698 went by this name; they also extended the vineyard and seem to have enjoyed much success with the sale of the wines.

After the property was sequestered at the Revolution it passed through several owners, several of whom appear to have been able in maintaining the vineyard and who also ran other estates in the absence of their owners; however, the property was not classified in 1855 – some writers appear to think that the disastrous effects of the oidium, which hit the vineyards just before the phylloxera, were the reason why the only Graves estate that was included in the famous classification was Haut Brion. La Mission had been put down as a fifth classed growth by Wilhelm Franck in 1845.

In 1903 a Victor Cousteau bought the estate. He became friends with Frédéric Woltner, who was working in Schröder & Constans, from whom Cousteau had acquired La Mission; Woltner, like so many distinguished Bordelais, was an outsider – from a family in Riga, Latvia. He held many agencies whose names are still well known and respected and he arranged with Cousteau that he should have first refusal if it was ever decided to sell La Mission. This occurred on Cousteau's retirement in 1919 and Frédéric Woltner then ran the property, increasing its reputation although, in the period between the two wars, it was difficult to regard such a small estate as a profitable investment. Cousteau's widow and Madame Woltner became friends and the latter left her property of La Tour Haut Brion to Madame Woltner when she died in 1934. Henri Woltner, Frédéric's son, was a progressive wine maker, installing glass-lined steel fermentation vats as early as 1926 – to the astonishment and shock of the traditionalist (and few are as traditional and conservative as wine makers already established and successful). It was at this time that white wine began to be made at the estate; this, as Edmund Penning-Rowsell in *The Wines of Bordeaux* points out out, is quite different in style from the white wine of Haut Brion – I would say it is more elegant, if comparisons have to be made. Henri Woltner's brother, Fernand, had two children, the daughter, Françoise, and her husband, François Dewavrin, taking over the estate with great success in 1977. All the wines have achieved high prices in recent years and a great pre-sale tasting of some of them at Christie's in November 1986 resulted in crowds of the discriminating jostling around the bottles and spittoons; curiously, although my tasting notes are ecstatic about many, notably the glorious 1961 La Mission, some of the lighter vintages, which I sometimes find mean and shrill, were pleasant, amiable and far more attractive than certain Médocs of the same years. Michael Broadbent's tasting notes repeatedly stress the longevity of both the red and the white wines.

In 1983 the Dewavrin-Woltners sold the property to Haut Brion. François Dewavrin, himself of a distinguished Flemish family, has many different interests in wine, but now he and his wife have bought property in the Napa Valley, California, where, says a French commentator, everything is perfect for growing Chardonnay. The estate here, too, is old, first laid out in the 1860s by two Bordeaux wine makers – a pleasant coincidence. Although no wine could be made during the Prohibition period, the close relationships maintained with Bordeaux today make the prospects bright for this new property.

As all books stress, the wines of these estates in Talence are quite different from those of Haut Brion – another mystery of wine, but the *croupes* or ridges in the vineyard probably account for at least some of this distinctive character. Everything is admirably maintained and the heads that were shaken when 'modern' equipment was put in – such as the rectangular white vats in the 1950s – have since copied what were then revolutionary methods. The house at La Mission is also totally different from that of Haut Brion, with many works of art on display, including a collection of holy-water stoups. Clive Coates recounts a pleasant story of La Mission in World War II: after serving as a U.S. embassy, it became a German headquarters, the general in charge making his bedroom in the chapel, Madame Woltner living on the first floor. When the war was nearly over, the general asked Madame Woltner if he might listen to the Allied broadcasts on her radio. Eventually – as occurred with some of the occupying forces in the Bordeaux region who were able to renew contacts with former friends in the wine world – they apparently used to dine together, while risking fearful penalties when tuning in to the outside broadcasts.

CHÂTEAU LA TOUR MARTILLAC (GRAVES LÉOGNAN)

Owner G.F.A. du Château La Tour Martillac. Director, Jean Kressman

Vineyard

25 hectares *vignes rouges*
  60% Cabernet Sauvignon
  25% Merlot
   6% Cabernet Franc
   5% Malbec
   4% Petit Verdot

 5 hectares *vignes blanches*
  60% Sémillon
  30% Sauvignon
  10% 'various vines from the last century'

Production
  80 t. red (about 8,500 cases) (120,000 bottles)
  15 t. white (about 2,500 cases) (30,000 bottles)

This is an ancient property and as a *domaine* it was at one time in the Montesquieu family, who built, probably in the twelfth century, the creeper-coated pointy-topped tower that stands, islanded, on a lawn in the courtyard. Because of this tower, the estate used to be called 'La Tour', but in order to avoid confusion with the great first growth of the Médoc and the numerous other 'La Tour' names that occur in the Gironde, the name of the nearby village of Martillac was added.

The vineyard itself seems to have been laid down in the 1880s and it is all in one piece, some of the vines being reputedly very old. The Kressmann family – Alfred Kressman bought the property in 1930 – came to the Bordeaux region from Germany in the middle of the nineteenth century and they are now one of the great wine 'dynasties', influential, with many branches, and much respected in various sections of the wine trade. Jean Kressmann, the present owner of La Tour Martillac, is most erudite and scholarly, his *régisseur* is Loïc Kressmann. When the Kressmanns first bought the estate the stress was on white wines, today made in accordance with the most modern techniques. The reds are traditionally made, vinified in wooden vats, sometimes for more than a week at a time; they go into wood for maturation for 18–22 months, the *barriques* being renewed in the proportion of one-third each year.

Until all the finer wines of the Bordeaux region began to be bottled at their respective estates, the La Tour Martillac wines were bottled by the Kressmanns in Bordeaux itself, but now they are all bottled at the property, with much enlargement of the premises being necessary. Yet the slightly remote, aged charm of the overall atmosphere remains and all those members of the Kressmann clan whom I have been fortunate enough to meet are equally delightful and conscientious. It is my loss that I have not often been able to drink the wines except at intervals, but they have always rewarded a sampling. The whites are fine, full and aromatic, capable of development long term (which unfortunately they do not always get, such are the pressures on both merchants and restaurateurs in export markets as well as in the region), and, like many other white Graves of top quality, they combine the Graves's special individuality with a certain complexity that I have found very attractive, although sometimes they pass through a reserved, withdrawn stage prior to attaining their prime. The reds are also full – needing time, but with agreeable fruitiness even at the beginning of their lives; perhaps they are a little more direct than the whites, as can occur in the wines of an estate that makes both red and white. Only the first vattings are entitled to the label of the estate; the *deuxièmes cuvées*, which may make use both of the *vin de presse* and the grapes from vines that are under ten years old, are sold as 'La Grave Martillac'.

CHÂTEAU MALARTIC-LAGRAVIÈRE (LÉOGNAN)
Owner G.F.A. Marly-Ridoret. Director, J. Marly
Vineyard
12 hectares *vignes rouges*
   44% Cabernet Sauvignon
   31% Cabernet Franc
   25% Merlot

   1.5 hectares *vignes blanches*
   100% Sauvignon

Production
   60 t. red (6,000–8,000 cases) (85,000 bottles)
   10 t. white (800–1,000 cases) (10,000 bottles)

This vineyard, facing that of Fieuzal, is another all in one piece. (In former times it was the Domaine de Lagravière.) It is named after the Malartic family, who owned or had associations with it before the French Revolution – the town of Malartic, north-west of Montreal, in the Canadian province of Quebec, gets its name from the Vicomte Maurès de Malartic, who went there in 1756. During the nineteenth century, the estate was sold several times, passing into the hands of other well-known proprietors of the region and, today, being owned by the Marly-Ridoret family, who also have traditions of wine making among their forebears. In the recent past it has undergone considerable rehabilitation – particularly necessary after four years of occupation by the Germans, who kept motor-cycles in the drawing-room and did a great deal of damage. The château itself is cream, trim and pleasant rather than imposing, with a large white *chai* a little distant from it, on the edge of the vineyard.

It is rather odd that the wine is seldom seen on lists in the U.K., for all authorities agree on its quality. However, it has a tradition of being somewhat austere until it is thoroughly matured, which may have put off some drinkers, who prefer clarets that are markedly *bouqueté* and almost soft in character. The recent association of the great Professor Peynaud with the estate, to whom he is the oenological consultant, may, it is thought, be slightly altering the style so as to give the wine wider appeal. As I have only drunk rather old vintages, I cannot pronounce on this, but my memories of them are quite impressive – a little aloof and reserved, perhaps, but with definite nobility and firm, well-bred character, the flavour being inclined to remind me a little of certain Pauillacs – possibly because of the high proportion of Cabernet Sauvignon. The white wines also apparently require time to demonstrate their quality, but I cannot speak from experience about them.

CHÂTEAU OLIVIER (LÉOGNAN)

Owner The P. de Bethmann family. Director, Jean-Jacques de Bethmann
Vineyard
19 hectares *vignes rouges*
   70% Cabernet Sauvignon
   30% Merlot

16 hectares *vignes blanches*
   65% Sémillon
   30% Sauvignon
   5% Muscadelle

Production
   100 t. red (10,000 cases)
   110 t. white (11,000 cases)

This is an old-fashioned, historic property, somewhat secluded in a wood. It has certainly been known as a vineyard since the twelfth century, and in the fourteenth century one of the Olivier or d'Olivey sons married into the La Brède family, the bride being Elisabeth de Lalande, daughter of Arnaud de La Brède. The Black Prince, son of King Edward III of England, apparently used to frequent the place because of the excellent hunting – wolves, boar and a variety of game in the surrounding forests.

When, in 1409, says James Seely (*Great Bordeaux Wines*, 1986), the Jurats of Bordeaux became owners of the *comté* of Ornon, they laid claim to the various estates there, including that of Olivier. The owners of Olivier resisted and the resulting lawsuit, eventually settled in their favour, continued for centuries.

In 1663 the property formed part of the dowry of Marie de Lasserre, who married Pierre Pesnel, Baron de La Brède; her daughter married Jacques de Secondat, father of the great Montesquieu (see p. 307). But between 1687 and 1886 the estate changed hands many times and there were many alterations: one of the owners 'restored' the building in a way that we can now say was far from ideal, another one, for no apparent reason, attempted to destroy many of the records, although fortunately some of the material was safely at La Brède. At least no one tried to drain the moat, which makes Olivier an outstandingly picturesque property.

The Frankfurt banking house of de Bethmann had become connected by marriage with the family then owning Olivier; the bank was only one of many finance houses well established in Bordeaux. In 1945 the de Bethmanns took over the estate and for a time the wines made there were sold through the Bordeaux establishment of Louis Eschenauer. From November 1981, however, the de Bethmann family have become solely responsible for the development and promotion of both the red and the white wines. They are also carefully maintaining the estate overall, its beauty certainly meriting attention.

The red wines are made traditionally, about a third of the number of *barriques* in which they age being renewed each year. There are plans to extend the vineyard as well. The white wines, say the de Bethmanns, are extremely individual because of the high proportion of Sémillon in the vineyard, whereby length is given to the finished wine. It will be of great interest to watch the progress of this formerly important estate from now on; although a highish standard has been maintained for the wines, I have tended to find them lacking in personality and excitement – maybe their individuality has been somewhat suppressed in the past and now will be allowed to develop.

CHÂTEAU PAPE CLÉMENT (PESSAC)
Owner Montagne & Cie. Director, Bernard Pujol
Vineyard
29 hectares *vignes rouges*
   60% Cabernet Sauvignon
   40% Merlot

 0.3 hectares *vignes blanches* (wine very seldom on sale)
   33% Sémillon
   33% Sauvignon
   33% Muscadelle

Production
  Red (130,000 bottles)
  White (1,200 bottles)

A description and account of the early history of this venerable estate is given in the chapter devoted to 'The Gascon Pope' – Clément V (Chapter 9). In accordance with Clément's wishes, it remained the property of the Archbishops of Bordeaux until the French Revolution. The reputation of the wine always seems to have been high, but, as it was reserved for the Archbishops' use, it seldom came onto the market, although Clive Coates thinks it possible that it is the wine referred to by Rabelais as *vin clémentin*, which, as he points out, would antedate Pepys's mention of 'Ho Bryan' by a century and a half, because Rabelais's dates are – approximately – 1494–1553. The high-ranking clergy of the medieval and later centuries did a great deal of entertaining, both of other clerics and of the nobility; often their 'palaces' or main headquarters were the places where eminent persons, including royalty, could stay when travelling. The wine was mentioned in the *Chronique bordelaise* in 1619.

Together with all church property, the estate was sequestered in the Revolution and then, when sold, it passed through many hands. By the middle of the nineteenth century it was considered second only in importance to Haut Brion; while the property of a J.-B. Clerc, it won important awards in 1861 and 1864 and the vineyard was extended. Prices of the wine were on a level with Médoc second growths.

An M. J. Cinto bought the estate after Clerc and, rather unfortunately, built the angular, grey, Victorian Gothic mansion – it was a bad time for architecture, except, I suppose, for municipal buildings and railway stations. Then Pape Clément was bought after World War I by an English family called Maxwell, but this was the period of the world-wide Depression and the whole estate was allowed to run down – to rehabilitate a wine property requires both a lot of money and informed use of it, for vines need time to become established and what may have been successful in one vineyard is not always ideal for one even near by. The final blow occurred in 1937, when the vineyard was badly damaged by hail, in June. The estate was about to be sold and used for building but fortunately in 1939 it was bought by Paul Montagne.

This was a remarkable man, a poet, able in a variety of ways. He devoted himself to restoring the place, although it was not possible to achieve much until after World War II and the 1950s. Since then progress has been steady and although Paul Montagne was blind for the last fifteen years of his life – he was 94 when he died – he lived to see the wines become famous and respected once more.

The courtyard, with the *cuvier* and *chais* around it, is progressively being put in order and extensions are being made to buildings around. The house is not much used at present and suffered badly in a fire in 1983; when renovations are complete it will be used as a conference centre, although the *régisseur* will have an office in it and some rooms will be used by the administration.

The wine making is traditional, those in charge stressing that a large band of pickers are engaged, so as to get in the fruit fast, within three to five days. It is also pointed out that, although modern technology contributes to both equipment employed and procedures followed, the wine maintains its established style and, although it used to be made in concrete vats, given one-third new oak, this has been increased since 1985, now being about 70 per cent. Clive Coates comments pertinently, in his monthly periodical *The Vine*, that Pape Clément is 'the most Médocain in taste of all top Graves properties. While Château Haut Brion and Domaine de Chevalier are characterised by their elegance, La Mission by its firm masculinity, and Haut Bailly by its rich plumminess, Pape Clément has a certain reserve one does not often find in Graves. This is allied with a more obvious Cabernet ripe fruitiness, a decisive cut from the new oak ... and, when young, quite a lot of tannin for a Graves, mellowing into a wine of great complexity, only after ten years or so in a good vintage showing its best.'

This is a Graves I myself have always found rewarding: the way in which it unfurls its delicate but pervasive fragrance, the soft, ripe fruit with overtones of spice and undertones of warm, firm clarety 'breed' is delectable. Some of the wines of the vintages of the 1920s I have been lucky enough to try have been memorable – but they, like some vintages made more recently, always seem to need time to reveal themselves.

CHÂTEAU SMITH HAUT LAFITTE

Owner Société Louis Eschenauer. Director, René Baffert. *Régisseur*, Claude Guérin

Vineyard
45.4 hectares *vignes rouges*
   69% Cabernet Sauvignon
   20% Merlot
   11% Cabernet Franc

  5.60 hectares *vignes blanches*
   100% Sauvignon

Production
   225 t. red (22,500 cases)
    30 t. white (3,000 cases)

This is a very old property, under vines in the twelfth century, but it seems to have been first known as a separate plantation in 1549, when it belonged to the Verrier family. Then, in 1720, it was bought by one George Smith, a very English name! The word *fitte* or *faite* is Old French for a mound or hillock. The Mayor of Bordeaux, Sadi Duffour-Dubergier, owned the property from 1856, winning many awards for its wines. Then it seems to have passed into various hands, coming partly into the portfolio of Eschenauer in 1902, who became owners in 1958. The estate had dwindled for lack of capital and it took some time before the revived investment could affect the wines.

     The wines of Smith Haut Lafitte that I have tasted have been pleasant – but they have not, in my limited experience, yet achieved more than agreeable and typical Graves quality. The white wines are straightforward Sauvignon and therefore – straightforward Sauvignon from Bordeaux. This estate does make wines that appeal to a wide market, yet could they maybe aim at anything more than a safe, typical standard? The trim property may have a future that will be of greater interest and the huge, subterranean *chai* should be able to nurture wines that, in its air-conditioned atmosphere, may be more excitingly interesting in the future.

SOME OTHER PROPERTIES

CHÂTEAU LA LOUVIÈRE AND LES VIGNOBLES ANDRÉ LURTON
Owner André Lurton
Vineyard

Among the estates owned by André Lurton are Château Couhins-Lurton (see p. 269), Rochemorin, the former property of Montesquieu (see p. 307), its name supposedly deriving from 'The stone of the Moors', and Château de Cruzeau, at Saint-Médard-d'Eyrans. This last, making red and white wines, is another of the historic estates, certainly under vines since the eighteenth century and possibly earlier. André Lurton, who comes of a wine family and was born at Château Bonnet, Grézillac, in the Entre-deux-Mers, where he still lives, acquired Rochemorin and Cruzeau in 1973 and a long-term programme of replanting, restoration and general rehabilitation was begun, so that the wines merit serious attention by now.

The diadem of the collection, however, must be La Louvière. This is another estate rather hidden in a forest, but the château itself is an eighteenth-century masterpiece, which André Lurton is restoring at the same time as constructing gigantic installations near by, which will enable many more wine lovers to enjoy the wine. He bought this estate in 1965.

La Louvière gets its name from the wolves (*louves*) in the local forests and made the region a favourite place for hunting with the medieval nobility. It was bought in 1550 by Jean de Guilloche, according to the elegant account of it in a remarkable tasting organised by Sotheby's at the London Wine Fair in 1986. Guilloche was an important man in the Bordelais and his daughter, Joanne, became 'Dame de Roquetaillade et de La Louvière', extensive holdings. In the seventeenth century an Armand de Gascq, who obviously was of the region, bought the estate when he was Abbot of St Ferme, at Chartres, and the Carthusian monks of the order ran the property until the Revolution – another example, among many, of the importance of the religious holdings in this region.

In 1798 La Louvière was bought by J.-B. de Mareilhac and to this event it probably owes its exquisite château, for de Mareilhac was in the building and construction business in Bordeaux and it is said that it was thanks to him that the magnificent Grand Théâtre was built in the centre of Bordeaux, although as this dates from immediately before the Revolution, I am inclined to agree with M. André Lurton's theory, as cited by James Seely in *Great Bordeaux Wines* (1986), that it was a pupil of the architect Victor Louis and not Louis himself who built La Louvière. It is pure eighteenth century in style, with a mirror-like lake at the back; those familiar with Château Margaux may well find resemblances here, for the Médoc château was also designed by a pupil of Louis in 1795.

During the nineteenth century the property, although not the wines and their reputation, was somewhat neglected, and in 1911 it was bought by the then Mayor of Léognan. In 1956 it was declared a *monument historique* and, after André Lurton bought it, the restoration of the interior, where there are important painted ceilings, was begun as well as the repair of the outside.

Today, the vineyard is made up of sixty-two hectares, of which fifty-five are under vines, the majority being devoted to the production of red wine. At present the proportions are: 70% Cabernet Sauvignon, 20% Merlot, 10% Cabernet Franc. The black grapes are machine picked and fermented in either epoxy-lined concrete vats or stainless steel tanks. They go into oak for a year – one-third of the casks being new wood – and then have another year in tanks. The grapes for the white wines are: 85% Sauvignon, 15% Sémillon, and unlike the reds, are picked by hand. The fermentation, says the Sotheby's brochure, 'takes place in a number of vessels. A part is fermented in epoxy- or glass-lined *cuves*, some in stainless steel and the balance in new oak *barriques*. Temperature is controlled by pressure at between 16–18°C. New oak *barriques* are used for ageing for a few months and the wine is bottled within a year to keep it as fresh as possible.'

The red wines, in very general terms, have seemed to me to achieve a taut, often charming style, the bouquet sometimes indicating a massive flavour which they do not always attain. Again, like most fine Graves, they need time to show themselves. The whites, however, which François Lurton, who conducted a tasting of both white and red in May 1986, stressed are, like other good white Graves, capable of surprising longevity. Since 1984 they have all gone into new oak. Some vintages attain a very large-scale flavour, many display a delightful bouquet that I have sometimes noted as 'honey and gingerbread' with the spicy, vanilla aroma often emerging. This is an estate to admire, to watch and, in most instances, to find the wines that make most enjoyable Graves drinking.

An estate I have also been told to watch for is LARRIVET HAUT BRION, a very trim-looking estate, with the *chais* on one side of the road, the house on the other. Apparently it once formed part of a bigger property belonging to the Canolle family, for whom it was overall named. It has belonged to the Guillimaud family since 1941 and the previous year the name was changed round from Haut Brion Larrivet, as the result of proceedings by the great first growth. The property was sold in 1986. (The 'Larrivet' part of the name refers to one of the local streams.) Mostly red wine is made, plus a very little white and at least one shipper on the lookout for up and coming claret is seriously interested, so this is a name to note in the future.

At Pujols-sur-Ciron is CHÂTEAU SAINT-ROBERT, an estate I have missed seeing. It produces both red and white wine, and an odd story about it is told by P. Joseph Lacoste in *La Route du vin en Gironde* (1948). Apparently when Prince Bismarck, at that time military attaché in Paris, was going down to Biarritz, he somehow heard that the wine made at Saint-Robert was specially attractive. He got himself invited there and the hospitality laid on was to such effect that he was quite incapable of returning to Bordeaux, but had to be put up for the night at Saint-Robert.

However much one makes notes when travelling, there is more satisfaction in studying a range of wines altogether, which is what I was able to do in London, at a showing of 'Lesser-Known Graves' in June 1986. There were several recent vintages shown, also both white and red wines, and I have here merely summarised what I noted then plus what I later jotted down while I was in the Graves in September 1986. In some instances, however, only either the white or the red was on show at the large-scale tasting, so my overall impressions could not always be registered at one time – another of the endless difficulties of 'fixing' tasting reactions.

The 1985 white CHÂTEAU SAINT-AGRÈVES, at Landiras, I thought an important wine, made on a large scale, obviously matured in wood (which it is) and almost 'meaty' in substance on the palate. The 1985 CHÂTEAU GENSAC, white, was a light, neatly made wine, well in balance. It comes from Pujols-sur-Ciron. The red Saint-Agrèves of 1984 was also a wine of substance, on a large scale, but, maybe because of the vintage, I did not find it as attractive as the younger white.

CHÂTEAU DOMS, from Portets, showed both its white and red wines at the London tasting and I drank it on several occasions in the region. It gets its odd name from the Latin 'dominus' and Alexandre Deleyre, editor of the *Encyclopedia*, was born there in 1726 and owned the estate. The overall style of Doms is full and four-square, maybe a little lacking in delicacy.

Another Landiras property is CHÂTEAU D'ARRICAUD, owned by M. and Mme Albert Bouyx. It is all in one piece, extending for about 40 ha with 25 ha under vines. Before the Revolution, the handsome house was begun by Comte Joachim de Chalup, at one time one of the Présidents of the Bordeaux Parlement; he was imprisoned in the Terror at Cadillac but fortunately survived and completed the building, which, together with its vineyard, has a fine view over the Garonne. Thirty tonneaux of red, 80 tonneaux of white wine are made and I particularly liked the white of 1984, well made, full and proportioned, the presence of the Sémillon discreet but definite in the back taste and underneath the immediate dryness. This is not surprising for, according to Féret in *Bordeaux et ses vins* (revised edition, 1986), the white wine vines are in the proportions: 70 per cent Sémillon, 25 per cent Sauvignon, 5 per cent Muscadelle. The reds have 65 per cent Cabernet Sauvignon, 30 per cent Merlot, 5 per cent Malbec.

CHÂTEAU CABANNIEUX, at Portets, is also an estate making red and white wines, with marked fragrance of warmth and spice, and an open, trim, pleasant style. CHERET-PITRES, CRABITEY and the CLOS DE LA TUILERIE are other Portets growths that I have often drunk with enjoyment. The red 1984 CHÂTEAU LAFARGUES, at Martillac, is another spicy-smelling wine and the 1983 DOMAINE DE LA SOLITUDE, from the same place, was fairly open textured and full, although the white 1985 of Domaine de la Solitude was an immediately full, almost fat wine, definitely for drinking soon, although I did not manage to follow up this impression in the region. There was even more charm and pleasant aroma about the 1985 white CHÂTEAU LA CROIX, from Langon, although the red of 1983 seemed a little 'pushy', trying too hard to impress. On so many occasions it is the white wines of the 'baby' Graves that provide interest, showing that the belief in their future by such as Pierre Coste (see p. 217) is justified and that their past reputation is well founded. My tasting notes about the white CHÂTEAU BRONDELLES, from Langon, are much the same – crisp, fresh, with a pleasing back taste that I describe as 'minerally'.

CHÂTEAU ARCHAMBEAU, at Illats, is a wine that I drank with enjoyment on several occasions in the region: making more white than red, it is one of those estates that have a foot in several camps – for it is, according to U.K. wine merchant Philip Tite, who delightedly introduced it on his autumn wine list in 1986, on the edge of Barsac and wines made here may, as was explained (p. 255), be marketed as 'Cérons'. Significantly, Dr Jean-Philippe Dubourdieu, the owner, is the nephew of Pierre Dubourdieu (p. 214) of Doisy-Daëne. Archambeau's sweet white I haven't tasted, but the red is direct and fresh, the dry white also pleasant. Another small-scale but agreeable wine is the CLOS D'UZA, which once belonged to Château

Yquem, from Saint-Pierre-de-Mons; it makes both red and white, as does CHÂTEAU DE CARDAILLAN, at Toulenne, which nestles against the estate of CHÂTEAU DE MALLE – in fact it is the 'Graves' part of this impressive property and it is at Malle that the wine is made.

At Mazères, there is the imposing site of ROQUETAILLADE-LA-GRANGE, where MM Pierre and Jean Guignard make red and white wines, in addition to handling some from near-by properties and, as far as Pierre Guignard is concerned, doing much promotional work for the Graves. The white wine is fresh and light, the red of the 1984 vintage surprisingly full, with a crisp fruity acidity, the overall style being thoroughly engaging. It is not wood matured and the make-up of the red wine vineyard is 25 per cent Cabernet Sauvignon, 40 per cent Merlot, 25 per cent Cabernet Franc, 10 per cent Malbec, which doubtless accounts for the unusual and appealing flavour.

The property of CHÂTEAU LES JAUBERTHES, at Saint-Pardon-de-Conques, is one whose wines I have not yet tasted, but its history makes it sound interesting. It now belongs to the Marquis de Pontac, and, in the very distant past, was part of an estate actually belonging to Paulinus (p.62), who gave it to the chapter of Saint-Seurin in Bordeaux. In the twelfth century it came into the hands of Armand de Gassies, the overlord of Saint Pierre, in return for an annual payment of twelve lampreys, due at Easter!

The Langon growth of CHÂTEAU LUDEMAN LA CÔTE makes red and white wines, the white wine here interesting me somewhat less than the red which, from the 1983 vintage, was endowed with a flowery charm and fruity taste. But inevitably I have had to omit many more names.

The estate that greatly impressed me, even before I was fortunate enough to meet the owner, was CHÂTEAU MAGENCE, from Saint-Pierre-de-Mons. Monsieur Guillot de Suduiraut, as his name implies, is one of the famous first growth of Sauternes and he is both respected and deservedly popular throughout the region. The first time I tasted the 1985 white Magence I noted 'very classic white Graves' and, on future occasions, had my impression of a finely made wine, full and notably fragrant confirmed. The red, too, is extremely fresh and crisp, the blackcurrant fruitiness being topped by what is almost a peppermint herb-tinged bouquet. Slightly more white wine is made than red, the *cépages* of the red being 46 per cent Cabernet Sauvignon, 27 per cent each of Merlot and Cabernet Franc; the white is half and half Sémillon and Sauvignon. The vineyard, meticulously maintained, is on a slightly elevated site.

293

At a time when 'organic' wines are attracting attention – although no definition of what such a term means has been established, so that there are, at the time of writing, some wines that would seem to be more 'organic' than others – I have found a red Graves that does come into this category, at least in a number of ways. This is the CLOS LA PÉRICHÈRE which, according to the latest edition of Féret, is in Castres, although its label says it is in Portets. The owner is Gabriel Guérin and the production is 20 tonneaux of red wine. The 1982 had a pleasant, definite bouquet, almost flowery but very firm, the initial fruity flavour making a charming initial impact on the palate. According to the shippers, West Heath Wine of Pirbright in Surrey, this, like the other wines shown in London in October 1987, contained no additives apart from the bare minimum of SO_2. But because, up to now, I have not been able to compare wines categorised as 'organic' alongside those from the same region and the same grapes, it is not fair to draw any conclusions from only a few samplings. The Clos La Périchère was both agreeable and well made, as far as I could judge.

But as so many people have begun their serious acquaintance of the Graves at Portets, at Château Rahoul, it is right to conclude with an account of this estate, just off the main road at Portets itself.

CHÂTEAU RAHOUL seems to have been built by Guillaume Raoul in 1646, according to an inscription on what is certainly an old-established property, although it has been added to in various ways throughout the centuries, fortunately without the basic classic lines of the house being distorted; the orangery and walled garden are hidden from the entrance, as is the swimming pool on the other side. When the estate acquired the 'h' in its name is not known, nor, nowadays, does anyone know how to interpret the shadows cast by the indentations on the ancient chunky sundial, which is supposed to give dates, phases of the moon and other information as well as the hours of the day. After the Revolution the very famous Bordeaux family Balguerie became the proprietors, then in 1862 a Comte de Camiran, another name that recurs in history. But until quite recently the estate seems to have been somewhat undistinguished, unless one can count a lawyer who, James Seely in *Great Bordeaux Wines* (1986) says, was sent to prison for fraud.

In 1972 David Robson, an Englishman, bought Rahoul, but sold it in 1978 to an Australian concern, led by the well-known writer and wine maker, Len Evans, and his partner, Peter Fox; in the previous year a Dane, Peter Vinding-Diers, had been brought in to run the estate, his knowledge of wine making having been enriched by study in South Africa and Australia. (He owns another property, Domaine la Grave, which makes red wine also at Rahoul.) Tragically, Peter Fox, the financial genius behind the concern, was killed in a car accident and what had been apparently an expanding set of wine estates – including property in California as well – had again to change hands and Rahoul now belongs to another concern.

Peter Vinding-Diers has introduced many innovations at Rahoul, in spite of the vicissitudes of the ownership and, although the estate makes more red wine than white, it is the whites that have attracted enormous attention – from other producers as well as from the wine-loving public. His work with yeasts and the use of skin contact with white wines has once again provided the injection of inspiration that the 'outsider' can sometimes bestow, and he also experiments with different types of oak in which to mature the white wines. Significantly, in view of what I have written elsewhere about the white grapes of the Graves, the Rahoul white wines are made wholly from Sémillon, although when fermented with the yeasts of some of the other fine properties, the differences that emanate are astonishing – Peter would say that he has no time to write about his achievements but it is to be hoped that someone will do so before too long, so that this major alteration in wine making will be recorded in detail.

The comment of a South African journalist after visiting the Graves is well worth quoting (from *Wynboer*, August 1987): 'Anyone who underestimates the influence of yeast on flavour need only taste one of Peter's experiments to convince them otherwise. He believes each property "houses" its own composition of yeasts which give a particular character to its wines. To prove his point and to stress the importance of individuality, he pressed Sémillon from one piece of vineyard at Rahoul, split the juice into three and inoculated with natural yeasts from Ch. Rahoul, d'Angludet and Lynch Bages. Vinification for each was identical. Broad, rich peaches; fresh, fruity "Sauvignon"; artificially perfumed, acidic, are my respective comments on these three totally different wines.'

The red wines of Rahoul are very charming, maintaining a balanced style, with the fruitiness of good Graves. Their charm probably derives much from the 70 per cent of Merlot in the vineyard, with 30 per cent Cabernet Sauvignon. It would be impossible to mention Rahoul at all without at least a reference to Susie Vinding-Diers, whose considerable achievements at one of England's great teaching hospitals, where she was theatre sister at a time when history was being made there, have adjusted themselves to transforming the hospitality of Rahoul to delectable heights and making of the vintage-time fare something that creates great satisfaction.

As will have been realised, even some of the least-known names of Graves properties can call up a proud past, rich in history and traditions. It is exciting today to observe a revival and progress of so many.

As this book goes to press, it is sad to hear that Peter Vinding-Diers and his family are severing their association with Ch. Rahoul. The contribution he has made to the wines of the region is widely admitted and his work, as well as the delight many have enjoyed of the friendship of Peter and Susie, will remain as one of the important recent achievements in the evolution of Graves wines today.

19

LILLET

THE GRAVES APERITIF

ANY wine regions have their own local aperitifs, liqueurs, or 'occasional' drinks. Where wine is made, variations on table wine usually tempt the wine maker or technician to experiment, using such materials as are cheap or surplus to ordinary requirements. Some of these extra drinks fulfil a useful rôle, utilising wine, must, fruits that might otherwise be unsaleable or, in their original form, unsuitable for immediate consumption. Such variations are pleasant, novel and, often, a small-scale, home-made drink can swell into big business.

The concept of the inn, tavern, café, 'pub' is, of course, very old. Even in a locality where wine might be available, except to the very poor, as part of daily fare, some kind of alcoholic drink taken outside the home has always appealed to a wide market: the drink might be taken on the way back from work to what could be a somewhat cheerless home or – as is often forgotten – the drink could be welcome on the way from home to work, when something to warm up the system of a consumer who maybe had had no breakfast and might have only a piece of bread for a midday meal must frequently have been much craved. The café, the bar or, in parts of Britain, the alehouse, were places of casual refreshment of importance and what they purveyed had considerable social significance.

The armies of cleaning women who, in the earlier part of this century in parts of the U.K. revived themselves after an overnight stint with port and lemon (lemonade), the navvies and market porters in the City downing their 'shorts' of spirit with a 'chaser' of some kind of beer, the dockyard workers adding a tot of rum to a mug of tea or, in Scandinavia, those who laced their morning coffee with schnapps and the executive who, having worked for most of the previous twenty-four hours, orders some brandy or Scotch as a 'pipe opener' or 'heart starter' are all following the same inclination.

It was in the bars of Turin in the eighteenth century that vermouth, essentially aromatised wine, came commercially to life. All around the Mediterranean spirits or some form of wine – often sweet, comforting and higher in strength than table wine – catered for this need for a drink before or after work. The modern businessman, who sends his secretary for a cup of coffee and a biscuit on arrival at the office, is doing the same thing. The place where the 'occasional' drink was available historically fulfilled a social need; the coffee houses and clubs of Europe and North America in the not too distant past and to the present day were places where rumours were appraised, deals were often done, plots and plans were hatched. So too in the *auberge*, *estaminet*, *taverne*. For various reasons people often need to meet and conduct certain activities away from their homes, but in a semi-public place.

The first French café was set up in 1672 by an Armenian in Paris, but the café as we should now recognise it – a place where other refreshments than just coffee were on sale – was first established there in 1686 and named after its owner: the Café Procope. Cafés became enormously popular; in addition to drinks, newspapers were available for anyone to read and, as publications of this type were expensive, the café was a type of reading-room. Montesquieu inveighed against cafés in his *Lettres persanes*: 'Those who frequent such places stir up silly thoughts in each other's minds.' It sounds as if he preferred salon rather than café society. Well-to-do men had their clubs which, in many instances, were the descendants of the guilds and trade associations of former times, but for the ambitious the occasional visit to a café could be important to anybody hoping to make his way, via useful contacts, in both business and local affairs.

Some idea of the routine of life in and around Bordeaux after the Revolution is indicated in the accounts given by the French Consul at Civitavecchia, Henri Beyle-Stendhal who, in 1838, toured the south of France and the Gironde fairly thoroughly. By this time the café, the club and a fairly wide range of drinks therein were quite usual. He states that: 'A Bordeaux businessman sees his wife only at meals. On rising, he goes to his office; at five o'clock he goes to the Exchange which he leaves at six and goes home for dinner. At half-past seven he is off to his club where he spends his time reading newspapers, talking with his friends and gambling. Not until midnight does he go home and often not until two o'clock in the morning. The women spend their evenings completely alone.... Many married men keep a mistress whose house they visit from seven to nine o'clock in the evening. These young women live in little one-storey houses, or sometimes in a house with only an entrance floor, but the whole house is theirs alone ... those young women are much happier than the married women, for every day they spend at least two hours with the man who prefers them.' Of course, such generalisations risk being far too sweeping, but a similar routine could have been observed in other regions and other countries at the period. The absence of public holidays, except for church festival days, plus the increase in trade and commercial life in the nineteenth century put considerable stress on businessmen and agricultural workers alike. The 'pause for refreshment' was one of the necessary 'bread and circus' alleviations of toil at the time – and the 'occasional' drink was increasingly in demand.

Paul and Raymond Lillet, merchants of fine wines and spirits, founded their business at Podensac in 1872. Theirs was (and remains) a family firm. At a time when the annual *per capita* consumption of wine in France was around 200 litres, they did well. They supplied numerous bars, cafés and other similar establishments. Podensac being where it is, they had plenty of customers on their doorstep, for traffic continued to pass along the former pilgrim route between France and Spain even after the coming of the railway. The wine that the Lillet brothers sold to be dispensed by the glass was, as might be expected, mostly sweet, providing the 'quick lift'. The Graves was well able to supply sweet or sweetish wines in quantity, not only from the immediate locality and from Sauternes and Barsac, but from the vineyards across the Garonne as well – Sainte Croix du Mont, Loupiac, the Entre-deux-Mers, the Premières Côtes de Bordeaux and St Macaire. The Lillet business prospered. Then, as tends to happen, innovations were inaugurated throughout the world.

Ever since the Egyptian campaign of Napoleon I, and in many countries where the French had established colonies, the use of quinine had been recognised, as both a form of tonic and a preventive; the herb itself seems to have been discovered in the sixteenth century by the Spaniards, when they conquered Peru. The word comes from 'kin-kina', the Indian expression for the bark of the tree with such useful properties and this became 'cinchona' in Spanish. Jesuit scientists are credited with bringing quinine back to various European cities, notably Montpellier, famous for medical research since early times; Louis XIV and Louis XV used quinine as a gift to favoured persons encountered in their royal travels throughout France and Napoleon I ordered that some quinine should be mixed into the daily wine ration of his army – it was known to be efficacious in cases of fever. Is it fanciful to suppose that the expression 'Chin-chin!' still often said in France when drinkers clink glasses is not, as many will suppose, a survival of 1920s jargon, synonymous with 'Cheers!' or 'Santé!', but a much older exclamation, dating from the time when a quinine-flavoured drink was indeed rightly associated with health?

In 1830, during the French campaign in Algeria, the army's chief medical consultant, Dr Maillot, ordered that the bark and powder of the quinquina herb should be distributed to the civilian population and the farmers, as well as to the troops; the therapeutic property of anything tasting of quinine became widely recognised – and, in consequence, bitter drinks became chic. I admit to thinking that the nursery dictum, 'It's just because it's so nasty that it does you good', may have had some additional appeal in circles where any lingering traces of gastronomic puritanism held sway.

A wide range of quinine-containing drinks now began to be made. St Raphaël was first registered in 1830, when Adhémar Jupet, losing his sight, prayed to Raphaël the Archangel, who is patron of the blind; Jupet, who had been perfecting the recipe for a drink of this kind, recovered completely – and, in gratitude, gave the well-known aperitif the Archangel's name. In 1835 Gaston Picon, in the French army in Algeria, evolved Amer Picon. Dubonnet was first offered as a 'tonic aperitif' by its maker, Paris wine merchant Joseph Dubonnet, in 1846. Byrrh was evolved in 1866 in the Roussillon region of the Pyrenees.

Quinine-flavoured drinks were made in France from the wines of the prolific region of the Midi and, at the outset, all were red; they were also sweet or sweetish, maybe because even then the mass market really couldn't always enjoy anything truly bitter, just as, today, many people who suppose that it is somehow 'better' to drink dry, in fact often consume quantities of sherry that is sweetened up to the legal limits for a fino and table wines that are 'medium dry' on the label but 'medium sweet' on the palate. In the Gironde, of course, even the officially dry white table wines tended in good vintages to have a slight softness, a rounded flavour, a fatness that can develop when such wines are kept longer in wood than is usual in our time. The history of 'noble rot' and its effect on grapes and the history of wine is out of place here, but although some books give 1847 as the 'official' date when Château d'Yquem first made a wine from grapes subject to *botrytis cinerea*, there were various other wines, in other countries, that seem to have had the same action of the fungus years, even centuries, prior to this. What I venture to suppose is that the wines of the Sauternais were always tinged with lusciousness in good vintages, this being accentuated by the way in which the grapes were picked and the wine made. So,

300

within the overall Graves area, sweetish wines were locally available to the Lillet firm. They had begun to build up an export business from about 1870. Then, in 1887, they produced an aperitif, to which they gave their own family name of Lillet, which was based on the wines of Sauternes; a quinine addition, predominant among the other ingredients, cut the rich sweetness and, by skilful blending, a balanced, fresh-flavoured drink was achieved. Never before had an apéritif been based on an acknowledged quality wine – the wine used as the base for other apéritifs was admittedly cheap. So, with Lillet, the price was higher than the prices of what could have been competitive lines, but both the Lillet family and those in the firm concerned with promoting the new drink realised, even at this early stage, that one can create the initial appeal of a product at its introduction as a luxury line and then, later, if need be, go down the market, though it is not feasible to launch something that is cheap and then try to increase its status and prestige.

The French colonies, many of which were already Lillet customers for wines and spirits, were the first targets for the new drink as well as the home market: Morocco began to buy Lillet in 1907, then Mexico and, in 1910, the Congo. Kenya and Madagascar were subsequently to be opened up for the aperitif. The drink was shown at the Franco–British Exhibition in 1908, but as early as 1904 an arrangement was made with a British firm to launch Lillet, together with certain other top-quality French lines, on the Indian market. Exports to the United States began in 1910 and although the Prohibition era hampered progress here after World War I, other markets in Norway, Guernsey and Jersey began to thrive in the between-wars period; from 1933 Lillet was again being shipped to the U.S.

It was in 1939 that the family firm of Twiss, Browning & Hallowes began to sell Lillet in Britain, with marked success; the importers bottled the aperitif themselves – this was often done even with fine estate wines until quite recently, as a mark of confidence between the producer and importer, though the fact was always stated on the label. Significantly, Twiss, Browning & Hallowes made Lillet slightly less sweet for the U.K. market – as had been found earlier in the history of Champagne, the British have always genuinely opted for a dry drink as far as the upper echelons of the market are concerned.

In New York and, subsequently, in the entire continent, Lillet's success was much influenced by one of the remarkable personalities of the British wine trade – Michael Dreyfus. His firm, Dreyfus Ashby, are still of great standing, a few of their current agencies in the U.K. being Hugel, Drouhin, Don Zoilo. Mike Dreyfus was faced with competition in the U.S. from the mighty vermouth firms from the south of France – Marseilles – and Italy – Turin – the numbers of Americans boasting Italian ancestry being sufficient to intimidate anyone not an inspired salesman. But Mike was just that. He began to create a chic atmosphere around Lillet, so that smart Americans felt impelled to drink it and be seen doing so; barmen were encouraged to ask customers if they wanted Lillet 'straight', as opposed to 'on the rocks', this preference indicating to people looking on that the drinker had been around and knew how the aperitif was taken in France itself. Mike also devised the use of a sliver of orange peel, twisted over the glass of Lillet so that the oils in the skin of the orange enhanced the drink – it was 'different', it was a gesture that made an impression, attracted inquiries.

Back in Podensac the firm were equally progressive about publicity – in many small but effective ways ahead of their time. For example, postcards advertising Lillet were printed in colour and distributed to Lillet agents to give to potential customers, so that these cards, already addressed, could be used to place orders by post.

The firm, like many other family concerns, endured many vicissitudes in and since World War II. Sometimes, to older drinkers overseas, it may have seemed that Lillet had become one of the aperitifs of their youth, now almost forgotten, along with certain other once-fashionable drinks whose names are now either unknown or only recalled when a dusty bottle in an out of the way French bar is sighted; the drinking scene has changed, social life has suffered pressures and taken up new crazes; foods and drinks have been transformed in the past fifty years, both in what is eaten and drunk and how; publicity has been revolutionised. The gigantic corporations in the drink world have swallowed up many smaller firms and, alas, 'big' in many such business transactions can often mean destruction and the disappearance of an otherwise pleasant and interesting commodity. It hasn't happened to Lillet. Though many must have thought it might.

Founders of the firm Paul and Raymond were succeeded by André and Marcel Lillet and André's four sons, Paul, Raymond, Pierre and René, ran the business until 1985. Then came another change. But this time it took place within the Bordeaux region, instead of coming from outside via some international combine dominated by its accountants, knowing little or nothing of traditions and caring not at all for the aesthetics of wines

302

and spirits. The impeccable St Julien estate of Ducru-Beaucaillou, in the Médoc, had been bought by François Borie in 1941 and continuously rehabilitated and revived so that, when his son, Jean-Eugène, took over on his death in 1953, the property was beginning to regain its former renown and today merits the respect and affection of all lovers of fine claret. Jean-Eugène's son, Bruno, brought up with fine wine, wished, on attaining maturity, to 'do his own thing' and not just follow the rest of the family in the Médoc. The prospect of management appealed to him and, eventually, he was able to become the present Président of Lillet, while Christophe Lillet, fourth generation of the family since the firm's foundation, is General Director. Together with them works Hervé Romat, their oenologue, and his rôle is an example of how life and business organisation in the Gironde has changed, for Hervé is a Doctor of the Institute of Oenology in Bordeaux – a post that might not have been understood by the Lillet founders and could have been regarded as 'new-fangled' by the firm before 1914. But its existence and work is valued today but while Hervé Romat is constantly in touch with the latest scientific developments affecting wine, at the same time, he is brought down to earth (as it were) when he visits the Lillet establishment in Podensac. The result indicates the evolution of a family concern into business in the latter part of the twentieth century.

The Lillet building, white, plain, rectangular to the view, is situated at the main crossroads in Podensac. It cannot have changed much since the turn of the century and indeed photographs taken then show the background of Podensac as hardly altered: one can recognise other buildings, although the main road is blocked with bullock carts and horse-drawn chariots, the oxen drawing the heavy loads often wearing neatly secured coats, to protect them against the early morning and evening chill and damp – the local climate has not undergone changes!

Inside the Lillet headquarters, however, there are few people today. No longer do vast quantities of wine, formerly brought in by casks loaded onto the horse-drawn or ox carts, now have to be stored in the huge vats, though these still remain. Nowadays wine can be moved briskly from wherever it is made by somebody lifting a telephone or operating a telex and put to immediate use on arrival. The aisles between the giant vats are quiet on most days. Nor are the areas within which the spices, peels, barks and herbs, plus other ingredients in the secret formula, were formerly stored now rustling with arrivals of precious and fragrant consignments; the premises here remain aromatic from the century and more during which

303

such stores remained here; they have impregnated what are now empty bins and walls where unregarded numbers and tags hang, so that the comparatively smaller quantities of today's flavourings bask in the perfumed atmosphere of an older bouquet. One is tempted to linger and, indeed, the vast areas make at least this visitor long to pause, relax in the quiet of the scented air ... what a situation for someone setting up an establishment for aroma therapy today!

Reassuringly, the young men now in charge of Lillet have made few changes involving the major reconstruction of the premises – no chrome and pseudo-leather, no slick reception area, only a counter with a pleasantly courteous clerk and, in the room where meetings are held and information is provided, there is an impression of nineteenth-century brownish-green décor, slightly dimmed light falling on glass-fronted bookcases and on the substantial leather-topped desks that would have been familiar to Christophe Lillet's grandfather or any frock-coated businessman of the 1890s.

Essentially, Lillet is still made according to the turn-of-the-century recipe. It is based on the local wines, of the Graves and the Sauternais; for the red version, the local reds are used. The wines arrive and receive the addition of the secret formula of both the aromas and flavours derived from fruits, spices, herbs and, of course, quinine, in a compounded state, termed 'liqueurs'. About 85 per cent of Lillet – all versions – is wine, the 15 per cent remainder being these 'liqueurs'. The only major change that has been made in the product of Lillet is concerned with the ageing of the wine, which is the base of the aperitif. These days less SO_2 (sulphur dioxide) is used in the production of wines destined to form the foundation of Lillet. The wines are less oxidised – that is, they have suffered less from the action of the air to which they are exposed, as was often inevitable in the past; the result is that they are fresher in style, zippier, with more 'lift' and crispness, such as appeals to drinkers of today. The blend of base wines is made earlier now than it used to be and, throughout the development of the wines in bulk, strict regulation by temperature control plus a modern cooling system safeguard their progress. Thus the fruitiness of Lillet at its best can be emphasised.

Lillet is, as some people do not realise, a perishable product. It is a form of wine and, like vermouth, won't last indefinitely once the bottle has been opened. If anybody has tried it from a long-opened bottle, kept maybe under the light of a warmish bar, then the taste cannot be altogether

304

pleasant. At the establishment, my hosts showed me the marked difference in taste between Lillet served at room temperature on a stuffy, damp day (which is not weather wholly peculiar to the Graves region either) and the same drink poured from a bottle previously chilled in the refrigerator, both bottles being newly opened. The first version was adequately drinkable, the second dryish with undertones of bitterness and spice coming out markedly in what, without chilling, had been a somewhat medium-style drink, the sweetness tending to blur the other subtleties of the taste when the apéritif was not chilled.

It is the aromatic character of Lillet that is one of its particular charms, the citrus fruit bouquet appealing greatly to me. This applies to the pale-toned Lillet. The red version, which was first made about a quarter of a century ago and is based on the local red wines, is somewhat softer than the white version, though it should not be thought of as definitely sweet; it has a pronounced lingering after-taste.

One of the questions I asked my long-suffering hosts on my visit must be recurrent among travellers in France; why the posters and the advertisements (sometimes faded by the sun) painted on walls proclaim 'Lillet' in the north of France, while those in southern regions use the phrase and spelling 'Kina Lilet'? It seems that, in the early days of the aperitif, it became extremely popular in the south, where Catalan workers – Catalonia straddles the Pyrenees and the former kingdom only ceased to exist in 1714 – took a particular liking to it; the freshness, plus the underlying quinine flavour, seemed to have a marked appeal to the sturdy mountain people. But the Catalans still cherish their own language – friends there have told me how, when forbidden during the Franco régime to speak it, they often preferred to speak English (learned from the BBC) in public rather than Spanish – and although the versions spoken in France and Spain vary slightly these days, Catalans pronounce the 'll' in a word as 'ye'. This presented problems of pronunciation of the word 'Lillet', the result being difficult to understand in French and unattractive in sound. So, in areas where Catalan people were numerous, the drink went out labelled as 'Lilet'. It was also, jokes Bruno Borie, a small economy – for one letter less makes the name cheaper to paint on a wall or side of a house!

Many would say that Lillet is essentially a type of vermouth – aromatised wine – and, therefore, can and should be drunk as vermouth is drunk: chilled, with various additives to taste. Diluting agents may be soda, Perrier water, tonic and it's up to the individual and the barman to put a twist of lemon or orange peel in as well. When poured into a goblet or medium to large wine glass it can be topped up with Champagne or dry sparkling wine, the slightly 'tonic' taste appealing to some drinkers in search of a 'different' cocktail. Or it can be combined with such fruit liqueurs as those based on strawberries (*fraise*), raspberries (*framboise*), blackcurrant (*cassis*) and similar spirits, the Lillet pleasantly cutting any excess sweetness; I would not, though, try mixing it with any *alcool blanc*, such as *kirsch, framboise*, or *poire Williams*, as the intense fruitiness of these fine spirits seems best enjoyed alone – which is how I, personally, also prefer to drink Lillet, chilled, with a sliver of orange or lemon peel twisted over the top of the liquid. You can, if in a show-off frame of mind, copy one of the devices by which Mike Dreyfus used to attract attention to Lillet: he would set light to the twist of orange peel as he dropped it into the glass. It does not seem to affect the flavour much more than unignited, but it looks pretty – though do not use the thinnest crystal.

Lillet, still a family business, has survived and prospered because of the basic quality of the product, plus the perseverance and quiet loyalty of those concerned with making and promoting it. It is *the* Graves aperitif and should be included in all taste experiences of the region.

20

TOURISM

Possibly the most important place to visit – and certainly among the most picturesque – is the Château de la Brède, which is only a short drive from Bordeaux and pleasantly sited amidst a forest. A detailed account of why it is so important is given here, for the benefit of the visitor who has no previous knowledge of its most famous owner – Montesquieu.

THE LORD OF LA BRÈDE

A plane coming in to land at Mérignac – where the airfield now covers an area formerly under vines – may circle southwards; the traveller looking out will then see a clearing among the wooded landscape which seems to be a park, surrounding an irregular patch of water. A building, topped by pointed, dumpy towers, arises from this moat, like a huge stone water-lily. This is the Château de la Brède.

It is shown on numerous postcards and some of it is open to visitors. The vineyards make 70 tonneaux of pleasant white wine and 2 tonneaux of red, although these wines are not widely known. And the visitor who knows no French may find it difficult to discover anything about La Brède save that it was the home of Montesquieu.

Who, as might well be remarked, was he?

Outside academic, philosophical and legal circles, few English-speaking people may know anything about him. Yet he is the third of the great personalities of the Graves in history (for obvious reasons I cannot select one from our own times).

It is not easy for us today to establish a sympathetic contact with some of the thinkers and writers of the late seventeenth and eighteenth centuries, even those of the British Isles. We can tag Isaac Newton because of the apple falling on his head and maybe some will recall his reproach to his dog who had destroyed a manuscript – 'Oh Diamond, Diamond, what hast thou done?' Do the names of Hobbes or Locke evoke any response? Easier to delight in the deeds of the soldiers and sailors, and the writings of the poets and dramatists. What went on at the courts of

France and England has been adeptly chronicled and we enjoy such accounts as we enjoy well-written gossip columns and lavish books of social history, but what about the men and women who wrote and talked – and how they talked – about the social and political problems of the period?

An Australian wine trade friend of mine was escorted to La Brède by one of the Vinding sons at Rahoul and, as they emerged, the willing-to-be-informed visitor inquired 'Who *was* this Montesquieu, anyway?' The French-educated child, astounded, eventually stammered that 'He was – he was – well he was a *splendid* chap!' In the autumn of 1986 I found myself trying to explain something about the owner of La Brède to a young British couple and an older American husband and wife, who were baffled by what the French-speaking guide was saying; none of us was ill-educated, but we would all have appreciated some background and enlightenment – 'un bref aperçu', as Michelin often says.

As one walks from the tree-shaded parking space up the slightly curved way to the Château, some knowledge of why Montesquieu is so respected may enliven the commentary of the 'visite'.

Charles Louis de Secondat was born at La Brède in 1689 and was baptized in the village church, a beggar standing as godfather, so that he should never forget the poor and needy. His family were noble, though not of the top rank and all of them seem to have been able and intellectually inclined. As was usual then, Charles Louis was sent to a near-by hamlet to be cared for by a wetnurse and it was in his infancy that he learned to speak Gascon, which he always enjoyed speaking to his servants and the workers on his estate.

The title of Montesquieu was inherited from an uncle while Charles Louis was still young and with the title came the office of Président of the Bordeaux Parlement. Montesquieu's brilliance had already been evident during his studies in Bordeaux (where people who could tended to move for the winter, rather than being isolated out in the country) and the legal-political activities of the city were of importance. As my colleague, Edmund Penning-Rowsell has pointed out, becoming a member of a 'parlement' – more akin to a local governing body than our 'Parliament' in London – was a way of rising in the world. 'Joining this elect body', says Edmund, 'was rather like becoming a member of a very select club and the rewards were social rather than pecuniary.' Members of a parlement had special privileges and 'the means to obtain entry to this aristocratic legal club normally came from land, including vineyards'. In fact one bought one's way in as a matter of course.

Montesquieu sold his presidential office in 1726 but, somehow, he tended to retain the title of 'Président' thereafter. We know that he was always precise about inserting the significant little 'de' in his wife's name – that particle so important to the French to this day! Jeanne de Lartigue was a Calvinist. She produced a son and two daughters; the marriage was definitely both arranged and 'convenient'. She was an admirable manager, controlling affairs at La Brède when her husband was away with such efficiency that it's a pity we know so little about her. For there was always much to be done. Madame's dowry had included property in the Entre-Deux-Mers and Preignac and there were plantations of vines at sites in Martillac and Léognan. Possession of these was not a sinecure. In his study, *Montesquieu et La Vigne* (Delmas, 1935), Émile de Perceval quotes the saying 'Qui terre a, guerre a' (Landowners have battles) and accounts of the lawsuits, purchases, sales and recovery of debts outstanding concerning the overall holdings occupy many pages, as they must have occupied much time of the original owners.

In 1721 Montesquieu's work *Persian Letters* was published – anonymously – in Holland. This book enjoyed a huge success. An earlier work, *Le Temple de Gnide*, which I have not read, seems to have been vaguely fantastic with some enlivening amorous descriptions. The *Persian Letters* is another piece of eighteenth-century writing that may be hard for many twentieth-century readers to appreciate: travellers from Persia comment on France and French life, with interpolations of what I tend to dismiss as Lower Fourth smut. It is, I am informed most reliably, witty writing. Yet these letters became so popular and the renown of the provincial lawyer-politician was so established (in England as well as France) that it is fair to include some of the comments of Christopher Betts, who edited the Penguin translation in 1973.

'The vivacity of the reaction against him (Louis XIV), the outburst of high spirits after the gloomy, ritualistic and religious decline of the "great century", the extension of interest to lands and customs outside the limits of Versailles and France, the taste for experiment in all public affairs as in science, the frivolity and calamities of Regency life are all to be found here. The book also inaugurated that eighteenth-century phenomenon known as the Enlightenment, a literary and intellectual movement which, in the name of freedom and humanity, attacked almost every traditional value in sight.' This explains much, even if we cannot feel stirred by the text, as does Mr Betts's percipient comment on the seventeenth- and eighteenth-century concept of 'l'honnête homme', which he defines as being 'a type who observed the social conventions with elegance and never paraded his individuality'. This, I think, is why some of us today find that we simply cannot feel any sympathy with Montesquieu. Where, in such a being, is the passion, the blood and guts? Where is the person standing up to be counted?

Fontenelle, nephew of Corneille, said of Montesquieu when asked if the Président really loved anyone, 'Il n'aime personne ... Il n'est que plus aimable' (He doesn't love anyone – though he's always most agreeable' – but the wordplay of 'aimer' and 'aimable' is lost in translation). Émile de Perceval writes, 'He pushed nothing to the extreme ... A stoic, without having ever endured suffering, he knew nothing about grief and kept out of the way of involvements of the heart.' Yes, says the more emotional Anglo-Saxon of the twentieth century, he was a cold fish, a skater on the surface of a comfortable life, someone who tittuped through society.

I had just reached this section of my book when, before a dinner given by friends in the wine trade in London, I began to talk to one of the aristocratic directors of one of the greatest Médoc châteaux. Hardly had I mentioned my difficulty in beginning to understand Montesquieu as a person than he launched into an illuminating series of comments on the eighteenth-century mind and its mode of thought. The intelligentsia at that time, often being the nobility and owners of property among the bourgeoisie, were percipient enough to realise that the whole of society as they knew it would – must – undergo a radical change. Many aspects of society had reached points of crisis. There were already indications that any alterations in the attitude of one section of a previously ordered and controlled society to another might result in violence; this inculcated fear in those who saw no means of controlling or directing the changes that they knew to be imminent – they anticipated Armageddon. With their heads they knew that a big upheaval was due. With their hearts they clung to what they had and what, often in spite of themselves, they wished always to have – a life that, if not always without complications, was materially comfortable and one which gave them opportunities to express themselves freely, even daringly, if they were tactful and did not cite examples from the immediate present.

This accounts at once for the admiration of many French philosophers and writers for 'freedom', both as an abstract ideal and for what they saw as freedom exemplified in Britain where, in fact, life was not always

310

as 'free' as it seemed to the outsider. The French had had certain rigidities imposed upon them and now they imposed these on themselves. In England there seemed not to be such constrictions, or the French were not aware of them, and it had already had its 'Glorious Revolution' by cutting off the head of its King! The search for 'freedom', which many French thinkers sincerely supposed they sought, would have resulted in a rude shock had servants and tradesmen addressed them as 'tu' – the intimate second personal pronoun that was beginning to be abandoned across the Channel!

The way in which so many of the thinkers of the eighteenth century indulged in what, at least to me, seem pastimes rather than pursuits, points of doctrine rather than practical religion, attitudinising instead of a considered attitude to life, now can be understood as whistlings in the bloody dark that, as many were becoming aware, was about to overwhelm them.

Many great thinkers have fallen short, in their lives, of what they formulated and professed in their writings. When Montesquieu, visiting Venice, threw his notebooks into the Grand Canal because he thought the police were after him, he was not heroic – but he was human. As a father he was mean – well, maybe he had seen how children wasted their patrimony. As a host he was parsimonious – perhaps he had noticed how some of his neighbours had lavished their incomes just to make a fine figure in the locality. His carriage horses were scornfully described as broken down – the consideration of the animal as a sentient being, worthy of respect, is a recent notion and he might have logically supposed that a means of transport need not be showy, as long as it got him to his destination. Yet – he had the capacity of having and expressing in his writings many great ideas. His imagination lit up what he thought about society, his personal amiability and apparently at least adequate feeling for religion do make him pleasanter to my eyes. None of this would I have been able to perceive until this necessarily brief conversation with a well-educated Frenchman who commanded an international perspective.

At this point I will also append the comment of another dear Bordeaux friend, someone who knows far more about Montesquieu than I: the period, he remarked, was one when, as possibly never before or since, writers were impressively intimidating at describing evil – notably in *Les Liaisons Dangereuses*. This awareness of evil was there in Montesquieu's time and those who had begun to shudder about the future should perhaps not be too harshly criticised now for amusing themselves while they could. Whereas once I had been prepared to criticise Montesquieu's superficial spirit, I can now venture to begin an understanding of a being whose mind and sensitivity was, in many ways, greater in scope than that of his feelings and his personality.

Montesquieu travelled extensively, in Hungary, Italy, Holland. He was elected to the Académie Française – even then an august body. From 1729 to 1731 he was in London, mixing with court and fashionable society, meeting intellectuals and politicians. His grandson seems, exasperatingly, to have burned his London diaries (he kept detailed accounts of his Italian sojourn), but some notes remain. The streets of London were apparently very dirty and carriage travel was dangerous because of the condition of the roads. But then, as now, everyone expected another country to be like his own – which was impossible! The French complained that the English did not like strangers. Well, why should they? The English did not even like each other! Montesquieu tried to take people as they come – in France he made friends with everybody, in England with no one. But he studied English institutions and profoundly admired the 'liberté et égalité (already, but the 'fraternité' was yet to come – and he might not have liked that). Though he felt the English did not deserve their unique freedom and commented: 'I never saw a nation that thinks less.' He also deplored the English lack of manners and the way in which a man was content if he has 'a good dinner, a girl and reasonable comfort'.

Back in France, he devoted much time to his properties in the Gironde, though he usually wintered in Bordeaux (La Brède must certainly have been damp then). Often he went to Paris, where he followed a fashionable routine, possibly basking in the praise attracted by his writings. In 1734 the huge study, *Considérations sur les causes de la grandeur des Romains et de leur décadence*, was followed by his masterpiece, *De l'Esprit des Lois*, in 1750. To us outsiders many chunks of these are of interest, especially his theories of the ways in which climate affects the national characteristics of various people. But the enormous scale of the latter work makes it intimidating to tackle.

He seems always to have been happy in the country, although his sessions in his library at La Brède were sometimes impaired by the eye trouble that afflicted him for much of his life. His property included forests – of which he was particularly fond – a variety of crops, game and domestic animals; Madame de Montesquieu managed very well, with the aid of the *régisseur* whose name, Éveillé ('Wideawake') seems particularly appropriate, but the proprietor liked to take an active part in things when he was there.

Prompt to call in debts and collect rents, he was nevertheless ready to supply food to his tenants in periods of hardship for, as always, anyone engaged in farming was at the mercy of the weather, which can be surprisingly wet and cold in the Gironde.

In 1709 a severe frost trapped many ships in the Garonne, freezing them into the ice formed on the river. In 1725 it was also a hard winter: a local annalist commented with relief on 22 January: 'No ice formed on my chamberpot!' In 1729 La Brède was badly affected by frost. The Intendant of Guyenne wanted many vineyards to be pulled up and replanted with food crops – he was the ancestor of many who, today, cannot wait for the result of a well-laid down and intelligently tended vineyard, but insist on a rapid return on capital and satisfactory 'cash flow'. Montesquieu wrote a memorandum about this, which indicated his true passion for vines. In it he warned against the competition that threatened Bordeaux with the increase of wines from other regions of France, and he noted with alarm that countries such as Italy, Portugal and Germany, were extending their areas under vines.

He was definite that a vineyard owner was more qualified to know what to do than any minister in the capital. His notes about the suitability of certain terrains for vines were detailed. A set of questions written in his own hand (published as recently as 1886), which Montesquieu circulated among his friends in the locality, gave precise indications as to what should be considered by the owner of a vineyard: method of pruning, trimming, thinning out, the allocation of work within the plantation, the style and type of the wines produced, their prices and so on. A particular friend, the Abbé de Guasco, was an appreciated 'sounding board'; it was de Guasco who, Montesquieu says, was the 'father of my meadows', because he had advised on the layout and planting of certain sections of the estates, including various woods.

Montesquieu gave detailed instructions for the handling of his wines. Author Charles de Lorbac, writing in the middle of the nineteenth century, quotes a letter referring to an English customer who had ordered some wine. Montesquieu says, 'He can keep it as long as he likes, even fifteen years if he wishes, but he must not mix it with other wines and he can be certain that he has it now in exactly the same state as I, when I received it from God's hand.'

There were grumbles in his memoirs about having to leave 'the most beautiful countryside I know' for Paris, where 'people make out they are enjoying themselves, because they tend to forget what real life is like'. For all that, he often did leave the Gironde for Paris and the chic salons of the *beau monde*. (People not obliged to live in the country in the winter and who are able to play at being farmers while many others incur the sweat and daily labour often attitudinise in this way!) He could be confident that his wife and the estate staff would care for the property and he also knew that his literary fame was useful to the sale of the wine he made – 'The success that my book has had in this country' (England), he writes to Guasco, 'has contributed to the success of my wine.' For, as Émile de Perceval says, 'Tout Bordelais est commerçant, tout viticulteur est marchand' (every Bordeaux man is a dealer, every wine grower is a businessman). Once Montesquieu remarked, 'Let nothing interfere with business!' (Napoleon I, with his supposed slighting reference to the British as a 'nation of shopkeepers' was not a native of the Gironde.) And Montesquieu's wine did not come from one of the great estates already enjoying fame, sure of ready sales in both France and export markets – he had to exert himself to popularise, publicise and sell it.

Ever since the great Dukes of Burgundy had been allies of the Kings of France the French court had drunk Burgundy wines. By the reign of Louis XV, serious attempts were being made to have Bordeaux wines widely accepted in France and the satyr-like Duc de Richelieu, when Intendant of the Gironde, eventually managed to establish red Bordeaux as a smart tipple – though he may well have slantingly publicised it as a drink partly responsible for his sexual vitality, which kept up to a somewhat surprisingly advanced age and, in a society where conquests of this kind were a type of sport, anything that was even vaguely aphrodisiac would have been as sought-after as a new face cream is today. Montesquieu saw how the Médoc wines would compete with those of the Graves, notably on the English market. He said proudly that he had 'substantial orders from England', happily reflecting that, with the profits therefrom, he would be able to 'complete my "maison rustique" ' – his 'little place in the country' – La Brède. 'False modesty!' comments Émile de Perceval.

He indulged in the forecasts of ruin and disaster common among farmers – 'Provincial France is ruined, nothing anywhere is worthwhile now.' Not that, I have to comment, he seems to have done much by way of improving the conditions of his workers and tenants at the little place in the country, which his wife and factor kept going. He wails, as those who enjoy a fairly regular private income often do, that his work (on *L'Esprit des Lois*) was interrupted by the dinner parties and suppers in the capital – but he went to them. 'O rus, quando te aspiciam!' (Oh countryside, when shall I behold thee? – with the 'understood' clause 'How happy I should be!' added). Well may today's visitor wonder why he ever left the place if he loved it so much. There he had his books, his vineyards and forests and no social distraction from his entourage and his family. Maybe the subserviance of these was not quite enough – maybe he wanted to compete and challenge the higher echelons of the nobility and the wits and thinkers of the capital? A feeling of inadequacy pushes people on, sometimes against their true inclinations.

For he continued visiting Paris where, in 1755, he died of some sort of fever. His last days were made terrible by the insistence of the Jesuits who wanted to make the enfeebled man revoke some of the theories expressed in his writings. There was conflict around him, and a friend siezed his work so as to protect it. But there were few of his intimates there at the last. As de Perceval says, it was a shabby sort of deathbed. He was buried at St Sulpice but the tomb was broken open and his bones scattered at the Revolution.

Montesquieu's son had no descendants and it was Denise, one of his daughters, whose arranged marriage had been a penny-pinching affair (her father forbade any wedding presents being given), whose children perpetuated the line and who, today, in the person of the Comtesse de Chabannes, own La Brède.

The building of La Brède is old. The word 'brède' means swamp or marsh or 'lande', which as the dictionary says, is 'sandy moor, waste'. The Lalande family were established there as early as 1079 and then, as they suffered progressive attacks from the local people (possibly because they were oppressive overlords or there was some incited family feud), the premises became dilapidated. At one stage the Lalandes of the La Brède branch – the name is famous in both Graves and Médoc history – seem to have gone to England; this might have been during the English occupation. A Cathérine de Lalande married one Gaston de l'Isle and their granddaughter, according to Florence Mothe (*Graves de Bordeaux*, 1985), married a Pesnel, an ancestor of Montesquieu.

Throughout its history, the château underwent many reconstructions. The surrounding curtain wall, blocking the path of any besiegers who might have crossed the moat, was eventually taken down, so that the inner keep now has a pleasant view. The place in fact looks more fairy-story picturesque from the outside than it proves to be within – historic buildings may look remarkable, but if people have to live in them modifications must often take place. Today's visitor, having crossed the moat, comes into a somewhat sombre entrance hall; there, at intervals, are several thick, twirly pillars of an almost black wood. They are some of the most interesting features of the place, because they date from the seventeenth century when they were installed to prop up the weight of the library overhead; they are of oak, hardened by being submerged for ten years in water.

Some of the rooms on view contain family portraits and the Secondat likeness is apparent through the generations: an elongated face, with a thin, not always straight long nose, a mouth that often seems about to twitch with nervousness, even though the lips are firmly closed. These faces could be those of business or professional men, reserved, critical, sensitive and sharply intellectual – no uncontrolled passions here. Jeanne de Lartigue's somewhat static portrait is of a firm, benevolent visage.

At the side of the fireplace in the room said to be Montesquieu's bedchamber there is a groove worn in the stone, which is supposed to be where he liked to prop his feet up at the edge of the hearth. In his time the long room above the entrance, formerly the guardoom, was the library. The curved ceiling makes the acoustics excellent and nowadays concerts are given here at the time of the Bordeaux 'Mai Musicale'. On the shelves there are still some books but Montesquieu's library was sold at the beginning of this century – and before anyone exclaims in horror at such a dispersal – remember that only recently John Evelyn's library was also sold in Britain and was scattered among many buyers. Need for money is one thing, the breaking up of a collection of books that a great man has owned, used and some of which may bear his markings is, even to a modest writer, a tragedy. Still, there are some books relating to Montesquieu at La Brède and it's clear that this library was planned by a real user of books, for the great roof beams are of chestnut, which is not only resistant to the attacks of various insects, but spiders will not spin webs on it.

La Brède is still inhabited, although the 'visite' is a little mournful, with few indications of family occupation, no twentieth-century trivia; the place seems arrested, as if under glass, the liveliness of the former most famous occupant seemingly embalmed here. Perhaps, after the beauty of the setting, the interior must be somewhat of an anti-climax?

The most famous account of a visit to this stone water-lily is that of Henri Beyle – Stendhal – who, while consul in the papal city of Civitavecchia, frequently took time off to travel. In 1838 he went on a longish tour for four months through the southern regions of France. His notes about Bordeaux are lively – 'Beautiful eyebrows', he says of the local ladies. (His write-up of La Brède is given in Appendix XI.)

Of Montesquieu Stendhal said – a little as I do – 'It is not precisely love that I feel . . . but rather veneration. He never bores me by expatiating on an idea I have already understood.' (Alas, I cannot claim that much!) Another comment is to the effect that 'the present owner could install a professional guide, whose wages could be paid by sightseers, for according to the bad-tempered servant girl' (who had showed Stendhal and his companion round) 'visitors come almost every day in the summer'. When Stendhal and his woman companion walked back to the village, they were attracted by the sign 'Beer' over the door of a café – 'but there was no beer'. When Stendhal inspected the little church he recalled an anecdote about Montesquieu, who once left behind a book that he had taken to Mass; the priest who found it was sure that it must be a text about magic, because of the diagrams of circles, triangles and so on – but it was actually a volume of Euclid. Stendhal also talked with several people who remembered Montesquieu's son, Jean-Baptiste, so informative about vines. It was said of him that he would go through the market, picking up and eating anything that took his fancy – followed by a servant, who paid for things taken.

As today's visitor recrosses the moat and wanders in the park, it is pleasant to be reminded of how, in Montesquieu's lifetime, two young Englishmen arrived at La Brède, anxious to see the great man of whom they had heard so much. An account is given in E. H. Young's *Montesquieu, a critical biography* (Oxford 1961). They probably arrived on horseback and gave their animals into the charge of somebody before they entered the keep, where they were shown into the library on the first floor where they noticed that a volume of Ovid was open at 'pages galantes' – was this, I wonder, done deliberately for the amusement or shocking of callers or did the philosopher really enjoy the vaguely titillating soft pornography of this classical writer? When the master of the house appeared he asked the two if they would like to join him for luncheon but, perhaps fortunately for them, they had already eaten on the way – Montesquieu's table tended to be frugal and he does not seem to have taken pleasure in sharing food and wine, even his own wine, with others. (Was this shyness or selfishness?) In his *Pensées*, he actually stated that 'Friendship is a contract in which we engage ourselves to provide small services to someone, so that he should give great services to us.' Anyway, either he also had already eaten or was not going to bother – they did not get even a drink.

Montesquieu invited the visitors to accompany him on a walk around the property. They noted that he was in high spirits, merry, courteous and, when they arrived at a locked gate, he foraged in his pocket, then said alas he'd forgotten the key, but doubtless they could get over – and he vaulted in fine style. Probably the Englishmen were shown the cuvier or presshouse, for this was of stone, something of which the estate must have been proud; elsewhere the majority of such buildings were very simple, more like low barns, with wooden walls, roofs and earth floors.

At this period, wines were still given four to six years in wood before they were considered to have arrived at their prime. They were shipped in bulk – in cask – for, although in 1663 Samuel Pepys wrote that he went to see 'some of my new bottles being made, with my crest upon them, filled with wine, about five or six dozen', this type of bottle, which certainly could not be laid down, on its side, acted as a carafe or serving vessel, being used again and again for smallish amounts of wine required for current usage.

It is possible – though this is only a theory of my own – that those who drank such 'wines from the wood', prior to the age of maturation in bottle, did not write much about what the wines tasted like because drinkers were then primarily concerned merely with whether a wine was good or bad, young or old, fresh or fading. Was there really anything more that could have been noted? The ancient Romans had written accounts of different wines, including those able to develop in sealed amphorae and it is perhaps somewhat odd that, when any adequately educated man of Montesquieu's period could have read the authors of classical times, no one appears to have experimented in ageing wine as recounted in such writings. Detailed accounts of foods and recipes are also infrequent until after Montesquieu's time and, though chefs and stewards did compile instructions about food preparation and wine making routines, there do not seem to have been any of the details and 'fine writing' that bejewel the gastronomic prose of a century later.

Neither Montesquieu nor any of his contemporaries wrote about what their wines tasted like when drunk. Régisseur Éveillé kept no records that have survived but, even if he had, would these have been much more than notes about the climate? Even within my own time of learning about wine it was, early in this century, thought remarkable that the owner of one great Médoc estate kept notes on the temperature at morning and evening, when his wines were racked, dates of fining and so on. The countryman often only makes a note when something out of the ordinary – a triumph or disaster – occurs. Maybe the eighteenth-century drinkers would have been laconic commentators even if we could find their tasting or cellar notes.

At La Brède, Montesquieu liked to wander around, wearing a straw hat in summer, a white cloth cap at other times; he would chat with the workers and often those who didn't recognise him would address him familiarly – using the 'tu' which, when he was enjoying being a Gascon countryman, he didn't resent. If he forgot to take a stick when he came out for a walk, he would pick up a vine prop to use. He said, and obviously thought, that his 'fortune was under his feet'.

Yet sometimes there is a hint that maybe he felt something else as well. When *Manon Lescaut* came out in 1734 he commented in his *Pensées* that 'I'm not surprised that this novel, of which the hero is a rascal and the heroine a tart, should be popular; all the despicable acts of the hero are inspired by love, which is always a noble incentive, although the actions thereof are bad. Manon loves as well – which makes one forgive her for being the creature that she is.' Does one detect a touch of wistfulness here – for an emotion that does not seem to have been experienced? There is certainly no involvement, no yielding to emotion. *De l'Esprit des Lois* has been tagged as being a warning to the monarchy and aristocracy, something that the author considered should be said, although indirectly, as so much had to be indirectly stated at that time; might he have not wished, even momentarily, that his work were more 'popular' and, maybe, influential? For many of the Revolutionaries were from the Gironde – did he ever feel that he might have been more passionate? Had he lived too remote from the life he admired in his own lands?

La Brède is as gently welcoming today as in the lifetime of its most famous owner. He wrote that 'the château is gothic in fact, but has several pleasant little touches about it, for which I got the idea in England. Here you'll find Nature – in her dressing-gown, as if she'd just got out of bed.' This is more appealing than much of his scholarly and worldly writing. And, it should be remembered, he also wrote, in the *Dossier de l'Esprit des Lois*: 'Great and immortal God! Humanity is your finest work. To love is to love You and, in bringing my life to its end, I consecrate this love of mine to You.'

PLANNING A VISIT

To this day, the Graves remains a somewhat hidden region. Even business people who have been visiting Bordeaux regularly for many years may not have explored much beyond the southern suburbs of that city. So it is not over-exploited as a tourist area. There are many places of historic and artistic interest, there is a quiet charm about the countryside that, in good weather, is appealing and relaxing to anybody able to detour from the main roads.

In a nineteenth-century book, *Les Fleuves de France*, the author, Louis Barron, dealing with 'La Garonne' in an undated edition of the Librairie Renouard, describes his railway journey through the Garonne as being 'a huge bouquet of flowers and fruits, of which the flavours, scents, colours are a delight to the taste, the sense of smell, the eyes'. It is surprising that he should have been able to smell anything, but he manages to note various places, including Roquetaillade, which he thinks 'wonderful', Langon 'a pretty little town', although it is near to others that seem to him more attractive. Of Bazas he says it is 'Built not on turf but on dust' and, apropos Uzeste, it is 'huge, richly decorated, enclosing its desecrated tomb'.

Although there are a number of pleasant hotels, notably at Langon and Bazas, and delightful small places to stay in Podensac, Villandraut and other little towns, as well as some hotel-restaurants out in the country, it is worth remembering that not all of these will be able to give more than basic service to the traveller who cannot speak French. Nor is there much 'night life' out in the country, where people go to bed early. So, if your French is somewhat elementary and you like to wander about and look at shops and perhaps have a drink after dinner, then it may be more satisfactory to stay in Bordeaux itself and make excursions. The hotels there are numerous and of all types although Bordeaux receives large numbers of travellers throughout the year and accommodation can be difficult to find at short notice.

The Graves has easy access from Bordeaux. Either take the autoroute to the south, following the signs for Langon and Toulouse until you can branch off to any desired destination, or else go down on the 'old road', the N.113, which is not as fast but facilitates detours to the villages and estates along the way. It is not easy to explore this area without a car – ideally, for the first-time visitor, one with a driver; this saves stopping to look at the map – and a detailed map of the area is essential, for the tiny winding country roads can be confusing. There is at least one signpost

320

in the *Circuit du Sauternais* which has two arms pointing to the same village in opposite directions! Even the Bordeaux brokers often get lost down here.

Just north of Podensac and on the main N.113 road, the Maison des Vins de Graves is a particularly helpful place to visit and obtain directions, should you have not been able to get information in Bordeaux itself from the Maison du Vin in the centre of the city (Cours du XXX-Juillet, at the corner of the Allées de Tourny). This establishment houses the Comité International du Vin de Bordeaux (C.I.V.B.). The Maison des Vins de Graves can provide a detailed map of the wine estates and will usually know which properties are open to visitors – this can vary according to seasons, so check before going to any; outside the 'high season' some may be closed in spite of printed information that they are open. (Or check with anyone in your hotel who can telephone to ascertain opening hours.) The Maison des Vins de Graves is competently staffed with at least some English-speaking personnel. They can also help with advice as to which estates have an English-speaking guide. Remember, though, that everything stops for the sacred lunch hour. This may begin at midday or one o'clock and last for an hour or slightly longer, rather depending on the place and the time of year. The public holidays, which include various religious festivals, mean that most places of business will then be closed all day and most French *monuments historiques*, which often include certain wine estates, are closed on Tuesdays, as are many museums and art galleries. The 'high season', which may be taken as beginning mid-June and lasting until mid-September, is when visitors are expected but, of course, during vintage any wine establishment will be working and working hard – unannounced visitors are not usually welcome at such a time, when everyone is busy and many firms close in August. The Graves vintage will generally take place slightly earlier than the vintage in more northern regions of the Bordeaux vineyard but it can continue until some way into October.

People wishing to arrange travel and visits for groups should, of course, try to do this through a travel agent. Your hotel may be able to contact a suitable firm experienced in touring the locality.

TIMING

Although this naturally varies, some approximate idea of what is involved can be given, and people wanting to make frequent stops or prolonged visits will, of course, take this into account. Some visits to wine estates or historic properties can involve quite a lot of walking, although there is usually somewhere to sit for anyone disinclined to accompany a regular *visite* or tour, which may take up to an hour or even more.

STARTING FROM BORDEAUX

In two or three hours – morning or afternoon – you can see at least one of the great estates actually within the Bordeaux suburbs and if you wish to go round others in the northern region of the Graves, then make an early start.

In a long day it is possible to traverse the Graves from north to south and detour to see at least one of the historic properties or castles and have a meal. But try to plan such a trip so as to include travelling back to Bordeaux by a different route instead of going over the same road twice. From the N.113 several estates may be seen from the main road and although some of the great properties near Bordeaux do sometimes seem elusive to the traveller, preliminary study of the map should enable several to be seen at least from the outside, if a pause on the way can safely be made.

Three days allows for a reasonable amount of the area to be seen without hurrying. Perhaps one day should be allocated to the great properties in the 'Graves de Bordeaux', plus a visit to La Brède (see p. 307) and its château and maybe the Château de Mongenan (see p. 331) at Portets. A **second day** would enable the traveller to go further south, maybe include a brief visit to the Sauternes area, also the the Château de Malle and the church at St Michel de Rieuffret (see p. 327). A **third day** could be devoted to going straight down to the south of the region, including Bazas and the surrounding countryside, Villandraut (see p. 108), Roquetaillade (see p. 327), Uzeste (see p. 116) and some of the lesser-known properties, which are in very attractive landscape.

GUIDES AND VISITS

Admittance is usually charged and tickets issued before a guided tour begins. At the conclusion, it is usually made plain if an additional 'thank you' is expected. It is usually possible to buy postcards, souvenirs and sometimes wine at such places.

322

If, however, you are shown round one of the major wine estates or a cellar or part of a winery, a tip should not be offered unless it is quite definite that the guide expects it. And be careful – the 'guide' who escorts you, even if wearing espadrilles and overalls, may be someone in authority, even possibly the owner ... and may understand everything you say in English! An expression of thanks and, of course, the recurrent handshake is all that is required here.

Special arrangements can often be made in advance for seriously interested students of wine to see round a wine establishment and ask questions. But bear in mind that, at vintage time, attention is concentrated on the vineyard and in the press-house. In August, as in many parts of France, there tends to be a general shut-down when people go on holiday and although there may be some staff in the offices, anyone outside will be preparing for the vintage. It goes without saying that, should a specific appointment have been made, it should be scrupulously kept – if you are delayed, then telephone to explain or get someone to make the call for you.

These days it is not always possible for all visitors to wine estates to sample the young wine – too much of the precious stuff is wasted in the spittoon or on the floor! If you are particularly keen to see a particular wine, it may be wise to try to request a tasting in advance but don't arrive with a number of people and expect that you will all be able to taste; genuine enthusiasts are usually treated with much kindness but anyone not accustomed to tasting young wine may be very disappointed, because it can be quite unpleasant to drink and anyone shy about spitting it out may incur a tummy upset, should fermentation still be in progress. Nor, in Bordeaux *chais* or at estates, is it customary for casual visitors to be given a drink at the end of a tour of inspection – you will have to arrange this for yourself afterwards.

MAPS

The Michelin map 79 covers the Graves, from Villenave-d'Ornon on the outskirts of Bordeaux down to the south of the region. But for Bordeaux itself and the surrounding area, you should also have Michelin map 233. There are various other maps, of course, but as, in the pursuance of many of the places mentioned in this book, you need to follow small country lanes, a mere *grandes routes* or overall map of France is inadequate.

The Michelin Green Guide *Côte de l'Atlantique* is very helpful. It is in French but other books listed in the bibliography on p. 373 may prove helpful guides as well. The annual *Guide Michelin* to hotels and restaurants contains most helpful town plans, even of quite small places, indicating one-way systems, approaches and bypasses, plus mentioning anything of special interest in the various towns.

SOME CENTRES AND PLACES OF INTEREST

In addition to places mentioned and described in detail in other parts of this book, it is my own hope that readers will try to see more – though the selection here represents my personal taste. Someone on holiday, with accompanying family and friends, may certainly want to spend time on the coast, also to go shopping and picnicking, because, it has to be admitted, anyone who is only casually interested in wine may find that one vineyard and one winery tend to seem similar to many others – and a more lasting impression will be gained, without fatigue, if you visit just one or two estates, rather than try to 'do' several in a hurry. The serious wine lover may not notice if those around begin to fidget and their attention wander – but this can happen early on and it is unfair to subject anybody on holiday to an excess of instruction and torrent of technicalities.

If possible, even a little advance 'homework', via this book or others, can encourage people to approach wine without timidity and postpone the moment when they become bored. But as the places mentioned in this chapter are not always well documented in English guidebooks, my notes may add to the general pleasure of getting to know the Graves.

Bazas
This is a delightful old town, with a huge, fan-shaped area in front of the Cathedral, bordered by picturesque old houses. Under the arcades that run along the sides there are the sorts of shops that invite one to linger. A market takes place here and under the arcades and there are displays of local arts and crafts. Go in the morning – and remember that cafés and restaurants will fill up early on such occasions. Public celebrations of various kinds take place on this spot, as they did in very early times and at midsummer St John's Day (24 June) is honoured by all manner of spectacles and displays. Some of these must be very ancient, even of pagan origin, as the

festival is particularly associated with bulls – but the visitor need not fear that the proximity to Spain means that such events involve the sort of bull-fight that is understandably a subject of much controversy.

Whether or not the cult of the bull was brought to this part of France by the Romans, whose bull deity, Mithras, certainly had adherents within the Roman armies, I have not been able to discover. But the bull is a very ancient symbol of power and courage. Like other tourists in Crete I have visited the excavations at Knossos and seen the bull figures in the Heraklion Museum; in many strange portrayals women as well as men apparently leap through the horns as the bull charges. Yet, commentators have asked, how could this be done? Was the actual leap performed sideways, across the bull's back, rather than a somersault directly over its head after a hand-stand on the horns – something that, it has been argued, would require more strength than could have been possible, even if bulls were smaller in those days. There is one picture in Crete where a woman seems to be talking soothingly to a stationary bull which may have become partly domesticated (Ernest Hemingway somewhere writes about a huge bull that was photographed with all the breeder's family cosily nestling up against it). 'Ferdinand', Disney's bull who didn't know how to fight, is charmingly shown in a picture on a vase in Cyprus, where a bull delicately sniffs at a flower. Even for a trained athlete, many authorities are agreed, it would seem impossible for the leaper to grasp the horns of a charging bull and vault over its back – maybe, some suggested, the artists of the ancient Mediterranean were employing their customary 'licence'.

Then I read *Small Boat in Southern France* (1965) in which author Roger Pilkington described one of the many inland voyages he had under-taken. He arrived at Castets where he saw a 'Race for ducks' on St Luke's Day (18 October), when apparently children race for ducks in the water; this is harder than it sounds but, once grabbed, the bird is either kept as a pet or given to Maman for culinary use. But after this Pilkington tied up at Bordeaux and he and his family went off into the Landes where, in some small village close to the coast, they saw true 'bull-jumping'. The man about to jump apparently first hauls on a rope tied to the bull's horns then, when the rope is released, the bull charges – and the 'young man hurdles, passing right over the horns of the creature, all down the length of its steaming body and landing lightly on the ground behind its tail'. So – bull vaulting can be done, though whether it still is I do not know. Pilkington also saw 'Le Tauroball', a game that he thought was essentially soccer, but played with a bull loose on the pitch – a fearful complication I should suppose!

While this book was being prepared for press I came across one published in 1890, *Wayfaring in France*, by Edward Harrison Barker, a man who walked around that country and in a number of volumes commented most intelligently on many regions travellers today will know well. In a section on the Landes, he saw an announcement in Dax of *Courses landaises*, when bulls and cows were teased by energetic locals, who always managed to get out of the way before they could be hurt. These men, writes the author, are *écarteurs*, but he also mentions that there are some who are additionally *sauteurs*: he saw one, 'the son of a pork-butcher ... famous throughout the Landes.... As the cow lowers her head to strike he leaps into the air, and drops on the other side of her.' Cows, he notes, were often used 'because they afford better sport by the greater facility with which they can turn round'. Although a Spanish team also displayed its agility when this writer attended the *Courses*, it was the men of the Landes who seemed to be the stars of this occasion. The lack of information about the prehistory of this area probably explains why no other traces of bull (or cow) leaping have been found, as the tradition is obviously very old.

The Cathedral of Bazas, originally very ancient, was rebuilt in 1233 and again much later, also having to be considerably repaired after the religious wars of the sixteenth century, when Bishop Arnaud de Pontac and, subsequently, his heirs, undertook much reconstruction.

An hour or more can be passed pleasantly wandering around Bazas and there are plenty of attractive-looking eating-places.

Langon

This is a rather quiet town today, but it is worth looking at the former busy port and, if you can effect entry, seeing Zurbarán's *The Immaculate Conception* in the Church of St Gervais – which I have never managed to do. Langon restaurants have a high reputation and in the centre of the town there are pleasant shops and cafés. It is an agreeable place in which to stay and many excursions are easy from there.

Villandraut

This (see p. 108), with its huge keep and charming little *place* with the delightful hotel-restaurant De Goth, is within easy reach of Bazas and Langon and a short drive from Uzeste (see p. 116).

EXCURSIONS IN THE SOUTH

To the east of Langon and Bazas there is the remote Abbaye du Rivet, with a plain, ancient church and peaceful enclosure.

At Castets-en-Dourthe, a sleepy small town, there is a fine view over the river from behind the church.

Le Nizan is virtually a hamlet but there is a wonderful panorama from the church – note the porch able to shelter pilgrims – and the small roads around offer a variety of scenery – the Graves is not all flat by any means! The great Château de Roquetaillade, built in 1307 by one of the nephews of Pope Clément V, is poised above the Brion valley and the views from its grounds are magnificent. Restored by Viollet-le-Duc in the nineteenth century (though his assistant, Duthoit, did most of the work), the château is still lived in. The château consists of two separate buildings (quite a lot of walking and going up and down stairs here) and there is a display of nineteenth-century costumes as well as historic exhibits. The great kitchen will probably appeal as much as these to the present-day visitor. Opposite the entrance to Roquetaillade there is an open-air museum or reconstruction of what a farm, with its buildings and outbuildings, would have been like in former times in this somewhat isolated place. You can buy souvenirs and wine at Roquetaillade itself.

The Château de Malle, just off the main road and well signposted, is an elegant seventeenth-century building, the appearance of the front being, somewhat oddly, quite different from that of the rear – it is as if the architect changed style completely. Malle is still lived in and the *visite* or guided tour includes several attractive rooms, the library, the chapel, with numerous family portraits, including one of the Duc d'Épernon who owned the imposing Château de Cadillac across the river. It is well worth while making a tour of the Italian gardens at the back of the château; these are now somewhat dilapidated, but the balustrades and statues augment a landscape of formal charm. There was, as may be imagined, an outcry when the autoroute cut across the bottom of the garden!

The vineyard of Malle is partly in the Sauternais and, for red wine, partly in the Graves. You can buy the wine of the property at the Château, the dry white and sweeter white, also a sparkling white wine made locally for the owners which is pleasant and shows how methods of making wine sparkling attain a high standard today.

If the tourist is planning an off-the-main-road return to Bordeaux, the route could pass via Noaillan and Léogeats from Villandraut. Some of the other pleasant places at which stops may be made are listed alphabetically, in the admirable guide prepared by the Maison des Vin de Graves. In this, the 'Pays de Podensac', comments Philippe Dubourg, Conseiller Général du Canton de Podensac, is beautiful, varied and rich in both history and prehistory. Arbanats has a fifteenth-century church on which there is a statue of St Hippolyte. This theologian and martyr is now hardly known, but his work in the third century, notably for the text now known as the 'Apostolic Tradition', is of outstanding importance on early Christian worship and customs.

Barsac, on the main road, possesses a sixteenth-century church, also on the main road, typical of the style known as 'Renaissance de la Gironde'. In former times there was much traffic here, where the Ciron joins the Garonne, and the place enjoyed much commercial importance.

Budos is dominated by a gigantic castle, which, from the twelfth century, belonged to one of the relations of Pope Clément V.

Cérons (see p. 255) is another port of former importance – in the sixteenth century the Benedictines diverted the course of the Ciron to join the Garonne between Preignac and Barsac. The special Cérons stone from the local quarries became widely important as a commodity in the nineteenth century, more than the casks made from the oak forests that had previously been much in demand. There is an impressive church porch in the old section of Cérons.

Guillos, a tiny hamlet, has the strange legend that a herd of cows vanished into the Lac des Troupins – to appear later at Arcachon!

Illats, another village, has a twelfth-century church and, on the outskirts, there is the sixteenth-century Château de Cagès. It is said that the former owner, Hélène du Cos, paid homage to the overlord of Landiras with 'a kiss on the right cheek'. Illats was a former pilgrim stop, notably for sick animals – the place-name, in Latin, is Illatum, signifying refuge.

Landiras also has a Romanesque church of the twelfth century of interest. Because Jeanne de Lestonnac, Montaigne's niece, married the Marquis de Landiras and founded the Institut de Notre Dame, Landiras consequently became another place of pilgrimage, even before Sainte Jeanne who died in 1640, was canonised in 1949. At Landiras there is also the establishment Fines Spécialités S.A., a subsidiary of Moët et Chandon, now producing the recently created Petite Liquorelle drink, made from Sémillon grapes, old Cognacs and other mature wines, which is lightly sparkling. As the installation is very modern, students of drink technology may wish to see round and visitors are welcome, but it should be stressed that this innovative drink is not to be thought of as in any way a Graves speciality. The name Landiras derives from a local saying: 'Quand tu passeras là, dans Les Landes tu iras'; [When you have got past that point, you'll be in the Landes].

Podensac might seem, to the driver in a hurry, as a rather plain place but it is full of interest – even if you miss the market alongside the main road when this takes place. It was here that, in 1615, the delegates from the Bordeaux Parlement came to present a welcome to Anne of Austria, the future Queen of France, as she arrived from Spain. Louis XIII, who was to marry her in the Cathedral in Bordeaux, is supposed to have come here secretly to get a glimpse of her – readers of Dumas's *Les Trois Mousquetaires* will know of her great beauty, although in real life she does seem to have been a somewhat dull lady. In addition to the Maison des Vins de Graves, just north of Podensac, and the Lillet establishment at the main crossroads, Podensac has a fine public garden and a water tower which is notable for having been one of the earliest works of Le Corbusier, who built it in 1918.

Portets gets its name from having been another port on the river. A look-out tower remains from the time when boats loading up were surveyed by the local officials. On this tower is the coat of arms of the town, with the motto that, translated, is 'A port I was, a vineyard I remain'. The final 't' of the name Portets is sounded – some suppose this to be a relic of the English occupation of the region. Many fortunate wine lovers may know this place because of visiting Château Rahoul, just off the main road to the west, where the dedicatees of this book were once in residence. The curious indented and ridged sundial in the garden there is supposed to indicate the phases of the moon and various other forms of the celestial calendar, but no one has so far been able to interpret it.

In *La Seigneurie de Portets, Castres et Arbanats* (1934) there are some interesting statements that appear sufficiently scholarly to be cited here. The authors of this collection of accounts state that first the Ligurian tribes and then the Spaniards peopled the locality and that it was Vercingetorix, a Gallic chieftain and hero, executed for leading a revolt against Julius Caesar in 46 BC, who first planted both fruit trees and vines at Portets. The place was a barony in the Middle Ages and the Goth family built many châteaux in the vicinity; by 1270 it had become a *comté* (county) and it paid an annual tribute to the English crown of three pigs and forty loaves of white bread. Portets was definitely one of the stopping places for pilgrims going to or coming from Santiago and, in 1525, King François I of France was given 'Graves wine' there when he was returning from imprisonment in Spain. Anyone travelling to Spain would have had to go through Portets on what was the main road and among the voyagers should be mentioned La Grande Mademoiselle, cousin of King Louis XIV, when she came back from the wedding of the King to the Infanta of Spain at St Jean de Luz.

The first steamers began to ply along the Garonne around 1818 and the quarries of the east (as well as the west) banks of the river provided plenty of building stone. The former importance and prosperity of what is now a small, somewhat sleepy place may be judged by the *dîme* or tithe (one-tenth) of the rate exacted from the people to pay to the local clergy: in 1736 this was as much as six tonneaux of wine, each tonneau costing around 180 *livres* (not quite the same as the 'livre sterling' of today!).

Preignac is another small town formerly bustling with business, mainly connected with the local wine trade, so that the manufacture of casks and implements to do with making them employed a number of people.

Pujols-sur-Ciron has an odd church, perched on a mound, which building is supposedly a protection against storms – of considerable importance, even today, when a sudden downpour or, worse, hail, can destroy a year's crop of grapes in minutes. St Michel de Rieufret is a tiny village, in flat land, apparently of scant note. Even people living quite near have not visited it. But the traveller *must* stop – the church, in the centre, does not seem particularly beautiful, although the exterior altar and the seats on the outside of the building indicate that this was one of the pilgrim stopping places. Get the key of the church or ask someone to unlock the door – the shop opposite will be helpful (and they sell admirable Landes honey).

This church was one of the most famous places of pilgrimage in the Gironde from the fifth to the ninth centuries; people came to go nine times round the interior altars and, in passing those of the Virgin and St John, they would crawl underneath – in commemoration of the appearance of St Michael the Archangel at Monte Gargano in Italy, towards the end of the fifth century. Michael, 'Captain of the Heavenly Host', was a protector of Christians and of soldiers, but also of the sick and parents came to St

Michel de Rieufret to put their children specially under his care. This church is also long-term associated with the intercessions of sufferers from stomach complaints. The interior combines plainness with some attractive baroque décor, with vines carved around some of the pillars. In one of the side chapels – get someone to turn on the lights if you can – the decoration is exquisite, the colouring and design as delicate as embroidery on satin. Note the representation of St Antony, with his associated piglet and bell (the order of Hospitallers of St Antony was founded around 1100 at Constantinople and the Saint is a protector of anyone likely to suffer from ergotism – 'St Antony's fire', a disease of cereals and certain grasses, causing burning pains, itching, gangrene and convulsions in those eating them, something often resulting in supposed daemonic possession in medieval times). There is also a portrayal of a curious dog with a stone in its mouth. The church, carefully tended and kept in better order than many in provincial France, is clearly a place of enduring devotion.

Virelade, another small town, is mainly noticeable for its eighteenth-century château, on the site of a much older building. This was formerly the property of Joseph de Carayon la Tour, whose bust is on a plinth in front of the church; he was in charge of the mobilised forces of the Gironde in the Franco–Prussian War of 1870–71.

The Château de Mongenan is just to the east of the main road, slightly north of Portets, down a lane. There is a trim little house, which is not open to visitors, but visitors pass through and may wander in a delightful garden, now carefully planted or replanted with fruits and flowers that would have been familiar to the man who laid out the original – Jean-Jacques Rousseau (1712–78), the great philosopher and writer, who was engaged by the then owner as a music teacher. Rousseau's precise drawings of plants, in his *Herbier*, are carefully preserved here and he would certainly have known the great cedar tree, reputedly the oldest in France.

Mongenan was built as a hunting lodge in 1736 – hence its elegant style – by Baron Antoine-Alexandre de Gasq; he was at that time Président of the Parlement of Guyenne, Directeur of the Compagnie des Indes and associate of the great financier and political figure, Jacques Necker (1732–1804), father of the remarkable Madame de Staël. It was this Baron de Gasq who founded the Bordeaux Academy of Music – hence his employment of Rousseau. The former stables of the château now house a small but interesting museum, opened in 1983. In addition to displaying historic and popular works of art, including the printed cotton Toile de Beautiran

(Beautiran is a little further up the road to Bordeaux) which, but for the French Revolution, might have become as famous as Toile de Jouy, the museum is mainly concerned with Valdec de Lessert. His mother was de Gasq's niece and many of his personal effects are on view, including his odd bath, like a sabot, in which the bather would sit, covered up but not easily able to use his arms or get out – which gives one an entirely different notion of the assassination of Marat in his bath by Charlotte Corday and a reason for the odd term 'slipper bath', a portable bath somewhat akin to the hip bath still in use in my childhood in country houses. The unfortunate de Lessert seems to have been rather too scrupulous in financial dealings to please the authorities of his time and he was eventually imprisoned and then, dragged out to be sent to Paris for trial, was torn to pieces by a mob at Versailles. One is shown the pamphlet denouncing him, also an early model of *La Louisette*, forerunner of Dr Guillotin's 'humane killer'. In addition to the Rousseau drawings, the gastronome will see a list of dealers in spices of the period and those who were permitted to buy and import Dutch cheese – an important commodity, for the Gironde has no local cheese of its own. Mongenan was also the home of the contemporary writer, Florence Mothe, whose several historical novels are on display there; and who has most recently written the book *Graves de Bordeaux*.

JUST OUTSIDE THE GRAVES REGION

There is an attractive although narrow main road on the east bank of the Garonne, which can provide an alternative route for anyone exploring the Graves. Cross the river at Langon and then turn right to St Macaire, a charming small town, taking its name from St Macarius, friend of St Martin of Tours (to whom so many French churches are dedicated). During the Hundred Years War, St Macaire remained faithful to the English crown and was awarded the proud title of *Ville royale* in 1341. The old houses and arcades, the Romanesque church and cloister make it a pleasant place to wander in and there is also a Museum of the History of the Postal Services of Aquitaine in the former Relais de Poste Henry IV, Place du Mercadiou.

Also on the east bank of the Garonne, but further inland, there is the Château de Malromé, occupying a commanding site; this was the home of the family of the painter Toulouse-Lautrec and there is a display of sketches, photographs and mementoes of him, which a conducted tour allows visitors to see. His tomb is in the nearby village of Verdelais, the road thereto passing by the Château de Malagar standing above its vineyard. This was the home of the distinguished writer and Christian apologist, François Mauriac (he wrote in 1937 that he neither understood nor liked the English – which many of the bulldog breed may say goes double for some of his works!). Malagar is not open to visitors but some of Mauriac's descriptions of the Landes in his novels and, even, of Bordeaux itself and the *noblesse de bouchon* are bitterly perceptive and interesting to wine lovers. Another place of interest at Verdelais is the Cave de Vinification, down a side lane, the first installation of its kind in the Gironde and the creation of Peter Sichel, of Château d'Angludet in the Médoc. It is not open to visitors except by arrangement with the office of Sichel & Co., 19 Quai du Bacalan, in Bordeaux.

The Entre-deux-Mers is most attractive countryside, with many delightful estates and country houses, to be viewed from the numerous winding roads leading up from the river. If you keep on the main road, eventually Cadillac is reached and this is well worth a halt, so as to see the impressive Château des Ducs d'Épernon (one of whom was Grand Admiral of France) and wander around the narrow streets in the centre of the town. This east bank road leads back to Bordeaux, but the latter part is narrow and winding and passes through some somewhat dreary industrial areas after the cessation of the pretty little country houses. So anyone in a hurry to return to the city should cross the Garonne at Langoiran or before and return by the wider main road on the west bank.

APPENDICES

THE CLAIMS TO THE ENGLISH CROWN

This simplified family tree shows how the English crown was claimed by both Matilda 'Empress' and Stephen, Count of Boulogne and how the Plantagenets, from Anjou, became involved with the succession through Geoffrey's marriage to Matilda.

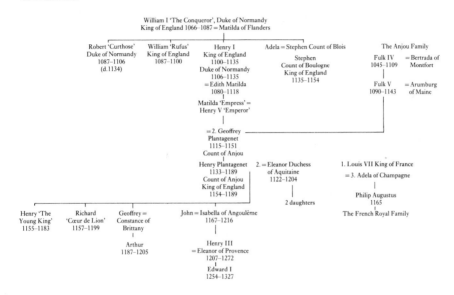

THE MAIN DESCENDANTS OF EDWARD I

This indicates how the English royal house was involved with France. John of Gaunt, Duke of Lancaster, was the titular King of Castile. He married three times, and his daughter Philippa by his first wife Blanche married John I, King of Portugal. His second wife, Constance, heiress of the King of Castile and Leon gave him a daughter Catherine, who married Henry III of Castile; their children included John, King of Castile (whose daughter Isabella married Ferdinand of Aragon) and Prince Henry 'the Navigator'. By his third wife, Catherine, widow of Sir Hugh Swynford, there was the Beaufort family, who included the Duke of Somerset, whose son Edmund, Earl of Richmond, married Margaret Beaufort and was the father of Henry VII. Other marriages within this family included John of Gaunt's granddaughter Philippa, who married the King of Denmark and Sweden, and Joan Beaufort who married Ralph Neville and became the ancestor of Edward IV, Richard III and Warwick 'the Kingmaker'.

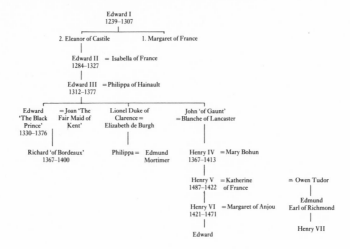

STOW'S SURVEY OF LONDON
VINTRY WARD

WARDS ON THE WEST SIDE OF WALBROOKE,
AND FIRST OF VINTRY WARD

Now I am to speak of the other wards, twelve in number, all lying on the west side of the course of Walbrooke. And first of Vintry ward, so called of vintners, and of the vintry, a part of the bank of the river of Thames, where the merchants of Burdeaux craned their wines out of lighters and other vessels, and there landed and made sale of them within forty days after, until the 28th of Edward I., at which time the said merchants complained that they could not sell their wines, paying poundage, neither hire houses or cellars to lay them in; and it was redressed by virtue of the king's writ, directed to the mayor and sheriffs of London, dated at Carlaveroke, or Carlisle, since the which time many fair and large houses, with vaults and cellars for stowage of wines, and lodging of the Burdeaux merchants have been built in place where before time were cooks' houses; for Fitzstephen, in the reign of Henry II., writeth, that upon the river's side, between the wine in ships, and the wine to be sold in taverns, was a common cookery or cooks' row, etc., as in another place I have set down; whereby it appeareth, that in those days (and till of late time) every man lived by his professed trade, not any one interrupting another: the cooks dressed meat, and sold no wine, and the taverner sold wine, but dressed no meat for sale, etc.

This ward beginneth in the east at the west end of Downegate ward, as the water-course of Walbrooke parteth them, to wit, at Grantham's lane, on the Thames side, and at Elbow lane on the land side; it runneth along in Thames street west some three houses beyond the Old Swanne, a brewhouse, and on the land side some three houses west beyond St. James' at Garlicke Hith. In breadth this ward stretcheth from the Vintry, north to the wall of the west gate of the Tower Royall; the other north part is of Cordwayner street ward. Out of this Royal street, by the south gate of Tower Royall, runneth a small street east to St. John's upon Walbrooke, which street is called Horshew bridge, of such a bridge sometime over the brook there, which is now vaulted over. Then from the said south gate west, runneth one other street, called Knightriders' street, by St. Thomas Apostle's church on the north side, and Wringwren lane by the said church, at the west end thereof, and to the east end of the Trinitie church in the said Knightriders' street, where this ward endeth on that south side the street; but on the north side it runneth no further than the corner against the new built tavern and other houses, in a plot of ground where sometime stood Ormond place; yet have ye one other lane lower down in Royall street, stretching from over against St. Michael's church, to, and by the north side of St. James' church by Garlicke Hith; this is called Kerion lane. And thus much for the bounds of Vintry ward. Now, on the Thames' side, west from Grantham's lane, have ye Herber lane, or Brikels' lane, so called of John Brikels, sometime owner thereof.

Then is Simpson's lane, of one Simpson, or Emperor's head lane, of such a sign. Then the Three Cranes' lane, so called not only of a sign of three cranes at a tavern door, but rather of three strong cranes of timber placed on the Vintry wharf by the Thames side, to crane up wines there, as is afore showed. This lane was of old time, to wit, the 9th of Richard II., called The Painted Tavern lane, of the tavern being painted.

Then next over against St. Martin's church, is a large house built of stone and timber, with vaults for the stowage of wines, and is called the Vintry. There dwelt John Gisers, vintner, mayor of London, and constable of the Tower, and then was Henry Picard, vintner, mayor. In this house Henry Picard feasted four kings in one day (as in my *Summary* I have showed). Then next is Vanner's lane, so called of one Vanner that was owner thereof; it is now called Church lane, of the coming up from the wharf to St. Martin's church. Next is Brode lane, for that the same is broader for the passage of carts from the Vintrie wharf, than be the other lanes. At the north-west corner of this lane is the Parish Clerks' hall, lately by them purchased, since they lost their old hall in Bishopsgate street. Next is Spittle lane, of old time so called, since Stodie's lane, of the owner thereof named Stodie. Sir John Stodie, vintner, mayor in the year 1357, gave it with all the quadrant wherein Vintners' hall now standeth, with the tenements round about unto the Vintners; the Vintners built for themselves a fair hall, and also thirteen alms houses there for thirteen poor people, which are kept of charity rent free.

The Vintners in London were of old time called Merchant-vintners of Gascoyne; and so I read them in the records of Edward II., the 11th year, and Edward III., the 9th year: they were as well Englishmen as strangers born beyond the seas, but then subjects to the kings of England, great Burdeaux merchants of Gascoyne and French wines, divers of them were mayors of this city, namely John Adrian, vintner, Reginold at conduit, John Oxenford, Hen. Picard, that feasted the kings of England, France, Scotland, and Cypres, John Stodie, that gave Stodie's lane to the Vintners; which four last named were mayors in the reign of Edward III.; and yet Gascoyne wines were then to be sold at London not above four pence, nor Rhenish wine above six pence the gallon. I read of sweet wines, that in the 50th of Edward III., John Peachie, fishmonger, was accused, for that he procured a license for the only sale of them in London; which notwithstanding he justified by law, he was imprisoned and fined. More, I read, that in the 6th of Henry VI., the Lombards corrupting their sweet wines, when knowledge thereof came to John Rainwell, mayor of London, he in divers places of the city commanded the heads of the butts and other vessels in the open streets to be broken, to the number of one hundred and fifty, so that the liquor running forth, passed through the city like a stream of rain water, in the sight of all the people, from whence there issued a most loathsome savour.

I read, in the reign of Henry VII., that no sweet wines were brought into this realm but Malmesies by the Longabards, paying to the king for his license six shillings and eight pence of every butt, besides twelve pence for bottle large. I remember within this fifty-four years Malmsey not to be sold more than one penny halfpenny the pint. For proof whereof, it appeareth in the church book of St. Andrew Undershafte, that in the year 1547 I. G. and S. K., then church-wardens, for eighty pints of Malmsey spent in the church, after one penny half-penny the pint, paid at the year's end for the same ten shillings. More, I remember that no sacks were sold but Rumney, and that for medicine more than for drink, but now many kinds of sacks are known and used. And so much for wines.

(From John Stow's '*Survey of London and Westminster*', 1598, 1603)

SYNONYMS OF GRAPES OF THE GIRONDE IN FORMER TIMES

LOCAL NAME	WINE	WHERE THE NAME IS IN USE	MOST WIDELY USED NAME
Agreste	Rouge	Podensac (Gironde)	Merlot
Alicante	Rouge	Rhin	Malbec
Anereau	Blanc	G. Couderc	Blanc Ramé
Angélicaut	Blanc	Gironde	Muscadelle
Angélicot	Blanc	Gironde	Muscadelle
Arribet	Rouge	Eaurel	Petit Noir
Arrouya	Rouge	Haute et Basses Pyrénées	Cabernet franc
Auxerrois	Rouge	Lot	Malbec
Balouzat	Rouge	Cubzaguais, Carbon-Blanc, Entre-Deux-Mers	Malbec
Béquignaou	Rouge	Gironde, Lot-et-Garonne	Fer
Béquignol	Rouge	Gironde, Lot-et-Garonne	Fer
Bigney	Rouge	Graves, Cadillac	Merlot
Blanc Auba	Blanc		
Blanc Auba	Blanc	Gironde	Ugni-Blanc
Blanc beou	Blanc	Alpes-Maritimes	Ugni-Blanc
Blanc Berdet	Blanc	Guyenne	Blanc Verdet
Blanc de Cadillac	Blanc	Gironde	Ugni-Blanc
Blanc de Cadillac	Blanc	Lot-et-Garonne	Pelegarie
Blanc doux	Blanc	Libournais	Petit Sauvignon
Blanc fumé	Blanc	Nièvre	Petit Sauvignon
Blanc de Gaillac	Blanc	Lot-et-Garonne	Pelégarie
Blanc Ramé	Blanc		
Blanc Verdet	Blanc		

LOCAL NAME	WINE	WHERE THE NAME IS IN USE	MOST WIDELY USED NAME
Blanche douce	Blanc	Dordogne	Muscadelle
Blancours	Blanc	Alpes-Maritimes	Ugni-Blanc
Bona	Blanc	Alpes-Maritimes	Ugni-Blanc
Boubet	Rouge	Basses-Pyrénées	Cabernet franc
Boucarès	Rouge	Haute-Garonne	Malbec
Bouchalès	Rouge	Lot-et-Garonne	Grappu
Boucharès	Rouge	Haute-Garonne	Malbec
Boucharès	Rouge	Lot-et-Garonne	Grappu
Bouchy	Rouge	Basses-Pyrénées	Cabernet franc
Bouillon	Blanc	Bas-Limousin	Folle Blanche
Bourguignon noir	Rouge	Rhin	Malbec
Bouscalès	Rouge	Haute-Garonne	Grappu
Bouschet-Sauvignon	Rouge	Libournais	Cabernet-Sauvignon
Boutignon	Rouge	Blayais	Pardotte
Bouton blanc	Blanc	Gironde	Petit Verdot
Bouyssalès	Rouge	Dordogne	Malbec
Bouyssalet	Rouge	Dordogne	Malbec
Braquet blanc	Blanc	Charente	Jurançon
Breton	Rouge	Vienne, Indre-et-Loire	Cabernet franc

CABERNETS

LOCAL NAME	WINE	WHERE THE NAME IS IN USE	MOST WIDELY USED NAME
Cabernet blanc	Rouge	Médoc	Cabernet franc
Cabernet franc	Rouge		
Cabernet gris	Rouge	Médoc	Cabernet franc
Cabernet-Sauvignon	Rouge		
Cabernelle	Rouge	Médoc	Carmenère
Cadillac	Blanc	Gironde	Ugni-Blanc
Cahors	Rouge	Gironde	Malbec
Cahors	Rouge	Blayais	Petit Noir
Cannut de Lauzun	Rouge	Agenais	Folle Noire
Carbouet	Rouge	Bazadais	Cabernet-Sauvignon
Carbouet	Rouge	La Brède, Bazas	Cabernet franc
Carmenère	Rouge		

343

LOCAL NAME	WINE	WHERE THE NAME IS IN USE	MOST WIDELY USED NAME
Carmenet	Rouge	Médoc	Cabernet franc
Camerouge	Rouge	Gironde	Fer
Catape	Blanc	Créon	Muscadelle
Cauny	Rouge	Divers	Malbec
Castets	Rouge		
Cau	Rouge	Divers	Malbec
Cavalié	Blanc	Castres	L'Enc de l'El
Chalosse noire	Rouge	Gironde	Fer
Chalosse blanche	Blanc	G. Daurel	Prueras
Chalosse de Bordeaux	Blanc	G. Couders	Blanc Ramé
Chausset	Rouge	Gironde	Fer
Chenin blanc	Blanc	Blayais	Pinot de la Loire
Chevrier	Blanc	Dordogne	Gros Sémillon
Clairette Vence	Blanc	Alpes-Maritimes	Ugni-Blanc
Clairette ronde	Blanc	Alpes-Maritimes et Var	Ugni-Blanc
Claverie noire	Rouge	Landes, Basses-Pyrénées	Malbec
Clavier	Rouge	Landes, Basses-Pyrénées	Malbec
Cô	Rouge	Divers	Malbec
Coly	Rouge	Vienne	Malbec
Colle Musquette	Blanc	Varsac, Sainte-Croix	Muscadelle
COLOMBARD	Blanc		
Colombier	Blanc	Gironde	Colombard
Coq rouge	Rouge	Divers	Malbec
Cors	Rouge	Divers	Malbec
COT à queue rouge	Rouge		Malbec
Cot de Bordeaux	Rouge	Indre-et-Loire	Malbec
Cote rouge	Rouge	Le Réole	Malbec
COT VERT			
Coulant	Rouge	Gironde	Cot Vert
Coulon gros	Rouge	Gironde	Cot Vert
Coulon timbré	Rouge	Gironde	Cot Vert

344

LOCAL NAME	WINE	WHERE THE NAME IS IN USE	MOST WIDELY USED NAME
Courbin, Courbinotte	Rouge	Gironde	Pardotte
Crabutet	Rouge	Bazas	Merlot
Cujas	Rouge	Lot-et-Garonne	Grappu
Dame Noire	Rouge	Lot-et-Garonne	Folle Noire
Damery	Blanc	Chablis	Folle Blanche
Dégoutant	Rouge	Poiton	Petit Noir
Donne rousse	Blanc	Divers	Colombard
Donne verte	Blanc	Divers	Colombard
Douçanelle	Blanc	Lot-et-Garonne	Muscadelle
Douce blanche	Blanc	Libournais	Petit Sauvignon
Enrachat	Blanc	Montpon	Folle Blanche
Enragé	Blanc	Montpon	Folle Blanche
Enrageade	Blanc	Coutras	Folle Blanche
Enrageade	Rouge	Agenais	Folle Noire
Enrageat	Blanc	Gironde	Folle Blanche
Etaulier	Rouge	Gironde	Malbec
Etranger	Rouge	Médoc-Graves	Malbec
Espagnolet	Blanc	Alpes-Maritimes	Ugni-Blanc
Estrangey	Rouge	Gironde-Médoc	Malbec
Feingentraube	Blanc	Allemagne	Petit Sauvignon
FER	Rouge		
Fer Béquignaou	Rouge	Lot-et-Garonne	Fer
Fer Servandou	Rouge	Lot-et-Garonne	Verdot
Fer Servandou	Rouge	Tarn-et-Garonne	Cabernet franc
Fert	Rouge	Dordogne	Gros Verdot
Fié	Blanc	Loire-Vienne	Petit Sauvignon
Franc Moreau	Rouge	Vienne-Yonne	Malbec
Fo ou Fou	Blanc	Montpon	Folle Blanche
Folle	Blanc	Charente	Folle Blanche
FOLLE BLANCHE	Blanc		
FOLLE NOIRE	Rouge		

LOCAL NAME	WINE	WHERE THE NAME IS IN USE	MOST WIDELY USED NAME
Fou (petit)	Rouge	Daurel	Cot Vert
Gamput	Rouge	Bas-Médoc	Cabernet franc
Giranson	Rouge	Carbon-Blanc	Petit Noir
Got Noir	Rouge	Divers	Malbec
Goulu blanc	Blanc	Isère	Petit Sémillon
Gourdoux	Rouge	Ludon-Macau	Malbec
Grais	Blanc	Gensac	Folle Blanche
Grande Parde	Rouge	Beautiran-Lioquau	Cabernet franc
Grande Vidure	Rouge	Médoc	Carmenère
Grappe rouge	Rouge	Lot-et-Garonne	Malbec
Grappu	Rouge	Quinsac	Petit Noir
GRAPPU	Rouge		
Gredelin	Blanc	Vaucluse	Ugni-Blanc
Gregeoir	Blanc	Abbé Rozier	Prueras
Grey	Blanc	Abbé Rozier	Prueras
Grifforin	Rouge	Charente	Malbec
Gros blanc doux	Blanc	Divers	Colombard
Gros blanc verdet	Blanc	Cazeaux-Cazallet	Blanc Verdet
Gros Bouchet	Rouge	Saint-Emilion	Cabernet franc
Gros Bouches	Rouge	lot-et-Garonne	Grappu
Gros Cabernet	Rouge	Médoc	Cabernet Noir
Gros Grappu	Rouge	Ambarès	Petit Noir
Gros de Judith	Rouge	Bordeaux	Grappu
Gros Marty	Rouge	lot-et-Garonne	Grappu
Gros Meslier	Blanc	Centre	Blanc Ramé
Gros Noir	Rouge	Lesparre	Malbec
Grosse Blanche	Blanc	G. Couderc	Blanc Ramé
Grosse Vidure	Rouge	Graves	Cabernet franc
Guenille	Blanc	Gironde	Colombard
Guepié	Blanc	Ste-Foy-Castillon	Muscadelle
Guilhan Musqué	Blanc	Lot-et-Garonne	Muscadelle
Guillan doux	Blanc	Clairac	Muscadelle
Guillan rouge	Rouge	Cadillac	Malbec

346

LOCAL NAME	WINE	WHERE THE NAME IS IN USE	MOST WIDELY USED NAME
Here	Rouge	Lot-et-Garonne, Gers	Gros Verdot
Herrant	Rouge	Lot-et-Garonne, Gers	Gros Verdot
Herre	Rouge	Lot-et-Garonne, Gers	Gros Verdot
Herrant (Grand)	Rouge	Gers	Gros Verdot
Hert	Rouge	Lot-et-Garonne	Gros Verdot
Hourcat	Rouge	Divers	Malbec
Jacobin	Rouge	Vienne	Malbec
Jurançon	Blanc		
Jurançon noir	Rouge	Carbon-Blanc	Petit Noir
L'Enc de l'El	Blanc		
Luckens	Rouge	Médoc et Graves	Malbec
Magret	Rouge	Médoc	Malbec
Magrot	Rouge	Corrèze et Lozère	Malbec
Malaga	Blanc	Lot	Gros Sémillon
Malbec	Rouge	*Cot à queue rouge*	
Malbec	Rouge	Gironde	Malbec
Mancin	Rouge	Gironde	Cot-Vert
Mansain	Rouge	Gers	Cot-Vert
Manseng	Rouge	Basses-Pyrénées	Cot-Vert
Marchoupet	Rouge	Castillon	Cabernet-Sauvignon
Maouran	Rouge	Gironde	Fer
Mauron	Rouge	Gironde	Fer
Mausat	Rouge	Gironde	Malbec
Massoutet	Rouge		
Mauzac	Rouge	Gironde	Malbec
Médoc	Rouge	Ardèche	Malbec
Mellé vert	Blanc	Orléans	Blanc Verdot
Merlau	Rouge	Médoc	Merlot
Merlot	Rouge		
Merlot blanc	Blanc		
Meslier de Saint-François	Blanc	Centre	Blanc Ramé

347

LOCAL NAME	WINE	WHERE THE NAME IS IN USE	MOST WIDELY USED NAME
Monbadon	Blanc		
Montils	Blanc	Blayais	Blanc Ramé
Mourane	Rouge	Carbon-Blanc	Malbec
Moussac	Rouge	Gironde	Malbec
Mousat	Rouge	Abbé Bellet	Teinturier
Moussin	Rouge	Gironde	Malbec
Moustère	Rouge	Gironde	Malbec
Moustousère	Rouge	Gironde	Saint-Macaire
Moza	Rouge	Gironde	Malbec
Muscade	Blanc	Sauternes-Graves	Muscadelle
Muscadalle	Blanc		
Muscadet aigre	Blanc	Loupiac et région	Ugni-Blanc
Muscadet doux	Blanc	Gironde	Muscadelle
Muscat Doux	Blanc	Gironde	Muscadelle
Muscat fou	Blanc	Bergerac	Muscadelle
Musquette	Blanc	Gironde	Muscadelle
Nanot	Rouge	Ambarès	Petit Noir
Navarien	Rouge	Divers	Malbec
Nègre de Préchac	Rouge	Libourne	Malbec
Nicouleau	Rouge	Gironde	Castets
Nochant	Rouge	Carbon-Blanc	Petit Noir
Noir de Chartres	Rouge	Divers	Malbec
Noir de Pressac	Rouge	Libourne	Malbec
Noir Doux	Rouge	Carbon-Blanc	Malbec
Œil de Tourd	Blanc	Clairac	Pinéras
Pagnière	Rouge	Gironde	Cot-Vert
Parde	Rouge	Cadillac	Malbec
Pardotte	Rouge		Pignon
Pelégarie	Blanc		
Petit blanc Verdet	Blanc	Cazeaux-Cazalet	Blanc Verdet
Petit Bouschet	Rouge	Libourne	Cabernet-Sauvignon

LOCAL NAME	WINE	WHERE THE NAME IS IN USE	MOST WIDELY USED NAME
Petit Cabernet	Rouge	Médoc	Cabernet-Sauvignon
Petit Fer	Rouge	Libournais	Cabernet franc
Petit Fer	Rouge	Gironde	Fer
Petit Noir	Rouge		
Petit Pelégarie	Blanc	Gironde	Pelégarie
Petit Pelgrie	Blanc	Gironde	Pelégarie
Petite Vidure	Rouge	Graves	Cabernet-Sauvignon
Périgord	Rouge	Vienne-Yonne	Malbec
Picpoul	Blanc	Gers, Basses-Pyrénées	Folle Blanche
Picquepouille	Blanc	Gers, Basses-Pyrénées	Folle Blanche
Piec	Rouge	Gers	Verdot
Pied Noir	Rouge	Gironde	Malbec
Pied de Perdrix	Rouge	Lot-et-Garonne	Malbec
Pied tendre	Blanc	Gironde	Colombard
Pienc	Rouge	Gers	Gros Verdot
Piet	Rouge	Gers	Gros Verdot
Pignon	Rouge	Basilédac	Pardotte
Pineau	Rouge	Bourgogne	Massoutet
Pineau de la Loire	Blanc	Blayais	Chenin Blanc
Piquepoul	Blanc	Gers, Basses-Pyrénées	Folle Blanche
Plant de Dame	Blanc	Condom-Nérac	Folle Blanche
Plant Médoc	Rouge	Bazas	Merlot
Plant de Palus	Rouge	Gironde	Verdot
Plant du Roy	Rouge	Vienne-Yonne	Malbec
Plant Touzan	Rouge	Lot-et-Garonne	Grappu
Préchat	Rouge	Libournais	Malbec
Pressac	Rouge	Libournais	Malbec
Prolongeau	Rouge	Lot-et-Garonne	Grappu
Pueras ou Runelat	Blanc		
Prunieral	Rouge	Corrèze-Lozère	Malbec
Puinéchou	Blanc	Gers	Petit Sauvignon
Punéchau	Blanc	Gers	Petit Sauvignon
Quercy	Rouge	Gironde	Malbec

LOCAL NAME	WINE	WHERE THE NAME IS IN USE	MOST WIDELY USED NAME
Queue de Renard	Blanc	Var	Ugni-Blanc
Queue tendre	Blanc	Saint-Palais	Colombard
Quille de Coq	Rouge	Vienne-Yonne	Malbec
Rebauche	Blanc	Castillon	Folle Blanche
Rochalin			
Sauvignon (gros)	Blanc		
Sauvignon (petit)	Blanc		
Sauvignonnasse	Blanc		
Sauvignon fumé	Blanc	Indre-et-Loire	Petit Sauvignon
Sauvignon jaune	Blanc	Gironde, Charente	Petit Sauvignon
Sauvignon vert	Blanc	Bourges	Gros Sauvignon
Sauvignon à grains verts	Blanc	Corrèze	Sauvignonnasse
Savagnin	Blanc	Bourgogne	Petit Sauvignon
Saint-Emilion noir	Rouge	Divers	Malbec
Saint-Emilion des Charentes	Blanc	Gironde	Ugni-Blanc
Saint-Hilaire	Rouge	Divers	Malbec
Saint-Macaire	Rouge		
Saintongeais	Rouge	Poitou	Petit Noir
Seme	Rouge	Gironde	Malbec
Sémillon	Blanc		
Sémillon Petit	Blanc		
Sémillon à bois noir	Blanc		
Sémillon blanc	Blanc	Gironde	Petit Sémillon
Sémillon crucillant	Blanc	Bergerac	Gros Sémillon
Sémillon mol	Blanc	Bergerac	Petit Sémillon
Sémillon Muscat	Blanc	Sauternes	Gros Sémillon
Sémillon rouge	Rouge	Médoc	Merlot
Sémillon roux	Blanc	Gironde	Gros Sémillon
Serine	Rouge	Côte-Rotie	Syrah
Servayeur	Blanc	Yonne	Petit Sauvignon

LOCAL NAME	WINE	WHERE THE NAME IS IN USE	MOST WIDELY USED NAME
Soumansigne	Rouge	Gers	Cot Vert
Surin	Blanc	Gers, Val-de-Loire	Petit Sauvignon
Surin	Blanc	Bourges	Gros Sauvignon
Sylvaner	Blanc	Allemagne	Petit Sauvignon
Syrah	Rouge		
Syrac	Rouge	Pulliat	Syrah
Tarney coulant	Rouge	Gironde	Cot Vert
TEINTURIER	Rouge		
Teinturier	Rouge	Blayais	Malbec
Terny	Rouge	Macau	Cot Vert
Terranis	Rouge	Cadillac, Saint-Macaire	Malbec
Trebbiano	Blanc	Corse	Ugni-Blanc
Tripet	Rouge	Bazadais	Pardotte
UGNI BLANC	Blanc		
VERDOT GROS	Rouge		
Verdot petit	Rouge		
Verdet	Blanc	Cazaux-Cazalet	Blanc Verdet
Verdot blanc	Rouge	Gironde	Gros Verdot
Verdot colon	Rouge	Gironde	Gros Verdot
Verdot rouge	Rouge	Gironde	Petit Verdot
Veron	Rouge	Nièvre, Deux-Sèvres	Cabernet franc
Véronais	Rouge	Saumurois	Cabernet franc
Vidure	Rouge	Graves	Cabernet-Sauvignon
Vidure Sauvignone	Rouge	Graves	Cabernet-Sauvignon
Vitraille	Rouge	Blanquefort	Merlot

(From Germain Lafforgue's *Le Vignoble Girondin*, Vol. I (Larmat, 1947).

THE GROWTH OF A DRY WHITE BORDEAUX

This experimental wine, La Tour Alain, was described by the late Allan Sichel in *Wine & Food* (No. 129, Spring 1966) under the heading 'The birth of a dry white Bordeaux' (the publication then edited by Julian Jeffs, Q.C.). In this article, the author (who died before it appeared in print) recounted how, from 1950, together with his associates, he tried to make 'what wine drinkers in Britain wanted. I pointed out that a lot of German wine was drunk in England despite its relatively higher price, that cheap wines from Yugoslavia were becoming popular and that taste was veering from the sweet to drier wines. I also pointed out that white Burgundies were more in demand than Sauternes and Barsac (a somewhat distorted view if applied to the whole field of wine drinking, but true amongst the more sophisticated groups) and commented that the great Barsacs and Sauternes of Bordeaux fitted in less and less well with British eating habits.' Allan continued: 'Then began three years of experiments in wine making, which produced unbelievably peculiar wines.' When questioned as to what was required he stated: 'The best I could do was to say "A Chablis at half the price and tasting of Bordeaux" '

The wine was produced, says Peter Sichel, 'by the Gasqueton family who at that time owned Ch. Couhins in the Graves and did produce the wine exclusively for my father from pure Sauvignon. It was certainly one of the very first pure Sauvignons produced in the area.' It was, wrote Allan, 'not until 1953 that the first cuvées of Château La Tour Alain were made and got a good reception in Britain in 1955'. The wine, according to Peter Sichel, 'was discontinued, probably because Château Latour started attacking anybody using this [the words "la tour"] as part of their wine name, but mainly because my father's great friend Edouard Gasqueton died in the early 1960s. The vineyard was taken over by other members of the family with whom we did not have the same relationship and ultimately the vineyard was sold to André Lurton.'

My personal recollections of La Tour Alain were of a fairly golden-looking wine with a pronounced bouquet. It was this flowery initial impression that prejudiced many people – 'oh I don't like sweet wines' – although, in most of the vintages, La Tour Alain was fullish in style but with a finish that was definitely dry, after what could sometimes be a mouth-filling, ripe taste. I once went to the property but can remember little (it was a dreary, damp day) except that the stone doorposts to the estate were topped with rounded shapes, like the pepperpot towers often seen in the Gironde.

The Edouard Gasqueton mentioned was a great personality and the proprietor of Calon-Ségur, at St Estèphe; it was once said of him that, even if nothing but water were available, he would somehow manage to make wine! In his article, Allan Sichel mentions Lionel Gasqueton as prime mover in the eventual creation of La Tour Alain.

DÉCRET OF 8 JULY 1984 RELATING TO THE PRODUCTION OF WINES APPELLATION CONTRÔLÉE 'GRAVES'

Le Premier ministre,

Sur le rapport du ministre de l'économie, des finances et du budget et du ministre de l'agriculture.

Vu la loi modifiée du 1ᵉʳ août 1905 sur les fraudes et falsifications en matière de produits ou de services, ensemble le décret nᵒ 72-309 du 21 avril 1972 portant application de ladite loi en ce qui concerne les vins, vins mousseux, vins pétillants et vins de liqueur;

Vu la loi du 6 mai 1919 modifiée relative à la protection des appellations d'origine;

Vu les articles 20 et suivants du décret du 30 juillet 1935 relatif au marché du vin et au régime économique de l'alcool;

Vu la loi du 13 janvier 1938 complétant les dispositions du décret du 30 juillet 1935 sur les appellations contrôlées modifiée par la loi du 3 avril 1942;

Vu le décret du 3 avril 1942 portant application de la loi du 3 avril 1942 sur les appellations contrôlées complété par le décret du 21 avril 1948 sur les appellations d'origine contrôlées;

Vu le décret nᵒ 74-871 du 19 octobre 1974 modifié relatif aux examens analytique et organoleptique des vins à appellation d'origine contrôlée;

Vu le décret nᵒ 74-872 du 19 octobre 1974 modifie relatif au rendement des vignobles produisant des vins à appellation d'origine contrôlée;

Vu le décret modifié du 4 mars 1937 concernant l'appellation d'origine contrôlée Graves;

Vu les délibérations du comité national de l'Institut national des appellations d'origine des vins et eaux-de-vie en date du 15 septembre 1983 et du 4 novembre 1983.

Décrète:

Art. 1ᵉʳ. – L'article 1ᵉʳ du décret modifié susvisé du 4 mars 1937 définissant l'appellation contrôlée Graves est ainsi complété:

«L'appellation d'origine contrôlée Graves peut être suivie du nom de Pessac ou de Léognan pour les vins qui répondent aux conditions de production fixées ci-après et sont récoltés :

«Pour Pessac : à l'intérieur de l'aire de production délimitée conformément à l'alinéa ci-dessus sur les territoires des communes de Mérignac, Pessac et Talence ;

«Pour Léognan : à l'intérieur de l'aire de production délimitée conformément à l'alinéa ci-dessus sur le territoire des communes de Cadaujac, Gradignan, Léognan, Martillac, Saint-Médard-d'Eyrans et Villenave-d'Ornon.»

Art. 2. – L'article 7 du décret modifié susvisé du 4 mars 1937 est abrogé et remplacé par le texte suivant :

«Art. 7. – Les vins pour lesquels, aux termes du présent décret, sera revendiquée l'appellation d'origine contrôlée Graves suivie ou non du nom de Pessac ou de Léognan ne peuvent être déclarés après la récolte, offerts au public, expédiés, mis en vente ou vendus sans que, dans la déclaration de récolte, dans les annonces, sur les prospectus, étiquettes, récipients quelconques, l'appellation d'origine Graves soit inscrite et accompagnée de la mention Appellation contrôlée, le tout en caractères très apparents.

«Les noms Pessac et Léognan ne peuvent figurer dans l'étiquetage et la publicité des vins qu'immédiatement en dessous de l'appellation Graves et dans des caractères dont les dimensions ne dépassent pas, aussi bien en hauteur qu'en largeur, les deux tiers des caractères composant cette appellation.»

Art. 3. – Le ministre de l'économie, des finances et du budget, le ministre de l'agriculture et le secrétaire d'Etat auprès du ministre de l'économie, des finances et du budget, chargé de la consommation, sont chargés, chacun en ce qui le concerne, de l'exécution du présent décret, qui sera publié au *Journal officiel* de la République française.

Fait à Paris, le 6 juillet 1984.

PIERRE MAUROY

Par le Premier ministre :
Le ministre de l'économie, des finances et du budget.
JACQUES DELORS

Le ministre de l'agriculture
MICHEL ROCARD

Le secrétaire d'Etat auprès du ministre de l'économie, des finances et du budget, chargé de la consommation,
CATHERINE LALUMIÈRE

355

DÉCRET OF 9 SEPTEMBER 1987 DEFINING THE CONDITIONS GOVERNING THE PRODUCTION OF APPELLATION D'ORIGINE CONTRÔLÉE 'PESSAC-LÉOGNAN'

Le Premier ministre,

Sur le rapport du ministre d'Etat, ministre de l'économie, des finances et de la privatisation, du ministre de l'agriculture et du secrétaire d'Etat auprès du ministre d'Etat, ministre de l'économie, des finances et de la privatisation, chargé de la consommation et de la concurrence,

Vu la loi du 1er août 1905 modifiée sur les fraudes et falsifications en matière de produits ou de services, ensemble le décret n° 72-309 du 21 avril 1972 modifié portant application de la loi du 1er août 1905 modifiée sur les fraudes et falsifications en ce qui concerné les vins, vins mousseux, vine pétillants et vins de liqueur ;

Vu la loi du 6 mai 1919 modifiée sur la protection des appellations d'origine ;

Vu les articles 20 et suivants du décret du 30 juillet 1935 relatif au marché du vin et au régime économique de l'alcool ;

Vu la loi du 13 janvier 1938 complétant les dispositions du décret du 30 juillet 1935 sur les appellations contrôlées, modifiée par la loi du 3 avril 1942 ;

Vu le décret du 3 avril 1942 portant application de la loi du 3 avril 1942 sur les appellations contrôlées, complété par le décret du 21 avril 1948 sur les appellations d'origine contrôlée ;

Vu le décret n° 74-871 du 19 octobre 1974 modifié relatif aux examens analytique et organoleptique des vins à appellation d'origine contrôlée ;

Vu le décret n° 74-872 du 19 octobre 1974 modifié relatif au rendement des vignobles produisant des vins à appellation d'origine contrôlée ;

Vu le décret n° 74-958 du 20 novembre 1974 modifí relatif à la fixation du plafond limite de classement des vins à appellation d'origine contrôlée ;

Vu le décret modifié du 4 mars 1937 relatif à l'appellation «Graves» ;

Vu les délibérations du Comité national de l'Institut national des appellations d'origine des vins et eaux-de-vie en date des 24 et 25 juin 1987.

Décrète :

Art. 1er. – Seuls ont droit à l'appellation contrôlée «Pessac-Léognan» les vins rouges ou blancs répondant aux conditions fixées ci-après.

Art. 2. – L'aire de production des vins ayant droit à l'appellation contrôlée «Pessac-Léognan» est délimitée à l'intérieur du territoire des dix communes suivantes du département de la Gironde : Cadaujac, Canéjan, Gradignan, Léognan, Martillac, Mérignac, Pessac, Saint-Médard-d'Eyrans, Talence, Villenave-d'Ornon.

Art. 3. – Pour avoir droit à l'appellation contrôlée «Pessac-Léognan», les vins doivent être issus de vendanges récoltées dans l'aire de production délimitée par parcelles, ou parties de parcelles, telle qu'elle a été approuvée par le Comité National de l'Institut national des appellations d'origine des vins et eaux-de-vie lors de sa réunion des 24 et 25 juin 1987, pour l'appellation «Graves» sur le territoire des communes visées à l'article 2 sur proposition de la commission d'experts. Les plans de délimitation sont déposés à la mairie des communes intéressées.

Art. 4. – Les vins ayant droit à l'appellation contrôlée «Pessac-Léognan» doivent provenir des cépages-suivants, à l'exclusion de tous autres :

Pour les vins blancs : sémillon, sauvignon, muscadelle.

Toutefois, la proportion de cépage sauvignon doit représenter au minimum 25 p. 100 de l'encépagement des superficies revendiquées en appellation d'origine contrôlée «Pessac-Léognan».

Pour les vins rouges : merlot N., cabernet franc, cabernet sauvignon, cot (ou malbec), petit verdot et carménère.

Art. 5. – Les vins rouges et blancs ayant droit à l'appellation contrôlée «Pessac-Léognan» doivent provenir de raisins récoltés à bonne maturité et présenter un titre alcoométrique volumique naturel minimum de 10 p. 100, la teneur en sucre résiduel des vins blancs ne doit pas excéder 4 grammes par litre. Pour les vins rouges, ne peut être considéré comme étant à bonne maturité tout lot unitaire de vendange présentant une richesse en sucre inférieure à 162 grammes par litre de moût. Pour les vins blancs, ne peut être considéré comme étant à bonne maturité tout lot unitaire de vendange présentant une richesse en sucre inférieure à 144 grammes par litre de moût.

En outre, lorsque l'autorisation d'enrichissement est accordée, les vins rouges et blancs ne doivent pas dépasser un titre alcoométrique volumique total maximum de 13 p. 100, sous peine de perdre le droit à l'appellation. Toutefois, le bénéfice de l'appellation peut être accordé aux vins d'un titre alcoométrique volumique total supérieur à la limite susvisée et élaborés sans aucun enrichissement, si le déclarant justifie d'un certificat délivré par l'Institut national des appellations d'origine, après enquête effectuée sur sa demande présentée au moins huit jours avant la vendange des vignes concernées.

Les notifications des dérogations visées à l'alinéa précédent doivent être

357

adressées aux services locaux de la direction générale des impôts et de la direction générale de la concurrence, de la consommation et de la répression des fraudes.

Les limites visées aux alinéas ci-dessus pourront être modifiées lorsque les conditions climatiques le justifieront, par arrêté conjoint du ministre chargé de l'économie et du ministre de l'agriculture, sur proposition de l'Institut national des appellations d'origine, après avis du syndicat de producteurs intéressé.

Art. 6. – Ne peuvent prétendre à l'appellation contrôlée «Pessac-Léognan» que les vins répondant aux conditions du décret n° 74-872 du 19 octobre 1974 modifié.

Le rendement de base visé à l'article 1er du décret susvisé est fixé à :

45 hectolitres à l'hectare pour les vins rouges ;

48 hectolitres à l'hectare pour les vins blancs.

Le pourcentage prévu à son article 3 est fixé à 20 p. 100.

Le pourcentage prévu à son article 6 est fixé à 60 p. 100 du rendement annuel de l'appellation «Bordeaux».

Le bénéfice de l'appellation contrôlée «Pessac-Léognan» ne peut être accordé aux vins provenant des jeunes vignes qu'à partir de la troisième année suivant celle au cours de laquelle la plantation a été réalisée en place avant le 31 août.

Art. 7. – Les vignes produisant les vins ayant droit à l'appellation contrôlée «Pessac-Léognan» devront être taillées et plantées selon les dispositions suivantes :

Le seul mode de taille autorisé est la taille dite «à cots» (ou courson) et «à astes» (ou long bois). Le cep doit avoir au maximum douze yeux francs. Le long bois ayant au maximum sept yeux pour le cabernet sauvignon, le cot, le merlot N., le petit verdot, le sémillon et la muscadelle, et huit yeux francs pour le cabernet franc, le sauvignon, la carménère. Les cots de retour étant au maximum au hombre de deux, tailliés à un œil franc ;

La densité de plantation doit être au minimum de 6 500 pieds à l'hectare.

Les vignes plantées conformément à l'arrêté du 15 février 1947 définissant les règles applicables pour l'A.O.C. «Graves» pourront avoir droit à l'appellation contrôlée «Pessac-Léognan» jusqu'au 31 août 2010 à condition d'avoir été plantées avant le 31 août 1990 et de respecter les règles de taille précisées au présent article.

Art. 8. – Les vins ayant droit à l'appellation contrôlée «Pessac-Léognan» doivent être vinifiés conformément aux usages locaux. Ils bénéficient de toutes les pratiques œnologiques autorisées par les lois et règlements en vigueur.

Art. 9. – Les vins d'appellation contrôlée «Pessac-Léognan» ne peuvent être mis en circulation sans un certificat d'agrément délivré par l'I.N.A.O. dans les conditions prévues par le décret n° 74-871 du 19 octobre 1974 relatif aux examens analytiques et organoleptiques des vins d'appellation d'origine contrôlée.

Art. 10. – Les vins pour lesquels aux termes du présent décret est revendiquée l'appellation contrôlée «Pessac-Léognan» ne peuvent être déclarées après la récolte, offerts au public, expédiés, mis en vente ou vendus sans que, dans la déclaration de récolte, dans les annonces, sur les prospectus, étiquettes, factures, récipients quelconques, l'appellation d'origine susvisée soit inscrite et accompagnée de la mention «Appellation contrôlée», le tout en caractères très apparents. Le nom de l'appellation doit être inscrit sur les étiquettes en caractères dont les dimensions, aussi bien en hauteur qu'en largeur, ne doivent pas être inférieures à la moitié de celles des caractères de toute autre mention y figurant.

Par ailleurs, les mentions «vin de Graves» ou «grand vin de Graves» peuvent figurer sur les étiquettes, prospectus et récipients quelconques. Les dimensions des caractères desdites mentions ne doivent pas être supérieures, aussi bien en hauteur qu'en largeur, aux deux tiers de celles des caractères composant le nom de l'appellation. Pour le cas particulier des crus classés, la mention «cru classé des Graves» peut être utilisée en remplacement des mentions «vin de Graves» ou «grand vin de Graves», dans le respect des mêmes conditions de présentation et de dimension des caractères.

Art. 11. – L'emploi de toute indication ou de tout signe susceptible de faire croire à l'acheteur que les vins ont droit à l'appellation contrôlée «Pessac-Léognan» alors qu'ils ne répondent pas à toutes les conditions fixées par le présent décret est poursuivi conformément à la législation générale sur les fraudes et sur la protection des appellations d'origine, sans préjudice des sanctions d'ordre fiscal, s'il y a lieu.

Art. 12. – Les vins de la récoïte 1986 qui ont été revendiqués avec l'appellation contrôlée «Graves» peuvent être admis au bénéfice de l'appellation d'origine contrôlée «Pessac-Léognan»:

– s'ils répondent à toutes les prescriptions du présent décret, à l'exception des conditions de rendement, qui, à titre exceptionnel, pourront être celles appliquées à l'appellation contrôlée «Graves» l'année considérée;

– s'ils obtiennent, dans un délai de cinq mois à partir de la date de publication du présent décret, le certificat d'agrément prévu à l'article 9 ci-dessus, délibré dans les mêmes conditions après examens analytiques et organoleptiques. Les marchands en gros qui détiennent des vins de Graves de la récoïte 1986 susceptibles d'être admis au bénéfice de l'appellation «Pessac-Léognan» doivent les soumettre aux mêmes contrôles, mais dans ce cas les prélèvements seront effectués par les agents de la direction générale de la concurrence, de la consommation et de la répression des fraudes.

Art. 13. – Le dernier alinéa de l'article 1er du décret du 4 mars 1937 modifié est abrogé.

Les dispositions relatives à l'indication des mentions «Pessac» et «Léognan» figurant à l'article 7 du décret du 4 mars 1937 modifié sont abrogées.

Art. 14. – Le ministre d'Etat, ministre de l'économie, des finances et de la privatisation, le ministre de l'agriculture et le secrétaire d'Etat auprès du ministre d'Etat, ministre de l'économie, des finances et de la privatisation, chargé de la consommation et de la concurrence, sont chargés, chacun en ce qui le concerne, de l'exécution du présent décret, qui sera publié au *Journal officiel* de la République française.

Fait à Paris, le 9 septembre 1987.

JACQUES CHIRAC

Par le Premier ministre:

Le ministre d'Etat, ministre de l'économie,
des finances et de la privatistaion,
ÉDOUARD BALLADUR

Le ministre de l'agriculture,
FRANÇOIS GUILLAUME

Le secrétaire d'Etat auprès du ministre d'Etat,
ministre de l'économie, des finances et de la privatisation,
chargé de la consommation et de la concurrence,
JEAN ARTHUIS

THE NON-CLASSIFIED GROWTHS OF THE GRAVES

The following, listed by communes, are the non-classified growths of the Graves, as supplied by the Maison des Vins de Graves of the members of the Syndicat Viticole des Graves et Graves Supérieures. For reasons of space, it has not been possible to subdivide each property into the details of production, although the Maison des Vins de Graves will always supply such particulars on request. The estates do not always coincide with those listed in the latest edition of Féret, so I have added any extra properties separately, after a line of demarcation. To anticipate criticism, I must point out that this is not a technical account of the Graves, nor an up-to-the-minute statistical survey – anyone requiring such particulars will be able to obtain them. What this list does indicate is the great number of Graves properties, making both red and white wines, accounting for an increasing area, notably in the south of the region. It is from such growths, many of them as yet little known, that many wines of interest and quality may originate in the future.

There are also several repetitions of names – because the property is split between different owners. The other form of nomenclature that may seem strange is that sometimes places are simply referred to as 'At . . .' (A . . .).

Then there are some members of the Syndicat registered outside the actual region, plus some who have properties within, for example, the Sauternes region and others, where the demarcation between the wines of the Graves and others is not strictly according to the boundaries of the actual area.

Commune: Arbanats	Ch. des Places	Ch. Pavillon de Boyrein
Dom. des Garbères	Dom. Teychon	. . . .
Ch. Carris	Dom. de Gingean	Ch. Boyrein
Ch. Lagrange		
Ch. Biot	**Léogeats**	**Mazères**
Ch. Coulon	Peylebe	A Cap Blanc
Ch. Toureau–Chollet	Le Bourg	Labarthe
Ch. Expert	. . . .	A Lamanieu
Dom. de Berot	Ch. Trillon	Ch. La Vigneronne
Ch. de Virelade		A Tucau
. . . .	**Roaillan**	Ch. Lamourette
Ch. Moron-Lafitte	Ch. Pujol Marceau	A. Rançon

Dom. Latrille
Chaloupin
Ch. Ramonas
La Testère
Ch. de Roquetaillade
Ch. Roquetaillade-la-
  Grange
Dom. Le Tuilerie Peyrous
Ch. Beauregard-Ducasse
. . . .

Dom. du Paysan
Abbaye de Larame
Aux Carmes, au Moutha

Budos
Le Bourg
Le Roy
Jouba
Ch. Le Roy
Le Liot
Fontbaue
Ch. Pouyanne
Ch. Mouyet
Dom. de l'Hermitage
Ch. de Budos
Marots
Les Mouliets
Le Bourg
Cru Castera
Le Chot
Ch. Pouyanne
Le Bourg
Baulin
. . . .

Clos d'Aramajan
A Virecoupe
A Cazenave
Clos de la Garenne

A Pingoy
A Couchire
A Massé
A Lapeyrouse
Dom. du Roy

Martillac
Bernedon
Lamorelle
Dom. de la Solitude
. . . .

Ch. Haut–Nouchet
Ch. Ferran
Ch. de Rochemorin
Ch. Malleprat
A La Salle
A Mirebeau

Podensac
Clos Graoères
Ch. Chantegrive
Ch. Le Cossu
Ch. de Mauves
Ch. Mayne d'Imbert
. . . .

Ch. de Madère
Ch. d'Anice
Ch. Ferbos-Lalanette
Ch. L Bon Dieu des
  Vignes
Ch. Bédat
Ch. Larroquey
Dom. de Brouillaou
Cru Manaut-Larroqueyre
Au Bourg
Cru de la Maoucouade
Cru de Bruilleau

Pujols-sur-Ciron

A Videau
A Colas
Au Bourg
Ch. Le Blanc
A Hazembert
A Menant
A Viteau
A Marouil
Ch. Saint Robert
A Videau
A Pingua
Les Tauzins
. . . .

Ch. Pinzas et Ch.
  Saint-Jean
Ch. Graville-Lacoste
Ch. Montalivet
Ch. Riverdon
Ch. Cherchy
Cru Bourrut
Clos de Gensac
Ch. du Haut-Blanc
A Cap-de-Hé
A Jean-de-Bos
Cru Lamoignan
Ch. du Marais

St Médard d'Eyrans
Dom. d'Eyrans
Ch. Lafargue
Dom. de Bruilleau
Dom. du Blayès
. . . .

Clos la Gravette
Dom. de l'esterrolle

St Michel de Rieufret
Ch. Lugaud

362

Ch. de Grenade

· · · · · · · · · · · · · · · · · · · ·

A Tobaerts

St Pardon de Conques
A Legues
A Saupiquet
A Laulan
Ch. Vignolles
A Nonnde
Ch. Pavillon-Lagrange

· · · · · · · · · · · · · · · · · · · ·

Ch. Les Jaubertes
Ch. Liché
A Viaut
A Mondic

St Selve
Ch. Mont St. Pey
A Jeansotte
A Jeansotte
Ch. Bonnat Jeansotte
Dom. du Barque

· · · · · · · · · · · · · · · · · · · ·

A Arzac
Ch. de Grenade
A Civrac
A Gaillardas

Toulenne
Ch. Latourte
A Maillard
Ch. Rougement
Dom. de Courbon
Ch. La Tourte des Graves

· · · · · · · · · · · · · · · · · · · ·

Ch. Respide
Ch. Chicane et Clos
  Louloumet

Ch. de Cardaillan
A Perrouquet
A Patiras
A Vincennes

Villenave d'Ornon
Ch. Baret

· · · · · · · · · · · · · · · · · · · ·

Ch. Pontac-Monplaisir et
  Ch. Limbourg
Ch. Couhins
Ch. Couhins-Lurton
Ch. Guiteronde

Virelade
Ch. du Cros la Gravière
Dom. de Lugey

· · · · · · · · · · · · · · · · · · · ·

Ch. de Virelade
Dom. de Nouet
Ch. des Tuileries
Clos de la Coye
Dom. de Bertet
A l'Escaloupey
Au Bourg
A Mounine
Dom. de Gayon

**Ayguemortes-Les-
Graves**
Ch. St Jérôme
Ch. Lusseau

· · · · · · · · · · · · · · · · · · · ·

Ch. Boiresse
A Maison Blanche

Auros
Ch. Montalivet

· · · · · · · · · · · · · · · · · · · ·

Ch. d'Auros
Ch. Mayne de Lacour
Au Pin
Dom. de Poncet

Beautiran
Ch. le Tuquet
Ch. Ballton
Ch. Martignac

· · · · · · · · · · · · · · · · · · · ·

Ch. Haut Callens
Dom. du Haut Callens
Cru Callens
Ch. de la Limagère
Clos Cachot
A Figueys

Guillos
Le Bourg
A Guillemin

· · · · · · · · · · · · · · · · · · · ·

A Guillemin
A Brot

Castres
Ch. Ferrande
Ch. Haut-Pommarède
Ch. Foncla
Clos La Périchère
Ch. St Hilaire
Ch. Sansaric
Les Jacquets
Ch. Nouchet
Clos de l'Hospital
Dom. Périn de Naudine

· · · · · · · · · · · · · · · · · · · ·

Ch. Lognac

Ch. Pommarède
Dom. de Samsarric
Aux Lilas

Isle-Saint-Georges
Le Bourg
Cru Lauriole
· · · · · · · · · · · · · · · · · · · ·
Ch. Turpeau
Clos l'Hospital
Clos Lauriole
Au Bourg
Au Bourg
A Boutric
A Pont-Castel
Au Rabey
A La Brède
A Boutric
Au Bourg
A Ferrand

Cérons
Ch. Le Peyrat
Ch. Larroc
Ch. Tour de l'Avocat
Quartier de l'Eglise
Clos Moulin à Vent
Crus Voltaire
Ch. Moulin à Vent
Dom. d'Expert
Ch. Haut-Mayne
Clos du Barrail
Ch. Huradin et Ch. du
  Salut
Clos Bourgelas
A Huradin
Ch. l'Emigré
Ch. la Salette

Quartier La Pire Nord
Clos Cantemerle
Ch. Peyrague
Ch. du Caillou
Dom. de Salvané
A Expert
Cru Voltaire
Harouet
Harouet
Le Frayon
Grand Enclos du Ch. de
  Ciron
Cru Branly
Ch. de Cérons
Ch. Haut-Mayne
Ch. le Peyrat
· · · · · · · · · · · · · · · · · · · ·
Ch. du Moulin de Marc
Ch. Mayne Binet
Ch. Lamoureux
Ch. Ferbos
Ch. Bourgelas
Ch. Lanette
Ch. Sylvain
Ch. Barthes
Cru di Pineau
Cru Larroquey
Ch. Larroquet
Ch. Balestey
Ch. Cantemerle
Ch. Méric
Ch. des Grands-Chênes
Ch. des Bessanes
Ch. Beaulieu
A Menaut
A Barreyre
Ch. Gravaillas
A La Palus

Illats
Maingeon
Ch. la Nontasse
Dom. Citadelle
Ch. Pryrères
Clos Baraille
Ch. Laroche
Condrine
Dom. de Calas
    Clos Pins Francs
Dom. Arrouats
Dom. de Lionne
Dom. Arrouats
Ch. d'Ardennes
Ch. Brousterot
Dom. Deux-Moulins
Ch. La Rouille
Dom. de Maingeon
Le Tauzin
Ch. de Navarro
Ch. le Merle
Ch. Peyragué
Ch. d'Archambeau
Cru St Roch
Brouquet
La Fontaine
Hillot
St Roch
Cru Belair
Merle
Cru Carbon
· · · · · · · · · · · · · · · · · · · ·
Ch. la Tuilerie
Ch. Beaulac
Au Merle
Ch. Thome-Brousterot
Ch. du Prouzet
Ch. Cantau

364

A Condrines
A Condrines
Au Bourg
Cru de Cabiro
Clos Courrèges
Cru Bel-Air

Langon
Ch. Montalivet
Dom. le Maine
Dom. Roland
Ch. Fernon
Clos Arquet
Sargade
Le Teighney
Ch. Ludeman La Côte
Pelot
Ordonnat
Aux Rochers
Ch. Lehoul
Ch. de Maine
Ch. de Respide
Ch. Le Teigney
Ch. La Croix
Ch. Castain
Ch. Brondelle
Ch. Brondelle
Ch. des Guillemins
Gaillat
Ch. Gaillat
Dom. Les Cluchets
Ch. Noguey
Ch. Camus
Ch. Tourmilot
· · · · · · · · · · · · · · · · · · ·
Ch. Chanteloiseau et Ch.
  l'Etoile
Clos la Maurasse

Ch. Tour de Boyrein
Clos Tegney
Clos de Casseuil
Clos de Tegney
Ch. le Brule
Ch. Lehouit
Clos de Tegney
A Ordonnat
Au Teigney
A Lajordy
Quartier la Carrade

La Brède
A Avignon
Clos du Pape
Dom. du Reys
Le Gars
Ch. Lassalle
Ch. Chante l'Oiseau
Le Chec
Ch. Magneau
A Beaucaillou
Ch. Les Fougères
Ch. de la Brède
Ch. Méric
Ch. Picot
Ch. la Blancherie
Clos Beney
Bergey
Dom. de Ricotte
· · · · · · · · · · · · · · · · · · ·
Ch. Guillaumot
Cru Bichon
Clos Haut Rey

Landiras
Ch. Manine
Grand-Boiste

Dom. des Plantes
A Artigues
A Laignasse
Clos St Robert
Ch. de Leyre
Ch. Batsères
Ch. Clare
Dom. Bassiouey
Ch. St Agrèves
Dom. Camegaye
Dom. de Perran
A Arrougets
Ch. de l'Argulère
Dom. du Moulin à Vent
Ch. Carbon d'Artigues
Cru Dujardin
Dom. des Aounades
Ch. d'Arricaud
Le Château
A Bassiouey
Ch. des Plantes
A Menon
Cru Fontaine de Manine
· · · · · · · · · · · · · · · · · · ·
Dom. de Terrfort et Ch.
  La Capère
Ch. Montgarede
A Jeangoiste
A Jeannets
A Pessilla
A Pessilla
A Jeannot de Lègue
A Artigues
A Artigues
A Barreyre
A Jeannot de Lègue
A Le Carpoula
A Lucat

365

A Artigues
A Lousteauneuf
A Artigues
A Artigues
A Cabiros
A Artigues
A Jeamnets
A Jeannot de Lègue
A Artigues
A Jeamnets
A Jeamnets

St Pierre-de-Mons
Belle Fontaine
Ch. Lubat
Les Jennets
Ch. Les Jaubertes
Ch. Mons
Ch. Lafon (Sauternes)
Clos Cabanne
Les Sarocs
Ch. Gassies
Cros Cantalot
Viex Ch. Bruhaut of Ch.
  Grave-Janilles
Rivière
Ch. Toumilon & Ch.
  Cabanes
Clos de la Magine
Dom. Peyron-Bouche
Clos Toumilon
Ch. Moulin à Vent
A Rousseau
Ch. Mounette Bruhaut
Ch. Magence
Ch. Cazebonne
Ch. St Pierre les Queyrats
. . . .

Ch. d'Arche
Ch. de Saint-Pierre et
  Clos d'Uza
A Camboutch
Cru de Lubat
Clos Maragnac
A Haut-Grava
Clos Viaut
A Camboutch
A Peydebayle
Cru la Madeleine
A Tamboy
Clos Cabanne
A Peydebayle
A Boritz
A Mons
A Peyron
A Saphore
A Lamédecine
Ch. Peydebayle

Portets
Ch. Pingoy
Dom. de la Grave
Ch. Rahoul
Ch. Millet
Ch. Crabutey
Courneau
Ch. Tardieu
Clos Moulon
Ch. Gueydon
Clos des Gravières
Dom. des Lucques
Ch. Pessan St Hilaire
Cru de Beausite
A Daroubin
Dom. de Lucque
Dom. de la Girafe

Ch. des Gravières
Ch. Lamothe
A Daroubin
Clos La Bonnetière
Ch. Graveyron
Ch. Durse
Ch. La Vielle France
Ch. Guérin-Jacquet
Dom. de May
Gueydon
Ch. Jean de Maye
Ch. Clerget La Gravière
Ch. Madelis
Ch. du Grand'Abord
Ch. Jean-Gervais
Clos Bellevue
Ch. de Portets
Ch. du Mirail
Le Courneau
Ch. des Lucques
Ch. Cabannieux
Le Courneau
Dom. Durse
Ch. Cheret-Lamothe
Clos Lamothe
Dom de Béquin
Ch. Lagueloup
Ch. La Tour Bicheau
Ch. Doms
Ch. de Mongenan
. . . .

Ch. l'Hospital
Dom. du Haut-Courneau
Ch. de Mirail et Ch.
  Maure Bellevue
Clos de la Tuilerie
Clos Saint-Hilaire
Clos de la Borderie

366

Clos Moulon

Ch. Bel-Air

Ch. Moutin

Ch. de Chaye

Ch. Jean de Maye

Dom. de Cheret

Ch. Port-du-Roy

Ch. du Clos Renon

The following are properties owned by members of the Graves syndicate, which, as will be noted, are in regions with different A.O.C.s. For reasons of courtesy and so as to provide a complete list, they are given here, but, because this book is solely concerned with the Graves, the other properties in the various areas that are listed in Féret are not included.

Fargues-de-Langon

Ch. Les Claveries

Ch. Pilotte

A Baylieu

Bommes

Ch. Haut Bommes

Ch. La Capère

Dom. de Terrefort

(Two additional owners)

Barsac

Ch. Roland

Ch. Brochon

Ch. La Pinesse

Ch. La Trelotte

Ch. Maron

Ch. St Jean & Ch. Liot

Ch. Coutet

Cru Jauguet

Cru Mercier

Ch. Caillou

Ch. Simon

Ch. Granville Lacoste

Ch. Menota

Ch. Doisy Daëne

Ch. Villefranche

Ch. Barssens-Guiteronne

Ch. Carles

Dom. de Maron

Sauternes

Ch. Lamothe

Ch. Trillon

Preignac

Cru du Seigneur

Ch. Haut-Bergeron

Cru du Blanc

Ch. Medeville et Ch. Gillette

Semens

Le Galouchy

Ch. Gravelines

Note: There are some inconsistencies in the spellings of names, also some variations in the prefixes 'Cru', 'Dom.', 'Au' or 'A'. Anyone comparing names with the versions given in Féret and other works of reference will see these, but it should be remembered that, when properties change hands there may be a slight alteration in the 'official' version of a name and that prefixes or the insertion of the 'de' are also variables. No list such as this and no book of reference can be immutable. It is sincerely hoped that any misreading of proper names may not be regarded as a discourtesy.

PRODUCTION OF VINTAGES IN THE GRAVES
FROM 1976 TO 1986

Vintages	(in hectos)					
	1976	1977	1978	1979	1980	average
White Graves	48,243	19,938	31,507	59,568	25,551	36,959
Graves Sup.	13,708	6,054	11,640	13,363	21,714	13,296
Red Graves	57,760	31,935	59,457	89,748	62,098	60,200
Total	119,711	57,917	102,640	162,679	109,363	110,455

* The overall average annual production is therefore: 100,000 hectolitres.

Vintages	(in hectos)					
	1981	1982	1983	1984	1985	1986	average
White Graves	22,469	64,043	43,202	48,708	48,814	60,415	47,941
Graves Sup.	12,356	20,100	25,953	19,434	14,516	28,822	20,197
Red Graves	66,469	100,869	94,868	60,073	98,585	132,303	92,194
Total	101,294	185,012	164,023	128,215	161,915	221,540	160,333

* The overall average annual production is therefore: 160,000 hectolitres.

As has been mentioned in the text, the increase in the production of red wine has been steady since 1962. This has occurred mostly in the south of the overall region, where many growers were previously concentrating on white wines. Apart from the famous properties in the north, this trend reflects the popularity of red wines with many of the foods traditional in export markets, where a French wine, notably from the Bordeaux area, enjoys much prestige, particularly for special occasions. The situation as regards the white wines shows greater variation – the competition from other French regions and other wine-producing countries is keen in the lower price ranges.

EXPORTS OF GRAVES WINES (SOURCE: C.I.V.B.) FROM 1980 TO 1986

White Graves

	1980/81	1981/82	1982/83	1983/84	1984/85	1985/86
Total marketed	32,775	41,546	46,554	49,361	46,978	47,348
France	6,812	16,436	17,853	15,388	13,454	16,440
Export	25,963	25,110	28,701	33,973	33,524	30,908
U.S.A.	10,478	8,001	9,476	11,831	11,829	10,245
Great Britain	3,495	3,467	4,891	5,100	5,462	3,836
Belgium	2,537	3,661	2,907	2,823	2,457	3,312
Canada	1,843	2,903	2,512	4,388	3,824	4,890
Japan	1,960	2,671	3,413	3,004	3,608	2,346
Holland	763	722	985	815	729	807
R.F.A.	825	605	832	996	942	1,227

Graves Supérieures

	1980/81	1981/82	1982/83	1983/84	1984/85	1985/86
Total marketed	14,256	17,877	23,446	23,843	22,519	18,511
France	3,334	3,830	2,181	1,516	2,243	3,031
Export	10,922	14,047	21,265	22,327	20,276	15,480
Holland	8,685	11,787	18,128	20,020	17,349	13,628
Great Britain	315	280	341	406	598	253
U.S.A.	335	162	176	191	213	72
Belgium	716	377	418	112	301	664

Red Graves

	1980/81	1981/82	1982/83	1983/84	1984/85	1985/86
Total marketed	59,153	61,604	61,577	59,785	75,706	68,330
France	34,329	40,050	42,797	34,194	44,662	41,150
Export	24,824	21,554	18,780	25,591	31,044	27,180
Belgium	6,452	5,799	4,737	5,495	7,262	6,269
U.S.A.	5,083	2,639	2,768	6,345	5,025	3,674
Holland	2,831	2,753	2,398	2,481	3,080	2,422
Great Britain	2,588	1,629	2,054	3,170	4,428	3,839
Switzerland	2,671	2,692	2,033	2,134	2,910	2,752
R.F.A.	1,197	1,923	1,175	1,489	2,453	2,496
Denmark	778	1,176	920	1,081	1,600	2,563

STENDHAL'S VISIT TO LA BRÈDE FROM 7 APRIL, 1838

It is not precisely love that I feel for Montesquieu, but rather veneration. He never bores me by expatiating on an idea I have already understood. This morning when I visited La Brède, I was filled with an almost childlike respect as once before on visiting Potsdam and touching Frederick II's hat that had been pierced by a bullet. This day at La Brède will be a red-letter day in my life; ordinarily a visit to a king's palace merely makes me feel like scoffing.

The property of La Brède where Montesquieu was born, and which he cultivated and increased, lies on the extreme edge of farmed lands on the right-hand side of the road from Bordeaux to Bazas and Bayonne. A little farther on, one comes to that vast desert of sand known as *les Landes*. It is the dreariest region in the world; the water is the color of coffee like the Spree that flows through Berlin and the sand is sparsely covered here and there by pine trees that are scraped for the resin. But even when it has not been scraped, this pine is the dreariest tree imaginable. It has only the name in common with the magnificent umbrella pine that is the glory of the Villa Ludovisi in Rome.

An ancient avenue, planted by the author of *L'Esprit des Lois*, leads to the château where he was born; they have just sold some of the trees to advantage. However, one hundred pines are still left on this avenue at the point where the traveler leaves the wretched country road as he comes from the village of La Brède and runs right toward the chateau.

I was all eyes and ears as I caught a glimpse of an almost round building without a façade, surrounded by very wide moats filled with clean but coffee-colored water. That water comes from les Landes and not even fish can live in it. This harsh and gloomy sight reminded me of the chateau where Armide held prisoner the Christian knights she had led from the field of the Crusades.

La Brède is a noble and apparently very strongly built château. At the broadest part, the moats are seventy feet wide and thirty or thirty-five feet at the narrowest. The water is on a level with the banks and the moats are not deep.

To enter you must cross three drawbridges, passing from one drawbridge to the other between two stout walls pierced by loopholes. Today, those little bridges are made of wood and are stationary. After the first bridge, and directly opposite the gate, is a little island that has been made into a garden no bigger than a hand. It is guarded by three round towers, two of them on the other side of the moat. The waters are held back by a dam; if the dam were destroyed the moats would go dry. Two of the towers defend this very essential dam. The manor walls are not rounded, but form a polygon of perhaps twelve sides. Beyond the moats are a meadow and some wheat fields and then the forest of oaks surrounding on all sides the chateau which sits triumphantly in the center of that great empty space. After crossing the third bridge, you come to a courtyard twelve feet wide by twenty feet long which overlooks the moats. To enter, you pass into a beautiful round tower rather elegantly machicolated. This is the only elegance on the severe exterior of this chateau without a façade. Prudence has obviously dictated the use of narrow windows.

As you enter the little courtyard you find yourself facing a door and windows with pointed arches. A little servant girl, slatternly but not ugly, showed us grumpily into a walnut paneled dining room where everything is ogival in shape, even to the armchairs and the straight chairs. There is no vaulted ceiling but a strangely low ceiling. Passing to the left, we entered an equally sombre Gothic salon, paneled in walnut. But there was nothing grand about this decoration; it was a rather shabby Gothic, like the ogival decorations in the little theaters on the Boulevard. This salon is papered and in good condition. On the paneling I noticed engravings of seaports by Joseph Vernet, thin, scratched engravings that make a poor effect against the dark wainscotting. As the fireplace is high and without a mirror, a modern lock has been hung high on the left on a level with Vernet's marine sketches. Above the clock are two oil portraits, extremely pleasing to the eye for they do not interfere with the general décor. One of those portraits, in an excellent color, is of a pretty woman with heavy eyelids and rather round eyes like some of the women's faces by Sebastiano del Piombo. She is portrayed as the Magdalen gazing at a crucifix, with her hand on a skull in the shadow. The other portrait is of a terrible warrior with a face fierce enough to frighten children. He wears the court costume of the Louis XIII era. This rather low salon, with only one window, is dark, gloomy, and a good preparation for the adjoining room, Montesquieu's bedroom. Here, so the slatternly servant girl told us, nothing has been changed.

The bedroom testifies to the extreme simplicity of the great man who understood the great painters of Italy and to whom all bourgeois and petty ornamentation was an abomination. This room has only one window though, to be sure, a fairly large one, which faces south overlooking the narrower part of the moat at the point where it is about thirty-five feet wide. It is paneled in a rather light walnut which is by no means impressive. The paneling itself is made of little square panels measuring two feet on the side.

There is a four-poster bed covered in faded green damask. Montesquieu died in Paris in February, 1755, a few months after arriving from La Brède. This bed was, therefore, used for the last time eighty-three years ago. The servant girl repeated that none of the furnishings in this room had been changed. The bed is supported by four very stout walnut posts that are absolutely plain. There is no tester, but a very ordinary and not very high step. Nor is there any mirror above the Gothic mantelpiece. Now the absence of a mirror in this spot is something to which I have never been able to accustom myself; to me it is the last degree of cheerlessness and misery.

Facing the mantelpiece, however, and at a man's height, is a mirror two feet square with beveled edges and a glass frame four or five inches wide; a fashion that was doubtless good taste in the provinces around 1738, a century ago. It is the direct opposite to that horrible pretty-pretty style of Louis XV's court. But the right-hand post on this Gothic fireplace, whose mantelpiece stands fully four or five feet high, is worn by Montesquieu's slipper, for the President was in the habit of sitting by the fire and writing on his knee.

The history of Bordeaux by that good old man, dom Devienne, printed in Bordeaux in 1771, sixteen years after President Montesquieu's death, states that Montesquieu spent the years 17... and 17... at La Brède and it was there that he wrote *La Grandeur et la Décadence des Romains*.

Neither Madame S. nor I could tear ourselves away from this room which, compared with modern luxury, looks plain almost to the point of poverty. Beside the bed is a huge false bronze medallion which appears to me to be a poor copy of the Dassier medallion. Near one window in the room is a terra-cotta bust with its eyes open: it looks like Montesquieu, but the peevish servant girl told us it was a friend of Montesquieu's. It seems to me that the present owner of La Brède could install a professional guide whose wages could be paid by sightseers, for according to the bad-tempered servant girl, visitors come here almost every day in the summer. The owners might even entrust the guide with one of the volumes from Montesquieu's library that had been annotated by his hand. Our reception at La Brède reminded me that in the past visitors were very badly received at Ferney on orders from the Genevan citizen who had bought Voltaire's château. Such successors, living in these celebrated places, keep alive the glory of the great men who made them famous; the proximity of the vulgar offers a contrast.

On the table in the center of Montesquieu's bedroom, is a book containing the names of visitors; the same stupid phrases, the same orthographic mistakes one sees in the Brocken (Harz) and in Weimar, but no well-known names.

Near the bed is a portrait, very badly executed, of a rather pretty woman with a sweet expression. She is said to be one of Montesquieu's mistresses. I made

372

the mistake of not copying the name which, according to good usage in the seventeenth century, was on the upper part of the portrait. But I was somewhat moved, I admit, and in this case reverie was so sweet that any manual effort would have been too great.

Near the window is a very poor sketch of the statue of Montesquieu that is in the royal courtyard in Bordeaux and which I have not yet been able to bring myself to go and see; it is undoubtedly a caricature of that great man.

The servant girl led us into the library, an immense room, as simple as the bedroom, with a semicircular dome covered by planks painted a light color. This room is possibly fifty feet long by twenty feet wide. The books, in small glassed-in cases are simply bound, the bindings, in my opinion, dating from a period much later than Montesquieu's century. I noticed quarto editions of most of the good Roman and Greek authors.

Then the servant, grumbling, said: "Someone is waiting for me." A manservant, probably hoping to appropriate our tip for himself, had come in to give her the message.

Above the library window nearest the door are some very bad family portraits; they have been hung against the light and it is probably just as well. Among the portraits are two plaster medallions with hair and beards highly colored which might cost four sous each and which seem to me from a much later date than Montesquieu. Since I avoid all contact with provincial literati and scholars as I would the plague, it is quite possible that I may not see any contemporary portrait of Montesquieu in Bordeaux. He held an important position; he became famous early in life and the century abounded in portrait painters. It is therefore probable that a man with better connections than I have would discover some of those portraits. All the caricatures in the front of the editions of Montesquieu's works that I own are poor copies of the Dassier medallion.

In spite of the servant girl's impatient frowns, we lingered on, unwilling to leave those three rooms a great man had honored by his presence. In the drawing room there is a cartoon of Monsieur Lainé with all his titles enumerated. Nothing diminishes the stature of a dead man so much, especially since the monarchy which invented those titles has been driven out.

Free at last of the servant girl, we made a slow tour of this strange polygonal chateau without a façade. In the moats the coffee-colored water was gently ruffled by the wind.

From Stendhal: *Travels in the South of France*, trans. Elizabeth Abbott, (Calder and Boyars, London, 1971).

GLOSSARY

Appellation contrôlée (abbr. to A.C., or A.O.C.): strictly the term is Appellation d'Origine Contrôlée, defining the area from which the wine comes, plus the permitted vines and method of cultivation, training, pruning, planting and density of vines per hectare; also the minimum amount of sugar in the 'must' (unfermented grapejuice), minimum degree of alcohol in the finished wine and maximum production of wine permitted.

Ban: usually with the suffix 'des vendanges', this is the announcement or proclamation of the vintage and, in former times, the date when picking of the grapes might begin. Anyone who began before the official date, in the hope of getting their wine to customers early, was penalised because this might involve harvesting unripe grapes and consequently letting down the quality of a region. Today, Alsace is the only French region where the Ban des Vendanges is still an official permission to pick, but most areas celebrate the start of picking in the autumn – even if – as in some years, most of the crop is in by the time the formal celebrations begin.

Une barrique de Bordeaux: cask holding about 214–223 litres.

Le chai: the above-ground store for wines – distinct from *le cave*, which is a true cellar.

Collage: a fining agent. *Coller* – to fine (not to be confused with *filtrer* – to filter).

Le cuve: this is the vat; *la cuvée*: the contents of the same. *La cuverie* is the vathouse, *le cuvier* the overall place in the installation where the wine is both made and, usually, where it is stored at least at the outset of its life.

Égalissage: the procedure whereby, in the spring after the vintage, the various vattings of different pickings (different grape varieties and the crop of different plots) are combined so as to compose one whole wine for subsequent maturation.

L'Égrappoir: a device that strips the grapes off their stalks. *Un égrappoir-fouloir* is a stripper plus a crusher (*fouler* – to crush).

Faluns: chalk deposit rich in fossilised shells.

Fleuraison: the flowering (of the vine).

Gauging: the method of assessing the contents of a cask, very much the concern of the customs officers, the organisations supervising shipments of wine unloaded in export markets, and, of course, the buyer.

Galets directeurs: stones that have been smoothed by the action of various waters.

Greffer: to graft. *Une porte-greffe* is the aphis-resistant stock onto which the 'national' vine is grafted. There are various types and the suitability of the *porte-greffe* is of considerable importance to the yield of the vine.

Hectare (ha): 2·471 acres.

Hectolitre (hl or hecto): 1,000 litres, 22·4 U.K. gallons.

Lie: literally 'lees', the deposit in the bottom of a cask. To bottle *sur lie* means to draw off the wine directly from where it lies on its lees, thereby often retaining a certain liveliness or 'working' style.

Palus (pronounced with the final 's' sounded): the western slopes on the alluvial shore of the Garonne and Gironde where, in the past, the wines from the vineyard cultivated there enjoyed high reputations. The steeper banks on the east of the Garonne are the *costes* or *côtes*.

Parcelles: small plots of land. Because many wine estates are made up of different segments of land permitted for vine cultivation, it is not usual for a property to be 'all in one piece', although certain of the great Graves estates are. The *parcelles* can be small patches some distance away from the winery.

Régisseur: estate manager.

Remplissage: the process of topping up the cask so as to minimise the amount of air inside.

Soutirer: the term used for racking, i.e. drawing off wine from where it rests on its lees.

Un tonneau: cask holding about 4 *barriques* (hogsheads) of wine. The capacity of an estate is often given in *tonneaux*, although today when estate-bottling is usual for fine wines, the capacity may be given in *caisses*, 12 bottles of wine, (in a wooden box if the estate is a fine one).

Trier: means 'to select'; *triage* is the process whereby a selection (of grapes) is made prior to crushing.

Veraison: the set of the fruit.

Z.A.D. (Zone d'Aménagement Différé) Technopole: an area chosen by the government as the proposed site for extensive development – both urbanisation and industrialisation.

BIBLIOGRAPHY

In addition to the books cited in the text, the following have been consulted:

Andrieu, Pierre, *Petite Histoire de Bordeaux et de son Vignoble* (La Journée Vinicole, 1952)

Appleby, John T., *Henry II* (G. Bell, 1962)

Barronne, Louis, *La Garonne* (Henri Laurens, Paris, undated, 19th century)

Barber, Richard, *Henry Plantagenet* (Barrie & Rockliff, 1964)

Chastenet, Jacques, *L'Épopée de Vins de Bordeaux* (Perrin, 1980)

Cocks, C., *Bordeaux, its wines and the claret country* (Longmans Green, 1846)

Crosland, Jessie, *William the Marshal* (Peter Owen, 1982)

Desgraves, Louis, *Evocation du Vieux Bordeaux* (Les Éditions du Minuit, 1960)

Louis Desgraves, *Montesquieu* (Éditions Mazarine, 1986)

Dion, Roger, *Histoire de la Vigne et du Vin en France des origines aux XIX siècle* (Paris, 1959)

Dovaz, Michel, *Encyclopédie des Crus Classés du Bordelais* (Juillard, 1981)

Duggan, Alfred, *Devil's Brood – the Angevin Family* (Faber, 1957)

Dumay, Raymond (ed.), *Le Vin de Bordeaux et du Haut-Pays* (Montalba, 1976)

Freson, Robert, *Le Goût de la France*, trans. as *The Taste of France* (Stewart, Tabori and Chang, New York, 1981)

Galet, Pierre, *A Practical Ampelography*, trans. Lucie Morton, (Cornell University Press, 1979)

Galet, Pierre, *Cépages et Vignobles de France* (1958–62)

Galy, Roger, *Promenades dans Bordeaux* (Raymond Piquot, 1962)

Galy, Roger, *Nouvelles Promenades dans Bordeaux* (Raymond Piquot, 1965)

Got, Armand, *Visages de la Gironde* (Delmas, 1956)

Guyot, Dr J, *Etudes des Vignobles de la France* (Paris Imprimerie Nationale, 1876)

Harvey, John, *The Plantagenets* (Batsford, 1948)

Higounet, Ch. (ed.), The great *Histoire de Bordeaux*, VII volumes (Fed. Hist. du Sud-Ouest, up to 1969), has been consulted throughout.

Hodge, Eleanor C., *Gascony under English Rule* (Methuen, 1926)

Hutchison, Harold F., *The Hollow Crown, a life of Richard II* (Eyre & Spottiswoode, 1961)

Jullien, André, *Topographie de Tous les Vignobles Connus* (Slatkine, réimpression de l'Édition de Paris 1886, en 1985)

Jullien, Camille, *Historie de Bordeaux* (Féret, 1895)

Keen, Maurice, *A History of Medieval Europe* (Routledge & Kegan Paul, 1968)

Kelly, Amy, *Eleanor of Aquitaine and the Four Kings* (Cassell, 1952)

Kingston, William Beatty, *Claret, its Production and Treatment* (Vinton, 1895)

Lacoste, P. Joseph, *La Route du Vin en Gironde* (Delmas, 1948)

Lamaison, P. E., *Recettes et Paysages* (Larousse, 1938)

Laporte-Castôde, Georgette, *Pain de Seigle et Vin de Grives* (Ducasée-Dahon, Dax, 1980)

Malvezin, Frantz, *Bordeaux* (Delmas, 1919)

Mothe, Florence, *Graves de Bordeaux* (Nathan, 1985)

de Perceval, Émile, *Montesquieu et la Vigne* (Delmas, 1935)

Pernoud, Régine, *Aliénor d'Aquitaine* (Éditions Albin Michel, 1965)

Perroy, Edouard, *The Hundred Years War* (Eyre & Spottiswoode, 1951)

Pongrácz, D. P., *Practical Viticulture* (David Philip, Cape Town, 1978)

Robinson, Jancis, *Vines, Grapes and Wines* (Mitchell Beazley, 1986)

Roger, J.-R., *Les Vins de Bordeaux* (Compagnie Parisienne d'Éditions Techniques et Commercials, no date, presumably post-World War II)

Root, Waverley, *The Food of France* (Cassell, 1958)

Seeley, James, *Great Bordeaux Wines* (Secker and Warburg, 1986)

Slocombe, George *Sons of the Conqueror* (Hutchinson, 1969)

Starobinski, Jean, *Montesquieu* (Écrivains de Toujours, 1982)

Stendhal, Henri, *Travels in the South of France*, trans. Elizabeth Abbott (Calder & Boyars, 1971)

Suffran, Michel, *Histoire de l'Aquitaine* (Hachette, 1976)

Taine, Henri, *Voyage aux Pyrénées* (Hachette, 1860)

Vital, Pierre, *Les Vieilles Vignes de Notre France* (Société Civile d'Information et d'Édition des Services Agricoles, 1956)

Warren, W. L., *King John* (Eyre & Spottiswoode, 1961)

White, Freda, *Ways of Aquitaine* (Faber, 1958)

Willan, Anne, *French Regional Cooking* (Hutchinson, 1981)

Young, Arthur, *Travels in France during the years 1787, 1788 & 1789*, ed. Constantia Maxwell (Cambridge, 1950)

Young, E. H., *Montesquieu, a critical biography* (Oxford, 1961)

Note : All Château names appear under Châteaux.

ageing 145, 182, 232, 285, 304
Agen 54, 136
Agenais 31, 100
Aigue-mortes 238
alcoholic strength 173, 184, 201, 229, 249, 251
Aldington, Richard 76
Aligoté 216
Alsace 27, 45, 212
Amer Picon 300
ampelography 178, 185
amphorae 54, 55, 56, 58, 318
Andrieu, Pierre 185, 190, 233
Appellation d'Origine Contrôlée 47, 158, 164, 165, 169, 171, 192, 218, 249–56, 260, 261, 262
Aquitaine 21, 35, 38, 54, 58, 63, 64, 65, 66, 70, 73, 74, 75–81, 87, 88, 89, 96, 98, 100, 103, 104, 118, 121–3, 130, 136, 180, 182, 332
Aquitaine, Eleanor of 73, 76–88, 106
Arbanats 163, 169, 238, 329
Armagnac 135
Armines 169
arrégailles 179
Arros, Arnold 233–4
Association pour la Sauvegarde des Graves de Bordeaux 169
Ausone 245
Auvernat 183
Aveyron 144
Ayguemortes-lès-Graves 169

Baffert, René 287
Balouzat 182
Baring-Gould, Sabine 77
Barker, Edward Harrison 326
Barrères 87
barriques 105, 134, 136, 145, 147, 205, 206, 208, 209, 260–1, 262, 263, 270, 271, 274, 282, 284, 290

Barron, Louis 320
Barsac 15–16, 26, 27, 45, 132, 134, 143, 150, 159, 198, 213, 238, 239, 255, 263, 292, 299, 328
Barton, Ronald 238
Barton, Thomas 146
Bayonne 53, 89, 103, 127, 152
Bazadais 31, 100, 102, 163, 189
Bazas 98, 107, 118, 134, 320, 322, 324–6, 327
Béarn 107, 202
Beaujolais Blanc 27
Beaumartin, Gabriel 172, 266
Beaumartin, Paul 271
Beaune 148
Beaurein, Abbé 143
Beautiran 25, 169, 238, 331–2
Bègles 144, 169, 238
Belin 137
Bellaterra 200
Bellet, Abbé 182, 184
Bellot de Minières, Alcide 271
Béraud-Sudreau, Hervé 171
Bergerac 215
Bernard, Olivier 265, 267
Bernardy de Sigoyer, Christian de 171
Bernkastel 148
Bethmann, Jean-Jacques de 173, 284, 285
biturica 181, 182, 185, *-basilisca* 57
Blanquefort 139, 158, 163, 189, 238, 239
Bocke, Erik 270
Boisredon, Laurent de 215
Bommes 132, 159, 232
Bon Bourgeois 239
Bonnel, Jean-Claude 171
Bons Crus 243
Bord, G. 189–90
Bordeaux 15, 19, 21, 23–5, 28–9, 31–2, 38, 40, 43–7, 51–5, 59–67, 70–1, 73–7, 79–80, 86–7, 89–93, 96–103, 106, 109–11, 113–14, 116, 121–59, 163–7, 169, 174–5,

179–80, 182–3, 185, 187–91, 193, 199–
  202, 204–6, 209, 213, 217, 222–3, 225,
  229, 230–6, 238–50, 254–60, 264, 266,
  270–1, 273, 275, 278–85, 288–9, 292–4,
  298–9, 302, 314, 319, 320–3, 326–7, 329,
  331–3
  map 14
Borie, François 303
botrytis cinerea 46, 198, 213, 300
bottle
  evolution of 144–6, 148, 154
  maturing in 144
Boucher, Claude 142
Bouchet, Bouschet 186
bouquet 156, 196, 197, 224, 227, 229, 241,
  270, 272, 277, 283
Bouquier, Jean 172
Bourg 24, 132, 144
Bourges 182
bouteiller 96, 99
brandied wines 145
Breton, Abbé 185
Brittany 103, 151
Broadbent, Michael 230–1
Budos 169, 189
Burgundy 27, 35, 73, 75, 77, 80, 121, 122,
  127, 129, 140, 183, 195, 207, 216, 229,
  236, 245, 314

Cabernet Franc 181, 184, 185, 186, 188,
  190, 191, 196, 251, 262, 263, 266, 268,
  269, 271, 273, 277, 278, 281, 283, 288,
  290
Cabernet Sauvignon 41, 157, 181, 182, 184,
  185, 186, 188, 190, 191, 194–6, 197, 198,
  204, 222, 227, 228, 251, 262, 263, 266,
  268, 269, 271, 277, 278, 281, 283, 284,
  285, 288, 290, 292, 293, 295
Cadaujac 148, 165, 166, 169, 171, 238, 242,
  251, 262
Cadillac 292, 327, 333
Cahors 182, 197
California 210, 206, 280, 295
Canéjean 165, 169, 173, 238, 251

Carignan 186
Carmenère 184, 186, 188, 191, 201, 251
cassis 195, 227
Castres 150, 169, 238, 294, 329
Catalonia 149, 305
Caudéran 238, 239
Célestin, Pierre 255
cépages 163, 187, 189, 293
Cérons 163, 169, 189, 238, 239, 255–6, 292,
  328
Cestas 169
Chablis 23, 27
chai 46, 105, 147, 164, 208, 221, 250, 270,
  283, 287, 323
Champagne 74, 75, 122, 133, 144, 176, 301,
  306
Chardonnay 216, 280
Charles VII, King of France 125, 126, 127,
  128
Châteaux
  Ch. Bahans 277
  Ch. Bardins 171
  Ch. Baret 171
  Ch. Bouscaut 171, 242, 262–3
  Ch. Cabannieux 292
  Ch. Carbonnieux 147, 148, 171, 237,
    241, 242, 263–5
  Ch. Cheval Blanc 25, 245, 276
  Ch. Climens 27, 263
  Ch. Couhins 171, 242, 268–9
  Ch. Couhins-Lurton 171, 231, 269, 289
  Ch. de Cruzeau 171
  Ch. Ferran 171
  Ch. de Fieuzal 171, 237, 242, 269–70,
    283
  Ch. de France 171
  Ch. Gazin 172
  Ch. Haut Bailly 172, 187–8, 236, 237,
    242, 266, 271–2
  Ch. Haut Bergey 172
  Ch. Haut Brion 24, 37, 44, 105, 132,
    137–9, 143, 147, 151, 154, 156, 172,
    210, 230, 232, 236, 237, 238, 239, 240,
    241, 242, 253, 261, 262, 263, 272–8,

280, 281, 286, 287
Ch. Haut-Gardère 172
Ch. Haut-Nouchet 172
Ch. Haut Ponteil Bergey 172
Ch. Lafite 32, 143, 144, 146, 154, 237, 239
Ch. Lafite-Rothschild 249
Ch. La Garde 172
Ch. La Louvière 147, 172, 236, 248, 252, 262, 288–90
Ch. La Mission Haut Brion 24, 148, 149, 172, 232, 236, 239, 241, 260, 262, 274, 276, 278–81
Ch. Larrivet Haut Brion 172
Ch. Latour 32, 144, 154, 239, 249–50
Ch. La Tour Haut Brion 172, 236, 241, 262, 278
Ch. La Tour Léognan 172
Ch. La Tour Martillac 172, 242, 281–2
Ch. Laville Haut Brion 172, 210, 242, 262, 278
Ch. Le Pape 173
Ch. Le Sartre 173
Ch. Les Carmes Haut Brion 173
Ch. Malartic-Lagravière 173, 231, 237, 242, 283–4
Ch. Margaux 154, 237, 239, 274, 276, 289
Ch. Olivier 173, 242, 284–5
Ch. Pape Clément 40, 105–6, 109–10, 125, 137, 173, 230, 236, 237, 241, 285–7
Ch. Pétrus 25, 254
Ch. Pique Caillou 173
Ch. Pontac Monplaisir 173
Ch. de Richemorin 173
Ch. de Rouillac 173
Ch. Smith Haut Lafitte 173, 242, 287–8
Chenin Blanc 216
Chevalier Domain de 171, 210, 236, 237, 242, 253, 260, 265–8, 271, 287
Ciron 35
claret 28, 88, 92–3, 105, 135, 137, 140, 141, 152, 155, 174, 195, 197, 229

Clarke, Moma 153, 155
Clarke, Oz 231, 243
climate 43–7, 58, 151, 191, 198, 253, 261
    floods 39
    frost 27, 133
    micro-climates 45–6, 192, 222, 246
    rainfall 37, 43–4, 45, 134, 182
    temperatures 43–5, 46
clonal selection 17, 174–5, 202
Coates, Clive 40, 106, 137, 152, 187, 210, 213, 214–15, 237, 238, 239, 266, 272, 276, 281, 286, 287
Cognac 271, 328
Coste, Pierre 210, 211, 217, 218, 292
Cot 251
Côtes 136, 142, 143, 189
coulure 197–8, 201, 251
courtiers 234
Cousteau, Victor 279–80
coutumes 90, 97, 122
Crawford, Anne 104
croupes 31, 36, 37, 192, 280
Cru 165, 171, 238, 240, 243
Cru classé 232, 235, 236, 254
Cru classé des Graves 251
cruchinet 186, 190
cuisines des vendangeurs 234
cuve autovidante 214
cuvée 204, 248, 250, 261, 282
cuverie 204, 210, 246
cuvier 105, 222, 246, 287, 318

dèbourage 212, 214
Delmas, Jean-Bernard 263, 272, 277, 278
Deschamps, J. 172
Dillon, Clarence 276
Dion, Roger 56, 156
Doisy-Daëne 213, 214, 215
Domaine Clarence Dillon 172, 278
Domaine de Grandmaison 172
Domaine de Hannetot-Grandmaison 172
Domaine de Petit Bourdieu 173
Dordogne 51, 97, 123
Dordogne, River 52, 61

Dovaz, Michel 105
Dreyfus, Michael 301–2, 306
Dubonnet 300
Dubourdieu, Pierre 205, 213, 214, 218
Dubourg, Philippe 328
Ducru-Beaucaillou 303
Dumas, Alexandre 107, 329
Dumont 239
Dupuy, M. 270

eaux-de-vie 135, 136
échoppes 142
Edward I, King of England 99, 108, 116
Edward III, King of England 98, 100, 101,
　104, 121, 122, 123, 124
égalissage 45, 206, 209
Elizabeth I, Queen of England 26, 77, 129
encépagement 187
Enjalbert, Henri 37, 40
Enragéat 183, 187, 189, 190
Entre-deux-Mers 52, 126, 137, 189, 252,
　289, 299, 309, 333
Épernon, Duc d' 333
Eschenauer, Louis 172, 173, 285, 287, 288
Étienne, Professor 62
Evans, Len 199, 294
exports 15, 88, 90, 91, 92, 93, 95, 100, 128–
　9, 133, 134, 136, 144, 145, 149, 151, 153,
　155, 167, 174, 178, 192, 216, 240, 247,
　301
Eyran 238
Eysines 87, 158, 169, 238

faluns 39
Fargues 132, 239
Féret 165, 189, 292, 294
fermentation 95, 102, 145, 204, 209, 213,
　218, 280, 290, 323
　controlled 205, 214
　malolactic 206
　see also macération carbonique; *macération*
　　préfermentaire
fertiliser 157
filleules 98

fining 208, 209
fouloir égrappoir 204
Fox, Peter 295
Frame, Donald M. 106–7
Franck, William 156, 229, 238, 239, 275,
　279
François I, King of France 129
French Revolution 31, 112, 114, 118, 121,
　128, 131, 141, 149, 151, 152, 155, 164,
　179, 239, 265, 274, 279, 283, 286, 289,
　291, 294, 315, 319, 332
Frescobaldi, Leonardo de 54, 181
Fronsac 24

Galet, Dexter 195
Galet, Pierre 163, 185, 201
galets directeurs 40
Galy, Roger 90
gardes-femmes 234
gardes-vignes 234
Garonne, River 31, 32, 38, 39, 40, 43, 44,
　45, 46, 51, 52, 54, 58, 61, 62, 89, 90, 98,
　104, 132, 142, 153, 158, 184, 292, 299,
　320, 328, 330, 332, 333
Gascon wines 92, 99, 102, 103, 104, 111,
　136
Gascony 64, 65, 70, 73, 81, 96, 97, 98, 100,
　106–7, 117, 127, 128, 157
Gasqueton family 269
Gay-Lussac 255
George II, King of England 139
George VI, King of England 27
Gironde 15, 23, 31, 43, 44, 45, 46, 51, 52,
　56, 58, 60, 62, 63, 64, 76, 87, 90, 100, 101,
　102, 104, 105, 107, 115, 127, 131, 133,
　135, 140, 148, 149, 151, 163, 167, 178,
　179, 184, 189, 191, 193, 196, 197, 200,
　202, 229, 234, 276, 282, 298, 300, 313,
　314, 319, 328, 330, 331, 333
Gradignan 165, 166, 169, 171, 238, 239,
　251
Grand Cru 232, 243, 244, 252
Grand Cru Classé 252
Grand Noir de la Calmette 201

Grand, Roger 233
grand vin 192, 205, 210, 237, 246, 248, 250, 261, 268, 277
grandes Graves 143, 189
grape varieties 181–202, 204, 205–6, 253
Graput 182, 190
Gratecap 87
Graves, maps of 34, 168
Graves Supérieures 255, 256
Gribelin, G. 269
Gros Bouchet 186
Guignard, Pierre 164
Guillos 169
Guyenne 31, 73, 108, 111, 124, 125, 128, 134, 181, 182, 331
Guyot, Jules 176, 184, 185, 186

Haillan (Le) 35
harvesters, mechanical 17, 175–6, 181
Healy, Maurice 138, 229
Henderson, A. L. 240
Henri II, King of France 132
Henri IV, King of France 107, 273
Henry II, King of England 94–5
Henry III, King of England 121, 122
Henry IV, King of England 124–5
Henry V, King of England 125
Henry VII, King of England 125
Héritiers Chantecaille 173
Hermitage 23, 149, 187
Heywood, Thomas 135
Holinshead 127
Hundred Years War 98, 332

Illats 163, 169, 255, 256, 278, 328
Isle Saint Georges 169

jalles 142, 163
Jefferson, Thomas 146, 151, 152, 238, 274–5
Johannisberg 189
Johnson, Hugh 25
Johnston, Nathaniel 149, 151, 152
Josephine, Empress of France 152, 264

Julien, M. 240
Jullien, André 154, 158
Jullien, Camille 51, 96
Jurançon Blanc 189, 190
jus de presse 214

Kelly, Amy 86
Kressman, Jean 281, 282

La Brède 24, 25, 35, 142, 169, 183, 189, 284, 285, 307–9, 312, 313, 315–16, 319, 322
Lacoste, P.-Joseph 109, 291
Lafforgue, Germain 35, 43, 44, 178, 186, 187, 191, 202
La Lagune 253
Landes 15, 31, 36, 38, 39, 60, 77, 106, 126, 128, 132, 152, 157, 325, 326, 333
Landiras 35, 163, 169, 239, 291, 328, 329
Langon 24, 31, 76, 86, 90, 98, 132, 133, 134, 136, 143, 150, 152, 159, 163, 169, 217, 239, 292, 293, 320, 326, 327, 332
La Rochelle 103, 104, 129, 135
La Tour Alain 200
La Tour de Mons 44
Le Bouscat 238
Léogeats 169
Léognan 35, 39, 40, 147, 165, 166, 167, 169, 171, 172, 173, 192, 232, 237, 238, 239, 242, 250, 251, 253, 266, 269, 281, 284, 290, 309
Les Chartronnais 97
Lesineau, Bernadette 172
Le Taillan 158, 239
Libourne 100, 144, 182
Lichine, Alexis 25, 230, 242, 246–7
Liebfraumilch 26
Lillet 297–306
Lillet, Paul and Raymond 299, 302
Lodge, Eleanor 98
Loire 65, 75, 77, 79, 124, 185, 199, 216
London 96, 99, 101, 102, 121, 127, 128, 129, 136, 137, 150, 249, 274, 310, 312
   Vintners' Hall 103, 155

Worshipful Company of Vintners 104
Longford, Lady 153
Lorbac, Charles de 156, 157, 229, 313
Louis VI, King of France 78, 79, 80, 81, 82
Louis IX (St Louis), King of France 121
Louis XIII, King of France 131, 329
Louis XIV, King of France 131, 140, 141, 299, 309, 330
Louis XV, King of France 32, 149, 314
Louis XVIII, King of France 153
Loupiac 239, 255, 299
Lowe, Sir Hudson 155
Ludon 253
Lurton, André 171, 172, 173, 210, 254, 262, 269, 288, 289, 290
Lurton, Lucien 172, 262, 263, 269
Lynch, Jean-Baptiste 152-3

McCann, Dom Justin 74
macération carbonique 194
macération préfermentaire 174, 213–16
Mâcon Blanc 27
Madeira 151, 155
Magence 44, 272
Maison des Vins de Graves 164, 321, 328
maître de chai 258, 274
Malbec 181, 182, 184, 186, 187, 188, 189, 190, 197–8, 251, 263, 269, 292
Malvesin, Frantz 271
Malvoisie 183
Mareilhac, J.-B. de 289
Margaux 40, 70, 140, 143
Markham, Gervase 135
Marly, J. 283
Marque du Vin 134
Martignas 169
Martillac 35, 165, 166, 169, 171, 172, 242, 251, 292, 309
martini, dry 26, 27
Mathew, Gervase 124
maturation 144, 147, 154, 191, 205, 206, 207, 209, 210, 238, 248, 269, 282, 283, 318

Maufras, Jean 173
Mauriac, François 15, 333
Maurois, André 121
Maxwell, Constantia 149, 150
Mazarin, Cardinal 131
Mazères 31, 169, 293
mechanization in vineyards 175, 180, 188, 204; *see also* harvesters, mechanical
Médoc 25, 28, 31, 38, 39, 40, 41, 45, 70, 106, 125, 127, 130, 131, 132, 133, 136, 137, 142, 143, 148, 151, 153, 155, 156, 157, 163, 165, 181, 184, 185, 187, 191, 193, 226, 229, 230, 231, 232, 237, 238, 239, 240, 243, 246, 247, 249, 250, 253, 276, 277, 280, 282, 286, 303, 310, 314, 315, 333
Mêlier 183
merchants 23, 52, 57, 58, 98, 100, 103, 128, 129, 130, 132, 135, 137, 139, 140, 150, 154, 220, 240–1, 248, 272, 300
Mérignac 31, 35, 87, 143, 165, 166, 167, 169, 171, 173, 217, 238, 239, 251, 307
Merlot 181, 184, 186, 187, 188, 190, 192, 196–7, 222, 251, 262, 263, 266, 268, 269, 271, 273, 277, 278, 281, 283, 284, 285, 288, 290, 293, 295
Meunier 183
Midi 300
Mitchell, Peter 144
Moët et Chandon 328
Montagne et Cie 173
Montagne, Paul 105, 286–7
Montaigne 106, 107
Montesquieu 106, 133, 142–3, 181, 182, 281, 284, 289, 298, 309–19
Morton, H. V. 68
Morton, Lucie T. 185
Mosel, River 47, 58
Mothe, Florence 15, 25, 250, 315, 332
Mouchy, Duc and Duchesse de 272, 276
Moustère 182
Mouton 144
Moza 182
Müller-Thurgau 200

Muscadelle 181, 187, 190, 201–2, 251, 284, 285, 292
Muscadet 27, 183, 201, 213, 215
Musquelle 182–3

Nantes 135, 136, 141
Napoleon I, Emperor of France 52, 125, 152, 154, 155, 264, 299
Narbonne 54, 56
négociants 149, 217, 245, 248

Obrion 140, 238, 274
Odart, Comte 186, 187
oenologist, role of 216–18, 246
oidium 166, 188, 251
Ordish, George 157, 158–9
ouillage 147

Palmer, Charles 153
palus 46, 130, 132, 143, 237
parcelles 175, 191–2
Paris 78, 80, 82, 83, 152, 153, 313, 314, 332
Parker, Robert 232, 236
Pasteur, Louis 145
Pauillac 28, 35, 152, 158, 226, 232, 249, 250, 284
Pays Basque 16, 31, 107
péages 100
Penning-Rowsell, Edmund 24, 92, 93, 128, 138, 139, 213, 231, 235, 237, 239, 240, 252, 280, 308
Peppercorn, David 248
Perceval, Émile de 181, 182, 183, 309, 314, 315
Pérignon, Dom Pierre 74, 144
Périgord 31, 73, 74
Perrin, Antony 164, 263, 264
Pessac 35, 109, 125, 133, 143, 165, 166, 167, 169, 171, 172, 173, 189, 192, 217, 232, 238, 239, 241, 242, 250, 251, 253, 272, 279, 285
Petit Fer 182, 184
Petit-Lafitte, Professor 182, 187
Petit Verdot 181, 188, 191, 198, 201, 251, 264, 268, 269, 281

Petite Liquorelle 328
petites Graves 143, 189
petites Landes 163
petits vins 29, 224
Peynaud, Émile 217, 283
Pez 137
Philip V, King of Spain 140
Philip the Fair, King of France 108, 109, 110, 111, 113, 114, 115
phylloxera 157, 166, 178, 187, 189, 195, 230, 251, 271, 279
Pijassou, Professor 237
pilgrim routes 52, 67–70, 79, 91, 101, 327, 330
Pilkington, Roger 325
pioche 157
Plantade, Alain and Francine 172
Plumb, J. H. 139
Podensac 25, 159, 163, 164, 169, 189, 255, 256, 299, 302, 303, 320, 321, 328, 329
Pointet, André 173
Poitou 73
Pomerol 28, 222, 226, 231, 246, 254
Pongrácz, D. P. 195
Pontac 140, 143, 147, 237
Pontac family 137, 138, 139, 240, 246, 273, 279, 293, 326
port 145
portes greffes 175, 253
Portets 169, 238, 250, 278, 292, 294, 322, 329, 330, 331
Portugal 191
Potensac 137
Poudensac 238
Pouilly-Fuissé 27
Poulsard 201
Preignac 132, 143, 238, 239, 309, 328, 330
Premier Grand Cru Classé 236, 252
prisage 99
privilèges 90, 97, 122, 155
Pruéras 183, 187, 190
pruning 159, 175, 176, 251
Pujol, Bernard 285
Pujols 132, 163, 238

Pujols-sur-Ciron 169, 330
Pyrénées 16, 32, 38, 40, 52, 64, 65, 68, 73,
    77, 107, 140, 300, 305

Quercy 182
Queyries 130
quillage 99
Quittanson, Charles 158

Rabache, Monsieur 240–1
racking 102, 147, 206
Rahoul 210, 213, 262, 294, 295, 296, 329
râpe 210
Rayet, M. 43, 44
reck 102
régas 179
régisseur 258, 276, 282, 287
rendement 174, 246, 248, 250, 251, 252
Réolais 189
Rhenish 104, 241
Rhine 58, 92
Rhône 149, 191, 216
Ribereau-Guyon, Pascal 217
Ricard, Abel 270
Ricard, Claude 265, 266–7
Richard II, King of England 104, 121, 123,
    125, 153
Richard Coeur de Lion 84, 85, 86, 89
Richelieu, Cardinal 149, 185, 314
Riesling 213
Rioja 149, 228
Roaillan 169, 171
Roberts, Lewis 135
Robinson, Jancis 181, 184–5, 186, 194, 195,
    198, 200, 201, 230, 251
Roger, J.-R. 25
Romat, Hervé 303
rootstock 158, 189, 197, 271
Roquetaillade 320, 322, 327
rosé 93, 269
rot 46, 197, 198, 201, 300
Rothschild, Baron Eric de 199
Roussillon 300
Rowley, Elmer B. 33

Runciman, Sir Stephen 74

saccharomyces cerevisae 215
Ste-Bazeille 182
Sainte-Croix 87, 147, 239, 264
Sainte-Croix-du-Mont 255, 299
St Émilion 28, 31, 123, 136, 153, 164, 179,
    182, 186, 193, 222, 230, 232, 244, 246,
    252
St Estèphe 28, 137, 246
Ste Foy 136
St Jean-d'Illac 171
St Julien 222, 250, 303
St Laurent d'Escures 87
Saint-Macaire 132, 190, 299, 332
St-Médard-d'Eyrans 165, 171, 251, 289
St-Médard-en-Jalles 35
St Michel-de-Rieufret 171
St Morillon 171
St Nicholas de Grave 87
St Pardon-de-Conques 171
St-Pey 239
St Pierre de Mons 31, 171, 293
St Selve 171
Sancerre 231
Sanders, Jean 271, 272
Sarthou, P. 173
Saucats 35, 171
Sauternes 15–16, 25, 26, 31, 35, 40, 45,
    132, 143, 159, 198, 213, 229, 238, 239,
    299, 300, 301, 304, 320, 322, 327
Sauvignon Blanc 181, 185, 187, 189, 190,
    193, 199–201, 202, 212, 213, 214, 224,
    231, 251, 263, 264, 268, 273, 278, 281,
    283, 284, 285, 288, 293
Savignac 239
Schröder & Schÿler 146
Scott, J. D. 23, 25
Seely, James 232, 263, 265, 279, 284, 289,
    294
Ségur, Jean de 273
Ségur, Marquis de 32, 143–4
Sémillon 27, 181, 187, 189, 190, 191, 198–
    9, 200, 212, 213, 224, 231, 251, 263, 264,

268, 270, 273, 278, 281, 284, 285, 290, 292, 293, 295, 328
Seward, Desmond 75, 97
Shaw, T. G. 240
sherry 145
Sichel & Co. 200
Sichel, Peter 333
Simon, André 92, 100, 133, 134, 135, 138, 237, 238
soil 31–41, 156, 157, 185, 189, 192, 232, 240, 269, 272, 277
Soult, Marshal 153, 154
Spurrier, Steven 232
Stendhal 298, 316–17
Stow, John 103
Sumption, Jonathan 67
sur lie 147, 205, 211, 213
Syndicat Viticole des Graves et Graves Supérieures 164
Syndicat Viticole des Graves Pessac et Léognan 165, 167

Talence 87, 158, 165, 166, 171, 217, 232, 238, 241, 242, 251, 278
Talleyrand, Charles Maurice de 275
Tarn, River 56
Tastet and Lawton 237
tastings 15, 19, 23, 27, 93, 101, 164, 193, 195, 219–32, 238, 245, 259, 268, 272, 277, 284, 287, 288, 290, 292, 293, 294, 295, 300, 306, 318, 323
taxation 90, 97, 98, 99, 100, 132–3, 134, 135, 136, 142, 150, 155
technopole 47, 169
  map 170
Teinturiers 201–2
terrasses 33, 35, 39, 53, 187, 253
Thomassin, Bernard 171
topping 139, 147, 237
Torres, Miguel Jnr. 200
Toulenne 171
Toulouse 16, 54, 56, 61, 76, 100, 114, 135, 153, 159, 278, 320
tourism 29, 32, 307–33

Tovey, Charles 240, 241
Tremaine, Edward 93
triage 213
Trier 58, 63, 148
Tucker, John 188
Tull, Jethro 150
Twiss, Browning & Hallowes 301

Ugni Blanc 198
Union des Crus Classés des Graves 164, 165
Uzeste 107, 116, 119, 320, 322

vendangeoirs 176
Verdelais 333
Verdot 187, 189, 190, 191, 198
vermouth 302, 305
Victoria, Queen of England 77
vigne dure 185, 198
Vilanova, Arnaud de 95, 110
Villagrains 35, 169
Villandraut 108, 112, 114, 118, 320, 322, 326–7, 328
Villenave-d'Ornon 147, 148, 158, 163, 165, 166, 171, 173, 241, 242, 251, 268, 269, 323
Vinding-Diers, Peter 205, 213, 294, 296
Vinding-Diers, Susie 295–6
vinegar 95
vines 33, 36, 37, 41, 46, 52, 54, 66, 94, 134, 141, 142, 143, 148, 150, 157–8, 159, 165, 167, 176, 198, 200, 202, 233, 240, 247, 257, 266
  age of 251
  Coculubis 56, 182
  colour 31, 36, 101, 158, 182, 185
  grafting 188, 189, 191, 197, 271
  varieties 178–9, 251
Vinet, Elie 185
vineyards 27, 31–3, 36–8, 40, 44–7, 56–7, 64–5, 87, 90–1, 93, 98, 101, 105, 122, 131, 133–4, 137, 140, 142, 147, 155–8, 164, 167–9, 171, 174–6, 179–81, 183–5, 187–8, 191–2, 196, 198, 202, 210, 217,

225–6, 228, 234–5, 238–9, 242–4, 246–7, 249–50, 253, 257, 279, 283, 290, 293, 296, 299, 315, 321, 323
  see also harvesters, mechanical; mechanization in the vineyards
vins de primeur 143
vintages 17, 19, 23, 44, 45, 95, 101, 102, 106, 127, 143, 153, 154, 155, 167, 176, 177, 196, 197, 204, 205, 209, 210, 222, 230, 234, 238, 248,251, 253, 257, 264, 266, 269, 271, 274, 277, 280, 283, 287, 290, 296
Virelade 163, 171, 238, 239, 331
Vital, Pierre 158, 179
viticulture 133, 153, 158

Waddell, Helen 61, 62
Warner Allen, H. 145, 146, 151, 152, 154, 229–30
Washington, George 146
Wellington, Duke of 125, 153, 154
Williams, Don Guido 26

wine-making 27, 45, 46, 56, 93–4, 133, 174, 177–8, 195–6, 202, 203–13, 228, 280, 287, 295, 300, 304
  new methods 174, 213–16, 282
  organic 17, 174, 294
wine presses and houses 102, 133, 183, 184, 197, 204, 210, 212, 246, 282, 318, 323
Wine Society 23–4
Woltner, Frédéric 279, 280
wooding 147, 154, 191, 196, 205, 206–7, 208, 209, 210, 212, 267, 269, 270, 274, 282, 318
Würzburg 148

yields 44, 57, 122, 151, 165, 180, 233, 246, 248, 255, 256, 262
Young, Arthur 149–50
Young, E. H. 317
Young, Gavin 155
Yquem 167, 300
Yugoslavia 26